T0331922

SOVIET
AIRCRAFT
INDUSTRY

SOVIET AIRCRAFT INDUSTRY

PETER G. DANCEY

FONTHILL

Fonthill Media Language Policy

Fonthill Media publishes in the international English language market. One language edition is published worldwide. As there are minor differences in spelling and presentation, especially with regard to American English and British English, a policy is necessary to define which form of English to use. The Fonthill Policy is to use the form of English native to the author. Peter Dancey was born and educated in the UK and therefore British English has been adopted in this publication.

Fonthill Media Limited
Fonthill Media LLC
www.fonthillmedia.com
office@fonthillmedia.com

First published in the United Kingdom and the United States of America 2015

British Library Cataloguing in Publication Data:
A catalogue record for this book is available from the British Library

Copyright © Peter Dancey 2015

ISBN 978-1-78155-289-6

Typeset in 10pt on 13pt Minion Pro
Printed and bound in England by CPI Group (UK) Ltd, Croydon, CR0 4YY

Contents

Acknowledgements

The compilation of this work has involved reference to many papers and documents originating from a number of Soviet aviation experts, correspondents and Soviet Cold War publications such as *Tekhnika Molodyezhi*, *Aviatsiya-Kosmonavtika*, *Grazhdanskaya Aviatsiya* and *Kryl'ya Rodiny*.

Introduction

In 1993, the new Russian Ministry of Aircraft Production, together with the Central Aerohydrodynamic Institute (TsAGI), published detailed figures of Soviet aircraft production for the period 1917-1941. Over the years there have been numerous publications on the subject of Soviet aviation and aircraft but little has been published with regard to Soviet aircraft industry and production. In fact, many quite a lot of publications appear to make little or no reference to these very important organisations in Soviet aviation history. This book aims to 'fill the gaps'.

With the start of the Cold War, the US Central and Defense Intelligence Agencies (CIA) and the USAF—thanks to their spies, special reconnaissance aircraft and satellites—managed to obtain a good and almost complete picture of Soviet aviation plants and production. But this information was, and still is, 'Top Secret'. Few details were published, and when or if they were, the figures were manipulated to conceal the danger of Soviet quantitative superiority, often for the purpose of obtaining finance from the US Senate for high-profile defence projects and the purchase of military hardware in order to maintain military aircraft procurement at a level perceived commensurate with the needs of the US and its allies. Things changed following the collapse of the Soviet Union, although not radically.

Now it is possible to obtain more accurate facts and figures on Soviet aircraft production—up until 1945. There is information on aircraft and helicopter plants, but nothing concerning their future programmes into the twenty-first century, and it is still impossible to obtain a good Order of Battle on the Russian Air Force. However, since the election of Vladimir Putin as the country's president, it is now possible to obtain data on Russian aircraft, particularly those intended for export, as Putin rightly recognises the importance of the industry to the country's economic standing.

In 1996, a new book was published in Moscow on the Voronezh aircraft plant, one of the biggest in Europe. The book includes much data on the number of Komsomolsks (youth communists) or Stalinnovists (workers liked by Stalin), but nothing on total manpower, covered area or numbers of aircraft built at the plant. It mainly contains the usual well-known technical descriptions with some historical development information on the aircraft built at Voronezh. Although there are numerous books on the development and description of Soviet aircraft and helicopters, nothing is available relating to the production of these machines, or the Soviet aviation industry and the production plants. In this book I hope to complete the picture for the reader on these exciting subjects, and to dispel completely this Soviet mystery.

The Soviet Union with its sealed borders remained for a long time an enigma, especially in respect of its aircraft and its aviation industry. Only propaganda, obscure photographs and vague outdated information were released to the western world. For a brief period from 1941, Hitler and his troops were able to obtain accurate data on Soviet aircraft and Soviet aircraft production, but it was not long before the Iron Curtain dropped for almost half a century.

It was a known fact in the early 1920s that the Soviets bought their aircraft from Holland, France and Italy, etc. But in the late 1920s, Stalin called for the development of a powerful indigenous aircraft industry to meet the country's aviation needs. This industry was to remain very secret, even in the 1980s. The Soviet Union maintained as much secrecy as possible on the location of its aircraft and helicopter construction plants and revealed no information at all on the number of aircraft produced or in service with either its military or civil air fleets. OKBs (design bureaux) and GAZs (production plants) were identified by numbers only, in an effort to conceal their locations.

The numerous books on the development and description of Soviet aircraft and helicopters, many written and edited by leading Soviet aviation designers and industrialists, contain very little on the history of the industry and its plants, or the production of its flying machines. One Soviet publication examined by this author even failed to acknowledge that Joseph Stalin ever existed and certainly made no reference to his directives and favours issued so freely to the industry throughout his tenure as Soviet President. The aim of this book is to go some way to correcting these anomalies.

1

Building an Aircraft Industry

The Soviet aviation industry, which had been nationalised in 1918, was administered between the wars by a number of different government departments and boards, ranging from VSNKh (All-Union Economic Council) to the Commissariat for the Defence Industries and the Commissariat for Heavy Industry, and at one time part of it was under the direct control of the GPU or secret police.

In 1939, a separate Commissariat for the Aviation Industry was created and the former Commissar for the Defence Industries, M. M. Kaganovich—later to shoot himself as a result of Kremlin purges—was appointed its head. The designer S. V. Ilyushin was a deputy. The last big reorganisation before the Second World War came in January 1940 when Kaganovich was replaced by A. I. Shakhurin, and A. S. Yakovlev became his deputy in place of Ilyushin. Prior to this, the two big design bureaux, TsAGI AGOS and TsKB, began to split up, and leading designers from these two centres together with other new designers established their own design offices. These changes were reflected in the adoption in 1940 of a new designation system for Soviet aircraft based on the names of the chief designers as opposed to the functional system that had been generally in use during the 1920s and 1930s (e.g. ANT became Tupolev).

A number of other factors helped to re-establish the Soviet aviation industry. On 16 April 1922, at Rapallo near Genoa in Italy, an agreement was signed between the Soviet Union and Germany, resulting in an immediate resumption of diplomatic relations between the two countries and marking the start of Soviet-German economic and military co-operation, although a few months earlier, on 6 February, the German firm Junkers had already made an agreement with the government in Moscow for the production of all-metal aircraft at the former Russo-Baltic Wagon Works (RBVZ) at Moscow-Fili.

The Dessau firm invested 500 million RM in rebuilding the plant, re-equipping and tooling, and provision of drawings and other materials as well as training of personnel, the German War Ministry providing 140 million RM. The refurbished plant became operational in 1923, and it was not long before the workforce had reached 1,350, including Germans and Russians. In just four years, Junkers accomplished a great deal towards the re-emergence of the Soviet aircraft industry, in realising the primary task of aircraft construction aligned with the training of qualified engineers, technicians and skilled workers. Moreover, the modern techniques associated with the construction of all-metal aircraft were quickly assimilated by the Soviet designers such as Andrei Tupolev and his associates. This enabled the Soviet aviation industry to develop its own modern designs and in a comparatively short time to efficiently produce its own aircraft.

By 1923 the Junkers Fili plant was building aircraft from German-and Russian-produced components: twenty Ju 20 (A-20) and forty Ju 21 (T-21) aircraft, which amounted to 41.1 per cent of all Soviet aircraft production at this time. In 1924, another twenty Ju 20 and fifty-three Ju 21 aircraft were constructed, representing 35.1 per cent of the total Soviet production, but by the following year this had reduced to only twenty-six Ju 21s and some Ju 22 single-seat fighters. Fili also assembled many Dessau-made aircraft, such as fifty-five Junkers Ju 13 (F-13) transport planes up until 1931—twenty-nine in 1923—although after receiving only three Junkers PS-4 (W 33) aircraft in 1928, many dozens were produced and delivered in the 1930s.

Assembly of military prototypes was also undertaken at the Junkers plant at Moscow-Fili—such types as the Ju G1 heavy bomber and the K 47 dive bomber—and there is no doubt that the Fili plant was responsible for the development of modern Soviet aviation. However, following a rather acrimonious period of relations with the Soviets regarding all-metal patents in the 1920s, and due to the prevailing deteriorating economic conditions, it became necessary for the Soviets to develop their own indigenous aviation industry.

The Tupolev OKB was established in 1922, in connection with TsAGI's Aviation, Hydro-aviation and Experimental Construction Section (AGOS), which was created for the production of experimental aircraft up until 1931, and the Experimental Aircraft Construction Section (KOSOS), which was tasked with aircraft development from 1932 to 1936. The latter was divided into ten separately numbered design bureaux (KB-1 to KB-10). The TsKB (Central Design Bureau) was established in 1926 and was made up of three large divisions with these responsibilities:

- OSS (landplanes) GAZ-1; after 1925 at GAZ-25, Chief Polikarpov;
- OOM (engines) GAZ-24, Chief Shvetsov;
- OMOS (seaplanes) GAZ-23; after 1927 at GAZ-22, Chief Grigorovich.

The Soviet aviation industry built 326 aircraft in 1925, of which 264 were military types. The target for that year was 500 aircraft but, in the event, only 65.2 per cent of this goal was achieved. To improve the situation more capital, machinery and manpower were mobilised for the aircraft industry, but in spite of this, only 469 aircraft were produced in 1926, which included 309 military types. Engine production was also low, but did represent a 574 per cent increase on the aero-engine production for 1923.

In 1926, eighteen I-2 fighters were built by GAZ-1 as well as 392 R-1s. GAZ-3 at Leningrad built forty-six Polikarpov U-1 trainers, and the Fili plant produced three Junkers Ju 21s, ten other series aircraft being built by other plants. Collectively the plants produced fourteen different prototypes, of which thirteen (including five light aircraft) were flight tested.

The following year saw an increase in production to 575 aircraft, including 495 military types. Forty-five fighters were built at GAZ-1 (thirty-four I-2s, seven I-2*bis*, two I-3s and two I-4s) and GAZ-1 also built 383 R-1 reconnaissance planes. GAZ-10 produced forty-nine MR-1s, GAZ-22 two R-3s, and GAZ-3 eighty-nine U-1s and twenty-five MU-1s. Additionally, nineteen prototypes were built, sixteen of which (including ten light aircraft) were air tested.

An important event occurred on 1 October 1927 with the reorganisation of the GAZs into Zavods (plants), but in 1927/28, the country's aviation industry was employing only 8,695 men.

In 1928, Soviet aircraft production saw a further increase when output rose to 870 aircraft, of which 610 were military variants. There were 259 fighters, including 170 I-4s and 508 reconnaissance types, among them 445 R-1s, although not all R-1s were used by the military. Conversely, the Red Air Force did not receive a single bomber at this time.

The industry actually had only one main aircraft plant, Zavod 1, at Khodynka, but this plant alone produced 704 aircraft—all the fighters and 445 R-1s. However, engine production in three plants totalled only 1,200 units, and to meet the shortfall it was necessary to resort to imports of engines and aircraft. Soviet aviation was still not self-sufficient. For this reason, on 29 April 1929, the first of the five-year plans was adopted, and the rapid development of Soviet industry, including the aircraft industry, started.

In 1929, there were only fifteen main plants, including four aircraft and three engine plants and one producing propellers. The rest were involved in producing parts and sub-assemblies and repair work. It was decided to invest 115 million roubles during the five-year plan to modernise and increase the size of existing plants and to build new ones. This amount was soon increased to 159 million, and then to the gigantic sum of 642 million roubles. Increasing capacity necessitated a similar increase in manpower, and the aim was to increase the 1927/28 total of 8,695 to 24,497 in 1932/33. In reality, however, by late 1932 the industry employed 79,894 personnel, or 84,064 if the workers at the new plants still under construction were included. Of these, 57,148 were production workers.

Not only did the objectives of the five-year plan continually increase but timescales were also shortened. The original plan was scheduled to run from the summer of 1928 to the summer of 1933, but completion was finally rescheduled for 31 December 1932, in spite of the fact that it would be impossible to achieve the objectives within this timescale. In the event, 426 million roubles were invested, 216 million less than promised. None the less, the value of the aviation plants increased from 45 million roubles in 1928 to 240 million in 1932. Of this total investment, 60 per cent was in the plants in the Moscow region, 15 per cent at Rybinsk (Zavod 26), 5.5 per cent at Taganrog (Zavod 31), 4 per cent at Leningrad (Zavods 23 and 47), 4 per cent at Zaporozhye (Zavod 29), and 11.5 per cent at other locations.

The fifteen main plants of 1928 had been increased to thirty-one in 1932, although nine of these were still under construction. This included nine for aircraft (Zavods 1, 22, 23, 31, 135) and four not yet finished (16, 21, 39, 43), six for engines (Zavods 24, 26, 29) and three not yet finished (18, 19?) as well as sixteen new plants for parts and prototype construction and repair work. In addition, in 1930, the Red Army (RKKA), Military Aviation Direction (UVVS) and the Pomvozduh trust transferred five repair plants to the aviation sector. These of course also received new Zavod numbers. Some plants were enlarged for aircraft production, including these:

- Smolensk (Zavod 35) which remained a repair plant;
- Khodynka (Zavod 39) for prototypes and later for aircraft building;
- Kiev (Zavod 43) later used for aircraft building;
- Sevastopol (Zavod 45) which remained as a repair plant;
- Leningrad (Zavod 47) later used for aircraft building.

The civil aircraft plant at Kharkov, which was building Kalinin aircraft, became Zavod 135.

The head of the aviation industry at this time was the extremely capable P. I. Baranov, who was unfortunately killed in an aircraft accident on 5 September 1933. However, there were many negative factors in the first five-year plan, mainly concerned with planning, which was subject to many changes. Early in the plan, two factories were scheduled to be built at Voronezh and Perm (Zavods 16 and 19). The first was to build attack planes, the second Bristol Jupiter engines, but before the plants were completed in 1933 the plans were changed. Zavod 16 was to build arms for the Red Army and Zavod 19 was to produce American Wright Cyclone engines; in 1934, Zavod 16 also switched to aero-engine production.

A further problem was the unprecedented increase in manpower levels. In 1931, manpower increased 230 per cent on 1930, and in some plants even bigger increases occurred. For example, during the period of the five-year plan, manpower at Zavod 29 increased by more than eight times and at Zavod 11 by nine times. As many of these were unskilled workers, the percentage of rejected material in the plants increased considerably. In 1930, rejects amounted to 4.2 per cent of output, rising to 7.8 per cent in 1931. Moreover, productivity in the same period decreased by 14.5 per cent.

In 1932, 51 per cent of the total workforce in the aviation industry worked in the aircraft plants, 35 per cent in the engine plants, 8 per cent in the plants producing parts and sub-assemblies, 3 per cent in the plants producing engine parts and 3 per cent in the repair plants. A positive factor was that within the five-year period the number of engineers and technical personnel increased tenfold.

Although output was uneven at times, overall production of aircraft did increase as a result of the five-year plan. Total airframe value rose from 42 million roubles in 1929 to 350 million in 1932. The plan had called for the production of 1,029 aircraft per year, and this was achieved, some of the fluctuations in output being attributed to the introduction of the heavy bombers into series production.

Production of 160 TB-3 heavy bombers, 884 modern R-5 recce aircraft, and 942 U-2 training aircraft in 1932 proved that the Soviets had in a very short time developed one of the most powerful aviation industries in the world. However, this was only the beginning. In September 1931, Soviet planners had started evolving their second five-year plan, to run from 1933 to 1937. Its target was to move the country's aviation industry well ahead of Britain, France, Italy, Japan and particularly the USA.

2

The Moscow Aircraft Production Organisation and Beyond

The Moscow Aircraft Production Organisation (MAPO) and Soviet aviation are virtually the same age. The history of Soviet aircraft production is considered to have begun in 1909, when after production of the first military dirigible, the First Russian Aeronautics Society (S. S. Shchetinin) factory went over to making aircraft. Outstanding Russian scientists such as N. Ye. Zhukovsky, A. Krylov and Sergey Chaplygin, a prominent aerodynamicist, collaborated with the works, and the first machines were produced in February 1910—the Russian 'A' and Russian 'B' aircraft.

From 1910 to 1912, Ya. M. Gakkel produced nine designs, a number of which recorded significant advances in Russian aviation. The Gakkel VII biplane of 1911 made five ferry flights from St Petersburg (later to be named Petrograd and Leningrad) to Gatchina at an average speed of 92 kph, the Gakkel VIII set up a Russian altitude record of 1,350 m, and the Gakkel IX was the world's first strut-braced monoplane. At the same time, a group of aircraft enthusiasts at Kiev had produced a number of experimental designs, and the first designs of the renowned Igor Ivanovich Sikorsky were also produced.

The Russo-Baltic Railway Car Plant started to build aircraft in 1912, with Sikorsky appointed as its chief designer. By May of that year, the Sikorsky 6 biplane had been produced, and two months later a second S-6 and an S-7 monoplane had been completed, the aircraft winning first and second places respectively in the August 1912 military competition. The first Russian flying boat, designed by Dmitry Grigorovich, was produced in 1913, and two years later the same designer produced the M-5 seaplane used primarily as a reconnaissance training plane at the naval flying schools. The M-9 that followed was considered to be the world's best military seaplane, and the prototype M-11 fighter seaplane produced in 1916 by Grigorovich was, the following year, the first fighter to be fitted with armour protection for the pilot and engine.

In the winter of 1912/13, the Russo-Baltic Plant produced Sikorsky's 'Grand Baltisky' (Great Baltic) and 'Russky Vityaz' (Russian Knight), the forerunner to the world's first four-engined bomber, the Ilya Muromets, which initially flew in 1913 with the first military bomber squadron of ten combat and two training planes established in the Imperial Russian Air Force in 1914. The aircraft bombed German troop concentrations, railway stations and airfields, and also used their machine guns to fire on marching troop columns and to attack German fighter planes. By 1918, around eighty Ilya Muromets aircraft had been built, and those that remained after the cessation of hostilities were used to inaugurate the country's first regular passenger/mail airline service on the Moscow–Orel–Kharkov route. From 1910 to 1912, Soviet aircraft production became more organised, with small batch production by a number of specialised factories.

By August 1911, the First Russian Aeronautics Society employed 100 people and could produce one aircraft every five days. In addition to the Russo-Baltic Plant, in 1912 the Duks bicycle factory in Moscow, established in 1893 with French capital at the big Khodynskoye field near the centre of Moscow, also entered into aircraft production and was scheduled to produce three aircraft per week under the supervision of engineer M. Evgrafov. Completed aircraft were flown by Russian test pilot S. Utochkin. In addition, two other aircraft plants were established, the V. A. Lebedev factory producing up to ten aircraft a month with 300 employees, and A. A. Anatr having 100 employees. The Duks Works made great progress and became one of the leading aircraft production plants in Russia (GAZ-1). The outbreak of the First World War stimulated the production of aircraft in Russia, but at the time there were already hundreds of personnel employed in aircraft manufacture, producing machines of French design—Farman, Nieuport and Morane types, etc.

In 1913, the Duks Works produced and delivered seventy-six Farmans, and the following year MAPO produced 180 aircraft with 1,871 employees. By 1917 this figure had risen to 492 with 7,385 people. Russia's aviation industry had comprised five airframe and two aero-engine factories in 1914, but by 1917 this had increased to eleven airframe, five aero-engine and two propeller factories that produced a total of 5,565 aircraft during the course of the war, and aviation industry personnel had increased from 2,100 to around 10,000.

By the end of 1917 the country's burgeoning aircraft industry had thirty-four factories together with seven under construction. Fourteen of these produced aircraft, seven produced aero-engines, three manufactured airscrews and one aircraft instruments. The three most productive plants had been Duks, producing 1,569 airframes, Shchetinin in Petrograd with 1,340, and Anatra in Odessa manufacturing 1,065. In late 1916 and early 1917, the Russian factories had produced around 230-250 airframes per month, with 1,800 aircraft and 4,000 engines supplied by the Allies. The Soviets also claim that with the Allied Expeditionary Forces (AEF) evacuation from Murmansk, some 139 Sopwith, forty-four Nieuport and thirty-one Farman aircraft and 300 aero-engines were seized.

The Duks Works was named State Aircraft Works No. 1 in 1918 and a new and vivid chapter was about to be written in Soviet aviation history. From then until 1923, the works built some 300 Sopwith 1½ Strutters, making it one of the most important aircraft in the early days of the Red Air Force. Earlier, in 1917, Strutters had been built at the Lebedev factory outside Petrograd, but shortages of engines limited production to around 140 aircraft.

However, the civil war that broke out in 1918 caused a serious setback to Russia's aircraft industry as the country became starved of foreign investment, supplies and up-to-date aeronautical technology. Many of the country's own aviation specialists went overseas, among them Igor Sikorsky, who settled in the USA and famously pioneered the development of rotary-wing aircraft.

During the civil war years the Ministry of Aircraft Production (MAP) continued with low-level production, mainly of aircraft of foreign design. However, in the early 1920s this was sharply reduced while the manufacture of aircraft of Russian design was increased. In 1918, 255 aircraft and 79 engines were produced, falling to only 137 aircraft and 77 engines the following year. The lack of resources to produce 'new builds' led to an increase in the repair and restoration of older designs, mainly British-designed DH.4, DH.9 and DH.9A aircraft under the supervision of Fiat engineers, with twenty-three DH.4s produced in 1920/21, the first twenty with 179 kW (240 hp) Fiat engines, and forty in 1921/22. For the entire civil war period only 668 new aircraft and 264 engines were built, although 1,574 aircraft and 1,740 engines were restored. In 1920, no new aircraft or engines were built and the industry's workforce fell to just 3,500 and continued to decline.

Following the civil war, which ended in 1921, Russia began a period of rebuilding its economy and industrial base, including the aircraft industry, and a three-year programme of state investment, retooling and expansion of the aircraft industry commenced in 1923. Three million gold roubles were allocated to regenerate the industry in 1921, and, in August 1922, a further 35 million for the purchase of foreign designs and the rebuilding of aircraft factories. Overseas licences were obtained for the more advanced technologies and the GAZ-1 plant in Moscow opened its own experimental aircraft manufacturing centre. The reality was that the situation was desperate.

In 1922, only forty-three airframes and eight aero-engines were produced, and by 1924 only thirteen military aircraft had been delivered. The Red Air Force possessed only 322 aircraft, of which thirty-six were naval planes. In order to supply the air force with the aircraft it needed, it was decided that the answer was to manufacture two or three fairly basic types—in fact copies of overseas designs, such as the DH.4, DH.9 and DH.9A fitted with a variety of Italian, German and British engines and later licence-built 298 kW (400 hp) American Liberty engines produced as the M-5.

The first Soviet series production aircraft, the R-1 (Reconnaissance 1—an improved and modified DH.9), was built under the guidance of the engineer Nikolai Polikarpov in 1923. More than 2,800 would be built (1,910 landplanes at GAZ-1 and 950 floatplanes at GAZ-10) with a variety of engines until production ceased in 1931. The R-1 was also the first Soviet aircraft to be exported, a number being delivered by Soviet pilots to Iran (Tehran) and Afghanistan (Kabul) in 1924. Also in 1923, the Polikarpov Department of Landplane Construction (OSS) was established at GAZ-1, its first design, the U-1, being produced the following year.

The U-1 was a reworked copy of a British Avro 504K that had been forced to land in northern Russia, following which it was taken to GAZ-1 where it was dismantled and analysed for Soviet production by Sergey Ilyushin. Powered by a 89.5 kW (120 hp) M-2 rotary engine, it was placed in production in 1922, initially at GAZ-5 in Moscow and later at GAZ-23 in Leningrad, where by far the majority of the U-1s were built. From 1923 to 1931, a total of 737 U-1 and seventy-three MU-1 floatplane trainers were built. The U-1 spawned a long line of home-produced Russian fighters. From 1926 to 1928, sixty Polikarpov I-2 fighters were built, and from 1927 until 1929, 102 I-2*bis* (*bis* = improved).

The first Soviet fighter aircraft were developed by Polikarpov and Grigorovich. However, Polikarpov's single-seat, low-wing I-1 monoplane displayed a number of insurmountable aerodynamic problems and consequently none of the thirty-three built entered service. On the other hand, in spite of Grigorovich's machine having a cramped cockpit and being generally overweight, the I-2 (initially also designated I-1) was ordered into series production in 1925 as the I-2*bis* to become the Red Air Force's first fighter, with 164 built at GAZ-1, and forty-seven at GAZ-23 from 1926 to 1928.

In 1927, the first series of U-2 [Po-2] trainers designed by Polikarpov were released. They became legendary and thousands of Soviet pilots trained on these aircraft. During the Great Patriotic War, the Po-2 was used as a night bomber, liaison, reconnaissance and air ambulance aircraft. The Soviets called it the 'partisan aircraft'—in the early 1920s the Soviet Union, like many other countries, including the USA, had bought its aircraft from France, Britain, Holland (500 from Fokker) and Italy etc.

The first indigenous all-metal fighter was the ANT-5 (I-4) developed by Pavel Sukhoi and Andrei Tupolev in 1927. At the same time, Polikarpov and his design team produced the I-3, and later, in 1929, the I-5, which was designed whilst Polikarpov, Grigorovich and other designers were incarcerated on fabricated charges by the state, such as the crash of the prototype I-6 (a re-engined I-3 with a Bristol Jupiter VI). They were accused by Stalin of conspiring to sabotage the aircraft industry—and forced to carry on their design work in prison conditions. As a consequence, the I-5, designed at the internee TsKB-39 design bureau, was also known as the VT-11 (VT being the Russian acronym for 'interior prison'). Three prototype I-5s were produced by April 1931, with seven pre-series (PP) models available by late summer. However, the portly mixed-construction I-5 soon showed signs of its enforced creation and most of 1931 was spent on exhaustive tests to cure the aircraft of its worst vices and preparing it for series production. As a precautionary measure, a licence was obtained from Heinkel for the production of the HD 37 biplane fighter at GAZ-1, where 134 were eventually built between 1932 and 1934. By late 1932, following intensive flying and testing at Khodynka airfield, which was often visited by Stalin, the I-5 entered production at the extensive new fighter plant at GAZ-21 at Gorky (Nizhny Novgorod), powered by a 358 kW (480 hp) M-22 radial engine built under licence from Gnome-Rhône at GAZ-29. Although difficult to fly, with inherent spin recovery problems (as with most early Soviet fighter designs), eventually the I-5 was an extremely successful aircraft. It was considered the best of the three (I-3, I-4 and I-5) and, with 803 built at the Gorky plant, the type remained in Red Air Force service for about nine years. Following the first flights the design team responsible for the I-5 were subsequently given their liberty as a reward.

Unfortunately this was not the last time the aircraft industry was to fall foul of the dreaded OGPU/NKVD Secret Police. In the late 1930s, Stalin again carried out a number of purges, with ironically the man most responsible for the modernisation of Soviet aircraft designs, Andrei Tupolev, a victim. He was interned in late October 1937.

In the 1930s, Soviet aviation was set a task (by Stalin) to produce aircraft capable of flying higher, farther and faster than any other. The Polikarpov OKB and the aircraft works started serial production of the R-5 aircraft that later become famous throughout the world. During the same period, Chkalov, Kokkinaki and Zhukov (test pilots at the Duks Works) set up the world's flight speed and payload-to-height records on Polikarpov-designed aircraft such as the I-15, I-16 and I-153 Chaika. The works collaborated with the design bureaux led by Ilyushin, Yakovlev, Petlyakov and Chizhevsky to produce the TsKB-26, TsKB-30, Yak-1, Il-4, Yak-3, Pe-2 and Il-2 aircraft.

The I-15 was considered to be one of the world's most outstanding and agile fighters. Series production of the type began in 1934, with 94 produced, and within a short time it had become a major part of the Red Air Force's combat inventory. As well as seeing combat in the Spanish Civil War in 1936, and China in 1937, in 1935 an unarmed I-15, flown by Kokkinaki, had established a world altitude record of 14,575 m. The introduction of an I-15*bis* into series production came in 1937, with a total build of 3,000 of various types of I-15 aircraft produced from 1934 until 1939. The I-153 Chaika, although still a biplane design, was a highly agile fighter with a retractable undercarriage, reinforced structure and an armament of four rapid-firing ShKAS 7.62 mm machine guns. It was fitted with a powerful M-62 engine and a variable-pitch AV-1 propeller. Having seen operational service in Mongolia, the aircraft was successively updated and in the hands of experienced Soviet pilots played a major part in the early years of the Great Patriotic War, in spite of the fact it was decidedly slower than the more up-to-date German aircraft that opposed it.

The Polikarpov I-16 was the world's first modern monoplane fighter, but its short, portly fuselage reduced its longitudinal stability to virtually zero, making it a tricky machine to handle. However, its high speed, agility, high survivability and ease of in-field maintenance ensured that it was soon ordered into production, with an initial batch of ten followed by a total series production run of some 9,000 examples built from 1934 to 1941. A modernised I-16 Type 29 was put into production in 1940, equipped to carry six under-wing rocket projectiles. The aircraft and its RS-82 rocket weapons successfully deployed against the Japanese in Mongolia. By 1933, Soviet pilots had reached heights of over 19,000 m, and pilots Kokkinaki and Gordienko made a non-stop flight in a TsKB-30 aircraft from Moscow to the USA in 1939.

In the mid-1930s the international situation became tense, and when Hitler's Germany and its allies eventually unleashed the Second World War in 1939, Soviet aircraft series production increased daily. From 1934 until 1938 the Soviet aircraft inventory had increased by 130 per cent and the total aero-engine aircraft power available had risen from 3.7 to 11.6 million hp. The average speed of bomber aircraft had increased by 56.5 per cent, short-range bombers by 88 per cent, and long-range bombers by 77 per cent. At the same time, the range of the short-and long-range bomber fleet had increased by 50 per cent and 61 per cent respectively. The operational ceiling of short-range bombers had increased by 83 per cent and long-range bombers by 77 per cent. In the autumn of 1938, however, Stalin realised that many Soviet military aircraft were obsolete, confirmation of this having been received from Spain where the German Messerschmitt Bf 109E 'Emil' fighters were proving to be vastly superior to the Soviet types deployed there. As a result, the third five-year plan (1938-1942) was to be even bigger than the previous two. Heavy industry, which included the aviation industry, was scheduled to increase production by 15.7 per cent each year.

Coal, petrol, steel, aluminium and electricity production was to increase considerably with the creation of 3,000 new industrial plants, many in the Urals and Siberia, far from the Soviet western border and far from future enemies. This massive expansion required eight million more skilled workers and an increase in productivity of 65 per cent, which meant that the country was to transform to a war economy with all emphasis on military production. Stalin was convinced that these measures would permit the Soviet Union to defeat the 'capitalist cannibals' and allow its domination of Europe and other parts of the world. When Hitler began his 'preventive war' against Stalin on 22 June 1941, it was too late. Soviet industrial production had already reached 86 per cent of that planned for December 1942.

In 1938, the Soviet Union had produced 7,727 aircraft, which included 2,379 fighters and 2,017 bombers. This compared to German production of 5,235 aircraft, of which 3,950 were military aircraft (including trainers). At the time, the USA built only 1,800 military aircraft (including trainers), many for export. Not only had Soviet production of aircraft and engines increased, but so had the manufacture of airscrews, equipment, arms and ordnance etc., and up to 1940, the industry had built 34,233 ShKAS-type machine guns for aircraft. Soviet aero-engine production was 17,034.

It was only the development of new aircraft that was static, sixteen prototypes built in 1936 but not tested having resulted in problems in development. This was the first indication of such problems and, in the years that followed, a number of prototypes were cancelled, due mainly to increasing costs of development. The loss of accepted prototypes actually resulted in less choice available for series production, but the decreases affected mainly new light aircraft (48 per cent), which was a bigger decrease than for the larger aircraft (32 per cent) which were mainly military. Stalin realised that in real terms series aircraft production had dropped, and in 1939 he ordered the creation of many new design bureaux, which were very often offered to young engineers. This soon reversed the situation, increasing competition between OKBs and resulting in an increase in some excellent prototype designs becoming available for evaluation for series production. These were to be the famous Soviet aircraft of the Second World War. Nevertheless, there was no overall growth in Soviet military aircraft production from 1939 to 1940, but there was a considerable increase in fighter and bomber aircraft production, the country at this time still being at peace.

In the period immediately preceding the Great Patriotic War, the Soviet aircraft industry developed very fast. In 1937, the People's Commissariat for War Industry in the Soviet Union had forty-two Zavods. These included twenty-one for aircraft production and ten for aero-engines, the others being for parts, equipment, armament and instruments, etc. In addition, the civil sector of the industry, e.g. Aeroflot, had fifteen plants dedicated to civil aircraft production. These were Zavods 81-89 and 240-245. Most of these were originally repair plants, although Zavod 81 at Tushino produced Stal-2 and Stal-3 transport planes and also DI-6 fighters, and started series production of the Yakovlev Yak-2 multi-role combat aircraft in 1940. Another civil plant, Zavod 84 at Khimki, had started to produce instruments in 1936 and was later adapted for series production of the American DC-3 airliners as the PS-84. In reality, however, production of the PS-84 was soon dropped and throughout the Second World War the 'civil' factory built Lisunov Li-2 (Douglas C-47) civil and military transports and long-range bombers.

Another 'civil' Aeroflot repair plant, Zavod 240 at Moscow, was producing the very modern Bartini I-240 fighter, which was a very advanced fighter for its time and was comparable to western fighters of the era. In 1939, Zavod 240 went over to production of the unique DB-240 diesel-engined long-range bomber, with which it continued until 1947. This aircraft was the Soviets' first mass-produced heavy bomber, well before the Tupolev Tu-4 Bull (a reverse-engineered B-29). In addition, the Red Air Force also had its own aircraft overhaul and repair bases, some of which were used as the war progressed for aircraft modification work and even production, and these were only the beginnings.

From 1939, the Soviet aviation industry developed on a very big scale. As a first step, in January 1939, the People's Commissariat for War Industry was divided into four independent commissariats: aircraft production, naval industry, armament industry and ammunition production. The Commissar for Aircraft Production at this time was M. M. Kaganovich. In September 1939, the Politburo adopted a policy to build nine giant aircraft plants and to increase the size and output of nine of the existing plants. This represented an increase of 260 per cent in aircraft production. The new plants were established at Kuibyshev (two), Tbilisi (two), Kazan, Novosibirsk, Minsk, Bykovo and Vnukovo. Yearly output rose to 10,000 aircraft in 1939, and to 26,000 in 1942.

On 26 October 1939, a Soviet delegation left on a seven-week visit to German aviation plants. This was followed a few weeks later by another delegation which, on 11 February 1940, ordered thirty-six modern German aircraft and helicopters, embracing twelve different types in all. Cross-licensed production was also negotiated: two-thirds for the Soviet Union and a third for Germany. When the German models were delivered to Moscow, in May-June 1940, they were examined in great detail by some 3,500 specialists from the Red Air Force, twenty-one different Zavods, three OKBs and many research institutes. The Luftwaffe soon had no more secrets for Stalin. Petrov, the Chief of TsAGI, having visited 219 'objectives' in Germany, informed Stalin that the production capacity of the German aircraft industry was seven combat aircraft a day; in reality, it was twenty-five a day.

Petrov's misinformation made Stalin feel threatened and he immediately ordered that Soviet combat aircraft production should be increased to fifty aircraft a day by June 1941, and to seventy a day by September 1941. The foregoing circumstances actually led Stalin to dismiss the 'incapable' Kaganovich from his position as Commissar for Aircraft Production and to appoint him as Director of Zavod 125 at Kazan. Later he was arrested because 'he had placed the aviation plants in the western regions, offering them to Hitler'. Finally, in Lubyanka prison in 1948, he shot himself with a revolver offered by his brother, who was a confidant of Stalin. The new Commissar for Aircraft Production was Shahurin, the Communist Party's secretary of the Gorky Region, who had little or no knowledge of aviation. It was for this reason that he had several deputies such as Gyementyev, Balangin for engine production, and the young designer Yakovlev for airframes.

In June 1940, seven factories that had absolutely nothing to do with aviation were converted for aircraft production. These formed Zavods 381-387. The Yaroslav automobile plant became Zavod 381, producing Ilyushin Il-2 Sturmoviks; the Tochizmeritel plant at Moscow became Zavod 382 for instrument and equipment production; Zavod 384 at Tashkent was for component production; Zavod 386 at Rostov was for LaGG-3 production; and the carriage works at Stalingrad as Zavod 387 started U-2 trainer aircraft (later Polikarpov Po-2) series production. In line with these changes, the length of the working day for employees in the aviation industry was increased from seven to ten hours a day. Moreover, if any worker arrived late twice or more at his plant, he was to be sent to the concentration camp.

By late 1940 the People's Commissariat for Aviation Industry had seventy-four finished plants—twenty-eight for aircraft, fourteen for aero-engine production and thirty-two for components propellers, undercarriage instruments, armaments, etc.—and the industry still awaited the nine new plants and the expansion of nine others. However, in February 1941, Stalin ordered that all plants still involved in civil production should be converted for military hardware production to prepare for the invasion of Europe on 6 July 1941. As a result, Soviet industry ceased to produce all consumer and domestic goods and any product considered by Stalin to be superfluous to the war effort. Only arms, guns, aircraft, ships, tanks, ammunition and bombs were to be manufactured in the still 'peaceful' Soviet Union. This was a situation that never existed in Germany, even when it faced certain defeat early in 1945. Following Stalin's decree, the industry grew to ninety plants with the capability of producing 60,000 aircraft a year. Part of the 1941 aircraft production schedule was for big assault gliders to help in the total invasion of Europe.

The Red Army had one million paratroopers, 250 times more than Germany, and Soviet engineers developed some ingenious methods for their transportation behind enemy lines. Many reconnaissance planes and bombers were transformed to carry between ten and fourteen parachutists in individual containers under the wings. Even army battle tanks were fitted with wings to carry troops deep into enemy territory. On 25 February 1941, the Council of the People's Commissars issued a new decree on the reorganisation of the Red Air Force: namely, 106 new regiments were to be created, each with sixty or more combat aircraft (6,700 new aircraft, plus reserves), and all existing regiments were to be equipped with new aircraft. During the first three years of the third five-year plan aircraft production increased by 13 per cent each year, the armament industry doing even better with a 39 per cent increase per year. The military budget was increased annually, with 25.5 per cent of the Soviet budget being allocated to the military in 1939. The following year this figure increased to 32.6 per cent, and in 1941 to 43.3 per cent, and during the second half of 1941 a 'one-off' allocation of an additional 20.6 billion roubles was made, over and above the normal annual budgetary allocation. This additional allocation was sufficient to produce 50,000 Pe-2 bombers. In the period from 1 January 1939 to 22 June 1941, the Soviet aircraft industry delivered a total of 17,745 combat planes. Yet, on the last day of June 1941, Stalin still ordered the industry to work day and night for victory.

It has been stated many times that Hitler was lucky to have made his attack against Stalin when he did, on 22 June 1941, as two weeks later it would have been too late. The concentration of the massive Soviet forces in the west, the one million paratroopers, ten times more aircraft, seven times more tanks, and the deployment of a number of unique weapons whose development had been ordered by Stalin, meant that the Germans would have been totally incapable of resisting the Soviet invasion, and Stalin would have realised his own aspiration to world dominance.

The massive build-up of Soviet hardware was being prepared for offence, not defence, and was subsequently amassed on the country's western border on 22 June 1941, in readiness for the big attack to commence on 6 July 1941. Preparations were made to evacuate Zavod 23 at Leningrad and Zavod 43 at Kiev out of range of the German bombers. Soviet glider factories had been producing hundreds of big wooden gliders for the big attack, but after the German assault all these aircraft were left completely destroyed and totally useless.

As the attack on 22 June continued, Stalin, realising he was in great danger of losing everything, immediately started secret negotiations with the Germans in an attempt to halt their advance. At the same time, he ordered the evacuation of the western territories, instrument plants were ordered to go to west Siberia, and he attempted to increase aircraft production. On the day of the German attack, the person responsible for aero-engine production was arrested and imprisoned for 'sabotage and spying'. However, forty days later, Balangin, who had lost many kilograms of weight in prison, was again in his office under direct instructions from Stalin to multiply production. Aero-engine production had remained the aviation industry's weakest aspect and had been a constant cause for concern. In 1928, 70 per cent of all the aero-engines used in the Soviet Union were imported, and attempts to improve and develop the Soviet

M-5 based on the American Liberty engine proved unsuccessful. The M-17, based on the German BMW VI engine, was already obsolete when quantity production was achieved in 1929, and had been supplemented by the purchase of the 358 kW (480 hp) 9-cylinder Gnome-Rhône 9ASB radial engines from France, and their eventual licensed manufacture as the M-22 was fortuitous.

Air-cooled radials with their high output and suitability to Russian climatic conditions were the best choice for the 'new' generation of Soviet combat aircraft, and the United States was approached as source of supply, as well as France. In 1929, a Soviet air delegation headed by Baranov and including Andrei Tupolev and Boris Stechkin, then head of TsAGI's Aero-Engine Division, had visited America to negotiate the purchase of aircraft and engines. The result was the acquisition of a number of 447 kW (600 hp) Curtiss Conqueror inline engines, but only in limited quantities, which were used in prototype and experimental aircraft. So, for the time being, only the M-22 was available to designers who wished to incorporate radial engines in their designs. A second delegation to the USA in 1932 was more successful, obtaining manufacturing rights for the 522 kW (700 hp) Wright Cyclone SGR-1820-F3 9-cylinder radial, which, along with a number of other examples, was used to power the I-14, I-15 and I-16 prototype fighters. In 1934, preparations were made to produce the Wright Cyclone as the M-25 at GAZ-19 at Perm (Molotov) under the supervision of Arkady Shvetsov, who later developed the engine into the more powerful M-62 series in 1937, and undertook development of the 14-cylinder two-row Wright Cyclone R-2600 radial at the same plant as the M-82.

In spite of the acquisition of the Wright Cyclone patent, contacts with the French aero-engine industry were maintained, and Vladimir Klimov and Sergei Tumansky were sent by TsIAM in a delegation headed by Sergey Ilyushin to discuss deals with a number of French firms in 1933. Two engines were chosen for licensed production in the Soviet Union: the 596 kW (800 hp) 14-cylinder two-row Gnome-Rhône Mistral 14 radial, and the 641 kW (860 hp) 12-cylinder Hispano-Suiza 12Y inline engine, developed as the M-85 and M-100 respectively. Tumansky produced the M-85 at GAZ-29, and Klimov, an experienced aero-engineer who had headed Soviet purchasing negotiations to BMW and Gnome-Rhône in the 1920s, was set up at the big GAZ-26 plant at Rybinsk (Shcherbakov), the former GAZ-6 Renault engine plant.

However, whilst these licence-built powerplants were destined to play a major role in the development of future Soviet aero-engine technology, the early years of the 1930s were dominated by the M-34, developed from the M-17 by Alexander Mikulin at GAZ-34 and used to power multi-engined and long-range aircraft as well as later versions of the Polikarpov R-5. Design work on the M-34 began in 1929, and after bench tests two years later the first flight tests were successfully completed in 1932. The 12-cylinder M-34 inline engine had the distinction of being the first Soviet aero-engine to be built on a production-line basis, with increased power variants from 520 kW (700 hp) to 890 kW (1,200 hp) built from 1932 until production ended in 1938.

Among the emerging technologies under the auspices of the new semi-autonomous organisations created by TsAGI to extend its aerodynamic development programmes was the Special Design Division (OOK), under A. M. Izakson, which was to concentrate on rotating-wing aircraft. The first Soviet autogiro, the KASKR, was designed by Nikolai Kamov and Nikolai Skrzhinski and built with the help of funds from the Osoaviakhim (military reservist and support organisation) in 1929. Test flights were made in 1930 and 1931, after a more powerful engine was installed. The first Soviet helicopter, TsAGI's 1-EA, was flown in August 1932 by its designer Aleksei Cheremukhin, but lacked stability and later crashed during tethered tests. As a result, in 1933, the OOK contained a helicopter brigade under Ivan Bratukhin and three autogiro brigades led by Kuznetsov, Kamov and Skrzhinski. Although the group made a promising start and a number of prototypes were built, only a small batch of Kamov A-7s had been built for the Red Army when the OOK was disbanded.

What was urgently needed was an effective anti-tank sturmovik. All efforts were concentrated in this direction, with the major design bureau being directed to submit prototypes for evaluation. At the TsKB four low-level ground attack or sturmovik prototypes were built on the basis of the R-5 recce aircraft, while Tupolev proposed a heavy twin-engined biplane which was a modification of the R-6. None of these proposals were accepted, and the only original design, the TSh-3 by Kocherigin and Gurevich, was eventually rejected in 1934, after prolonged testing, on the grounds of inadequate speed. In fact, its top speed of nearly 250 kph at sea level was only marginally lower than specified, but its more than generous armour protection for the crew brought its all-up combat flying weight to slightly over 3,500 kg and it was considered that the 620 kW (830 hp) M-34F engine would be inefficient in providing the aircraft with viable attack speeds.

The reality was that the powers that be expected the sturmovik to possess the turn of speed of a heavy single-seat fighter plane while incorporating extensive armour plating for crew protection and carrying a substantial load of armament. These requirements in reality stifled sturmovik development until Ilyushin produced its TsKB-55 in 1938. Even then, production was delayed by Stalin's insistence that the design should be revised as a faster single-seat aircraft, thereby denying the Red Air Force early experience with what was to become the greatest sturmovik of all time, the ubiquitous Ilyushin Il-2. In the interim, as usual, a number of existing types were adapted. There was a sturmovik version of the R-5, the R-5Sh, several hundred of which were built, while a number of Kocherigin's DI-6 two-seat fighter biplanes were converted to serve in the ground attack role. Two attempts were also made to adapt the I-16 for ground attack, but these did not proceed beyond the prototype stage.

One of the basic factors seriously affecting the development of the sturmovik was the lack of an effective anti-tank weapon. Batteries of 7.62 mm machine guns were useless, and low-level horizontal bombing at speed had proved to be hopelessly inaccurate. Eventually a breakthrough occurred in the form of a new large-calibre recoilless cannon devised by Leonid Kurchevsky for the Red Army, which could be adapted for installation in aircraft. After Stalin and Mikhail Tukhachevsky had witnessed the impressive demonstrations of the weapon, Kurchevsky was awarded vast funds for its development and was made head of a Special Weapons Development Directorate attached directly to Sergo Ordzhonikidze's Commissariat for Heavy Industry. He was also granted direct access to Stalin and given a Lincoln limousine to convey him between his experimental factory and the Kremlin. Stalin instructed the aircraft industry to work closely with him in the design of a special aircraft to carry two 76 mm APK-4 cannon and Sukhoi was instructed to mount weapons of the same calibre on the I-4 fighter for preliminary tests.

The I-4, with its Kurchevsky cannon, was demonstrated in December 1931, and despite a number of accidents in early test firings, results were considered good enough for a special 'Z' fighter to be built by Grigorovich, who decided to use an I-5 airframe converted into a monoplane. The major problem to be overcome was the dispersion of the explosive reactionary gases expelled from the cannon, necessitating a protective metal sheathing under the wings and the raising of the tailplane so that control of the aircraft would be unaffected by the blast. However, relocation of the tailplane gave rise to aerodynamic problems and completion of prototype testing was delayed until 1933, when the first of three Top Secret 'Z' fighters was demonstrated by NII VVS test pilots to Stalin and his close associates. Tupolev was immediately ordered to start production, despite the 'staged' demonstration masking a number of serious ongoing problems with the aircraft that no one was brave enough the reveal to Stalin.

In reality, the 'Z' was not easy to fly. It required expert handling and the Kurchevsky cannon proved to be highly unreliable, often jamming or bursting, with its muzzle velocity far below that needed for accurate air gunnery. None the less, following Stalin's directive, twenty-one 'Z' fighters were built at GAZ-1 in 1933, and a further fifty at GAZ-135 in Kharkov up until 1936, during which time relations between Grigorovich and Kurchevsky continued to deteriorate. They became decidedly worse when Stalin insisted that they work together on a new fighter project, the IP-1 (DG-52), along with a number of other aircraft designers who were forced to work with the new supremo of the Soviet armaments industry.

Pavel Sukhoi was instructed to provide for the fitting of two APK-4 cannon in his new I-14 fighter, while Arkhangelsky and Chernyshev were ordered to start on designs of heavier aircraft capable of carrying two 120 mm recoilless cannon. Chernyshev's I-12 fighter, a twin-boom puller-pusher design with two Bristol Jupiter VI radial engines, was soon abandoned due to objections from NII VVS pilots aware of the hazards of baling out and falling into the rear propeller. Arkhangelsky's two-seat DIP (ANT-29), a more conventional twin-engined aircraft, escaped Kurchevsky's influence as priority was given to the SB bomber with which it had a degree of commonality.

A number of other adventurous designs from other OKBs were proposed to accommodate Kurchevsky heavy armament, including a fighter with a retractable cockpit cover by Ilyushin and Lavochkin, and the BICh-7 flying-wing fighter by Boris Cheranovski as well as a project by Peter Grushin at the Moscow Aviation Institute. But, in February 1936, with almost all of Kurchevsky's ideas discredited, his design facilities were appropriated and later in the year he was arrested, to be executed or perish in one of the Gulag labour camps.

Stalin believed Kurchevsky had betrayed him and became deeply suspicious of all Soviet engineers and designers, particularly those involved in the aspects of new and unconventional military development. The Kurchevsky fiasco actually sparked further repercussions and arrests, which were soon accelerated by the unfavourable reports from the Spanish Civil War regarding Soviet aircraft performance compared with the opposing German machines. In fact, the full extent of Stalin's purges over the next three years has never been fully expounded.

Development of the I-15 and I-16 fighters had been in parallel with the development of the SB bomber to meet the 1933 requirement for a fast tactical bomber to replace the ageing TB-1, R-5 and R-6 aircraft still in service. The SB was designed by Alexander Arkhangelsky under Andrei Tupolev's supervision, with the first of the two all-metal ANT-40 prototypes appearing in 1934. Powered by two Wright Cyclone SGR-1820-F3 radials, the first was flown by test pilot Mikhail Gromov on 7 October 1934, followed by the second, with two Hispano-Suiza 12Y inline engines, on 30 December. The performance of the second aircraft was markedly improved, due mainly to the reduced drag offered by the inline engines and a fuel capacity increased from 940 litres (207 gallons) to 1,670 litres (367 gallons), with a top speed of 420 kph (260 mph) at 5,000 m (15,000 feet) altitude and an extended range of 1,250 km (777 miles) with a 500 kg (1,100 lb) bomb load.

Unfortunately, NII VVS testing did not proceed smoothly and there were innumerable acrimonious disagreements between Arkhangelsky and the VVS test pilot, Konstantin Minder. These reached such a pitch that Ordzhonikidze was asked to intervene, and when he and Tupolev arrived at the test field they found the prototype aircraft festooned in home-made posters indicating its many defects. Inevitably the affair reached Stalin's ears, and he rebuked Arkhangelsky for not listening to Minder's complaints and recommendations. However, NII VVS tests were finished in July 1935, the bomber entering series production at GAZ-22 (Fili) and GAZ-18 (Voronezh), with the first aircraft entering Red Air Force service in early 1936. At the peak of production, thirteen SBs were completed each day, and the aircraft was still in production when the Germans invaded in June 1941.

The SB was continually updated throughout the 1930s, with Soviet 626 kW (840 hp) M-100A and 716 kW (960 hp) M-103 engines in later variants. With some 6,456 built, it came second only to the Polikarpov R-5 as the most widely built of Soviet pre-war bombers. At its inception, with its monocoque fuselage frame and duralumin covering, it represented a great advance in Soviet aircraft design, although with further advances in fighter plane design and performance, as events in Spain were to prove, the SB was not safe from attack by the new generation of German fighters, such as the Messerschmitt Bf 109. It was soon pushed to higher altitudes in an attempt to avoid the enemy fighters to deliver its bombs—but at the expense of bombing accuracy. In the late 1930s, a civil freighter variant of the SB was introduced, designated PS-40.

From March 1941, the aircraft industry was required to work 24 hours a day in an effort to produce 1,500 aircraft per month by July of that year. Statistical evidence available at the time indicates that the industry had supplied no more than 7,500 combat planes annually in 1939 and 1940, although other figures give production at 10,382 and 10,563 for 1939 and 1940 respectively. Of the 17,745 combat aircraft produced between 1 January 1939 and 22 June 1940, only 3,719 were new types, with 2,653 being Yak-1, LaGG and MiG fighters, Pe-2 bombers, and BSh/Il-2 Sturmoviks were produced in the first six months of 1941. But then only a very low figure of just 1,166 new types including the Yak-4, Ar-2, Su-2 and DB-3F (Il-4) were built in the year 1939/40.

On 19 August 1941, Stalin was obliged to order the full-scale evacuation of the industrial plants behind the Volga River. In a few months, 2,539 Zavods were evacuated, and some 7.7 million workers—the lucky ones with their families—were installed in the eastern regions of the country by the spring of 1942. On the other hand, there are no records of the many hundreds of thousands who froze to death or died from hunger and disease in the massive evacuations that took place. But this, in Stalin's eyes, was a small price to pay in order to salvage the Soviet Union's aviation industry. On the same day, he again ordered an immediate increase in production of combat aircraft, mainly fighters. The evacuated Zavods actually worked day and night in two places at once —at their original locations up to the last moment until finally all parts, tools and machines had been removed, and at the new locations as parts, tools and machinery were recommissioned for use. Soviet railways carried 1.5 million wagonloads of plant, equipment and personnel eastwards from July until November 1941, involving 1,523 factories, installations and research establishments of all kinds from areas occupied or likely to be occupied by the enemy.

Responsibility for the evacuations was entrusted to Volodya Shakhurin, the Commissar for Aircraft Production, and his immediate specialised deputies, P. V. Dementiev and P. A. Voronin (fighters), A. I. Kuznetsov (bombers), A. A. Zavitaev (aero-engines), A. S. Yakovlev and V. P. Kuznetsov (the chiefs of prototype aircraft and experimental aero-engine development) and M. V. Khrunichev (in charge of factory buildings and raw material supplies). In all, 85 per cent of Soviet airframe and aero-engine production facilities were evacuated from the west of the country, with some plants moving a second time in the summer of 1942 when the Voroshilovgrad (Lugansk), Voronezh and Stalingrad areas were threatened.

The Soviets were fortunate in being aided in this massive undertaking to some degree. Firstly, the Luftwaffe was almost totally preoccupied with army support tasks, with no directives issued to switch to a campaign of strategic bombing. Those raids that were ordered against Moscow had little effect in hampering the industrial evacuation of the area. Between January and May 1942, Moscow, Gorky, Voronezh and Rybinsk—all centres of aircraft production—suffered only small and occasional air attacks which did little more than provoke the Soviets to strengthen their air defences in the area. Secondly, there was ready availability of new factories completed or near completion in the interior and east of the Urals, intended to supply machines for the Far Eastern Air Force, although it is true that many were far from completed at this time. However, in the execution of this massive evacuation and relocation the Soviets paid a heavy price, with hundreds killed.

The evacuation of aircraft plants from the Moscow area had been completed by October, but for those in the remote areas of the western Soviet Union the task was more complicated. A number of production plants, in particular GAZ-29 at Zaporozhye and GAZ-31 at Taganrog, were still moving out their heavy machinery and machine tools under heavy shell-fire, and many barges transporting GAZ-26 from Rybinsk to Ufa became ice-blocked in the frozen Kama, Belaya and Ufa rivers.

Having arrived at their designated new areas, conditions were diabolical with many schools, hospitals, cinemas and theatres requisitioned to house the thousands of workers until new special barrack blocks could be built. Many workers rarely left the factories and slept by their machines, the hastily erected factories working day and night with power provided by generators on railway wagons. Billboards were posted with slogans urging ever greater productivity—For the Front!—For the Motherland!—For Stalin! However, output of the component plants at this time was highly erratic, resulting in grave repercussions at the final assembly plants. At GAZ-153 in Novosibirsk, Yakovlev shared the production lines with Lavochkin where LaGG-3 fighters were already in production, and the factory, its airfield and surrounding areas were choked with aircraft awaiting undercarriages and propellers. Stalin ordered an investigatory committee, headed by General Petrov, to report on the reasons for the congestion in the assembly plants. Shakhurin was castigated by Stalin for the fall-off in deliveries—from a peak of over 2,300 in September 1941, to 800 in October, and to fewer than 450 in November, with most of the evacuations still in progress.

Early in 1942, Stalin ordered that monthly production totals should be based on the number of aircraft 'combat ready' and not on the number assembled. In addition, any directors whose factories fell short of requirements would receive a telegram of rebuke from Stalin. Already two such men, M. B. Shenkman and A. T. Tretyakov, the directors of GAZ-18 and GAZ-1, had been sharply reprimanded on 23 December 1941. Their personal telegrams read:

> You have let down our country and our Red Army. You are still not facilitating the production of Il-2s. The Il-2 is as vital to our Red Army as air or bread. Shenkman is producing one Il-2 per day and Tretyakov one or two MiG fighters. This is an insult to our country and our Red Army. We do not need MiG-3 fighters but Il-2 Sturmoviks instead.
>
> If GAZ-18 thinks it can fob us off with one Il-2 a day it is cruelly mistaken and will suffer the consequences. Do not make the government lose its patience. I demand the production of more Il-2s. This is my last warning! Stalin.

The rebukes and pressure placed on the aircraft plants and its directors by Stalin worked. Production had risen rapidly by April 1942, with 8,141 combat planes delivered by the middle of the year and a further 13,436 in the second half, to give an overall production total for 1942 of 21,577 out of the 25,240 planned.

In comparison 15,735 had been produced in 1941, of which 12,000 were combat planes, and combat plane production in 1943 reached 30,000 out of a total output of 34,884 aircraft, with a significant shift from bomber to Sturmovik production. GAZ-24, evacuated from Moscow and now co-located at the Frunze Aero-Engine Works producing inline AM-38 engines for installation in the Il-2, was producing four times as many engines in 1942 as the year before, becoming one of seven plants to win the Order of the Red Banner in 1945. But as Il-2 Sturmovik production increased, twin-engined bomber production plummeted.

In 1940, twin-engined bombers formed only 34 per cent of Soviet military aircraft production. The following year that figure fell to 24 per cent, and to just 14 per cent in 1942, with only 3,500 bombers built compared to 8,200 Sturmoviks. The largest bomber type was the Pe-2, of which a total of 11,427 were built. Even so, only two were built in 1940 at GAZ-22, followed by 438 in the first half of 1941, and 1,409 in the second half. This represented the total Soviet bomber production for that year, although some increase did occur the following year when GAZ-22 moved to Kazan, along with GAZ-16 from Rybinsk, to build the bombers' M-105 engines.

As in Britain, where at one time the Rolls-Royce Merlin engine was in short supply, Soviet bomber production suffered from having to compete for engines, as most of the Klimov inline variants were needed for Yak and LaGG-3 fighters. However, the phasing out of production of the LaGG-3 in 1943 did help to ease the situation. Even Tupolev's sophisticated Tu-2 had to compete with the Lavochkin radial-engined fighters for supplies of the Shvetsov ASh-82 engine. The only bomber not to be affected in this way was the Ilyushin Il-4 fitted with Tumansky M-88 radials, built as the standard long-range bomber at GAZ-39 at Irkutsk.

Despite all these problems, the Red Air Force had almost always maintained many more operational aircraft than the Luftwaffe, in spite of very heavy losses, with the Soviet aviation industry committed to their immediate replacement. On 22 October 1941, the Luftwaffe claimed 15,179 Soviet aircraft destroyed or captured, but according to the Soviets they possessed 32,100 military planes at the time of the German attack on 22 June 1941. However, as already mentioned, the situation changed at the beginning of December 1941. The Soviet troops advanced, evacuation of the works was stopped, and serial production of combat aircraft resumed. Workers and engineers achieved the 'impossible'. In three months the first series of attack planes were produced —the Ilyushin Il-2 Sturmovik, the legendary 'flying tank', referred to by the enemy as the 'Black Death'. In the second half of 1941, the country's aircraft industry had also produced a further 9,777 aircraft, giving a total of 41,900, of which (according to the Soviets) 21,100 were lost in 1941. Stalin could also of course mobilise many thousands of civil aircraft. There were also American (Lend-Lease) and British deliveries, although at this stage these were very small and certainly without influence on the ensuing battles. Soviet military aircraft production in the April-June quarter of

1941 increased to 3,546, which by the July-September period had further increased to 7,338, although by the October-December quarter there had been a dramatic fall to 2,439.

On 9 November 1941, the Central Military Council approved the reduced aircraft production plans for December 1941 and January 1942. However, in spite of the reduced target and every attempt being made to achieve this, the actual output for December 1941 reached only 40 per cent of the aircraft production target and only 23.6 per cent of the aero-engine production requirements. Output had followed the downward trend already established in November 1941, which was three and a half times less than in September 1941. In fact, only 693 aircraft were built in December.

The following clearly indicates the big increase in aircraft production immediately after the German attack of June 1941, but there were dramatic reductions following the evacuations. Aircraft production remained low in early 1942: 976 in January, 822 in February, 1,352 in March, and 1,423 in April.

Production period	Combat aircraft production	Total aircraft production	Percentage of combat aircraft in total
January-June 1941	4,177	5,958	70.1 %
July-Dec 1941	8,200	9,777	83.9 %
Total production 1941	12,377	15,735	78.7 %

Owing to the German advances in 1941, 63 per cent of the coal mines, 68 per cent of the iron foundries and 60 per cent of the aluminium plants and a large percentage of the electrical power stations had been destroyed. It was of the utmost urgency to replace all these lost mines and industrial plants with new ones behind the Volga, in the Urals, west Siberia, Kazakhstan, and other parts of the vast expanses of the Soviet Union. Another problem was the reorganisation of the supply system and communications between the aviation and other sub-assembly plants. Acute shortages of raw materials did not make this easy; sometimes it was impossible. Airframe production plants reverted to wooden construction as there was no aluminium, and even the 'all-metal' Il-4 bomber received wooden wings. All production of the excellent Mikoyan MiG-3 fighter stopped, as the aero-engine plants could no longer supply the engines, and the MiG-3 plant was converted to build engines for the Il-2 Sturmovik aircraft. Other models that Stalin did not like were removed from the production programme entirely, although this did have the positive effect of stemming the proliferation of models in production, thereby enforcing a degree of rationalisation.

What price did the evacuated Soviet workers have to pay to save Stalin and his dictatorial regime? Very often both aircraft and engines were built in cold, often unfinished plants or wooden barracks or at times in the open air at -30 °C. The evacuated workers were accommodated in cold barracks or tents, and at times even just holes in the ground. Sometimes it was necessary to travel up to 15 km through deep snow to the plant to work a 12-hour shift, having had only a single meal of three potatoes. They were obliged to work without food, medical care, or even proper clothing and footwear, even if sick. Any workers not able to produce the 'norm' were sent to the concentration camps, where the only liberation was death.

From March 1942, several more plants were organised at Moscow. These were mainly for the production of equipment, instruments, arms and aircraft. At Khodynka, and the empty workshops of Zavod 1, the new Zavod 30 was organised for Ilyushin Il-2 Sturmovik production. At the same time, Zavod 381, evacuated from Yaroslavl, was also sent to Khodynka, to the empty hangars vacated by Zavod 39. Zavod 381 built 243 Il-2s in 1942, but the following year switched to Lavochkin La-5FN fighter production. Zavod 23, which had been evacuated in 1941 from Leningrad to Moscow-Fili to build LaGG-3 fighters, was then sent to the East in September 1941, but returned to Fili in 1942 to build DB-3F bombers. It remained there until 1943, when it moved to Omsk to build Tupolev Tu-2s, taking the place of Zavod 166. This Zavod had been established in the autumn of 1941 especially for Tu-2 production, but was now required to build Yak-9s when they entered production in January 1943. Zavod 82 was also organised at Tushino, in the plant previously occupied by Zavod 81. These changes did not always seem to make sense and were contrary to Stalin's rigid order 'Do not touch the production lines'—an order which in itself was bad, as it often prevented the introduction of new or improved models, although production of combat aircraft in 1942 very nearly represented the total production of aircraft for the year.

In 1943, 14,600 fighters were produced and, the following year, Soviet fighter plane production peaked at 18,000 aircraft built. The Chkalov factory at Novosibirsk, GAZ-153, which was producing three Yak-1 fighters a day in February 1942, was by the end of the year producing twenty a day and by the end of the war had increased its output to fifty Yak-9 fighters. From January to March 1945 alone, it assembled 1,500 aircraft, which was 10 per cent of its wartime production. A second fighter plant, GAZ-292 at Saratov, was awarded the Order of Lenin in July 1942 for early fighter production and later Yak-7B production, leading to the Yak-9. Although fewer than thirty were produced in 1943, this led to an eventual total build of 16,700, which was 25 per cent of all Soviet wartime fighter production.

Of the Lavochkin designs the La-5 and its La-5FN development were the most numerous, with some 10,599 built, most at the Ordzhonikidze fighter plant, GAZ-21, at Gorky. GAZ-126 at Komsomolsk-on-Amur and GAZ-31 at Tbilisi also produced La-5s, GAZ-126 receiving the Order of Lenin in July 1942, and GAZ-31 the Order of the Red Star in July 1945. The new Zavods at Yaroslavl and Moscow assembled 5,753 La-7 fighters from 1944 onwards.

Transport plane production at GAZ-84, evacuated from Moscow to Tashkent, remained modest and the Soviets were glad to receive Lend-Lease Douglas C-47s from the USA. Even though transport plane production did continue to rise from 450 in 1942 to 1,260 in 1943 and just over 1,500 in 1944, these were only small utility planes such as the Shche-2, Yak-6, or transport variants of the Polikarpov U-2 training plane.

The planned replacement for the indigenous Lisunov Li-2 (DC-3) variant was the Il-12. Although work began in 1943, the type did not actually fly until 1946. At the same time production of training aircraft, which in addition to the Polikarpov U-2 and UT-2 were usually conversions of standard fighter planes, rose from an annual output of between 3,000 and 4,000 aircraft to 5,500 in 1944.

Up until the autumn of 1944, the Soviet aviation industry was meeting all the needs of the Red Air Force, and production of 8,000 training planes in 1945 meant that many older models could be passed on to the Osoaviakhim. The Achilles' heel of the 'new' Soviet fighter designs, however, was the substitution of wooden structures as the shortage of machine tools began to bite. Aircraft weights increased dramatically, with the commonly used M-105PF inline engine barely able to cope. In a desperate attempt to lighten the Yak and LaGG fighters to match the Messerschmitt Bf 109s on equal terms, fuel tankage and defensive armament was cut, putting the Red Air Force's fighter pilots at an even greater disadvantage. A further disadvantage with Soviet wooden airframes was brought about by the poor quality of protective paints and lacquers used. These caught fire easily and failed totally to arrest corrosion, many aircraft that had been set aside for the Battle of Kursk being found to be unairworthy due to deterioration of their airframes after prolonged exposure to the open air. Even so—despite Stalin's protestations that immediate steps should be taken to revert to metal production and his fury that the aircraft industry had put the country's fighter planes out of action, accusing them of being Hitlerites—it was not until 1943 that Yak-9 and La-7 fighters received metal wing spars, and 1944 until the first all-metal fighter plane, the Yak-9U, entered production. It would be late 1946 before the first all-metal Lavochkin fighter, the La-9, was supplied to the VVS.

The Lavochkin OKB also experienced a number of problems with its radial-engined fighters. Having adapted the LaGG-3 to accept the Shvetsov ASh-82, Lavochkin spent most of the summer of 1942 in eliminating overheating and vibration problems due to unbalanced propellers. Once the engine problems were resolved they were successfully fitted to the subsequent LaGG-5, but suddenly a new problem arose. There were two incidents of wings breaking off in flight. Initially it was thought that sabotage was to blame, but further investigations revealed that production engineers were using hammers to force wing-fixing bolts into undersized holes made by worn drill bits, overstressing the surrounding area and leading to the wing breaking off in flight. A crash recovery programme was put into operation to correct all the various anomalies, and by the end of 1942 a total of 1,129 LaGG-5s had been built. The type's performance was further enhanced the following year with the fitting of the more powerful ASh-82FN engine, the revised La-7 appearing in 1944.

The most powerful aero-engine available in 1944, the 1,492 kW (2,000 hp) Mikulin AM-42, powered the Il-2's replacement, the more manoeuvrable Il-10 from the same

OKB, around 3,000 of which were built by the war's end. The first, delivered to the Red Air Force in October 1944, was available in sufficient numbers for the Battle of Berlin in 1945. The only new bomber produced during the Second World War was Tupolev's Tu-2, the prototype having flown in January 1941. Although a pre-production batch of sixty-two aircraft were built for combat evaluation in 1942, production was then suspended until 1944, when a simplified version was produced and placed into production at GAZ-166 at Omsk, and later GAZ-22 at Kazan, with only around 800 to 1,000 built by the end of the war.

In 1942, Soviet aircraft production had easily outstripped German production. Germany produced 15,556 aircraft—including 5,565 fighters, 1,259 assault aircraft and 4,357 bombers—whilst the Soviet Union produced 25,436—including 9,918 fighters, 8,229 assault aircraft and 3,523 bombers. Stalin also received Lend-Lease aircraft from the USA. However, Hitler was forced to supply many of his allies with aircraft in exchange for desperately needed raw materials, and the Luftwaffe was fighting on three big fronts as opposed to the Red Air Force operating on just one. Another important factor in the increased Soviet production in 1942 was the great reduction in production costs due to the use of cheap labour in poor conditions and the rationalisation of models. The following gives a clear indication of this. A Pe-2 bomber costing 420,000 roubles in 1941 cost only 353,000 roubles in 1942, and the cost of an Il-4 bomber reduced from 800,000 roubles to only 468,000. As a result of these factors, in December 1942, 3.3 times more aircraft and 5.4 times more aero-engines were built in the Soviet Union than in December 1941.

Throughout the war the number of production plants did not increase overall, some plants closing whilst others were incorporated into bigger, already well-established ones. In any case, in 1942, the Soviets were not able to establish new plants, but in the recaptured territories many new, mainly repair plants were set up in 1943/44. However, none of these were well equipped and not one of them was able to change over to series production during the war, in spite of massive Allied supplies of machine tools and raw materials. In addition, lack of resources prevented Germany from establishing a strategic heavy bomber force, and luckily for Stalin, this kept the important military aircraft and tank production plants in the Volga and the Urals, albeit relatively low in number, safe from German bomber raids.

It was not until the summer of 1944 that Heinkel He 277 bombers were available, and by then it was too late. In the end, Stalin's plans and his determination to maintain and increase military production throughout the war, whilst not always achieving the targets set, did enable the Soviets to win the day, thanks to the ineptitude of the *Reichluftministerium* (RLM) and the German aircraft industry's shortcomings.

The relative success of the evacuation of the production lines to the Volga region and behind the Urals, along with modest Allied deliveries of aircraft, had resulted in a total Soviet aircraft inventory during the war of 62,800 fighters, 19,200 bombers, 33,700 sturmoviks and 22,900 other aircraft. From July 1941 to September 1945, the Soviet aircraft industry produced 136,838 aircraft, 108,028 of them combat planes, representing 79 per cent of the total. Nevertheless, without denying this tremendous achievement, often in the most horrendous conditions, most of the machines produced were single-engined aircraft, most were of wooden construction, powered by efficient but mediocre (in terms of performance) engines, and, in truth, the industry had lacked any real experience of all-metal construction, production of multi-engined types, electronics and radar, and development of gas turbine engines.

In spite of colossal losses, the Red Air Force finished the war with 27,500 fighters, 9,700 bombers, 10,000 sturmoviks and 16,900 other types still in service. Stalin was ready to realise his dream of world communist domination—starting in eastern and central Europe. Captured German aircraft plants were dispersed mainly in the Urals and Siberia. The Heinkel Rostock plant was sent to Kiselovsk, 40 km from Stalinsk, where a large bomber aircraft factory was established and Kiselovsk produced all the necessary parts for series production. At the war's end, 66 per cent of the German aircraft industry, together with its research and production facilities in Austria and Czechoslovakia, fell into Soviet hands.

However, the decision not to place any of the advanced German combat aircraft designs in production for the Soviet Air Force had already been taken, in December 1945, at a Kremlin conference attended by representatives from the Red Air Force and the Ministry of Aircraft Production, when the People's Commissariat for Aviation Industry and Soviet engineers promised that they could produce better aircraft for Stalin. The situation with captured German missiles was different, and Sergei Korolev was promoted to head German V-2 development and production projects at Kapustin Yar. For an industry well aware of its shortcomings and deficiencies in the field of aircraft engineering (airframe and aero-engine), rocket and gas turbine engines, and Top Secret optical and electronic equipment, there was now a chance to catch up with its western counterparts, the Americans and British. Not only to catch up, but to overtake them, as was to be evidenced in its first post-war designs, in particular the Mikoyan and Sukhoi fighters.

The first task post-war was to carry out a complete evaluation of as many of the newer German designs as possible. Andrei Kochetkov of the NII VVS Fighter Test Section headed the team assessing the Messerschmitt Me 262 jet. Kochetkov became the first Soviet pilot to fly a gas turbine engined aircraft, on 15 August 1945. Tests on the latest Focke-Wulf Fw 190 variants were made on behalf of the Lavochkin OKB by several NII VVS pilots. The Messerschmitt Me 163 rocket plane received particular attention, although most test flights were made unpowered due to a lack of hydrogen peroxide for the aircraft's Walter HWK 109-509 rocket engine. These flights were not popular with the NII VVS pilots, as the ballasted Me 163s towed aloft by a Tu-2 usually resulted in heavy landings. Later, in March 1946, an Arado Ar 234 twin-jet bomber was found at Damgarten and flown back to Rechlin, where a series of evaluation flights were made despite a number of engine and undercarriage failures.

In addition to the aircraft, the Soviets inherited expertise by way of Prof. Günther Bock, chief of research for the Experimental Aeronautics Institute at Berlin-Adlershof;

Rudolph Rental, project engineer for the Me 163 and Me 262 fighters; Dr Adolph Betz, a specialist in swept-wing research; Dr Brunolf Baade, former chief designer for Junkers; and Siegfried Günther, designer of the Heinkel He 162. Günther had been linked to the development of Kurt Tank's Focke-Wulf Ta 183 jet fighter and the preliminary design of the Mikoyan MiG-15.

Despite the Kremlin's decision not to place any of the Germans' advanced designs in production, early post-war prototype designs bore a marked resemblance to German aircraft, as might be expected. The Sukhoi Su-9 interceptor, first flown in 1946, appeared as a straight-wing version of the Me 262, and the Ilyushin Il-22 had many features of the proposed Heinkel He 343, itself a development of the Arado Ar 234. Particular attention was given to Dr Hans Wocke's Junkers Ju 287 V2 forward swept wing bomber prototype discovered at Dessau, which had been transported to the Soviet Union in 1945 to undergo a number of test flights. This led to a series of experiments with a small aircraft designed by Pavel Tsybin with a 30-degree forward swept wing; the aircraft was variously flown as a ballasted glider towed aloft by a Pe-2 or powered by a tail-mounted rocket engine. It is of interest that occasional authoritative reports still appear in western aviation magazines today that Sukhoi's forward swept-wing high-tech interceptor is still under development. Indeed a model was displayed on the Sukhoi stand at the 2001 Paris Air Show at Le Bourget airport, but nothing has been seen since. The order that indigenous Soviet fighter designs should be powered by German BMW 003 and Junkers Jumo 004 jet engines had been given in February 1945, and by late autumn the Yakovlev, Mikoyan, Lavochkin and Sukhoi OKBs had presented Stalin, Novikov and Shakhurin with a number of projects to consider.

Unbeknown at the time, Shakhurin was dismissed in December 1945 and replaced as Minister of Aircraft Production by one of his wartime deputies, Khrunichev. He was later arrested, tried and interned for alleged 'mismanagement' of the aircraft industry during the evacuations of 1941. Lavochkin also incurred the intense displeasure of Stalin at this time for refusing to testify against the former Minister of Aircraft Production.

Stalin made further changes in 1947, when Marshal Astakhov was replaced as the Chief of GUGVF by General Baidukov, a long-time confidant of Stalin. Chief Air Marshal Golovanov relinquished command of the Long-Range Air Force to Air Marshal Zhigarev, who was also First Deputy C-in-C of the VVS, thereby bringing bombers directly under Soviet Air Force control again. Rather perversely, Stalin appointed Zhigarev C-in-C Soviet Air Force in 1949, dismissing Vershinin and placing the control of the VVS for the next seven and a half years under the command of the man who had been at the helm at the time of the Red Air Force's almost complete destruction in 1941.

The first of two post-war jet prototype aircraft to be produced was the Yakovlev Yak-15, achieved quite simply by replacing the VK-107 piston engine of a Sukhoi Su-3 with an 8.8 kN (1,980 lbf) Junkers Jumo 004B jet engine exhausting under the fuselage. This was followed by the specially designed Mikoyan MiG-9, with two BMW 003s fitted side by side in the nose, both aircraft flying for the first time on the same day, 24 April 1946. Within six months these were followed by their unsuccessful competitors, the Sukhoi Su-9 and La-150. Three prototypes each of the Yak-15 and MiG-9 were displayed at the Tushino Air Day on 18 August 1946, and Stalin immediately ordered two blocks of fifty to be produced for the following year's May Day fly-past over Moscow. In the event, only 280 Yak-15 fighters and modified Yak-15U trainers with tricycle undercarriage were produced before they were superseded by the improved Yak-17 featuring a number of aerodynamic refinements and the uprated RD-10A engine.

A total of 430 Yak-17 fighters and Yak-17UTI trainers were built between March 1948 and August 1949, the type entering Soviet Air Force service in late 1948. In reality, early Soviet jet fighters were produced only in small numbers, with the VVS relying on its extensive reserve of extremely capable piston-engined types that remained on inventory at the war's end. In addition to the ASh-82 radial-powered La-9 close air support plane and the La-11 long-range escort fighter, both built post-war in 1946/47, Stalin expressed to Lavochkin a preference for the proven piston-engined fighters of the Great Patriotic War over the untested Mikoyan MiG-9 jet.

The reality was that the Yak-15, Yak-17 and MiG-9 were seen only as interim designs until the advent of a more advanced day jet fighter with high-altitude capabilities, for which the specification had been issued in 1946. Intended to counter the high-altitude strategic bomber, its design would draw on the vast amount of research and evaluation work undertaken post-war on German designs and swept-wing technology to produce a new fighter, substantially armed, with a high rate of climb, good manoeuvrability at altitudes over 11,000 m (33,000 feet) and an endurance of at least one hour. As is now well known, this emerged as the famous Mikoyan MiG-15, which is reported to have made its first flight on 30 December 1947 (although it is believed that an earlier prototype which later crashed had taken to the air in July of that year).

During the war the Soviet aircraft industry had experienced a dramatic change. Not only had it expanded greatly in terms of personnel and output, it had also undergone a great geographical shift. As we have seen, important centres of production had been developed in the Urals and Siberia, and to a lesser extent in central Asia and the Far East. After the war there was a brief period of conversion to civilian production, but this soon gave way to a renewed expansion of the industry, especially after the outbreak of the Korean War. Resources were allocated on a massive scale for the rapid development of jet aircraft, missiles, radar systems and nuclear weapons.

This extraordinary priority for military production was only briefly checked after Stalin's death in 1953, when Georgi Malenkov, the Prime Minister, sought to engage the aircraft industry in the manufacture of consumer goods. But after a relative short-lived episode, 'traditional' priorities were reinstated under the leadership of Nikita Khrushchev and Leonid Brezhnev. Only occasionally, when between two different series productions or in order to use spare capacity, would a plant turn to the production of consumer goods.

The post-war Ministers for Aircraft Production M. V. Khrunichev and P. V. Dementev, both of whom were Shakhurin's deputies, presided over an expanding industry, with new factories producing electronic equipment and missiles. Of the hundred or so MAP plants, five were given over to fighter plane production, nine produced bombers, transports and larger civil types, ten manufactured rotary wing types and light utility planes, and ten were used for aero-engine production. Most were newly introduced models, production of older but still useful types being handed over for licensed production in Poland or Czechoslovakia. Both countries re-exported Soviet or indigenous designs to the Soviet Union, Poland Mil Mi-2 helicopters and Czechoslovakia Aero L-29 Delfin jet trainers, advanced L-39 Albatros jet trainers and Zlin light training and aerobatic planes.

In 1949, delivery of new armaments to the communist satellite countries began, not only in Europe but in Asia as well. In June 1950, North Korea was able to attack the unarmed South, completely overrunning the country in two weeks as planned. Red China came into being in 1949, and by February 1950, Stalin had promised 3,000 combat aircraft to Mao Tse-tung, of which 750 were to be supplied by December of that year. The Chinese were able to use them to stop the UN forces in Korea, and the war turned into a stalemate. Indeed, without Stalin's death in March 1953, the situation could have been prolonged for many years, although an official cessation to hostilities has never been declared or officially signed. Even today in the new millennium, North and South Korea officially remain at war, with formal daily diplomatic exchanges undertaken by the US, and the North Korean military maintaining the border divided by a DMZ.

Stalin had earlier captured the Japanese nuclear installations in North Korea, and having received much 'illegal help' with development, the first Soviet atomic bomb was exploded at Semipalatinsk on 29 August 1949. Stalin immediately ordered Myasishchev and Tupolev to develop intercontinental strategic bombers capable of attacking the USA and also requested supersonic interceptors for blocking American long-range bombers, as well as simple but effective front-line jet fighters and light jet bombers. All were to be manufactured in such numbers as to establish numerical superiority over the western powers, and the first flights of these aircraft occurred just prior to his death.

The availability of these new aircraft led to a complete reorganisation of the Soviet Air Force. In 1953, Frontal Aviation had sixteen air armies, each having:

- three fighter divisions (three regiments) of 124 aircraft each;
- two sturmovik or fighter-bomber divisions of 124 aircraft each;
- one bomber division (some with jet bombers) of 93 aircraft;
- one reconnaissance regiment with 40 MiG-15s;
- one reconnaissance regiment with 30 twin-engined aircraft (some Ilyushin Il-28s).

This provided a total of 786 combat aircraft, plus a regiment or two of light transport aircraft. Antonov An-2s and Lisunov Li-2s were also available to each air army. A further 5,500 aircraft were in the north and west (Russia, Germany, Poland) and 3,000 in the south-west (Ukraine, Balkans, etc.), with another 3,000 in the Far East. The PVO (Air Defence Force) had 4,000 interceptors in more than 100 regiments, and the Long Range Bomber Force had more than 1,000 Tupolev Tu-4s in service (220 of them in the Far East) and 100 Tu-16s, but only twenty-five atomic bombs. Soviet Naval Aviation also had some 3,000 aircraft, of which 50 per cent were jet fighters the rest were jet bombers, reconnaissance aircraft and seaplanes.

Stalin was eventually succeeded by Nikita Khrushchev, 'the missile man', as leader of the Soviet Union. Following detonation of the Soviets' first super-bomb in 1953, they announced, on 26 August 1957, that they possessed an intercontinental ballistic missile (ICBM) and when, thirty-nine days later, they launched 'Sputnik 1' into space, the United States experienced its second 'Pearl Harbor'. On 17 December 1959, Khrushchev announced the formation of a new branch of the Soviet armed forces— the RVSN or Strategic Missile Force—and suddenly the Soviet Air Force had lost its strategic importance. Already, in 1957, Khrushchev had made many cuts in the aircraft building programmes, MiG-17 fighter and Il-28 light bomber production having been halted. In 1958, MiG-19 fighter production was stopped completely and the following year Tu-16 bomber production also ceased. Total bomber production dropped from 1,550 in 1955 to just 100 in 1959, and fighter production dropped from 4,300 in 1953 to 400 in 1959. Despite these cutbacks, the following new types were introduced: the Mikoyan MiG-21 fighter, the Sukhoi Su-7 and Su-9, the Tupolev Tu-22, and the Yakovlev Yak-28. However, production of these types never reached the previous high levels of output.

The production of transport aircraft was also reduced from 800 in 1957 to only 275 in 1963. However, the Antonov An-12 was introduced to replace the An-2 Colt biplane still in production, and the Ilyushin Il-18 four-engined turboprop was introduced in place of the semi-obsolete Il-14. Only helicopter production increased, from 150 in 1953 to 950 in 1959. As a result of this reduced production, the Soviet Air Force actually diminished in size during these dangerous years of the Cold War, when many times it could have turned to real war.

However, Khrushchev had many successes with his missile and satellite programmes, and many excellent new aircraft and helicopter designs were also introduced during his era. Aeroflot, the national airline, developed rapidly, but other industries such as agriculture failed to progress and develop and the general standard of living fell. The 'missile man' even made several visits to numerous capitalist countries to study 'the right way to progress'. By 1964, Soviet influence had become widespread in Africa, Asia and other parts of the world, through trade and economic aid and the supply of aircraft to Third World countries, and in this environment the Soviet aircraft industry appeared to progress well. The OKBs produced many new and interesting designs, such as the Antonov An-24, the Ilyushin Il-62 and Il-76, the

Mikoyan MiG-23, MiG-25 and MiG-27, and the Mil Mi-8 and Mi-24 helicopters, along with such types as the Sukhoi Su-17, Su-22 and Su-24, and the Tupolev Tu-22M, Tu-134 and Tu-154 airliners and the Yakovlev Yak-40 short-haul aircraft.

In the early 1980s, the Reagan administration in the USA was alarmed by the growth of the Soviet armed forces and of the country's military production base. There were 135 military industrial plants in the Soviet Union—over 40 million m^2 of floor space— producing more than 150 different types of weapons systems for the Soviet forces and for export to client states and other developing countries. In parallel with the build-up of its military strength, the Soviet Government had created and continually exploited situations of crisis and instability in the Third World and elsewhere, using force and intimidation in such countries as Vietnam, Czechoslovakia, Poland and Afghanistan. Experience in many, if not all, of these areas of hostility allowed the OKBs to develop the often inferior introductory model of a particular type of aircraft into a very superior weapons system. For example, the original fairly ordinary MiG-21F and PF models were developed into the vastly superior MF and *bis* variants. In this way new 'tools' were born for Soviet global expansionist policies. By this time the man in charge was the General Secretary of the Communist Party, Leonid Brezhnev. In 1976, he was awarded the country's highest military rank—Marshal of the Soviet Union.

It is interesting here to compare Soviet and US military aircraft production for the years 1976-1977/78. The Soviet aviation industry produced thirty extremely capable Tupolev Tu-22 bombers, whereas no bombers were produced by the Americans, and 1,250 Soviet strike/attack aircraft were manufactured compared to only 646 produced by the US. In 1978, Soviet fighter production was 1,300 aircraft, whereas the US combined fighter production for 1977 and 1978 was only 526. Soviet military helicopter production in 1978 was 1,400 aircraft compared to 348 in the US. Also in 1978, the Soviets produced 225 military transports, whereas only sixty-seven were produced by the Americans, and that was a good year for the US, as in 1975 they had produced only thirty-four aircraft in this category, and in 1977 only twenty-five. In the 'black year' of 1976, the Belgian general Robert Close, Chief of Staff of NATO, wrote his famous book *Europe without Defense?* wherein he demonstrated quite clearly that attacking Soviet forces in Europe could defeat the NATO alliance in 48 hours.

However, Soviet fortunes changed for the worse in the 1980s, with the country's economy in deep difficulties as it faced many competing priorities with scant resources. Problems included food shortages, low productivity, transportation disruptions and energy constraints. Externally, the high cost of supporting other communist regimes such as Cuba, Vietnam and Poland, which were often experiencing difficulties themselves, had also created many extra burdens. These difficulties peaked after two decades during which Moscow's policy had been 'guns before butter'. Now the country was sick and the leader was sick, Brezhnev dying in November 1982. At the time, nobody knew of course that the Soviet Union itself had only nine years to go.

In 1980, Mikhail Sergeyevich Gorbachev, born in 1931, became a full Politburo member and five years later he became General Secretary of the Communist Party.

The first Soviet leader who had not seen wartime service and was not filled with guilt over the wartime purges of his fellow countrymen, he soon revealed he could easily deal with rivals and gained a reputation as the 'man with the nice smile and iron teeth'. However, the struggle between developing the consumer industry and the arms industry continued, although overall production of military hardware remained unchanged in this period.

Gorbachev eventually placed his own men in all key posts to assist him in carrying out his economic and organisational reforms. His tools were *Glasnost* (transparency in affairs) and *Perestroika* (restructuring). Unlike his predecessors, he did not believe that war was 'fatally inevitable' and understood that what his people really wanted was 'order at home and peace abroad'. As an immediate start, Gorbachev withdrew all Soviet troops from Afghanistan—'Russia's Vietnam'—in February 1989.

However, one aspect of *Glasnost* and *Perestroika* that Gorbachev had not allowed for was that many minority groups within the Soviet Union now saw an opportunity to destabilise and weaken Moscow's grip on the country. Soon he himself was heading for trouble, and the collapse of the Soviet Empire would be very fast. Luckily it was a relatively bloodless coup, as Gorbachev understood that Soviet power lay not in the Kremlin but with the Red Army. For this reason, and not only for economic considerations, he cut the defence budget by 14.2 per cent and production of arms and military spending by 20 per cent from 1990. For almost a decade before, the Soviet military had been demanding new air defence systems to counter low-level intruders. By 1987, and at great expense, they had got them, along with a new generation of Soviet fighters, the Sukhoi Su-27 Flanker and the Mikoyan MiG-29 Fulcrum interceptors with full look-down/shoot-down capabilities to deal with low-flying targets, together with two new air-to-air missiles (AAMs) to be carried by the MiG-31 Foxhound and AA-10s for the MiG-29 and Su-27 aircraft.

Gorbachev, on the other hand, sought disarmament, and in 1986 he wrote a very important book entitled *For a World without Nuclear Arms*. In December 1987, he signed a treaty in Washington for the dismantling of nuclear missiles in Europe, the infamous American cruise missiles and the Soviet SS-20s, and he showed the way in September 1988 by dismantling the giant radar of Krasnoyarsk. The following month he proposed the closure of all foreign military bases, and a little later came the START Treaty and the reduction of all conventional armed forces in Europe.

For his outstanding contribution to world peace Gorbachev was rightly rewarded with the Nobel Peace Prize. But despite this, in August 1991, a *coup d'état* by Russian conservatives led to his arrest. His old friend but latterly political adversary Boris Yeltsin took command of the Army, which was shelling the Parliament building in Moscow, and managed to control the situation, although almost immediately one after another the Russian republics proclaimed independence. The *de facto* Soviet Union was no more. On 25 December 1991, Gorbachev resigned and told a stunned Western audience, 'I leave my post very anxious; the worst of this crisis is the collapse of the state.' Within twenty-four hours the hammer and sickle flag of the USSR was replaced by the new Russian Federation flag on the tower of the Kremlin. The Soviet Union had died, to be replaced by the Commonwealth of Independent States (CIS).

At that time the country's military forces were in total disarray and military production all but ceased. The CIS Air Force almost completely disintegrated, with few if any new pilots or other aircrew coming through, as its source—the DOSAAF, the successor to the Osoaviakhim—was disbanded. Most of the force's aircraft stood idle due to lack of spares and fuel. In fact, at those front-line units that could be considered 'operational', aircrew and operational safety was of great concern as the combat pilots were not getting enough flying hours to keep them proficient on type. In 1996, a senior general revealed that in his opinion the air force was in such disarray it would take at least fifteen years to restore it to a credible force again.

Aircraft production had all but ended. Only Sukhoi with its incredible Su-27 Flanker and Mikoyan with a number of new MiG-29 Fulcrum variants were able to sustain production. There was also some low-scale production of transport types by Antonov, Mil and Kavoc in the rotary field with their new attack helicopters, and Mil still produced upgraded variants of its famous Mi-8 and Mi-17 helicopters.

Defence of the realm (as with Britain's Trident) now rested with the Russian Navy and what remained of its nuclear submarine fleet. Russia's adoption of its SSBNs (nuclear submarine force) as its major deterrent was supported by its confidence as to the survivability of the SSBN force and its ability to respond quickly and effectively to launch commands. The SSBNs would be supported by the largely land-based Naval Aviation Force (AV-MF), particularly when operating in Soviet coastal waters. The Naval Aviation Force is larger than most other countries' individual national air forces, having in excess of 1,000 aircraft for the four Fleet Air Forces (Northern, Baltic, Black Sea, and Pacific).

Since the mid-1950s, when the force was first equipped with missile-carrying jet bombers, weapons systems and tactics have been progressively upgraded. The Tupolev Tu-22 variable-geometry swing-wing bomber, which entered service in 1974, was used by the Black Sea, Baltic and Pacific fleets in the strike/anti-shipping role and could carry missiles, bombs or mines. Current fighter attack aircraft in the Naval Aviation inventory are the Su-25 Frogfoot and Su-27K Flanker. Anti-submarine warfare (ASW) and reconnaissance is an important role for Naval Aviation, and turboprop Tu-95s were first introduced in the 1970s. The latest reconnaissance and ASW variants of this aircraft are the Tu-142 Bear F and the Tu-95 Bear D (RT) respectively. Ship-borne helicopters and fixed-wing aircraft are owned and operated directly by the Navy, as a sort of Fleet Air Arm as distinct from Naval Aviation proper, on the carrier *Admiral Kuznetsov*, the Navy's only aircraft carrier.

3

Soviet Cold War Production

Production at the Soviet series plants paralleled the specialisation existing in the research and design sectors. Plants specialised by type of aircraft (bombers, transport, fighter, helicopters) as well as by size. This prompted continuity and a good working relationship between series production plants and the OKBs responsible for developing a particular system. However, ties between particular bureaux and series plants were not rigid, and production assignments changed depending on MAP's commitments to customers and the floor space available. If the plant had spare capacity, it could enter into production agreements outside the aircraft industry and use available equipment and manpower to manufacture other items.

Generations of increasingly complex and sophisticated aircraft have been produced by the Soviet aviation industry since the beginning of the jet age. Military aircraft production made up the largest and most important portion of the industry's efforts, which included long-and intermediate-range bombers, air-to-surface missiles, long-range recce aircraft, ECM (electronic countermeasures) and ELINT (electronic intelligence), and in-flight refuelling tankers for Soviet Long Range Aviation (DA). The industry also produced fighters, fighter-bombers, recce aircraft and helicopters for Soviet Tactical Aviation and interceptors for the PVO forces. In addition to combat aircraft, large numbers of medium-and long-range troop carriers and logistic transports have been produced for Soviet Military Transport Aviation (VTA) and trainers have also been built for various flying training establishments.

Peak post-war production occurred in the early 1950s, with the production of more than 15,000 MiG-15 fighters, along with a smaller but equally significant amount of civil aircraft and helicopters built to meet the needs of Aeroflot. In 1977, Aeroflot operated over 2,000 large and medium-size passenger and cargo aircraft, as well as several thousand helicopters and An-2 light transports, and the combined totals of these aircraft reflect an extensive and substantial output of the industry from 1965 to 1980. There was an overall annual increase in output until 1975, followed by a slight decline. Temporary declines historically occurred during periods when older aircraft were being phased out as new-generation models entered production.

The aviation educational institutes are staffed by highly skilled scientific and engineering graduates recruited from specialist aviation establishments, state

universities and polytechnics, all under the aegis of the Ministry of Higher and
Secondary Specialised Education. The institutes listed below were originally founded
within the Ministry of Aviation Industry but were resubordinated to the Ministry of
Higher Education during Stalin's educational reforms in 1946:

- Kazan Aviation Institute
- Kharkov Aviation Institute
- Kuibyshev Aviation Institute
- Leningrad Institute of Aviation Instrument Construction
- Moscow Aviation Institute
- Moscow Aviation Technological Institute
- Ufa Aviation Institute.

These establishments are important major technical sources providing the
undergraduate and graduate manpower needs of the industry's research institutes,
design bureaux (OKBs) and series production plants (GAZs/Zavods) located in their
respective territorial regions. In addition, several educational institutes in a number
of cities—e.g. the Moscow Higher Technical School *imeni* Bauman and the Tashkent
Polytechnic Institute—have expanded their aeronautical curriculum throughout the
years and are an additional source of engineering and aviation graduates. Several of
the Ministry of Aviation Research Institutes have also been empowered by the Higher
Certification Commission of the Ministry of Higher Education to award Candidate
of Science degrees (roughly equivalent to a British PhD). This serves as an academic
qualification permitting the individual to study and perform research within one of
the many aeronautical fields that will contribute directly to the needs of the institutes
and industry.

Goals set by the Soviet leadership were instigated by the five-year plans. Achieving
the development schedules as laid down by the plans was essential, since the
individual and institutional successes were judged by these achievements and rewards
were based on 'plan fulfilment'. Development stages followed within the industry
conform to the 'Unified system of design documentation' (YeSKD—*Yedinaya sistema
konstruktivnoy dokumentatsii*) as outlined in several GOST (*Gosudarstvenny standart*)
state standards, and consisted of the following defined steps:

- Receipt of a technical assignment from the Ministry of Aircraft Production (MAP);
- Preparation of a technical proposal;
- Proposed co-ordination and approval by the Research Institute and the customer;
- Preparation of the draft project;
- Draft project co-ordination and approval by the Research Institute and the
  customer;
- Preparation of the technical project (mock-up) approval followed by detailed
  design);

- Prototype construction;
- Prototype testing (by the Design Bureau/Ministry);
- Pilot (PP) model production;
- State testing (operational evaluation by the customer and the State Commission);
- Approval for series production.

Design bureaux tended to minimise risks by using approved technology and off-the-shelf sub-systems and components whenever possible. Small steps in technological advancement were made, when and if required to meet the performance demands of the customer. One of the criteria set was to produce a design for ease of production. An example of a design objective overlooked by the West until the earlier 1980s, the English Electric Lightning, was a maintenance engineer's nightmare, but the Soviets, even until recently, avoided complicated design features, specifying only the essential tolerances, allowances and finishes. Industry-wide, design handbooks and specifications provided all information on approved technology developed and available for use.

Construction of the prototype, testing and evaluation prior to the new type entering series production (the fly-before-buy concept), of prime importance to the development process, are aimed at ensuring customer requirements are met. An additional and important factor that helps to ensure the customer (more often than not, of course, the military) gets what he wants, is a degree of competition between the design bureaux. The extent and nature of this competition varied, and could, depending on the complexity and importance of the aircraft, extend from a paper design competition in the initial stages up to a full-blown prototype 'fly-off' evaluation. Sometimes, of course, with political interference, particularly in the days of Stalin, it was not always the winner or best design that entered series production. However, close co-operation between research institutes and design bureaux was extremely beneficial to the industry and the product that was eventually presented for series production.

The Soviet aviation industry always supported the many scientific and research institutes with their theoretical studies and aircraft development. Each institute specialises in one or more domains, developing its own experimental base and publishing its own technical bulletins and documentation. The Central Aerohydrodynamic Institute (TsAGI), created on 1 December 1918 under the direction of N. Ye. Zhukovsky, plays an essential role in the study and development of a prototype. Initially located at Moscow, it later transferred to the town of Zhukovsky (Ramenskoye) where many laboratories, wind tunnels, libraries, prototype workshops and generating plants etc. were built. It assisted the first works of many of the chiefs of the OKBs, high-ranking design engineers such as Tupolev, Sukhoi, Myasishchev, Petlyakov, Arkhangelsky and Mil. Originally aircraft, engines and propellers were tested there, but today missiles and space vehicles can be included in this list. The TsAGI now also trains the necessary technical personnel required to work on the development and testing of ships, submarines, trains, metro trains, cars and medical equipment.

The institutes were divided into four groups, according to the function or role they played in the development of new aircraft or equipment. In the first group was the Central Institute of Aviation Motors (TsIAM), the Russian Institute for Aeronautic Material (VIAM), the State Institute on the Researches of Aeronautic Systems (GosNIIAS), the Siberian Institute on Aeronautic Researches (SibNIA), the Avionics Research Institute (NIIAO), and the Research Institute on Industrial Application of Glass (NITS). Sub-assemblies and structures are studied and constructed with the help of the Research Institute and Instrument Construction (NIIP), the Electronic and Automatic Institute of Moscow (MIEA), the Institute on the Research of Parachute Construction (NIIPS), and the Institutes of NIIAO and NITS in the first group. Flight testing is undertaken by the LII (Flight Research Institute) at Ramenskoye, although other organisations are also involved with tests.

To help with the introduction of prototypes into production other institutes exist, such as the Research Institute of Technology and Production Organisation for Aircraft (NIAT), the Research Institute of Technology and Production Organisation for Engines (NIID), the Technological and Research Institute (NITI) and the Obninsk Association for the Science of Production (ONPO). All of these are extremely diversified, and five of them—TsAGI, GosNIIAS, TsIAM, LII and VIAM—direct the work of the others. There are additional institutes to help with the work of the foregoing, such as the Research Institute of Economy, Organisation and Direction (NIIEPU), the Research Institute of Normalisation and Standardisation (NIISU) and the National Research Institute of Aeronautic Industry (Giproniiaviaprom).

Each institute carries out fundamental and advanced research in its respective domain. Some are relatively new; others, like TsAGI, are very old. TsIAM was founded in 1930 from some departments of TsAGI, the Institute for Automobile Engines, and Zavod 4. Originally working on piston-engines, it converted to other areas such as hypersonic jet engines using hydrogen, and has two departments: a research department in Moscow, and a research and test centre at Lytkarino near Moscow.

One of the most important institutes is the LII. Created on 13 June 1940 at Ramenskoye military airfield, it was directed by the famous pilot Mikhail Gromov. It carries out checks on each type of aircraft, including radio-controlled aircraft, by way of flight tests, technical investigations, development of methods and operating techniques, security, etc. Ramenskoye airfield is one of the largest in the world, with four runways, the largest of which is 5,403 m long and 70 m wide. In 1995, some 120 aircraft and helicopters were based here for experimental and test flying, more than 70 per cent of which were experimental and research aircraft. This institute was also responsible for the training and development of new test pilots and special pilots for other aircraft, helicopters and space vehicles. The centre could undertake tests on up to fifteen different aircraft types at any one time, but the days when this was a great advantage are long gone, and the reality is that nowadays the test work is becoming increasingly rare.

In recent years there has been a surprising lack of activity at Moscow's famous Ramenskoye test airfield, and the cancellation of many next-generation aircraft types supports the theory that, for the next decade or so, Soviet procurement and subsequent flight test programmes will be restricted to refinement of existing types. For this reason it is proposed to use part of the airfield as an international civil transport (cargo) airport.

4

Design Bureaux and Production Plants

Most of the OKBs were established in 1939, and were then normally known as Experimental Design Bureaux. Usually headed by a prominent chief designer, many of whom had already achieved national and international recognition for their accomplishments, they were responsible for developing new systems and improving existing systems in short timescales, at minimum cost, whilst maintaining high technical and tactical operating characteristics. Under Stalin, designers who failed to produce acceptable aircraft risked being shot and their design bureau closed. Later, however, they were comfortably shielded against competition and cutbacks, and a precedent was set in 1935 when a Sukhoi interceptor design that was clearly inferior to its Mikoyan counterpart was converted to the ground attack role instead of being scrapped. Some competition was encouraged between bureaux, although official policy was for continued parallel development, at least up to the prototype stage, as a form of insurance policy against any failure that might occur.

During the period from 1945 to 1974, around 140 aircraft designs are known to have reached the prototype stage, some sixty of which actually entered series production. In subsequent years this ratio decreased as a result of greater research and development costs. Costs up to this stage were borne by the Ministry of Aviation Industry, together with the development flying costs, but at times some competitors dropped out at the early stages of the project.

The design bureaux produced designs that went through all the usual model tests: a mock-up, prototype(s) and about five pre-production aircraft. Soviet regulations specified that there should be at least three prototypes—one for fatigue tests and two for flight tests—although often five prototypes were built. The results of the tests were reported to the Head of the Department of Experimental Design at MAP, who reported to the Commander-in-Chief of the Soviet Air Force or the Minister of Civil Aviation. If satisfied, he then authorised the NII VVS to begin state tests. On completion of these tests, a report went to the Commander-in-Chief of the Soviet Air Force or the Minister of Civil Aviation who, with the Minister of Aircraft Production, reported to the Deputy Prime Minister. He would then call a meeting of the Council of Ministers, attended by the Chief Designer and addressed by the Chief of the NII State Test Department. If it was decided to put the aircraft into production, the factory planners were brought in to discuss how the aircraft was to be produced, and to estimate the cost of production. The final price was agreed after negotiation between the intended operator/user and the factory.

The OKBs had some financial operating margins which allowed them to expand their facilities. As an example, the Tupolev OKB responsible for the development of the Tu-160 strategic bomber doubled in size between 1978 and 1987. Many of the great aircraft OKBs developed into family enterprises. Alexander Yakovlev's son Sergei became responsible for his father's YAK trademark, Andrei Tupolev's son ran the Tupolev OKB, and whilst there was no direct family descendant of Mikoyan to take control, it was later headed by the famous veteran in-house engineer Rostislav Belyakov.

At the start of production, the design OKB would assign a team of specialists to each GAZ involved in the manufacture of the new aircraft. This could be made up of anything between fifteen and fifty people, but usually comprised about thirty-five design engineers. Throughout the introductory phase they were accommodated at the plant, being replaced at the start-up of series production by the same number of GAZ production engineers who would have been working alongside the OKB designers at the introductory phase. In this way there was full co-operation between design engineers and production engineers. The GAZ management had experienced production specialists immediately available to speed production and ensure that the new type was quickly and efficiently adopted for series production.

Work in the OKBs was not unpleasant and, in many respects, quite stimulating, especially at the time when military production took precedence, with no defence cutbacks and when cancelled projects were unheard of, unless of course the aircraft failed completely to reach expectations or the OKB lost a competitive evaluation. But in Soviet industry there was no such thing as proprietary information or a patented design feature. It was not unusual for a selected design to be an amalgam of two original submissions, and in some cases a modern combat aircraft could have features incorporated that had been originally proposed by three or four different design bureaux. After the big purges of 1936/37, which provoked the deaths of many high-ranking officers, politicians and engineers, others such as Mikhail Tukhachevsky or the Kalinin OKB Chief, along with many other chief designers such as Tupolev and Petlyakov, found themselves in prison. After top-level conferences at the Kremlin, Stalin was obliged to reorganise Soviet Aviation and the TsKBs were disbanded.

Stalin ordered the creation of many 'new' design bureaux, and as a result of his directives sixteen were established. All those set up in 1938 were supervised by Stalin himself and Beria, his NKVD (Secret Police) Chief, but of the twenty projects at the new OKBs only three entered series production. Of these, the MiG-3 was also dropped in late 1941, and only two of the fighters were mass-produced in the Second World War—Lavochkin fighters with radial engines, and Yakovlev fighters with V inline engines.

Soviet aircraft were usually conservatively designed, with risks kept to a minimum, and were developed for ease of manufacture using proven technology whenever possible. There was close interaction between the user and the designer, which was often not the case in other countries, and Soviet aircraft design usually reflected the demands of the user. Mikhail Mil instructed his subordinates to 'make it simple, make it rugged, make it work, and make it reliable'. The Soviets also employed a high degree of standardisation, with off-the-shelf components used in successive designs. For instance, the Su-15 used the same radar and missile system components as the Yak-28 and engines of the type used in the MiG-21.

Prior to the 1970s, Soviet aircraft consistently weighed less than their US equivalents. However, with aircraft such as the General Dynamics F-16 and the McDonnell Douglas F/A-18 this trend was reversed, and the later Soviet types such as the MiG-29 and Su-27 were similar in size to their US counterparts and somewhat heavier. Soviet fighters of the 1950s, 60s and 70s were always smaller in volume than US fighters of the same era (e.g. the MiG-21 as compared to the McDonnell Douglas F-4 Phantom, and the MiG-23 compared to the F-15 Eagle). In reality, this left the Soviet types with less room for development, poor accessibility for ease of maintenance, and less fuel, limiting combat radius, often without any in-flight refuelling capability. A bonus was the automatic 'stealth' qualities, the aircraft possessing a smaller cross-sectional area, made possible by small diameter Soviet aero-engines. This also presented the airframe with much lower drag than US types, providing it with the speed, altitude and take-off performance appropriate to intercept missions and straight-line high-speed flight. But it has to be said that the MiG-29 and Su-27 are equal to their American counterparts in thrust-to-weight ratio and wing loading and, with the Su-27's thrust vectoring, greater agility. However, it has been estimated that a typical Soviet combat aircraft such as the MiG-27 could have been built in the US using modern construction techniques for only half of the cost in the former Soviet Union.

The simplicity of Soviet aircraft was a result of clever conceptual design, although in a few cases it was an indication of technological limitations, sometimes caused by constraints in manufacturing capability and capacity. The crude finish often apparent on various parts and sub-assemblies of the design (note the undercarriage wheels on even the Fulcrums and Flankers) was often the result of practical trade-offs between adequate performance and minimising production costs. The aircraft were designed to be manufactured using a minimum of exotic materials, parts and machine tools, using labour-intensive manufacturing techniques. Modifications in the series production phase were kept to a minimum, sometimes compromising operational performance for the sake of maintaining production output.

In general it can be said that Soviet combat aircraft are more reliable and more easily serviced by low-skilled personnel, reportedly requiring only a fraction of the maintenance man-hours needed by a comparable US combat type. The aircraft are specifically designed for use in a war scenario where their operational life is likely to be short but effective, and it is therefore quite likely that any specific type will remain serviceable throughout its (albeit short) operational life without the need for major servicing. Where necessary, combat damaged aircraft or aircraft that have reached maximum operational flying hours are returned to the Ministry of Aviation Industry factories where they are completely refurbished to 'new-condition standard'. The refurbished aircraft is then transferred to the main operating base for squadron use or to a war reserve stockpile. All new and rebuilt Soviet aircraft are supplied to their operational units by the Ministry of Aviation Industry partially assembled in large containers which also contain the spares to cover the specified guarantee period.

History has shown that the West has, until the advent of the MiG-29, Su-27 and the Su-25 sturmovik, generally underestimated the quality of Soviet aircraft and their weapons systems. In fact, Soviet aircraft are relatively proficient for the tasks they are designed for: they are easy to operate and maintain, and have the additional advantage of rough field operability. In spite of its apparent technological superiority, the US has not been able to achieve superior operability, which is reflected in the fact that its latest stealth bomber, the Boeing B-2 Spirit, requires eighty man-hours of deep maintenance for each operational hour of flight time.

However, an area of design where the West is ahead of its Russian counterparts is in the field of weapons systems and integrated avionics. Many of the Soviet systems take a good deal of pilot expertise and 'correct switch sequencing' to make the system combat-ready. Practised pilots may be able to cope, but even here poor instrument displays and poor sun-washout levels are hugely inferior and highly unacceptable to western crews. It is only recently that the Soviets have turned to 'all-electronic' cockpits and little use has been made of the head-up display. Whilst the MiG-29 Fulcrum has an impressive array of weapons systems, in terms of integration it lags far behind the West, little use having been made of HOTAS (Hands On Throttle And Stick), as confirmed by Luftwaffe pilots who flew ex-GDR MiG-29A Fulcrums.

An indication of American superiority in the weapons systems field can be gained from the following. Since 1979, US-built combat aircraft (F-14s, F-15s and F-16s) have taken part in at least 110 aerial combats involving 1,400 air-to-air and air-to-ground sorties, resulting in 147 confirmed 'kills' without any US losses. Almost all of the engagements involved aircraft of Soviet manufacture. The enemy aircraft managed to fire only sixteen missiles and made five gun-fire passes, with only one hit.

It is now of interest to examine in greater detail a number of the better known Soviet production plants and test facilities.

MAPO

In the early years of Soviet aviation, the Moscow Aircraft Production Organisation's Zavod 1 was the prime production plant for the country's indigenous combat types. The plant produced 389 Polikarpov I-3 fighters between 1927 and 1931; 172 I-4s in 1927/28; 142 I-5s in 1931/32; 131 I-7s (Heinkel HD 37s and 43s) between 1931 and 1934; 333 I-15s between 1934 and 1936; 61 DI-1s in 1937; 2,408 I-15*bis* in 1938/39; and 3,437 I-153s between 1939 and 1941.

When serial production of the R-5 recce bomber started at the Polikarpov OKB and Zavod 1, 4,914 were built between 1930 and 1935, as well as 111 seaplane variants, designated MR-5, in 1934/35, and 620 civil versions, designated R-5 SSS, and 1,031 bomber versions, the R-Zet, between 1935 and 1937. Zavod 1 also produced oil and water radiators, landing wheels, wire, bomb-release mechanisms, bomb racks and machine-gun rings for other plants.

The old GAZ numbers had been converted into Zavod numbers on 1 September 1927. For the aviation plants a complete block of numbers, 1-36, was reserved, as well as random numbers from 39. The apparently missing numbers were used for other military plants producing arms, gas, guns, munitions, ships, tanks and trunks, etc. GAZ-1 (Aviakhim) retained its number because it was both an aviation plant and a chemical warfare plant.

In 1938, one of the Communist Party's many purges of the plant began, the Chief Engineer, Dmitry Markov, being arrested and sent to prison. In fact, this fate befell almost all the key personnel at the plant, including Markov's deputy, the Director Ivan Kostkin, the heads of two design bureaux and the heads of four major workshops. However, as the international situation continued to worsen, Stalin started to prepare for his European War and most interned personnel were released. Production at the plant increased daily, with 2,362 aircraft built in 1940 as well as 120 Yak-4s and 3,220 MiG-1s and MiG-3s in 1940/41 (3,100 of them in 1941 alone).

Most of the male workers at the plant were called up for military service when Germany attacked the Soviet Union in June 1941, signifying the start of the Great Patriotic War, and women and teenagers took their places at the lathes and machine tools. In October that year the situation worsened dramatically as the battlefront neared Moscow, and it was at this time that the State Defence Committee took the decision to evacuate the works to the East, to Kuibyshev. Here the Director, Tretyakov, was ordered by Stalin to build large quantities of Ilyushin Il-2 Sturmoviks, particularly if he wished to keep his job. However, at the beginning of December 1941, the situation at the front changed as the Soviet troops advanced so the evacuations of the works ceased.

A new Zavod 30 was created in March 1942 and serial production of combat aircraft resumed. Within three months the first of the Il-2 Sturmoviks (ground attack aircraft), the 'flying tanks', were produced. In 1942 alone, 1,053 were built at Khodynka, and the total built between 1942 and 1945 was 8,865.

In recognition of its contribution to this achievement, on 2 July 1945, by decree of the Presidium of the Supreme Soviet of the USSR, Zavod 1 was rewarded with the Order of Lenin. After the war, in 1945/46, the plant started producing consumer goods such as oil-stoves, refrigerators, dishes and saucepans, although the main product was still aircraft. As is now known, of course, all the Zavods would return to full military production within a short space of time, Zavod 1 producing passenger types designed by Ilyushin such as the Il-12.

In 1950, the works produced the Ilyushin Il-14 advanced passenger plane and at the end of the decade it moved on to the Il-18, which became the pride of the country's civil air fleet and renowned throughout the world. At the same time, employees from the works were involved in a number of major construction projects in and around Moscow, such as the erection of the Kremlin Palace of Congress, the cinema 'Russia', the TV tower in Ostankino and the hotel 'Russia' as well as other well-known landmarks. The plant also produced large quantities of consumer goods and equipment for the food manufacturing industry, such as automatic machines for packing pepper and sugar, universal kitchen machinery, electric lamps, folding beds and souvenirs.

The year 1962 saw the introduction of the MiG-21 at GAZ-1, and later the MiG-23/-27, to be followed by the MiG-29 Fulcrum. Since 1988, the MiG-29 has been regularly exposed to the public at various international air shows and has now developed into an extremely potent aircraft with the 'all-electronic' cockpit, the MiG-29M variant for the Russian Air Force.

MAPO (Zavod 1) was awarded two Order of Lenin Banners in recognition of its achievements in the field of aircraft manufacture. One of the first aircraft manufacturing plants, it had remained the leader in the aviation industry after *Glasnost* and *Perestroika* in a country where the industry was in turmoil, with little or no requirement for its products until 2000.

Voronezh

The decision to build a new aircraft plant at Voronezh had been made in April 1929. Construction started in the autumn of 1930 on the outskirts at Pridacha, and the new GAZ-18 was opened in April 1932. Its first production task was building the TB-3 heavy bomber, although the plant initially undertook the repair of TB-1 heavy bombers. Already, in 1932, an employee at the plant, A. S. Moskalev, had designed a small all-metal five-seat transport plane, the SAM-5, the prototype being built in 1932/33. By order of the 'big constructor' (Tupolev), Kalinin arrived at the plant from Kharkov, setting up his design office with 135 staff, who completed a number of Kalinin designs such as the K-7 heavy bomber (which first flew in August 1933), two of which were built in 1935, with other machines only 66 per cent complete when all further work on the type was banned. Kalinin was ordered to concentrate on the K-12 tailless bomber, the design of which he finished in July 1936, but the aircraft was fated never to enter series production. Indeed, there were many confrontations at Voronezh between Kalinin and Tupolev. Early in 1938, work on a batch of ten K-12 bombers was started, along with a number of K-13 aircraft. However, before the first flights of his designs could take place, in 1938, Kalinin was arrested and later shot in Voronezh prison. His OKB was disbanded and all the aircraft were scrapped.

The first type to be built at GAZ-18 under the direction of Chief Engineer Baranov were five all-metal TB-3 heavy bombers in 1934, after which the plant received an order for twenty-four ANT-25 long-range aircraft (twenty by 1 May 1936), although only fourteen were built—eleven in 1936, and three in 1937. Of the bomber variant, the RDD, only one prototype was built. It had been planned to build thirty DB-2s, a heavily modified twin-engined version, but GAZ-18 began to build the new DB-3 long-range bomber variant in 1937. Twelve were built in 1937, 204 in 1938, 555 in 1939, 808 in 1940, and 328 in 1941. Between 1934 and 1938, thirty-seven Moskalev SAM-5*bis* ambulance aircraft were built, but 1938 saw the cancellation of a new order for a further 200 aircraft.

Moskalev's small design bureau developed a series of extremely interesting aircraft, but his work was sabotaged by his great adversary Yakovlev. All this rivalry and in-fighting meant that Voronezh came nowhere near producing its target output of 1,500 bombers annually. In 1940, the plant received new orders to produce Ilyushin Il-2 Sturmovik attack aircraft and Yermolayev Yer-2 long-range bombers, of which 1,510 Il-2s and seventy-one Yer-2s were produced in 1941 by 9,000 workers in a work area of 100,000 m^2. Unfortunately, on 19 September 1941, the plant was bombed, and with German troops attacking the city, GAZ-18 was hurriedly evacuated to Kuibyshev the following month. The evacuation was completed by 6 November and the plant again concentrated on Il-2 Sturmovik production, a task it continued with throughout the rest of the war.

In 1941, the Wehrmacht failed to reach Voronezh, but during the summer offensive of the following year the Germans occupied the city, although not for long. Voronezh was under the control of the Soviets again on 21 January 1943, albeit having suffered almost total destruction. The hard work of cleaning up the ruins of the plant, blown up by the Soviets themselves in July 1942, was started in earnest, and the new GAZ-64 repair plant was opened on 12 April. By 21 February 1944 it was producing wings for the Il-2, and by early 1945 it was assembling Il-4s. In 1946, the plant was working on production of Il-10 parts, and on complete assembly of the Il-10 in 1947. It had produced 255 aircraft by 1949, in which year it also undertook repair work on Il-12 transport aircraft.

In 1950, GAZ-64 started work on production of the Il-28 jet bomber, assembling 1,520 in total. The Voronezh plant started building the Tu-16 medium jet bomber from May 1954, although only 198 were built between 1955 and 1957. From 1958 to 1960, production switched to An-10 transport aircraft for Aeroflot, 110 being produced for the Soviet airline. Between 1961 and 1966, 280 An-12 heavy military tactical transports were produced, whilst from 1960 to 1964, GAZ-64 undertook modification work on Tu-16 bombers for missile-carrying, reconnaissance and ECM roles.

The plant at Voronezh started production of the Tu-28P heavy interceptor in 1965, and 198 of the type had been assembled by 1971. The plant, which lost its GAZ-64 designation in 1966, also built Tu-123 Yastreb pilotless reconnaissance vehicles, and the first Tu-144 SST Charger aircraft parts it had built were delivered to Moscow in 1968. At this time, VAPO was already one of the biggest aircraft factories in the Soviet Union, with 300,000 m^2 of covered areas. The high-bay final assembly hall was built in 1958/59, when 20,000 men worked at the plant, including 4,000 engineers and technicians. The plant was located 5 km south-east of the city, adjacent to Voronezh Airfield East, which served as a flight test and runway facility for the plant.

In 1971, Voronezh started building the first of seventy-five Tu-144 SSTs that had been ordered. The plan was to build fifteen a year, but due mainly to engine problems, only seventeen were built in total, which included the two prototypes. In reality, Aeroflot was relieved as it had never wanted the sophisticated Tu-144 aircraft, knowing that it would put a severe drain on its resources to operate. The aircraft was far too complex to be operated efficiently and cost-effectively. The result was that, in 1977, the plant started production of the Il-86 large civil jet transport aircraft for Aeroflot, eighty-three of which were built by the late 1990s. In parallel, it started production of the even bigger Il-96 in 1986, against an order for seventy aircraft. However, after the collapse of the Soviet Union, Voronezh experienced all sorts of problems, especially in relation to funding and raw material shortages. The plan for 1993 was production of three Il-96s, but only two were built, and the planned build for the following year was five aircraft. In reality, these were Il-96M & Il-96T cargo aircraft fitted with American avionics.

Fili/Kazan

Back in May 1921, Bolshevik Russia had made a cross-licence agreement with Germany for aircraft production. This had been followed in 1922 by another agreement between the Soviet Union and the Junkers firm for the production of 100 aircraft in Russia, and it was not long before work started on the Junkers factory at Petrogradskoye shosse 32 in the old Russo-Baltic Wagon Works at Moscow-Fili, which had been founded in 1917.

The agreement, made on 4 December 1922, was to build Junkers F 13 metal transport aircraft, and also fifty J 21s, fifteen J 22 Is and fifteen J 22 II military aircraft, to be delivered before April 1924. In October that year, more than 400 German engineers and skilled workers had arrived at the new GAZ-7 at Fili to work with and train Soviet personnel. In 1923, twenty Ju 20s and forty Ju 21s were built in the Soviet Union, but the J 22 that followed was rejected by the Red Air Force. GAZ-7 built only the all-metal aircraft. The following year another twenty J 20s and fifty-three J 21s were built, along with BMW IIIa engines. In 1925, twenty-six J 21s were produced, and the plant also assembled twenty-four K 30c aircraft from parts made in Sweden. The last three J 21s were completed in 1927, and the plant then began to build ten Junkers PS-4 (W 33) transport aircraft. However, on 1 March 1927, the plant, which employed in the region of 4,000 workers, was placed under state control and later that year was renamed Zavod 22 '10th Anniversary of October Revolution'. It almost immediately commenced building Soviet-designed R-3 reconnaissance planes, 101 of which were built up until 1929, including seventy-three in 1929 alone. Another 177 I-4 fighters were built between 1929 and 1931, 163 of them in 1930.

In 1929, production of the TB-1 twin-engined heavy bomber also started, with 216 built up to 1932, the first having been finished in July 1929. Two years later, TB-1 output had reached 146 aircraft. Also at this time, Zavod 22 built sixty-one ANT-9 three-engined high-wing transport aircraft, and forty-five R-6 reconnaissance versions of the TB-1 in 1931/32. The plant then embarked on its biggest programme to date—the production of four-engined TB-3s—delivering the first nine of 155 built that year on 25 April 1932. Another 270 were produced in 1933, 126 in 1934, 74 in 1935, and 115 in 1936. The last and 763rd was finished in 1938. Already, in 1934, a new product had been set down for production—the KR-6 cruiser—a heavily armed version of the R-6. A total of 270 had been built by 1935.

Throughout this period the plant had been enlarged several times. The original covered surface area in early 1933 was already 50,000 m^2, although this was to increase with the addition of an extra 30,000 m^2. Early in September 1933, the Director of the plant was killed in an air crash, and Zavod 22 received his name, Gorbunov.

From 1936, Zavod 22 built eleven ANT-35 small twin-engined transport planes. However, the profit remained in production of military aircraft, especially bombers. Between 1936 and 1941, the plant built 5,695 of the fast SB-2 twin-engined bombers: 268 in 1936; 853 in 1937; 1,250 in 1938; 1,435 in 1939; 1,820 in 1940; the final deliveries being made in 1941, of which the last 250 built were of the Ar-2 version. In 1938, the plant's Head of Construction, Nikolai Bazenkov, was arrested and sent to prison, and in August 1940, LaGG-3 development was started by Mikhail Gudkov, which on its conclusion led to work on the K-37 anti-tank aircraft and the Gu-82 fighter project. The plant switched to production of the new Pe-2 bombers in 1941, 1,120 of which were built until Zavod 22 was evacuated to Kazan from 16 October 1941. By this time the giant plant was employing over 25,000 workers. However, in this period many other things also happened at Moscow-Fili. For example in 1936, Arkhangelsky organised his own OKB at the plant for development of the SB-2 which, as we have already seen, led to the development of the Ar-2.

After Zavod 22 had been evacuated from Fili to Kazan, Zavod 124, which was already at Kazan, was absorbed into Zavod 22 on 26 December. The Director of the combined plants was Okulov and the Chief Engineer was Korneyev. Following on from 1941, the plant continued with production of the Petlyakov Pe-2, producing 1,937 in 1942; 2,423 in 1943; 2,944 in 1944; and 1,634 in 1945—a grand total of 8,938. Other Petlyakov designs produced were nineteen Pe-3s in 1944, twenty-two Pe-8s in 1942, twenty-nine in 1943, and five in 1944. From 1943, the massive Pe-2 production at Kazan was sufficient on its own to satisfy the needs of the Red Air Force, and between 1946 and 1952, 1,000 Tu-4 Bull strategic bombers were built and equipped to carry the first Soviet atomic bombs on Stalin's orders.

The Tu-16 was the first Soviet true large jet bomber, equivalent to the American B-47, and was in reality a superior aircraft, as the B-47 used six engines whereas the Tu-16 used only two. The success of the Tu-16, the Tu-95 and the Mya-4 meant that total Tu-4 production peaked at 847 aircraft. Included in this total were the 547 built at Kazan. Production of the Tu-16 ceased in 1958, but the production lines reopened three years later. In the 1960s, the Kazan plant was dominated by one large building complex which constituted the principal assembly and sub-assembly halls and the only final assembly building. It contained 70 per cent of the plant's covered area of 350,000 m². The Tu-104 airliner also produced at Kazan was the first successful jet transport built by the Soviets, although the Il-62 that followed was a much better aircraft. From 1963 until 1990, the plant produced 269 Il-62s.

In 1969, the Kazan plant had produced the first five Tu-22Ms and the planned annual output was reached in 1979, with a total of 507 produced by 1993. The Tu-22M swing-wing strategic bomber would pose a great threat to Europe in general for several decades. The 1980s saw a massive new development at the Kazan site in order to facilitate the production of 100 Tu-160s, although the reality was that only twenty-seven were finished between 1984 and 1992, instead of the planned 100 by 1995. The most recent designs earmarked for production at Kazan are the Tu-214 with its Rolls-Royce engines, and 10 Tu-330 planned to enter production as replacements for Russian Air Force An-12 aircraft.

Ulan-Ude

Ulan-Ude is situated deep in Siberia, near Lake Baikal, on the main Trans-Siberian railway line. The town had only 29,000 inhabitants in 1926, but in the industrial period several new plants were established there, including one large wagon plant, which resulted in the population increasing to 129,000 by January 1939. In July of that year, Zavod 99 repair plant was established for the overhaul and repair of M-25 and M-100 aero-engines. Soon the plant was also producing small parts for the Polikarpov I-16 fighters and, in 1941, sub-assemblies for other plants (e.g. Pe-2 bomber fuselages). The plant became more important after the evacuations caused by the outbreak of the Great Patriotic War, and Moscow decided that complete fighter aircraft should be built at Zavod 99. The plant received the name of Stalin, and the first of 184 Lavochkin La-5FN fighters were built here in 1943, followed by a further 102 in 1944. In that year Zavod 99 switched to production of the improved La-7, building forty of them, and the following year another 210 La-7s were built at Ulan-Ude.

After the war, in 1946, the plant started to build the more sophisticated La-9 fighter, and La-9UTI fighter trainers from 1948 until 1950, but in 1951 it began producing the MiG-15UTI jet fighter trainer aircraft, with a total of 2,755 built up to 1959, including 975 between 1956 and 1959. However, Zavod 99 was actually one of the smaller production plants of the Soviet Union, and it was not historically associated with any single designer or type of aircraft, producing a number of diverse designs from different design bureaux. Thus it was in 1953/54 that it also built Yak-12R light aircraft, and manufactured 670 Kamov Ka-15 two-seat light helicopters between 1957 and 1962, a small number of which were exported. From 1958 to 1960, another 370 stretched all-weather Ka-15 variants, designated Ka-18, were produced, but during the same period the plant also built 120 An-12 transport planes, and between 1959 and

1965 it manufactured no fewer than 165 Yak-25RV twin-jet reconnaissance aircraft. These were followed by 183 Yak-28Rs in from 1964 to 1966.

In 1960, the Kamov OKB arrived at Zavod 99 with a greatly expanded design team, and the plant became known as the helicopter plant, although this did not preclude the building of 120 An-24 transport aircraft in the period from 1965 to 1967, as well as a number of different missile types throughout the 1960s. During that decade the plant virtually doubled in size to 170,000 m^2 and had a considerable number of multistorey buildings not normally found at other aircraft production plants.

The number '99' was dropped in 1966 and the plant became known simply as Ulan-Ude Zavod. Between 1968 and 1975, 460 Kamov Ka-25 Helix ASW ship-borne helicopters were constructed in three different variants. However, with Kamov's death in November 1973, the plant was turned over to the production of the more competitive Mil helicopters and manufacture of the Mi-8 Hip multi-purpose helicopter commenced. Some 3,000 of the main variant, the military utility helicopter, were built up until 1992. In 1991, the capacity was for 100 Mi-8Ts a year, and until recently this helicopter was still in production but at a much lower output. From 1981, Ulan-Ude also started to build the improved Mi-8 variant, the Mi-17, which is still in small-scale production today as the Kazan 171 in its military transport and civil passenger variants.

In the late 1980s, in addition to the Su-25UT Frogfoot aircraft, the plant produced 200 MiG-27Ks (from 1988 to 1990), although the plant had also started production of the dual-seat attack trainer variant of the Sukhoi Su-25 sturmovik aircraft in 1985. Whilst all trainers were built at Ulan-Ude, production of the single-seat Su-25 at this time was at Tbilisi in Georgia, which of course is now no longer in Russia. Ulan-Ude underwent extensive alterations in 1994 to accommodate production of the Su-25T and Su-25TM anti-tank variants of the Su-25 sturmovik, the first of which were produced in late 1995. It was also proposed to build the new Kamov Ka-62 at Ulan-Ude, but only a very small number were produced. It is for this reason that the plant's spare capacity is now taken up with the production of consumer goods such as washing machines, kitchen furniture, pots and pans, etc.

Novosibirsk

The very large Siberian plant GAZ-153 at Novosibirsk was planned in the 1930s as a tractor factory. However, it was not long before the plans were changed and the finished factory commenced work immediately in 1937 as GAZ-153 on the production of the first of 809 I-16 fighters until 1941. The production peak occurred in 1940, with 503 I-16s produced that year, at which time the plant was also ordered to commence production of the Lavochkin LaGG-3 fighter. In the event, this was to present GAZ-153 with many problems, due mainly to late or missed deliveries of component parts, such as propellers, radiators and guns, from other factories. By the autumn of

1941 the plant had managed to finish only one aircraft, the remaining half-finished machines being stored outside on the airfield, completely covered in snow during the very harsh winter of 1941/42. It was not until the spring of 1942 that the factory was able to complete the build of these aircraft. Total LaGG-3 production was only 330.

From October 1941, four plants and OKBs were evacuated to GAZ-153, including the very energetic OKB Chief and Vice Commissar for Aircraft Production, Alexander Yakovlev. He was able to obtain an order to place his own Yak-7 into immediate production and also received all the necessary help and materials needed to start mass-production under a new plant director. By 1943, 4,888 Yak-7 aircraft had been produced at the Novosibirsk plant, but production of the Yak-9 also started late in 1942. A total of 12,536 were built up until 1948, making GAZ-153 the most important Soviet fighter production plant throughout the Second World War and beyond. After the victory, the plant produced a number of civil aircraft in parallel with reduced Yak-9 production: 697 Yak-9s were built in 1947, and a further 249 in 1948. From 1949, the plant was ordered to build MiG-15 jet fighters, of which 2,950 were produced until 1952, along with 400 MiG-15UTI training aircraft from 1950 to 1952. A total of 2,775 of the much-improved MiG-17 were built at GAZ-153 between 1952 and 1956, after which it switched to production of the first Soviet supersonic fighter aircraft, the MiG-19, of which 1,140 were built from 1956 to 1958.

In 1958, the plant was associated with the manufacture of Sukhoi designs, producing no fewer than 1,100 Su-9 interceptors for the Soviet PVO between 1958 and 1963. From 1963 to 1966 a further 700 of the improved Su-11 variant were built. GAZ-153 was the biggest Soviet fighter production plant at the time, with a floor space of 300,000 m^2 and 15,000 people working one shift, 40 hours per week. In 1966, the GAZ number 153 was dropped and the plant became known as V. P. Chkalov. Production of the sophisticated Su-15 interceptor began in the same year, and in 1967 the plant was the winner of the 'socialist competition' for its efforts on the Su-15 production programme. Floor space had increased to 400,000 m^2 and a new assembly line had been opened to produce the extremely capable Su-24 strike aircraft.

The Supreme Chief of the Soviet Union, Leonid Brezhnev himself, visited the plant in August 1972 for the roll-out of the first series production Su-24 aircraft. To enable continuance of Su-15 and Su-24 production simultaneously, a new large transhipment building was erected in the eastern part of the plant, and there were several smaller buildings and other minor constructions. Su-15 production was finally halted in 1983, with the completion of the 1,400th aircraft, but production of the Su-24 with its many sophisticated variants continued until 1992. A total of 1,100 of these excellent aircraft were built at Novosibirsk. However, along with all the other Soviet aircraft production plants, it suffered greatly from the collapse of the Soviet Union. Orders were cut, raw materials were in short supply, and funding for aircraft production was removed almost completely, with conversion to production of consumer goods necessary.

In 1994, it was planned to build ten An-38 transport aircraft, but ultimately none were produced. Other plans were made at the time to build the new Su-27IB fighter-bombers, but only a few prototype aircraft were produced. Later, it was planned to build the latest Su-27 derivative, the Su-34 multi-role aircraft, as a replacement for all Russian Su-24s by the year 2005, provided funding was available courtesy of President Putin.

As a matter of general interest, some American intelligence reports (*circa* 1972) that have recently become available state:

> Civilian test pilots at the plant, who checked out new aircraft before they were picked up by their military crews, received 500 roubles a month plus an amount for each flight. A mechanical engineer earned 160-180 roubles and a bookkeeper, 90-100 roubles and a production foreman 135 roubles. A production assembly mechanic earned 220-250 roubles, but when working on a pre-series model could earn up to 500 roubles a month. All workers received a 'Siberian' bonus of 15% on basic earnings. Security at the plant was provided by about 200 civilian guards, 60% of whom were women. Guards carried side-arms and in the main walked guard dogs. The perimeter fence was of reinforced concrete, about 9 feet high, topped with barbed wire; there was also an inner fence, about 4 feet high, topped with barbed wire, and the perimeter was fully illuminated at night. Later the Soviets also took precautions to avoid detection by US spy satellites.

Khodynka

At the time of nationalisation of the Duks plant (GAZ-1) in 1918, it employed 540 personnel. After use as a repair facility in 1920/21, GAZ-1 built twenty-three DH.4s followed by a further forty in 1921/22, and production of the R-1 (Soviet DH.9) started in 1923. It was the first aircraft to be mass-produced by the Soviets. In 1926, 392 were built at Khodynka, where at this time the airfield was very primitive, with no bitumen, only grass, and a number of wooden hangars. One hangar was for aircraft of the Military Air Academy, another for Dereflot aircraft, and the others were for the use of GAZ-1 and for the training aircraft of the Moscow School of the Red Air Force. On the eastern border there were several military stockrooms and at Leningradsky shosse 21 was GAZ-5, formerly Zavod F Moska, which had constructed a number of different aircraft and Polikarpov prototypes. In October 1927, this plant became Zavod 25. West of Khodynka was a military cemetery, to the north-west was a big dump full of destroyed aircraft, and to the north was Leningradsky shosse, later Leningradsky Prospect, a large boulevard 5 km long and 118 m wide.

Development at the plant occurred very quickly. Early in 1930, the Red Air Force repair shop at Khodynka became Zavod 39, and it was not long before Zavod 25 was incorporated. The Zavod also housed the infamous Vyacheslav Menzhinsky, Chief of the OGPU, the much-feared Soviet Secret Police. The Central Design Bureau (CKB) was created here, and it was in the secret hangar 7 that arrested designers like Grigorovich or Polikarpov designed some of the best Soviet military aircraft.

In 1931, Yakovlev worked here, although not as a prisoner. Soon 'series' construction of prototype aircraft was carried out, and the first five Tupolev TB-3 heavy bombers were built in late 1932. In the meantime, Zavod 1 and Zavod 39 received new brick buildings and hangars, becoming the largest aviation plants in the Soviet Union. Civil operations also received big new hangars and tarmacadam runways. However, these developments were nothing compared to those of 1934, when the two large plants and the airfield were increased in size and Khrushchev arrived to oversee the construction of the Moscow Metro. At the same time as the famous Metro was built, on Stalin's orders the Sverdlovsk Square–Central Airfield main line was constructed with two secret corridors: one from the Kremlin to Sverdlovsk station, and the other from Central Airfield station to a secret hangar. In an emergency Stalin or any important members of the Communist Party or Soviet Government could travel underground on the Metro in complete secrecy and security to Khodynka, where government aircraft would be waiting day or night in heavily guarded hangars to evacuate the Soviet leaders. The whole operation could be completed in 15 minutes. In October 1941, Soviet leaders were evacuated in this way to Kuibyshev, to a massive underground fortress capable of withstanding a nuclear attack. Stalin used this route out of the Kremlin over several decades, and Muscovites knew only too well how often and quickly this Metro line was closed without notice or explanation.

Khodynka has always been an important place for Soviet aviation, both for development and production. In 1941, Zavod 1 built 3,100 of the famous MiG-3 fighters. Zavod 39 built not only SB-2s but also 303 modern Pe-2 bombers and 196 Pe-3*bis* twin-engined fighters. In October/November of that year both plants were evacuated, although Khodynka did not remain empty for long. The new Zavod 30 was organised there in March 1942, eventually building more than 8,865 Ilyushin Il-2 Sturmoviks during the war.

After the Second World War, Zavod 30 built every kind of aircraft in very large quantities, including bombers and transport planes, and from 1960 most of the MiG variants, mainly for export. Even today, the famous MiG-29s for export are still in production at Khodynka, and it is planned that the MiG-AT jet trainer will also be produced there. It was also an important development centre, with the MiG OKB at Leningradsky Prospect and its production facility at Botkinsky Proezd in the former Zavod 1. After the death of Stalin the new Sukhoi OKB was also established at Khodynka. The Ilyushin OKB was in Zavod 30, and the new prototypes were built there.

Khodynka had been of such importance to the Soviet aviation industry that although within its vast boundaries there were many empty spaces and unoccupied buildings, even the infamous KGB with all its powers throughout the 1960s, 70s and 80s was not permitted occupancy. One wonders what the destiny of this famous airfield is under the Putin regime. Does Khodynka have more as yet undiscovered secrets to reveal?

Akhtubinsk

The test centre at Akhtubinsk—officially named the State Flight L Test Centre. (*Gosudarstvenny Lyotno Ispytatelny Tsentr*, GLIT)—is situated some 1,300 km (800 miles) east of Moscow close to the border with Kazakhstan, near the shores of the Akhtuba River and the town of the same name. It enjoys some 300 or more days of good weather each year, so test flying can be carried out almost constantly except on extremely hot days. The area, which lies between the towns of Volgograd and Astrakhan, was out of bounds to foreigners and even today special clearance is needed to enter the area. The airfield has two runways, including one which at 5,500 m (18,000 feet) is almost as long as the runway at the Zhukovsky test centre. Occupying an area of 10 km^2 (3.8 square miles), Akhtubinsk is the biggest test airfield in Russia, with a number of specially equipped areas to record a variety of test parameters. The OKBs use the centre for research work as well as for flight testing of aircraft.

Each year hundreds of studies are carried out by the various design bureaux and research institutes. Tests and evaluations involve aircraft, remote-controlled recce vehicles and armaments as well as modification and validation work, the latter often including work with civilian organisations. Almost every aircraft type (fighters, bombers, transports, reconnaissance and electronic warfare) currently in service, as well as those under development, can be found at Akhtubinsk, and a number of older types such as the MiG-23UB, the Su-17M4 and the Su-17UM3 are often used as chase planes when not used as test beds. Qualification tests of AAMs and their homing equipment is mainly undertaken using target drones. Most of the older Su-9 drones have now disappeared and currently early MiG-21 variants are used with undoubtedly more up-to-date models such as the MiG-23. A number of Czech Aero L-29s and some surplus Tu-16s have also been employed.

The GLIT centre at Akhtubinsk has not escaped the dire situation the country is in, and there are only a handful of pilots managing to maintain hours. However, a number of test pilots have continued training and have familiarised themselves with the multiplicity of types at the base in the hope of better times ahead.

***

Until the election of Vladimir Putin, the Soviet Union and the CIS experienced one of the most difficult periods in the history of its aviation industry, in the main due to a severe lack of funds. Civil aircraft makers had suffered most, passenger traffic having dropped by 77 per cent, and the fall in demand forced staff cuts at all levels but particularly in the production plants. Many workers went long periods without being paid, often up to twelve months at a time, and salaries were so low that many younger staff had second jobs. The industry's component suppliers were particularly hard hit, and many vital suppliers of undercarriages, electronic assembly, avionics and aircraft instruments were forced to close. However, many of the famous military plants

(GAZs) survived, but only just. Despite all this, at the start of the new millennium there were still some twenty-three factories manufacturing airframes, and many others building aero-engines, avionics and components, but not all of these plants could hope to survive in the modern competitive environment that the industry had been forced into.

As the country's leading civil aircraft manufacturer, Aviastar (now Taganrog Aviation) at the Ulyanovsk production complex currently survives, mainly on modification work of the Ilyushin Il-76 into the Mainstay A-50 AWACS aircraft, on contracts with India and Israel. The Israeli contract involves developing the type to help China meet its AEW/AWACs requirements, but the US has warned Israel that if it delivers modified Il-76 aircraft to China, it will withdraw $20 billion worth of defence aid. Aviastar was designated to build the Beriev Be-32K passenger regional airliner, but as yet there is no firm information as to the progress of this project.

Of the other civil aircraft plants, Smolensk (formerly GAZ-35) and Orenburg (formerly GAZ-464) are likely to close. Smolensk had built Yak-40s and early Yak-42s, and has since manufactured a number of elderly designed Yak-18T four-seat training aircraft and a few slightly modified SM-94s along with some Technoavia SM-92 utility aircraft. In addition, a few high-altitude Myasishchev M-55 Geofizika aircraft have been produced. Orenburg has built a number of Yak-3 fighter replica aircraft in anticipation of a market which has so far failed to develop, but may survive to build the new Kamov Ka-226 utility helicopter.

However, after the Kosovo crisis in 1999, the outlook for military aviation in Russia looked somewhat better. Russian leaders believed that NATO had chosen to ignore Russian opinion and, even before Putin's first election as president, they made the decision to rebuild their air force. It was decided to scrap all MiG-21 and MiG-23 variants and firm orders were placed for the lMiG-29M variant and several versions of the Su-27 Flanker. In addition, the first orders for the new An-70T transport aircraft were placed. In confirmation of its intent, for the first time in five years the government paid monies owing for previous deliveries to some of the aircraft plants that were to be involved in the production of these new aircraft. For example, the Kazan Gorbunov factory (GAZ-22) was finally paid for the last Tupolev Tu-160 Blackjack strategic bomber.

With the return of eight Tu-160s from Ukraine to the CIS, the new air force battle order had fifteen of these long-range bombers on operational strength, with a further six test and research aircraft in reserve, matching the USAF's Boeing B-2 Spirit inventory one-for-one. Many of the military plants have large numbers of completed or partially completed airframes in store. Kazan has two Tu-22M Backfires, whilst MAPO (RSK MiG—MiG Russian Aircraft Corporation) has a large number of MiG-29 fighters at its Lukhovitsi plant and two-seat MiG-29UBs at Nizhny Novgorod (formerly GAZ-21) where low-scale production of the MiG-31 Foxhound has continued.

The MiG-29 Fulcrum and the Su-27 Flanker have continued to be sold to a number of overseas customers throughout the period of austerity, earning valuable currency for the hard-pressed Russian economy. The Nizhny Novgorod factory also offers upgrades for MiG-21 Fishbed users worldwide. Additionally it has produced the Myasishchev M-101T Gzhel single-engined turboprop utility aircraft. Three factories have been involved in Su-27 Flanker production, including the Irkutsk Aircraft Manufacturing Association (formerly GAZ-39) and Gagarin Aircraft Manufacturing Factory (formerly GAZ-126) at Komsomolsk in the East where the ship-borne Su-27K variant is built. Irkutsk also produces the multi-role Su-30 variant, which has been exported to China, Ethiopia, India, Indonesia and Vietnam, with a licensed-production agreement with India for local assembly of 140 aircraft with Irkutsk-built parts.

The outstanding battle-proven Sukhoi ground attack Su-25 Frogfoot and Su-25UB variant are built at Ulan-Ude (formerly GAZ-99). Sukhoi set up a civil aircraft division in what was previously a purely military design bureau and has produced its world-renowned aerobatic aircraft since the 1980s. It has developed a 30-passenger airliner, the S-80, built at Komsomolsk, and a collaboration has also been agreed with the US-based Alliance Group to develop a range of 50- to 100-seat regional airliners.

An area of unprecedented success for the Soviet aircraft industry has been in the field of rotary aircraft. Its Mil Mi-8 and M-17 Hip family has been produced in a never-ending supply of over twenty-five types and variants. The Mi-8, a large twin-engined design capable of carrying up to thirty-two passengers or four tonnes of freight, had its maiden flight in September 1962, since when well over 8,000 have been produced. Since 1956 many have been exported, eventually to no fewer than fifty-seven countries, including China, India, Syria, Egypt and Peru, with many still in use today.

The Mi-8 and Mi-17 helicopters are built at the Kazan factory, where series production of Soviet helicopters first started with the Mi-1 in 1951. Production of the larger Mil types—including the Mi-24 attack helicopter, the Mi-26 heavy-lift, the Mi-38 attack helicopter and the updated Mi-28N Night Hunter all-weather variant—is undertaken at the helicopter factory in Rostov-on-Don. Production of the Mi-34 four-seat business helicopter began at Arsenyev in 1993, alongside small batch production of the Kamov Ka-50 Black Shark and Ka-52 attack helicopters. Earlier, some Mi-8s and Mi-24s had been produced at the Progress Joint Stock Company in Arsenyev, which post-war had been more usually associated with the production of Kamov Ka-32 helicopters and Antonov An-14 Pchelka business aircraft. The other Kamov helicopters were built at the Ulan-Ude Manufacturing Association or the Kumertau Aircraft Production Association, although the latest design, the 14-passenger Ka-60, which appears as a bigger version of the Eurocopter Dauphin, is built at the RSK MiG Lukhovitsi plant.

Those production plants hardest hit by the collapse of the Soviet Union were the manufacturers of military transports and civil airliners. With fewer than thirty new jet airliners delivered in five years, it is not surprising to discover that a number of civil airliner plants still have unfinished aircraft on their lines from when production began to run down more than a decade ago. However, in June 2000, President Putin affirmed his intention of setting up a properly constituted leasing organisation to enable regional airlines to re-equip their ageing fleets and more importantly to maintain desperately needed air services to the vast interior of the country.

Aeroflot agreed to purchase six Il-96-300 wide-bodied airliners, most of which were nearing completion at the Voronezh plant (formerly GAZ-240). The airline also signed letters of intent to purchase twenty Tu-334 twin-jets powered by Rolls-Royce BR715 engines and planned to be built at the RSK MiG plant at Khodynka in Moscow. Fifty An-140s are to be built at the Aviacor plant in Samara to re-establish the airline's internal feeder routes. The 102-seat Tu-334, first flown in February 1999, is intended to replace ageing Tu-134 and Yak-40 airliners. Standard aircraft are powered by two Ukrainian-built Progress D-436T turbofans with 73.57 kN (16,540 lbf) of thrust, while the 120 variant would be fitted with Rolls-Royce Deutschland BR715s. However, by the mid-2000s only the first prototype was flying, although the second and third were due to fly. The famous Kazan Gorbunov production plant, which still has five Il-62s unsold, has now begun to build the Tu-214, a long-range version of the Tu-204. Currently it has firm commitments for the twelve aircraft on final assembly and is in the process of setting up a new line to produce the Tu-324 regional jet.

The prime manufacturer for the Tu-204 was Aviastar at Ulyanovsk, building both variants, the Aviadvigatel PS-90-powered Tu-204-100 and the westernised RB211-powered Tu-204-120 for the Egyptian leasing company Sirocco Aerospace. In 1995, Aviastar had about twenty-four Tu-204s on final assembly, but by mid-2000 only four had been delivered, two of which were traded to Perm Motors in exchange for aero-engines, such was the sorry state of Russian civil aircraft manufacturing. One Aviastar-built Tu-204 which was redeveloped as a 160-seat longer-range Tu-234 was due to make its first flight in 2000. Aviastar had orders to build about fifteen. The company also builds the giant An-124 Ruslan freighter, having delivered one (the first for four years), to the Russian heavy-lift contractor Volga-Dnepr, two remaining on final assembly at this time but with no customers.

Aviacor at Samara was preparing to build An-70 transporters for the CIS Air Force, as well as the An-140 regional turboprop aircraft. Aviacor was also to build the Tu-334, but in 1999, by government decree, this project was transferred to MAPO MiG in Moscow, although Aviacor was to manufacture wing sets for the aircraft. The Saratov plant (formerly GAZ-292) had previously built Yak-24s, Yak-28Ps, Yak-38s, Yak-40s and Yak-42s, and had about nineteen Yak-42s in final assembly, but with no other aviation manufacturing work in the offing, the company was concentrating on the production of agricultural tractors. Novosibirsk (formerly GAZ-153) was building some 27-seat An-38 turboprop aircraft, and Polyot in Omsk (formerly GAZ-166) was producing an updated version of the An-2 Colt, the An-3, for a number of local airlines and agricultural work, as well as some An-74 transport aircraft.

Other aviation factories struggled to stay afloat. Aviant was building the An-32, had An-124 capability and was setting up for the An-70 and the Tu-334. KhAPO in Kharkov, the main producer of the An-74, was also building the An-140, the first of which was delivered in May 2000. TAPO at Tashkent (formerly GAZ-184) was still building Il-76 freighters as well as Il-114 regional turboprop airliners, and the Georgian Aviation Industry factory at Tbilisi (formerly GAZ-31) had begun production of the Yak-58, which was yet to receive certification.

5

Engine Design and Development

The Soviet aero-engine industry had been mainly engaged in producing engines of foreign design, notably the American Wright Cyclone (Soviet M-25 and M-63), the Hispano-Suiza Y Series (M-100) and the French Gnome-Rhône K-14 series (M-85). At the outbreak of the Great Patriotic War many of the fourteen plants engaged in aero-engine production, endangered by the imminent invasion, were evacuated to the Urals region.

During the war the Soviet Union produced between 175,000 and 185,000 aero-engines, including 38,000 in 1942, 49,000 in 1943, and 52,000 in 1944. The industry standardised on four basic types: Alexander Mikulin's inline AM-38 and its development, the AM-42, used almost exclusively in the sturmovik designs; the Klimov VK-105, developed as the VK-107 for fighter planes and Pe-2 bombers, with more than 97,000 produced at Ufa; Shvetsov's ASh-82 radial, used primarily by Lavochkin and by Tupolev for the Tu-2 bomber; and the 5-cylinder M-11 produced by a number of smaller factories.

In general, aero-engine development in the Soviet Union was not particularly successful at this time, and there were numerous frustrations and disappointments. Take, for example, Klimov's 12-cylinder VK-107 with its 300 kW (400 hp) increase in power over the VK-10. Although it underwent considerable development, any hopes that it might give a new lease of life to the LaGG-3 fighter were short-lived after it displayed constant overheating problems during tests in 1942. It was not until 1944 that the VK-107 was cleared for fitting to the Yak-9U and later variants of the Yak-3 fighter. Mikulin's AM-39, developed from the ubiquitous AM-35, showed more promise and from 1943 was used to power a number of prototypes, including Polikarpov and MiG high-altitude fighters, although post-war only limited numbers were built to power Tupolev's Tu-10 tactical bomber developed from the wartime Tu-2. The most successful Soviet Second World War designs were Shvetsov's ASh-82 and ASh-82FN 14-cylinder radials, although the 1,492 kW (2,000 hp) 18-cylinder ASh-71 and similar ASh-83 tested on a number of prototype aircraft were less successful and did not enter series production.

In order to address the acute shortage of aero-engines due to prolonged development of new models, all the major engine design bureaux were instructed to prepare enhanced versions of existing designs, despite the misgivings of the OKBs as to the likely reduced engine life and increased maintenance. At the same time, research into the field of auxiliary reaction engines was also encouraged—including ramjet and liquid-fuel rocket engines. Merkulov DM-2 and DM-4 under-wing ramjets had already been successfully tested on I-15*bis* and I-153 test beds in 1940, and seventy-four test flights had been made without incident. Similar tests were carried out on the I-207 biplane fighter prototype and on the Yak-1, and later, in 1942, on the LaGG-3 and Yak-7 fighters. However, it soon became apparent that the increased weight and drag and high fuel consumption did not justify the relatively short burst of speed provided. It was reported in 1967 that a number of PVO Yak-7 fighters had been equipped with ramjets in 1944 for operations against high-altitude Luftwaffe reconnaissance planes.

Khalshchevnikov produced a design where the ramjet was an integral part of the aircraft fitted in the rear fuselage, utilising power from the nose-mounted piston engine to drive the compressor. Later the Su-5 (I-107) and MiG I-205 mixed powerplant fighters with Klimov VK-107 engines were designed in a similar manner, and tested in 1945. A small number of MiG I-250s were series-produced for jet familiarisation training, but with the obviously superior gas turbine powerplants now in full-scale development and production, auxiliary engine design was abandoned.

At the same time, Soviet liquid-fuel rocket engines were developed by Valentin Glushko and his deputy Sergei Korolev, who was responsible for the installation and flight testing of the RD-1 which burnt kerosene and nitric acid. Having overcome inherent starting problems, the RD-1KhZ was developed using chemical ignition and installed in the rear fuselage of a Pe-2 bomber. Following the conclusion of initial tests in October 1943, it was decided to continue development to enable the engine to be used to facilitate expedited pursuit, evasion and climb, and take-off from short runways or with aircraft with excessive loads when long-range flights were to be made.

In late 1943, the appearance of Luftwaffe reconnaissance planes over Moscow created fears of a renewed German bombing offensive. With the knowledge that Messerschmitt Me 262 jets were about to enter series production, the Lavochkin, Yakovlev and Sukhoi OKBs were instructed to prepare rocket-assisted variants of their existing fighters to fly high-altitude air defence missions at around 13,000 to 14,000 m (30,000 to 40,000 feet). The first type to be adapted was the Lavochkin La-7R, which was ready for NII VVS testing in 1944. However, it proved to be a highly unpleasant and unreliable aircraft, as nitric acid and fumes penetrated into the cockpit and various leakages gave rise to a number of corrosion problems with the wooden airframe. A version with a metal rear fuselage, designated La-120R, was tested in 1945, along with rocket-boosted variants of the Su-7 and the Yak-3R, one of which exploded in mid-air, which led to further work on aircraft with auxiliary reaction motors being discontinued. Other equally unsuccessful projects by Korolev included the installation of RD-1KhZ units behind the engines of Pe-3 and Pe-21 fighters to convert them into high-altitude interceptors, as was the proposal to fit three RD-1KhZs to a Lavochkin La-5 to enable a top speed of 950 kph at 17,000 m.

Three designs of air defence fighters powered only by rocket motors were prepared. The first, designed by Alexander Y. Bereznyak and Aleksei M. Isayev at the Bolkhovitinov OKB, was designated BI and made its first powered flight in April 1942, having made an earlier flight in September 1941 as a glider. The BI was a very small aircraft with a wingspan of only 6.4 m (21 feet) and powered by a D-1A rocket engine of 10.8 kN (2,425 lbf) thrust designed by pioneer Leonid Dushkin. Most of the fuselage contained propellant, which accounted for almost half the aircraft's gross weight. The propellant of kerosene and red fuming nitric acid (RFNA) was housed in tanks in the fuselage centre section. As with the first American Bell X-1, nitrogen held under pressure was used to expel the fuel from the tanks. Following the BI's first flight, problems with the rocket motor prevented further powered flight tests until March 1943. Then, on the seventh powered flight, the original BI prototype made a low-level, high-speed run but dived sharply into the ground, killing the test pilot Grigori Bakhchivandzhi. Opinions were sharply divided as to the merits of the tiny wooden fighter plane with its fearsome engine. In his flight log Bakhchivandzhi had written:

> Flight in a reaction-motor powered aircraft is very pleasant as the pilot has no airscrew in front of him and fumes do not intrude into the cockpit. Engine noise diminished with the increase in speed and the engine functioned as required on take-off and in flight. The sudden cutting out of the engine did not affect control; that is, the aircraft showed no tendency to deviate from course, and the pilot felt deceleration as on any conventional aircraft. The ease with which the machine responded to its controls was better than on modern fighters.

However, another NII VVS test pilot who flew the BI, Krudin, described the BI as 'the devil's broomstick'.

Following the fatal accident, further tests with the BI prototypes were made, but as the reason for the crash remained unsolved and the Rocket Propulsion Research Institute (RNII) development team refused to refine the D-1A engine or develop a multi-chamber to give it controlled cruise, official interest in rocket planes declined rapidly. The initial batch of twenty BI airframes built at Nizhny Tagil were scrapped, and two other rocket projects were terminated. Stalin was obviously not impressed, and Bakhchivandzhi was posthumously awarded the title 'Hero of the Soviet Union' in April 1973.

The two cancelled projects were the Polikarpov Malyutka, a sophisticated design that did not get off the drawing board, and the Tikhonravov I-302P. It was a more ambitious project although similar in shape to the BI, with tail-wheel landing gear, unswept wing and fuel tanks in the centre section, but it was twice as heavy. It was powered by a RD-1400 rocket engine of 14.7 kN (3,307 lbf) thrust, used for take-off and acceleration, and two under-wing Zuyev rockets using much less fuel, to extend its flight time. Its armament of four ShVAK 20 mm cannon was double that of the BI. Maximum speed was estimated at 900 kph (560 mph), although this was thought to be somewhat optimistic. The prototype I-302P was completed in the spring of 1943, but none of the intended engines were ready and it flew only as a glider, and gliding tests with a Pe-2 tug were still in progress when the project ended.

While the BI and I-302P were in essence only experimental aircraft when compared to the Messerschmitt Me 163B Komet that did see operational service, they did stimulate a degree of interest in rocket-powered fighters which was rekindled in 1945, when captured German aircraft and information became available for analysis and testing at the end of the war.

The Soviets did lay claim to some wartime gas turbine engine development with their 600 kg axial-flow unit designed by A. Lyulka, I. F. Kozlov and P. S. Shevchenko in Leningrad in 1941, which gave rise to the wartime 700 kg VRD-2 development and the subsequent 1,300 kg VRD-3, designated TR-1, fitted in the Ilyushin Il-22 and Sukhoi Su-11 prototypes in 1947/48. Nevertheless, it is true that early gas turbine development and production relied emphatically on the import of British Rolls-Royce engines and the continued production of the BMW 003A and Junkers Jumo 004B axial-flow designs, under the Soviet designations RD-20 and RD-10, with the BMW 003 (RD-21) developed to give 9.8 kN (2,205 lbf) by increasing the fuel feed and the temperature of the gases at the post-turbine stage as well as increasing the rpm of the turbine. In a similar manner the power of the Junkers 004B was increased, giving rise to the 9.8 kN RD-10A and the 10.8 kN RD-10F.

The Soyuz Design Bureau at Moscow was founded by Mikulin, who worked there from 1943 to 1955. His successors were Tumansky (1955-1973), Favorsky (1973-1987) and Kobchenko (from 1987). It built 26,000 engines which flew 24 million hours. The Soyuz bureau is best known for its long series of fighter aircraft engines, and in the late 1980s and early 1990s it produced vectored thrust engines for Soviet naval VTOL fighters (Yak-36s and Yak-38s) along with fan-and shaft-powered engines for light aircraft.

The afterburning AM-9 Mikulin RD-9BF was developed for future Mikoyan OKB supersonic combat aircraft. When work began in 1950 on the preliminary design of a fighter capable of breaking the sound barrier in level flight, the Mikoyan OKB engineers decided to power it with a new, smaller Mikulin turbojet. Mikulin, the engine manufacturer and academic, had just developed a powerful turbojet, the AM-3, to power the Tu-16 bomber. At the time, rated at 8,750 kg, it was probably the most powerful jet engine in the world. However, it was of course much too large for a fighter so Mikulin decided to develop an engine with the same layout, operating cycle and architecture as the AM-3 but a third of the size.

On 30 June 1950, Mikoyan, Yakovlev and Mikulin were called to the Kremlin to discuss plans for the new engine with Mikhail Khrunichev, the Soviet Aviation Minister, and it was later announced by decree of the Soviet Council of Ministers that the AM-5 would power the new Yakovlev and Mikoyan fighters. However, the AM-5 engine was not an immediate success. Numerous adjustments were required, and it was obvious that proving and tests would be better carried out on a flying test bed than on the factory test bench. Mikoyan, who was extremely interested in the new engine, offered to install two AM-5 engines side by side in a MiG-15, a proven airframe. For his part, Yakovlev proposed to fit them in pods under the wing of his new fighter, the Yak-25. In the end, Mikoyan's suggestion was taken up and two AM-5s were fitted in place of the single VK-1 of the MiG-15*bis* aircraft, the design of which the MiG-17 was based on. The modification was approved on 20 April 1951 by the Council of Ministers and it was renamed the SM-1.

The prototype was rolled out at the end of 1951 for factory tests by test pilot Grigory Sedov. The object of the tests was to prove the viability of the dual AM-5A engine fit and to recommend any further minor modifications that might improve the performance of the MiG-17. The two AM-5As, without afterburner and with a maximum rating of 2,000 kg (4,409 lb) , delivered more thrust than a single VK-1F with reheat. Furthermore, the two engines weighed 88 kg less than one VK-1F. However, it quickly became apparent that the thrust of the AM-5A was inadequate to meet the design specifications. Mikulin then decided to add an afterburner to the engine, which subsequently became the AM-5F and was rated at a maximum dry thrust of 2,150 kg and a reheated thrust of 2,700 kg. Increased fuel was accommodated for by the fitting of a 1,220-litre and a 330-litre tank behind the cockpit, and a canister for a 15 m² (161 square feet) tail chute was attached to the fuselage under the tail section to assist with braking and minimise brake wear.

However, after a number of development flights with the SM-1, and later the SM-2, Mikoyan convinced Mikulin and other experts that the thrust of the dual AM-5F engine installation was insufficient for the next generation of Soviet aircraft. Mikulin therefore embarked immediately on the creation of a new afterburner and increased the engine compressor output from 37 to 43.3 kg/sec. Out of this came a much more powerful Soviet turbojet—the AM-9 (later RD-9B). This was the engine chosen by the MiG OKB for its new supersonic fighter. Another great engine design bureau at St Petersburg (formerly Leningrad, Factory 117) produced high-powered piston engines developed under Klimov.

In 1946, the plant was selected to build the Rolls-Royce Nene jet engine, later developed as the Klimov VK-1. Klimov was succeeded at Factory 117 by his deputy Sergei Petrovich Izotov, who initially developed gas turbine engines for helicopters but in 1968 moved into fighter engine development. Izotov died in 1983 and was succeeded by Valentin Stepanov, who on retirement was succeeded by Alexander Sarkisov, although the bureau has now been renamed after its founder Klimov. The 'Factory 117' title is included in the engine designations, e.g. TV2-117TG. Engines designed by NPO Klimov were manufactured at Perm by Sverdlov and at Zaporozhye by Motorostroitel, except for the TV7-117 produced at the Chernishov factory at Moscow and the Baranov factory at Omsk.

The Klimov Corporation developed a link in June 1993 with Pratt & Whitney Canada. The outstanding engine designer Arkady Shvetsov was responsible for the 75-150 kW (100-200 hp) M-11 5-cylinder air-cooled radials made in large quantities from 1928 to 1959, from which he developed the larger 746 kW (1,000 hp) ASh-62 and 1,492 kW (2,000 hp) ASh-82 units. The ASh-62 was made in large numbers, powering the Lisunov Li-2 (DC-3) and the Antonov An-2, with the ASh-82 powering the Lavochkin (La-) fighters, Tupolev Tu-2 and Tu-4 bombers, Ilyushin Il-12 and Il-14 transports and Mil Mi-4 helicopters. Another important power unit from this bureau was the 544 kW (730 hp) ASh-21, which powered the famous Yak-11 two-seat advanced trainer.

The Kuznetsov Engine Design Bureau at Samara (formerly Kuibyshev), 900 km (559 miles) east of Moscow on the River Volga, was established under General Designer Nikolai D. Kuznetsov and was probably better known for the production of aircraft and guns. It was also the centre to which the Soviet Government and foreign embassies were evacuated in the autumn of 1941. Later aero-engines, rocket engines and space vehicles were manufactured at Kuibyshev. Immediately following the war, engine design at Kuibyshev was concentrated in two bureaux: OKB-1, working on jet engines; and OKB-2, working on rocket engines. At this time there were about 800 German aero-engineers at Kuibyshev who had been forcibly transferred from the BMW and Junkers Jumo plants in their homeland. Engine production took place at Frunze, the large Kuibyshev manufacturing plant named after Mikhail Frunze, an early Bolshevik leader. The wartime BMW 003 and Junkers Jumo 004 turbojet engines, redesignated RD-20 and RD-10, were among the first Soviet jet engines to be produced in the country.

In 1949, Kuznetsov was still at Ufa, working on the RD-12 and RD-14 designs as Klimov's deputy, but was later moved by the Ministry of Aviation Industry to Kuibyshev as head of the design bureau. The engine OKB was at this time working on the Soviet version of the Junkers Jumo 012 turbojet, but Kuznetsov decided to concentrate his efforts on another Jumo project, the 3,730 kW (5,000 hp) 022 turboprop engine, under the Soviet designation TV-022. In the event, neither the TV-022 nor the twin version TV-2F that were developed for Tupolev's Tu-95 Bear entered service. By 1950/51 most of the German engineers had been repatriated, although a number still remained, including the former Junkers designer Ferdinand Brandner, who were required to work on a replacement for the cancelled TV-2F. With the promise that on completion of the project they would be permitted to return home, the German designers set about their task with gusto and by 1954 they had returned to Germany, leaving their 8,950 kW (12,000 hp) design behind them. The new engine, known as the 'K', was the world's most powerful turboprop, designed to drive huge contra-rotating propellers.

Under Kuznetsov's direction the 'K' underwent further development at OKB-1 and by 1957 it had been uprated to 11,190 kW (15,000 hp). In recognition of Kuznetsov's leadership of the project, the engine was given the designation NK-12 when the giant turboprop engine powered the Tu-20/95 Bear strategic bomber and maritime reconnaissance aircraft and the civil Tu-114 airliner. The Tu-20 first flew in 1954 and remained in operational service for nearly thirty years; the Tu-114 had its first flight in

October 1957 and entered service with Aeroflot in 1961. The military derivative of the Tu-114 was the Tu-126 Moss AWACS aircraft, which was powered by the NK-12MK. A further aircraft to be powered by the NK-12 was the An-22 Antheus long-range heavy transport, which had its first flight in February 1965. The type ultimately entered service with Aeroflot and the VTA, with some forty or more still available in 1994.

A second Kuznetsov single-shaft turboprop was developed in the 1950s, the 2,984 kW (4,000 hp) NK-4, at the request of the Ministry of Military Aviation Industry. In parallel, Alexander Georgievich Ivchenko, at Zaporozhye in Ukraine, was working on his AI-20 engine to the same specifications. The engines were intended to power the An-10 and Il-18 transport aircraft, both having made their first flights in 1957.

Having started its development ahead of the AI-20, the NK-4 entered pre-series production at the Frunze plant, with some 200 engines delivered for fitting to the Il-18. However, when Khrushchev became aware of the existence of the AI-20 he called the two designers to Moscow to explain why two engines had been developed to meet the same requirement. Kuznetsov presented Khrushchev with a full technical appraisal of the NK-4, to which he is said to have exclaimed, 'We are not students and you are not a lecturer.' On the other hand, Ivchenko simply explained, 'We have the engine and it works,' and Khrushchev, anxious to build up the aviation industry in Ukraine, ruled in favour of Ivchenko's AI-20.

Kuznetsov then turned his attention to another monster engine, the 196.12 kN (44,090 lbf) NK-6 two-spool turbofan with duct burning, intended to power the Tupolev and Myasishchev supersonic bombers. In the event, although the engine was developed to the point of preparation for state tests, the programme was cancelled. Kuznetsov moved on to the NK-8 commercial turbofan designed for the long-range Il-62 transport aircraft, and a further variant, the NK-8-2, with thrust reverser was developed for the Tu-154 medium-range airliner. Both aircraft joined Aeroflot in 1972.

Uprated NK-8 turbofans were developed for heavier versions of the airliner: the 102.97 kN (23,148 lbf) NK-8-4 for the Il-62, and the NK-8-2U for the Tu-154. However, operationally these engines proved less than satisfactory and were certainly less than economical. As a result, with the launch of the Il-62M in 1970, a switch was made to a version of the Soloviev D-30 turbofan. In 1982, a similar switch was made when the Tu-154M appeared. An upgraded derivative of the NK-8, the 127.48 kN (28,659 lbf) NK-86, was developed in the early 1970s to power the Il-86, the first Soviet wide-bodied passenger jet.

In parallel with conventional airframe applications, from the early 1970s Kuznetsov became heavily involved in the development of an entirely new type of airborne vehicle—the 'wing-in-ground effect' craft. These aircraft had been developed by the Central Construction Bureau for Hydrofoil Ships at Nizhny Novgorod under the Soviet pioneer of 'wing ships' Rostislav Alekseyev. The craft were designed to fly over water at a height of around 2-5 m (6 feet 6 inches-16 feet 5 inches) with support being provided by the air cushion under the hull and short-span wide-chord wings. Initially these wing ships were powered by eleven NK-8 turbofans, with two groups of four in pods on stub wings over the nose, to accelerate the craft into ground effect, and three for cruise, mounted on the vertical stabilizer clear of the sea spray. The NK-8s were special 'navalised' variants treated to protect them against the corrosive effects of saltwater, and ten of these mammoth 'Caspian Sea Monsters' were built. The largest, designated 'KM', weighed 500 tonnes, was 100 m (328 feet) long and had a span of 40 m (131 feet). During trials the 'KM' established a weight/speed record of 540 kph (335 mph), which was only bettered later by the giant An-225 Mriya heavy transport aircraft first flown on 21 December 1988. A second series of smaller wing ships, known as Ekranoplans, were produced in the 1970s, powered by two NK-8-4Ks buried in the nose for acceleration and take-off and a single 11,185 kW (15,000 hp) NK-12MK on top of the vertical stabiliser for cruise. In the 1980s, similar Ekranoplan designs reverted to the earlier multi-podded, nose-mounted installations of the K-series.

The engine design bureau at Kuibyshev also developed two unique versions of the NK-8: the 102.97 kN (23,149 lbf) NK-88 and NK-89. These were dual-fuel engines capable of operating on either normal aviation kerosene or cryogenic fuels such as liquid hydrogen, LH_2 (NK-88) or liquid natural gas, LNG (NK-89). The development of these engines began when the Soviets were concerned that global supplies of hydrocarbon fuels could run out early in the twenty-first century. The NK-88 engine was flown in the Tu-155 (a variant of the Tu-154) and the NK-89 was flown in the Tu-156. Whilst the Soviet Union, like a number of other countries including Britain, eventually realised that the perceived threat to global fuel reserves at the turn of century was, to say the least, somewhat premature and alarmist, the dual-fuel capability with regard to aero-engines in the Soviet Union was investigated thoroughly by virtue of the enforced logistics of delivering aviation fuel over long distances by surface transport to Vladivostok and other remote parts in the east of the country, often in sub-zero conditions.

With Siberia's gas fields providing a ready supply of LNG, it had made sense for the Soviet Union to investigate dual-fuel engines. These investigations were carried out in conjunction with the Tupolev OKB, Pratt & Whitney and Deutsche Aerospace, including MTU. A number of projected cryogenic-fuelled Kuznetsov designs were shown, along with the latest Tupolev aircraft designs at the Moscow Aerospace-93 Show. These included the 450-seat Tu-306 (a version of the Tu-304 airliner) fitted with the new NK-46 turbofan, the stretched 160-seat Tu-156M2 (a version of the Tu-154M2) and the Tu-214 and Tu-338 versions of the Tu-204 and Tu-330 freighter with the NK-94, and the stretched 120-seat Tu-336 (a version of the Tu-334) with the NK-112 turbofan. However, the NK-88 and NK-89 engines were not the first Soviet engines to operate with cryogenic fuels. Never one to resist a challenge, Kuznetsov was also heavily involved in work on high-performance, cryogenic-fuelled engines designed for the rockets and space craft involved in the Soviet space programme.

With regard to aero-engine design, it is fitting to mention here the challenges faced by the Kuznetsov OKB in designing the Soviet Union's first SST, the Tupolev Tu-144.

The NK-144 was essentially a supersonic version of the basic NK-8 engine, retaining the same 1.348 m (4 feet 5 inches) fan, with major design changes embodied to attain the necessary fuel economy, reliability and durability. The aircraft had its maiden flight in December 1968, and was the world's first SST to take to the air. However, it would be a further seven years before the Tu-144 entered service with Aeroflot, and even then only as a freighter, and its operational life was to be short-lived. The aircraft was bedevilled by safety, reliability and engine problems, and in an effort to overcome these deficiencies, uprated variants of the NK-144—the 196.13 kN (44,092 lbf) NK-144A and the 215.74 kN (48,500 lbf) NK-144B—had been developed prior to its final withdrawal.

It is thought that the NK-22 two-spool afterburning turbofans fitted to the Tu-22M Backfire bomber were direct descendants of the NK-144, and as some 350 Tu-22Ms are estimated to have been built it can be safely assumed that the military requirement was the driving force in the development of the common powerplant. In the early 1980s, Kuznetsov developed a completely new three-shaft generation of military afterburning turbofans, four of which powered the Tu-160 Blackjack long-range supersonic strategic bomber. The mighty NK-321 with its 245.16 kN (55,115 lbf) thrust is the world's most powerful combat engine, the first four NK-321s to take to the air having been fitted to the first prototype at Ramenskoye on 19 December 1981. It was originally intended to build about 100 Blackjacks, but production had been cut by 1994 to one aircraft per year and it is unlikely that the NK-321 will ever be produced in large quantities.

At the age of 87, Nikolai Kuznetsov finally handed over control of his design bureau to his deputy Evgeny Gritsenko. Kuznetsov must surely rate among the world's greatest aero-engine specialists, his team having designed the most powerful turboprop engine, the most powerful combat engine and the most powerful turbofan engine.

The Rybinsk Engine Building Design Office produced a complete range of engines— turbofans, jet and piston, and lift jets—for the naval VTOL fighters under four general designers: V. A. Dobrynin, P. A. Kolesov, V. I. Galiguzov and A. S. Novikov. It also developed the world's largest turbojet, the 196.12 kN (44,090 lbf) RD-36-51 non-afterburning replacement engine for the modified Tu-144D SST. The company's most up-to-date project is the TRDD D-777 which embodies the bureau's '77' experimental gas generator. The engine design is described as a low (technical) risk development, with high growth potential, high fuel economy, and noise and exhaust emission levels in line with current designs. It incorporates FADEC (Full Authority Digital Engine Control). Developing 123 kN (27,645 lbf), proposed applications are the Tu-34-II, the Yak-46 and the An-180.

The company's other major project is the 40 kN (9,040 lbf) RD-41 lift jet originally for the Yak-141 VTOL fighter. Although that was cancelled, the lift jet engine continues in the guise of the 26.98 kN (6,065 lbf) RD-60 take-off booster for the Beriev A-40 Albatros multi-role amphibian. The bureau's latest development is a small, high fuel economy 4-cylinder, 2-stroke diesel unit of 149 kW (200 hp), the DN-200, and it also undertakes research work on non-metallic materials, especially carbon composites such as silicon nitrate and silicon carbide.

Arkady Shvetsov founded the engine bureau at Perm, and was followed by Pavel Soloviev from 1953 to 1989. The bureau has specialised for some thirty-five years in turbofans for Soviet civil airliners, providing the powerplants for most of Aeroflot's fleet. Its new design was the 156.91 kN (35,275 lbf) PS-90A to power the Il-96 and Tu-204 airliners. Engines created by Shvetsov and Soloviev have powered twenty-six types of aircraft and helicopters, whose total flying time exceeds 48 million hours. Aircraft types include the Tu-124, Tu-134, Tu-154M, Il-76, Il-62M, MiG-31, and the Mi-6 and Mi-10 helicopters. The bureau's only known military engine, the 93.17 kN (20,945 lbf) afterburning turbofan D-30F6 for the MiG-31 Foxhound interceptor, was a development of the company's D-30 civil turbofan. Its success in the civil powerplant field has led to the Ilyushin and Tupolev OKBs' alternative replacement engine scheme proposal.

Perm engines are produced by the state enterprise Motorostroitel, which is adjacent to the engine design bureau in Perm, and by a manufacturing plant in Rybinsk, where there is a Perm branch design office. Rybinsk builds the D-30KP, D-30KU and D-30KU-154, whilst the Perm plant builds the PS-90A and the DF-30F6 plus a small number of the other D-30 models. It also produces Klimov TV2-117 turboshaft engines for the Mi-8 helicopter. At Perm, the Permskoe Agregatnoe Manufacturing Association produces the fuel systems and other parts for the Perm bureau and others.

The Stupino Machinery Design Bureau, although more commonly known for its propeller and propfan designs, from the 1960s through to the early 1980s was also heavily involved in the design and development of Auxiliary Power Units (APUs), its units being used in the Tu-134, the Tu-154 and the Il-62. However, in 1982, the Soviet Government declared that there was over-capacity in this sector of the industry and that Stupino should cease all APU work, but under the changed business conditions that now prevail there are indications that Stupino may re-enter this field of propulsion. Its first new design was a 67 kW (90 hp) APU TA-14 single-shaft unit for the Yak-UTS trainer. Stupino produces a wide range of propellers, including those for ultra-lights and micro-lights. One of its newest products is the SV-10 six-bladed unit of 2.5 m (8 feet 2 inches) diameter used on the An-28. Another interesting unit is the SV-27 contra-rotating, automatic-feathering, reverse-pitch propfan designed to absorb 10,000 kW (13,400 hp). It is 4.5 m (14 feet 9 inches) in diameter. The assembly has eight blades made from composite material at the front and six at the rear, and features electrical de-icing of the blades and spinner.

The Red October Design Bureau in Moscow is an independent design office within a manufacturing plant. It sometimes engages in the design of new engines; at other times it undertakes work to eliminate defects from engines already in service, or to improve their performance. The following engine types were originally developed by this bureau as demonstrators under its designer Tumansky and subsequently put into series production for a number of combat types: the R-27F2M-300 for the MiG-23;

the R-29-300 for the MiG-23M; the R-35 for the MiG-23ML; the R-29D-300 for the MiG-27; and the R-29BS-300 for the Su-27.

The Ufa Motor Building Corporation is a manufacturing plant and not a design bureau. As well as manufacturing the Lyulka AL-31F afterburning turbofan, Ufa also makes other fighter engines, all of which are turbojets and of Tumansky origin: the initial MiG-21 engine, the 64.5 kN (14,500 lbf) R-13-300; the 69.61 kN (15,649 lbf) R-25-300 for the improved MiG-21*bis*; the 112.78 kN (25,354 lbf) R-39B-300 for the MiG-23; and the 44.13 kN (9,920 lbf) R-195 for the Su-25 Frogfoot sturmovik.

The VOKBM Motor Design Bureau at Voronezh, under its General Constructor Prof. A. G. Bakanov, is the country's main centre for piston engine development. The plant took over the design of Ivan Vedeneyev engines, which included the M-14 family series of 9-cylinder, single-row radials with models for both fixed-wing and rotary aircraft applications. The M-14 family, derived from the earlier Ivchenko AI-14 series of engines, range in power from 235 kW (315 hp) to 298 kW (400 hp) and were used mainly in trainer and aerobatic aircraft types. Another engine produced by the company is the M-3, which appears to be an M-14 with six cylinders removed, leaving three in an inverted 'Y' configuration. Other engines produced by the company are the 150 kW (200 hp) M-16, the small 30-40 kW (40-55 hp) for ultra-lights and micro-lights, and the similarly configured 60 kW (80 hp) M-19. Production of all these various units is undertaken on the same site by the Voronezh Mechanical Plant.

In the wake of *Glasnost* and *Perestroika*, Soviet engine firms endeavoured to broaden their production base, some also turning to other industrial products and some to marine engines. In the West these units are generally based on well-proven commercial aircraft designs and not combat engines, which although built in large numbers, may not have flown the same number of proving hours as a civil airliner powerplant. It is more than likely that Russian engine design bureaux and manufacturing units will need to merge and pool resources if they wish to remain as viable competitors to western manufacturers such as Pratt &Whitney, Rolls-Royce, BMW, SNECMA and MTU, who are currently more interested in getting their own products into Russian airframes rather than engaging in collaborative ventures.

6

Soviet Designers and Aircraft

This section of the book describes the majority of Soviet aircraft produced since the 1940s, the reorganisation of the aircraft industry and the introduction of the 'designer's name' designation system. It is only since the 1960s that Soviet aeronautical achievements and details of the industry and its products have gradually been unveiled to the rest of the world. During that decade, Soviet aviation was making inroads into the international field by way of its military aircraft (with over 5,000 in service in about thirty different—mostly communist block—countries), and its civil types (with over 300 airliners and helicopters in service in about twenty countries). Aviation exports had risen from 3.82 million roubles to 100 million roubles in 1964, and had increased again to 131.4 million roubles by 1968, the last year for which figures are available. In 1973, Aviaexport claimed that 5-10 per cent of all Soviet civil aircraft built were exported and that sales were increasing at a rate of 15 per cent per annum.

At the end of 1973, the Soviet civil airline Aeroflot had an international route network of over 150,000 km and agreements with sixty-five different countries. With its domestic and international operations, the airline at the time was comparable in size with the four leading US airline companies. In addition, Aeroflot was responsible for all non-military and non-sporting flying in the Soviet Union and also acted as a Reserve Transport Force for the Soviet Air Force. Aeroflot's rate of growth was then greater than any other comparable airline, and in a country where road and rail links were limited and distances vast, there were immense possibilities for air transport, for the carriage of both freight and passengers. By 1973, Aeroflot had carried 88 million passengers, 102 billion passenger-kilometres, 1.8 billion freight tonne-kilometres and 11.3 billion passenger tonne-kilometres.

Defence expenditure was estimated to be 8 per cent of the gross national product in 1972, and was the third highest figure per head of population in the world. Soviet Air Force equipment inventory was estimated in the region of 10,000 aircraft, including 7,500 deployed tactically (Frontal Aviation) and in air defence (IA-PVO, Fighter Aviation/Air Defence Force).

The Soviet Union's expansion into world markets inevitably meant that, despite traditional secrecy, more information than ever before suddenly became available about modern Soviet aircraft—with information of the civil types particularly accessible. Military aircraft were now readily on show to the world, and, with the passage of time, were displayed at all the major trade shows such as Paris, Dubai and Farnborough. Mikoyan and Sukhoi in particular, with their incredible MiG-29 Fulcrum and Su-27 Flanker displays, revealed to western air force chiefs the real status of the opposition. A bonus for aviation enthusiasts, and others interested in the fascinating subject of Soviet aviation, has been that much more accurate information has become available with the co-operation of Soviet specialist writers, historians and leaders of the main design bureaux who have collectively brushed away many of the anomalies, guesswork and misinformation that had previously been associated with publications concerning Soviet aircraft.

It is the object of this section of the book to clarify any misunderstandings that might still exist, once and for all. Going against accepted protocol by most western aviation writers, little reference is made by the author in this section to NATO code-names, as of course in most instances these are not the names given by the Soviet OKBs.

Alekseyev (I-)

From 1942 onwards, Semyon Mikhailovich Alekseyev was Chief Designer in the Lavochkin OKB, and was largely responsible for the La-5 and La-7 design details. He was successful in establishing his own OKB in 1946, concentrating on the design of high-performance jet combat planes and producing a number of prototype designs, none of which entered series production. This was largely due to Yakovlev, who convinced Stalin that they were nothing more than Messerschmitt Me 262 copies, old-fashioned and obsolete, which was certainly not the case.

Alekseyev's initial design, the I-211, was a twin-jet fighter similar in appearance to the British Gloster Meteor, fitted with two locally produced 1,000 kg (2,205 lb) Lyulka AL-1 turbojets. These were replaced before its first flight in 1947 by two 1,300 kg TR-1 turbojets. The aircraft had ample fuel capacity and a maximum speed of 935 kph (581 mph) at sea level, with a 3-minute climb to 5,000 feet. It was armed with three NS-37 guns fitted below the floor of the pressurised cockpit.

Unfortunately the Lyulka engines were underdeveloped and inherently unreliable, and it is believed that the aircraft became the prototype I-215 that succeeded it on the drawing board, fitted with two imported 1588 kg (3,300 lb) Rolls-Royce Derwent 5 engines (later locally produced as the RD-500). It was intended to provide the I-215 with nose radar, although this was certainly not fitted to the prototype aircraft. It is known that the aircraft was fitted with an ejection seat in the pressurised cockpit, and also with a downward-pointing searchlight. Speed brakes were fitted in the wings with automatic opening at critical speed, as was normally incorporated in the early Mach-limited Soviet jets.

Flight trials of the I-215 began in November 1947, but it did not enter series production. The I-212 that followed was essentially a scaled-up I-215 designed to meet a requirement for an all-weather interceptor. The aircraft actually closely resembled the Canadian CF-100, with the unusual feature that the radar operator was seated behind the pilot in a rear-facing seat. In the event, however, the radar was never installed, and it is also thought that in spite of the government having awarded Alekseyev the assignment, it actually led to his demise in 1948, when the OKB was closed due to Yakovlev's vociferous criticism of the aircraft.

Just before the closure of the Alekseyev OKB, the frustrated designer had made one final attempt at designing a heavily armoured, ground attack and close support aircraft, the I-218. As jet engines suffer high fuel consumption at low level, Alekseyev chose a two-bank 1,490-1,640 kW (2,000/2,200 hp) Dobrynin VD-251 piston engine, driving a pusher AV-28 contra-prop with two three-bladed units of 3.6 m (11 feet 10 inches) diameter. The pilot was seated in an armoured cockpit with flat glass slabs providing excellent vision, while the back-seater again faced the rear to aim and fire his two defensive barbettes, mounted Messerschmitt Me 410-style in the tail booms, with an arc of fire 25 degrees above and below the horizontal and out to 50 degrees laterally. These guns were planned to be NR-23s with 120 rounds each. There were also various proposals for heavy forward-firing armament such as four NR-23s with 150 rounds each, two N-37s with forty rounds each, and two N-57s with thirty rounds each. In addition, wing racks were to be provided for sixteen rockets and under-fuselage pylons for carriage of up to 1,500 kg (3,307 lb) of bombs, presumably aimed in dive attacks. The highly stressed armoured parts were to be made of the new nickel steel 30 KhGSNA. The prototype is known to have flown in 1948, but there is no further history of Alekseyev or his aircraft after that date.

Antonov (An-)

Born on 25 January 1906, at Troitsy near Moscow, Oleg Konstantinovich Antonov designed his first aircraft in 1923 for a light plane competition organised by K. K. Artseulov. While at school, Antonov helped to organise a branch of the Moscow Glider Group at Saratov, and it was here that he designed the OKA-1 Golub glider. His reputation as a glider designer was established whilst he was still a student at the Leningrad Polytechnic Institute, where he designed a series of elementary training gliders, some of which went into production in 1929. On graduation in 1930, Antonov was appointed as chief engineer at the Moscow Glider Factory, and was later to become the chief designer from 1931 until its closure in 1938. During this time, Antonov designed or helped design over twenty gliders, including trainers and the high-performance Rot Front series. Some 5,000 gliders of Antonov design were eventually built.

In 1937, Antonov designed his first powered aircraft, the OKA-33 (LEM-2), a powered glider. Having failed in his attempt to gain entry to the Zhukovsky Aviation Academy in 1938, he joined Yakovlev's Sportsplane factory and was given the task of preparing the Fieseler Fi 156 Storch for licensed production at Kaunas in Lithuania, two or more aircraft having been received from Germany in June 1940. He was also tasked with producing an ambulance variant. However, the Kaunas factory was overrun in the first days of the German invasion and the project ceased, although after a brief period the factory was reorganised to produce Antonov's A-7 troop-transport assault glider. In total, 450 A-7s were produced, many being used to supply partisan forces behind enemy lines.

Antonov returned to the Yakovlev Experimental Design Bureau in 1943 as first deputy designer and spent the remainder of the war at Novosibirsk where he was in charge of Yak-3 development and production undertaken there and at other factories, also later working on the Yak-9 and the Yak-15 jet fighter. At the end of the war, whilst still at Novosibirsk, he was instructed to form an independent OKB for the design of a utility aircraft powered by a 545 kW (730 hp) engine. He recruited his OKB staff (formally established on 31 May 1946) mostly from members of his aeronautical course at the Novosibirsk Institute and eventually established its headquarters at Kiev.

The first aircraft designed by the newly established Antonov OKB was the SKh-1 (An-2) biplane. This won for Antonov and his three principal assistants a 100,000 rouble Stalin Prize in 1952, for work in the field of aircraft construction in the transport and commercial sector. More than 35,000 An-2s were built, some low-volume production still being undertaken in Poland in the early 1990s. Following the successful An-2, the Antonov OKB was responsible for a series of large-capacity turboprop transport aircraft, all of which conformed to a standard high-wing design, with maximum fuselage volume, rear loading in the freight versions and rough field capability. The designs included the An-8 in 1955, the An-10 in 1957 (and also the An-12 tactical transport for the VVS), the An-14 in 1958, the An-24 twin-turboprop airliner (which entered service with Aeroflot in 1962, carrying up to forty passengers on the medium-range routes), the heavy-lift An-22 in 1964, the An-26 military freighter in 1968, the An-28 in 1972, the An-30 photographic survey variant of the An-24 in 1973, the An-32 ('hot & high') in 1976, the An-72 in 1977, and the An-124 in 1982.

Today, Antonov transports are produced at Kiev, which was one of the first plants in the Soviet Union to have its own tank-testing and wind-tunnel facilities. Other GAZs producing Antonov aircraft were Arsenyev, Irkutsk, Kharkov, Moscow, Omsk, Tashkent, Ulan-Ude, Ulyanovsk and Voronezh, also under licence in China and Poland (An-28).

Antonov died on 4 April 1984, at the age of 78, and was succeeded at the Antonov OKB by Piotr Vasilyevich Balabuev. The Antonov OKB is the sole Soviet design bureau in what is now independent Ukraine, and is still currently working on a number of new designs. More than 22,000 aircraft of over 100 different types and versions of Antonov designs have been built, more than 1,500 of which have been exported to forty-two countries.

***

When the Antonov An-2 first appeared in prototype form in 1947, it was treated with derision in the West and regarded as something of an anachronism and a near-obsolete curio. Destined for nothing more than a very short lifespan, the unfashionable biplane configuration was actually chosen quite deliberately by Antonov, who was quite willing to accept drag penalties in order to exploit the many advantages of the configuration, such as the excellent low-speed handling characteristics, STOL performance and handling. The simple and straightforward engineering approach resulted in an easy to maintain and extremely rugged aircraft, ideally suited to the terrain from which it was primarily intended to operate—the vast tundra that comprises much of the former Soviet Union. Antonov later declared, 'These days I would have no chance of the Soviet authorities accepting such an aircraft for series production; this was only possible after the Second World War.'

In spite of its appearance, the An-2 incorporated many modern features, including full span slats and electronically operated double-slotted trailing-edge flaps. Designed primarily for agricultural use, the aircraft took its first flight on 31 August 1947 as the SKh-1 and was to prove very popular both with civil customers and the military. A subsequent series production run of some 29,000 aircraft turned the unspectacular An-2 into one of the greatest post-war Soviet aviation successes.

The requirement had been formulated in May 1946, by the Ministry of Agriculture and Forestry, and presented to the Antonov OKB on its establishment at Novosibirsk. In designing the aircraft, Antonov used high-tensile steel for the welded front fuselage carrying the engine and fixed landing gear, whilst the rest of the fuselage and fin were of stressed fabric to minimise weight and improve capacity and flexibility in providing doors and openings. The wings, with I-type struts, were made of light alloy back to the front spar and then of stressed fabric covering.

Two prototypes were built, the first fitted with a 567 kW (760 hp) ASh-21 engine but the second had a 746 kW (1,000 hp) ASh-621R radial engine. This engine caused a number of different problems on the first sixty series aircraft, the An-2Ts, delivered from October 1948. To overcome these, from the 61st aircraft on, the aircraft was fitted with wings of larger horizontal surface area, which allowed it to take off fully laden at 90 kph (56 mph) on grass and become airborne after travelling only 170 m (560 feet). In fact, these improvements and the 746 kW (1,000 hp) engine enabled the aircraft to perform superbly in many differing roles.

The aircraft had entered series production at four plants: Zavod 99 at Ulan-Ude, Zavod 116 at Arsenyev, Zavod 464 at Moscow, and Zavod 473 at Kiev. Up until 1964, 14,960 were produced, of which only 229 were exported. During the period between 1964 and 1971, the Moscow plant built another 506 aircraft of a modified variant, the An-2M, of which 226 were exported. Most of the early An-2s were of the T sub-type and were for agricultural use, replacing the Polikarpov Po-2, and as early as June 1948, it was realised that the An-2 could do as much work in three days as the Po-2 did in a month. In 1948, the aircraft was covering a total of 2 million hectares annually in the Soviet Union, and by 1963 An-2s had covered 64.4 million hectares for the Ministry of Agriculture and Forestry. The T sub-type was also used by the Soviet Air Force and Aeroflot.

Licensed production of the An-2 was almost as important as home-based output, as many were destined for the Soviet Union. In Poland, PZL at Mielec produced 11,730 An-2s from 1960 to 1987, mostly for export, with the biggest number destined for the Soviet Union. China built the An-2 as the Y-5 transport plane up until 1990. The Nanchang aircraft plant built 727 from 1958 to 1968, and later, from 1971 to 1986, the Shijiazhuang factory produced an additional 221 Y-5s, although in contrast to Polish production, the Chinese aircraft were mainly for home use. In fact, the aircraft was used in more than sixty different countries in very large numbers, in both civil and military roles, the largest military user being North Korea. Many aircraft, painted all-over black, were used on insertion missions, dropping special commandos behind South Korean lines in the Korean War.

The An-2 was built in forty different versions. The most important models were the An-2P 14-passenger transport, the An-2S air ambulance, the An-2SKh agricultural version, the An-2T military version (for light transport and glider towing), the An-2TD parachute transport, the An-2NRK night reconnaissance and artillery observation (including 'F' and 'K' variants), the An-2PP water bomber (for fire-fighting), the An-2TP 12-passenger airline variant, and the An-2V fitted with turbocharger etc. The Polish and Chinese aircraft were also produced in a number of sub-variants, and Polish production resulted in a number of improvements that increased serviceability and operability. PZL constructed 5,000 aircraft between the first flight of the Polish-built An-2 Antek on 23 October 1960 and February 1973, mean time between service having been increased to 2,000 hours as opposed to 900 hours in 1961 and 1,500 hours in 1970. The Mielec plant also produced the An-3 equipped with the turbocharged 1,080 kW (1,450 hp) TVD-20 engine, increasing payload by 40 per cent. Some An-2s were retrofitted with this engine.

The unusual biplane configuration of the An-2, nicknamed 'Annushka', actually belies its real dimensions, many people having the impression that it is a very small aircraft. However, this is most misleading, as anyone who has entered the aircraft will tell. Although the aircraft is obviously shorter, the cabin is as large as the Douglas DC-3 (C-47 Dakota) and the pilot's cabin is as roomy as in many airliners. The 746 kW (1,000 hp) engine permits good short-field performance and handling, and the aircraft is extremely popular with its users in the Soviet Union.

The M-15 was the most extraordinary aircraft of this type. Actually a jet biplane, it had a lengthened biplane wing and was fitted with an AI-25 turbofan engine. Only five were built and tested in the Soviet Union, the first prototype flying on 20 May 1973, and it was decided to end series production of this most extraordinary aircraft in 1981. However, the An-2 was still in production in the early 1990s in China with SAMC (Shijiazhuang Aircraft Manufacturing Corporation) as the Yunshuji-5 (transport aircraft-5) or Yun-5. SAMC has produced more than 225 An-2 (Y-5N) general-purpose types since 1970, but later concentrated on two main variants: the Y-5B, the dedicated agricultural and forestry aircraft that had its first flight on 2 June 1989, with the first nine series aircraft produced in 1990; and the Y-5B/C, thirty-five of which had been built by the end of 1994.

Antonov An-2 model designations

An-2D	Polish-built paratroop trainer
An-2M	Soviet agricultural variant for crop dusting/spraying (506 built)
An-2M	Polish variant of An-2V floatplane
An-2P	Basic general-purpose variant
An-2R	Polish designation of Soviet An-2S
An-2S	Polish-built An-2P ambulance version
An-2S	Soviet agricultural version of An-2P
An-2T	Polish mixed cargo general-purpose version equivalent to An-2P
An-2TP	Polish-built luxury passenger/cargo version
An-2V	Floatplane version
An-2ZA	Meteorological version for high-altitude research, with observer's cockpit mounted forward of the tailplane.
An-3	Turboprop conversion of An-2 agricultural version Glushenkov TVD-20 turboprop engine
Y-5B	Chinese-built agricultural and forestry version
Y-5N	Chinese-built civil transport variant

The big success of the German DFS-230 assault gliders in Belgium and the Netherlands in May 1940 led Stalin to request designs for a glider transport from at least ten different Soviet OKBs. The winner in December 1940 was Antonov's RF-8, which was a greatly scaled-up variant of the famous Rot Front family of gliders. The monoplane, featuring a simple high-cantilevered wing with a narrow fuselage, could carry up to ten infantrymen with armament and equipment, and had an all-wood, fabric-covered wing of 19 m (62 feet) span.

In January 1941, a special division was created at the People's Commissariat for Aviation Industry to oversee the manufacture of assault gliders. Production of the Gribovski G-11 and the RF-8/A-7 for the Red Air Force started immediately in the glider factories at Moscow and Saratov, the first being completed in the spring of 1941. Stalin wanted a large number of them for the planned offences against Germany, Hungary and Romania on 6 July, but Hitler discovered his plans and attacked the Soviet Union two weeks earlier than planned. As a result, Stalin was not able to use the A-7 as planned to counter the surprise attack. Many A-7s were destroyed by German bombing, the rest being destroyed by the Soviet Army due to the fact that they lacked towing aircraft to evacuate men and machines to the rear of the battle area. In 1942, another 450 A-7s were built for the new offensives, and with the German Army's spring/summer offensive of 1942, the A-7 was finally deployed to supply partisans behind the German lines. Old SB-2 or DB-3 bombers were normally used by the

Soviets as glider tugs, although a number of British Armstrong Whitworth Albemarle tugs were also employed.

Design of the Antonov An-10 started in November 1955, and the aircraft had its first flight at Kiev on 7 March 1957. The first prototype, reported as having civil registration CCCP-U1957, was a 90-seat high-wing aircraft developed for Aeroflot from the earlier An-8 of which nine were still in use in August 2000. The first aircraft flew with 2,984 kW (4,000 hp) NK-4 engines, later replaced by AI-20K turboprops of the same power. Although the prototypes were built at Zavod 473 at Kiev, the series aircraft were produced at Zavod 64 at Voronezh from 1958 to 1960 in twenty-eight batches of five, yielding a total of 140 aircraft (most of which were registered in the CCCP-11134-11229 serial range). The An-10 entered Aeroflot service on the Moscow–Simferopol route on 22 July 1959 in its 84-passenger seat configuration designed for operation over stage lengths of 800-2,500 km (497-1,553 miles). The aircraft carried a crew of five—two pilots, a navigator, a radio operator and a flight engineer.

In 1958, a stretched version, the An-10A, was awarded a Gold Medal at the Brussels International Exhibition. Configured for 100 passengers, it entered service with Aeroflot on 10 February 1960. Externally the aircraft could be distinguished from the An-10 by two small fins at the extremities of the tailplane and by an anhedral on the outer wing panels, and internally by a new cockpit layout. The two small fins were deleted in later variants and the single ventral fin under the rear fuselage was replaced by two ventral fins of larger area. In May, June and July of 1960, the An-10A made several record-breaking flights, the most significant of which was a round-trip—Moscow–Melitopol–Moscow— of 2,000 km (1,243 miles) at an average speed of 723 kph (450 mph) with a payload of 15,000 kg (33,070 lb). The aircraft also demonstrated successfully that it could fly on one engine with 100 passengers on board, and an An-10A established a remarkable record for propeller-driven aircraft in April 1961, flying over 500 km (311 miles) closed circuit at an average speed of 730 kph (454 mph).

Eventually the aircraft was available in 100-, 117-and 130-seat versions. The higher capacity was obtained by the removal of a toilet and a baggage compartment. The cabin was pressurised at sea-level conditions up to 5,150 m (16,896 feet), at 10,000 m (32,810 feet) the cabin altitude was 2,350 m (7,710 feet), and its height of 2.5 m (8 feet 2 inches) permitted films to be shown in flight. All fuel was carried in twenty-two bag tanks in the wings, giving a total capacity of 13,900 litres (3,058 gallons). Double-slotted slats and a multi-wheel undercarriage fitted with low-pressure tyres permitted grass strip operation, and it was also possible to operate the An-10 on skis. However, an accident at Katkov in May 1972 led to the type ceasing operations on 27 August 1973, by which date forty-two had crashed and twenty-five had been transferred to the Ministry of Aviation Industry. The aircraft was never operated by the military or exported and was one of the few civil types in the former Soviet Union to be given a name, 'Ukraina', as well as a designation.

The Antonov An-12 was the cargo version of the An-10A, conceived originally as a military transport directly descended from the An-8 and developed alongside the

An-10. It was distinguishable from the An-10A by a rear fuselage design incorporating a loading door large enough to embark vehicles and bulky loads. The gun turret at the base of the rudder in the military version was deleted in the civil An-12. The prototype (c/n 7900101) had its first flight from the Irkutsk factory airfield on 16 December 1957. The aircraft, piloted by 'Hero of the Soviet Union' Y. I. Vernikov, the chief test pilot at the LII at Zhukovsky near Moscow, carried out a short flight of approximately 9 minutes before it was forced to land after vibrations were felt in the forward fuselage. However, after this rather disappointing start a total of 1,243 An-12s were built and, like the American Lockheed C-130 Hercules, it was adopted by the military for a variety of roles. Some thirty were built or derived from existing versions, entering service with the Soviet Air Force in 1959.

Production began at GAZ-90 at Irkutsk in 1957, where 155 were built in eighteen batches, with testing and evaluation carried out at the NII VVS at Kiev in 1958. Four years later, production of the aircraft at Irkutsk ended and was transferred to GAZ-34 at Tashkent, where the majority (830) were built between 1962 and 1972, although GAZ-18 at Voronezh also built 258 of them. The factory was actually captured for a short while by the Germans in the Second World War, but after its liberation on 12 April 1943 it was renumbered GAZ-64, although aircraft produced at Voronezh were defined as produced at GAZ-40. Apart from early production aircraft built at Irkutsk, there were two basic models—the An-12A and the An-12B. About 800 An-12Bs were produced, all but about fifty of which were for the VTA. The aircraft formed the backbone of the VVS transport force for many years, at one time equipping some twenty regiments with thirty aircraft each. In some aircraft a 14-seat pressurised compartment was added behind the flight deck for handling crews and other passengers. However, a serious drawback of the An-12BP was that the cargo hold was not pressurised, which meant that when used as a troop-carrier the aircraft was restricted to an altitude of 5,000 m (16,400 feet), greatly reducing its range due to the fact that it had to fly at this much lower altitude.

Production of An-12As began in 1961, the main difference to the base An-12 being increased fuel capacity. The second and most prevalent model was the An-12B, again with additional fuel capacity and with a TG-16 APU. There were additional versions followed again by modifications to the 'A' and 'B' variants, whereby additional fuel tanks were installed in the fuselage under the floor of the cargo compartment. Two versions were built: the An-12UD (Extended Range) containing two extra fuel tanks, and the An-12UD-3, with three extra ranks. Fitting of the tanks obviously reduced the space for cargo. Aircraft with tanks fitted under the cargo compartment were designated An-12AP and An-12BP respectively. There were also a number of specialised models but most aircraft were modified to BP standard. Although fitted with a winch, the other equipment in the cargo hold was very basic and the aircraft did not feature a rear loading ramp, the rear cargo doors opening to the side and upwards and separate ground ramps required for loading and unloading of heavy equipment. A more sophisticated variant with improved loading facilities was developed at

Tashkent in 1967. Designated An-12BK, it incorporated a number of improvements on the An-12BP and around thirty-five were built. A number of other modifications were incorporated that did not affect suffix designations, most changes being associated with the fitting of upgraded secure communication and navigation equipment.

The An-12T was a variant for the transportation of special fuels, corrosive liquids and chemicals. Converted in 1961, the aircraft was fitted with special containers installed within the freight compartment. Another fuel carrier was the An-12BKT, which was modified in 1972 from an An-12BK. Capable of carrying 19,500 litres (4,289 gallons) of extra fuel, it was actually used as a ground-based tanker able to refuel two aircraft at once and was intended to support Frontal Aviation units operating from reserve airfields.

There were two Search and Rescue (SAR) variants, the first of which entered service in 1963 as the An-12PS. Based on the An-12B airframe, the aircraft was fitted with the 'Istok-Golub' emergency signal detection system. As the aircraft had two ball-shaped blister fairings under the fuselage, plus an array of antennae, it was mistakenly thought by NATO to be an ELINT variant. A more advanced SAR version entered service in 1969. The aircraft carried a life-raft and could be used to rescue downed aircrew in the sea, and to recover cosmonauts if necessary. A special reconnaissance variant was also available at this time, its task being to measure levels of radioactivity in the atmosphere. The aircraft is known to have been an An-12BP, although no specific type designation was allocated.

One of the most unusual variants was the bomber version, designated An-12BKV, capable of dropping missiles from the cargo compartment. A secondary role was to drop land-mines from the air. (It should also be mentioned here that many Indian Air Force aircraft, used as bombers against Pakistan, carried 16 tonnes of bombs on pallets which were pushed out of the aircraft by hand over the drop zone.)

In 1970, two versions entered service for the training of navigators. Both types were modified from An-12Bs or An-12BKs, designated An-12BSh and An-12BKSh respectively, and contained ten workstations in the freight cabin for the training of navigators. That same year, the An-12BK-VKP was introduced for the command post role, this version being known as 'Zebra'. One An-12BK was modified in 1975 for use by senior officers as a VIP transport and designated An-12BKK 'Capsule' by virtue of the fact that a hermetically sealed capsule with a VIP interior was fitted in the freight compartment.

Also in the 1970s, several versions for the electronic warfare role were introduced, the first of which was the An-12B-I. Seven An-12B aircraft were modified to this standard, equipped with an ECM system known as 'Fasol' (literally 'Stringbean'). Subsequent ECM aircraft were modified 'BK' variants and were the first to feature the four large external pods containing the 'Siren' jamming system. A total of forty-five aircraft were produced with this equipment, until the modernisation programme switched to the next variant, the An-12PP. Twenty-seven aircraft were modified, with ECM stations added to the airframe in the shape of four canoe-type fairings situated under the main fuselage. The aircraft also featured a bulged fairing on the rear fuselage in place of the gun turret, and there were also a number of inlet and outlet fairings added to assist with cooling of the equipment fitted in the freight compartment. In 1971, there was a further development when the An-12BK-PPS appeared. Basically this was a combination of both the earlier ECM types with the 'Siren' system and the four under-fuselage canoe fairings. The ultimate ECM variant, developed in 1974, was the An-12BK-IS which featured a new system, 'Barrier', in addition to 'Siren'. There were 105 An-12BKs modified to this standard, but it is thought that some were earlier An-12BK-IS aircraft updated with the new equipment. Operational details of electronic warfare variants are scarce, but it is believed that a number of An-12PPs were stationed in Syria in 1973, operating in full Syrian Air Force markings but flown by Soviet crews.

It was estimated in that at least 125 ECM aircraft were still operational in 1994, along with some 350 transports and an additional seven electronic warfare (ECM) aircraft with the AV-MF (Naval Aviation). In addition to the special variants, a number of aircraft were used on experimental programmes. The first of these was used for testing satellite communications, and four additional crew stations were included in the aircraft (An-12BM Molniya) used for long-range radio communication trials with the satellite Molniya-1. An aircraft involved in infra-red (IR) technology trials in 1969 was designated An-12B Kubrik.

In the 1970s, tests began to evaluate an anti-radar missile, Kh-28, against ground-based radars using an aircraft designated An-12BL. One An-12 was rebuilt in 1972 with uprated engines and redesigned propellers for evaluation purposes. The modified aircraft was designated An-12M, although no upgrades were ordered from this evaluation programme as the performance and handling characteristics were only marginally improved. Two aircraft were modified in 1979 as meteorological survey platforms, the modified An-12BKTs continuing in use until they were de-modified in September 1993. Finally, two An-12BKs were converted for research into in-flight icing trials, operating from the test centre at Zhukovsky, and some ejection seat trials were carried out using a specially modified An-12BK also operating from Zhukovsky.

It is believed that at one time Aeroflot operated more than 400 An-12s, many of which were ex-military aircraft. There were three civilian variants of the An-12B, known as the An-12MGA. Production of this version started in 1959 and continued for thirteen years. A distinguishing feature between the An-12MGA and the military An-12BP was that the rear gunner's turret was removed and faired over, providing extra storage for batteries, although it is reported that some An-12MGAs did retain the rear turret, making external type identification difficult. Succeeding civil variants, designated An-12BK-MGA and An-12BSM, were more easily identified, the An-12BK-MGA by the fact that the rear turret and the observation compartment were replaced by a large fairing contoured into the base of the tail. The containerised An-12BSM was the ultimate civil variant, featuring several important changes for the handling of freight and large cargoes. It included a roller-bed floor in the cargo compartment to accommodate two sizes of freight containers, plus two cranes with a 5,000 kg lift capacity.

Official figures indicate that some 180-200 An-12s were exported, but other records appear to show that closer to 260 aircraft were exported to some twenty-four countries. In addition to receiving twelve aircraft in 1965, China produced 667 Yunshuji Y-8s, a version of the Tashkent-built An-12BK. Production began in January 1980 at the Shaanxi Transport Aircraft Factory and continued until 1993. The Chinese aircraft actually featured a more pointed nose, which increased the overall length by 0.91 m (3 feet), and was fitted with slightly uprated 3,170 kW (4,250 hp) WoJiang-6 turboprop engines developed from the Soviet Ivchenko AI-20K units. China also developed a maritime patrol/surveillance variant using the nose of the Harbin H-6 (Tupolev Tu-16), which was designated Shaanxi Y-8MPA. Shaanxi also produced an export variant for Sri Lanka, designated Y-8D. In 1997, the company announced a stretched Y-8 (Y-8F-200) with a 2.4 m (8 feet) insert increasing its overall length to 36.25 m (119 feet) and its pressurised cargo compartment to 15.7 m (51 feet 6 inches).

In August 2000, the total number of civil-registered An-12s in use worldwide was estimated at 167, of which 147 were in Europe and the CIS. The little twin-engined An-14 Pchelka was a passenger/freight transport with STOL characteristics. A full-scale mock-up was available in July 1957, and CCCP-L1958 made its first flight on 15 March 1958, followed by the second prototype, CCCP-L1956, although large-scale production, mainly at GAZ-16 at Arsenyev did not begin until 1965. According to Antonov, this long delay was not caused by development problems but by uncertainty within Aeroflot as to specification requirements. Originally the specification called for an aircraft carrying three passengers and a pilot; this was later increased to five passengers and, later still, to seven passengers. The changed requirements led the Antonov OKB to replace the original rectangular planform wing with a trapezoidal design of longer span. The 194 kW (260 hp) AI-14R engines were replaced by 224 kW (300 hp) AI-14RF engines, and the tail unit was also redesigned.

Eventually four versions of the An-14 were available: the passenger version with accommodation for six or seven in the cabin and one more passenger alongside the pilot if necessary; an executive version, carrying four passengers and their baggage in a cabin equipped with an office desk and a fifth passenger seated alongside the pilot; a cargo variant; and an air ambulance carrying six stretchers in two tiers of three together with a medical attendant. The Pchelka was designed to give true STOL performance when operating from any type of terrain. To simplify the pilot's task, the wings were designed to provide high lift through the use of double-slotted flaps and leading-edge slats. The aircraft's powerplants provided a good reserve of power, and the tandem wheels had large low-pressure tyres. A ski undercarriage could also be used if needed. Aircraft could be configured for geological survey, aerial reconnaissance tasks and for SAR and training purposes; for the training role, dual controls were fitted.

In 1967, it was announced that a turboprop version was under development, and the first prototype, designated An-14M, flew at Kiev in September 1969, powered by two 604 kW (810 hp) TVD-850 engines. The aircraft had a fuselage stretch to accommodate fifteen passengers. However, in spite of the fact that official Soviet flight testing was completed in 1972, it was not until twelve years later that the first aircraft was built at PZL Mielec. An-28 SSSR-28800, as the series An-14M was designated, took to the air on 22 July 1984, receiving full Soviet certification on 7 February 1986. Polish production was licensed for domestic use only.

Total Soviet production of the An-14 amounted to 339, of which twenty-three were exported. Early in 1962, the Soviet Air Force and Aeroflot had issued a common requirement for a very large transport aircraft. In fact, at the time it was the biggest of its day, at 250 tonnes, and was powered by four 11,190 kW (15,000 hp) Kuznetsov NK-12MA turboprops. The unpressurised cargo section was 4.4 m^2 and capable of containing a payload of 45 tonnes. Accommodation for up to twenty-nine passengers was provided in a forward fuselage pressurised compartment. Five prototypes were built at Zavod 473 at Kiev-Svyetoshino—two for the air force and three for Aeroflot—the first of the latter (CCCP-46191) making its maiden flight on 27 February 1965.

The presence of the Antonov An-22 at the Paris Air Show at Le Bourget in 1965 caused quite a sensation as its attendance had not been announced beforehand. Series production of An-22Ms had started at Tashkent in 1966, and by the time production ceased in 1974, sixty-eight had been built. Of these, 50 per cent were Soviet Air Force aircraft fitted with larger navigation radar, and had the ability to carry main battle tanks or mobile missile systems. The remaining 50 per cent were for Aeroflot, although, as was normal in the Soviet Union, they were available to the military as and when required. Many were used by the military when it was deemed use of 'Red Star' VTA transport aircraft might prove provocative.

Many Aeroflot aircraft used in Siberia, based at Tver and Ivanovo, were operated mostly under military control. Although of limited strategic use within the Soviet Union, the aircraft proved to be a very useful long-range transport and were used on a number of occasions for resupply flights to Egypt and Syria during the Arab-Israeli War in October 1973, and also for delivery of military materials to Cuba. The An-22 Antei, named after the son of Poseidon and Gaia, was really a very useful giant transport for the Soviets. Sometimes aircraft overloaded by as much as 25 tonnes still clawed their way into the air. The proposed civil variant to carry 724 passengers on a double deck, weighing 273 tonnes, was never built. Neither was the proposed dual 350-passenger/30-tonne cargo freighter/transporter.

By 1993 the An-22 fleet had reduced to just forty-five. It is reported that all An-22s were grounded in January 1994, after an in-flight explosion on 18 January at Tver. The aircraft also experienced problems with it turbofan engines, but attempts to overcome this by importing engines from the West were blocked. One aircraft, CCCP-64460, was modified by Antonov for transporting An-124 wing sets between the Tashkent plant and Ulyanovsk, and still remained in use with the Antonov OKB in August 2000.

The prototype Antonov An-24, (serial L1959) first flew at Kiev on 20 December 1959, and although the type was intended as a 44-seat passenger transport it soon gained favour with the military as a dual-role passenger/cargo aircraft. After a second prototype and five pre-production aircraft had been flown and tested, the type eventually entered service with Aeroflot in September 1963.

From the outset the aircraft was designed for operation from smaller airfields and makeshift runways. It could also be fitted with rocket-assisted units to boost take-off performance if needed and was powered by two 1,902 kW (2,550 hp) Ivchenko AI-24A turboprops driving AV-72 four-bladed propellers. The aircraft carried a crew of up to five: the pilot, co-pilot, navigator, radio operator and flight engineer. Accommodation for up to thirty-eight equipped troops or thirty fully equipped paratroopers was provided. In the air ambulance configuration up to twenty-four stretchers and a medical assistant could be carried. The aircraft's military potential was soon recognised, and in addition to service with the VTA it was deployed by at least a further fifteen air arms. Production was undertaken at Irkutsk (GAZ-39), Ulan-Ude (GAZ-90) and Kiev (GAZ-473), the last aircraft, which included civil variants, being produced in 1979. In total some 1,465 were built, of which it was estimated in August 2000 that some 472 were still in use worldwide, of which 421 were in Europe and the CIS. China produced a reverse-engineered variant, the Xian Y-7, which made its first flight on 25 December 1970. There were several versions of the Y-7, all powered by the Dongan (DEMC) WJ5AI turboprop. Most were delivered to Chinese airlines, although a number were used by the Chinese armed forces.

The Antonov An-26 short-range utility and tactical transport although derived from the An-24RT specialised freighter was in fact a new design with a fully pressurised cargo hold, uprated engines and new rear loading ramp. Particular attention was paid to the rear fuselage design, with a full-width door/ramp to provide easy access for loading and unloading of cargo and the facility for the door ramp to be swung under the fuselage in flight to permit simple air-drops. Small vehicles can be driven directly into the hold, while other cargoes can be handled by an electrically or manually operated floor-mounted conveyor and winches. A large bulged observation window fitted on the port side, just aft of the flight deck, in all probability is to help with achieving greater accuracy when the aircraft is used in the para-dropping role. Optional tip-up seats can be provided for up to a maximum of forty paratroopers down either side of the fuselage, or twenty-four litters if the aircraft is used in the air ambulance role. Role conversion of the aircraft can be completed in 20-30 minutes in the field. The aircraft can carry a crew of five and there is also a station at the rear on the starboard side for a loading supervisor or load dispatcher. The An-26 is powered by two 1,902 kW (2,550 shp) Ivchenko AI-24VT turboprops driving four-blade constant-speed fully feathering propellers, plus a 7.8 kN (1,756 lbf) Tumansky RU-19A-300 auxiliary turbojet fitted in a starboard engine nacelle for use as required during take-off, climb and level flight and for self-contained starting of the main engines. There is no provision for drop tanks or in-flight refuelling.

Flight tests started in 1967, and the aircraft was first seen in the West at the Paris Air Show in 1969. In 1981, an improved version (Curl-A) with revised freight handling equipment was announced, so that the 5,500 kg (12,125 lb) maximum load placed on three standard pallets could easily be handled by just three men. A small number of aircraft (100) were converted to ECM (ELINT/SIGINT/EW) platforms and were designated An-26 Curl-B. Between 1969 and 1986, a total of 1,398 A-26s were built at the Antonov plant at Kiev, including 559 for Aeroflot, 400 for the Soviet Air Force, 100 ECM variants for Frontal Aviation, and fifty for Soviet Naval Aviation. A number of An-26s were built for export, and it was estimated in August 2000 that around 268 were in use worldwide, some 223 in Europe and the CIS. As well as various civil airlines the An-26 was used by twenty-seven different air forces. A Chinese derivative built by the Xian Aircraft Company, the Y-7H, was flown in late 1988, and although generally similar to the An-26, it featured winglets and slightly uprated WJ5E turboprop engines.

The Antonov An-38 was developed from the Mielec An-28 built in Poland. The new twin-turboprop made its first flight on 23 June 1994 from NAPO Chkalov production plant at Novosibirsk in Siberia. The export version is powered by two Garrett TPE331-14GR-801E engines rated at 1,312 kW (1,760 shp), fitted with Hartzell propellers, whilst the Russian aircraft is powered by two TVD-1500 turboprops fitted with reversible AV-36 propellers. The 26-seat light, multi-purpose commuter is intended to replace large numbers of ageing An-24s and Czech Let L-410s in service within the CIS for passenger and freight transportation. The aircraft has a high-wing, twin-engined layout and twin tail fins and is designed for operation using a normal fixed-wheel undercarriage, skis or floats. Easy conversion from passenger to full cargo configuration is provided by folding back the partitions between the cabin and baggage area to give an unobstructed cargo area for up to 2,500 kg (5,512 lb) of freight. Large clamshell rear doors allow for rapid loading and unloading of cargo.

The aircraft has an integrated avionics system that includes weather radar, an automatic flight control system and an ice protection system to enable round-the-clock operations even in adverse weather conditions. When the prototype was displayed to potential Russian customers during April 1994 at Novosibirsk and Aviaexport it received 279 preliminary orders, 200 of which were for the East Siberia Air Transport Regional Division. An An-38-100, c/n 3810001, was displayed at Zhukovsky in August 1995 and subsequently at Le Bourget as '352' of the Antonov OKB. The intention was to build fifty An-38s by 1997, but in August 2000 it was estimated that only six were in use in the CIS.

Design of the An-70 as a co-operative effort between the three states of Ukraine, Russia and Uzbekistan started in the mid-1970s to meet a requirement of the Soviet VTA for an advanced fuel-efficient military transport to replace the ageing An-12s and to take over many of the transport operations undertaken by the Ilyushin Il-76. Specific requirements called for short-runway operation and very fast loading/unloading procedures. Being slightly larger than the Euroflag Airbus A400M but considerably smaller than the American C-17 Globemaster III, the aircraft uses all the modern technologies such as a MIL-STD-1553B data bus, SKI-77 HUD and all-weather CAT IIIB landing aids and advanced aerodynamics. It is fitted with a fly-by-wire control system with three digital and six analogue channels. A unique innovative back-up hydraulic/electro-magnetic control system was developed by Antonov, along with increased use of the latest composites and carbon fibre tail assemblies. Power is provided by four Zaporozhye Progress 10,290 kW (13,800 hp) D-27 propfans fitted with distinctive contra-rotating scimitar-shaped propeller blades: eight 4.5 m (14 feet 9 inches) blades forward and four behind. The cargo hold is pressurised and air-conditioned, but the aircraft has no provision for any seating except for two loadmasters in the forward fuselage area. The crew door is situated in the port forward fuselage but there is no rear door, which presumably excludes any future para-dropping role. An internal cargo-handling system and cargo ramp with height adjustment eases loading and unloading. The cockpit has provision for a crew of three, including a flight engineer.

The aircraft is designed to operate from unpaved and concrete runways up to 2,000 m in length. Development of the An-70 began in the early 1980s, and it was planned to enter series production in 1988, but this was delayed by funding problems, despite Antonov OKB announcing at the 1991 Paris Air Show that it would be displayed at the 1993 show. The aircraft finally had its roll-out on 20 January 1994, but it was not until eleven months later, on 16 December at Kiev's Svyetoshino airfield, that the aircraft took off on its maiden flight bound for the Gostomel flight test centre. However, the flight lasted only a little more than 30 minutes, the aircraft being forced to land ahead of schedule due to worsening weather conditions and an approaching snowstorm. Unfortunately, after clocking up only three flying hours, the aircraft was lost on its fourth flight on 10 February 1995 with all five crew and two test observers following a collision with its An-72 chase aircraft, which despite severe damage and a fire was able to return to Gostomel for a safe emergency landing. Despite this severe setback, a lack of funding and numerous other problems that have bedevilled the whole An-70 programme, the Russian Air Force has indicated that it still needs and wants such a transport.

On 18 February 1995, Russia and Ukraine signed an agreement confirming continuation of co-operation on the aircraft's development and production of the second prototype, which had its first flight in April 1997. In fact, this was originally the intended static test airframe produced in 1994. A civil version of the aircraft is to be offered under designation An-70T, as well as a westernised export variant to be designated An-77, which interestingly resulted in an uninvited bid being submitted by Antonov to the British Ministry of Defence in connection with the RAF's need to replace the Lockheed C-130K Hercules.

Arkhangelsky (Ar-)

With Tupolev interned, Alexander Alexandrovich Arkhangelsky became responsible for development of the SB-2 in 1938. In reality, he designed this aircraft, the ANT-40, in the Tupolev OKB on his return from the US, as he had become *de facto* head of the ANT (Andrei Nikolayevich Tupolev) OKB when Tupolev was arrested.

About 120 USB (SB-3) or SB-UT dual-controlled trainers were delivered. These were deemed necessary as the SB initially suffered a high attrition rate from pupils converting from much slower aircraft. Following heavy losses of the SB-2 in the Spanish Civil War, Stalin ordered that improvements be made to the bomber. These centred on a more advanced wing which with the use of improved flaps could generate a much higher maximum lift coefficient and could therefore be reduced in size. This, combined with more powerful engines in reduced drag installations, resulted in enhanced flight performance, with the revised aircraft equalling the current fighter speeds. However, the Red Air Force, impressed by the Junkers Ju 87A Stuka's performance in Spain, demanded a dive bomber variant.

The new design was ready in 1939, with a slotted wing (RK) of only 40 m² having the inboard trailing edge in the form of large double-slotted flaps stressed for use as dive brakes. Unfortunately tight production schedules demanded the redesigned wing should be replaced by a simpler one, which was closer to the original design but utilised the new NACA 22 cross-section with reduced span and reduced surface area and electrically actuated dive brakes. The structure was strengthened, yet the empty weight was reduced compared with the SB-2*bis*. The engines were the new cowled M-105Rs, driving constant speed propellers. In order to reduce drag, the radiators were mounted behind the engines in the wing, and because of the greater torque and thrust, the chord of the fin and rudder was increased. Fuel capacity was 1,490 litres (328 gallons), with provision for two strap-suspended overload cells of 740 litres (163 gallons) total capacity. Other changes included lengthened nacelles, a redesigned nose with a central cupola mounting a ShKAS machine gun, and two similar guns in a dorsal turret and rear ventral hatch. Normal bomb load was one 500 kg, two 250 kg or six 100 kg bombs, but loads up to 1,500 kg (3,307 lb) could be carried with a reduced fuel load. The prototype flew late in 1939 as the SB-RK, even though the advanced wing had been dropped. The following year the aircraft was ordered into production at Fili and Irkutsk, but manufacture was paralleled with SB-2*bis* production and it was for this reason that only 128 SB-RKs were produced in that year.

In January 1941, with the introduction of a new designation system, the aircraft became known as the Ar-2. Early that year, GAZ-22 at Fili switched to Pe-2 production, after only sixty-nine Ar-2s had been built, but GAZ-125 at Irkutsk continued with Ar-2 production, 168 being built, until October 1941, when GAZ-39 arrived after having been evacuated from Moscow. Total SB-RK/Ar-2 production was 365 aircraft.

When the Wehrmacht attacked the Soviet Union on 22 June 1941, 42.2 per cent of the Red Air Force's bomber fleet comprised SB-2 aircraft. The Western Military District (MD) had 377 whilst Kiev MD had 300 of the newer Ar-2s; a further 218 Ar-2s were in service, mainly in the Western MD. This represented 2.6 per cent of the total Soviet bomber fleet. The Byelorussian MD, for example, had only twenty-two Ar-2s out of a total of 540 bombers (4.1 per cent), but after the heavy losses sustained on 10 July 1941 this MD still had twelve Ar-2 bombers out of a total of 201 (6 per cent). By then the Ar-2 inventory had declined very quickly. Later, in the Battle of Moscow, the type was used only in mixed regiments, and the Ar-2 had almost completely disappeared from the Red Air Force's inventory by early 1942.

Between late 1933 and early 1934, Special Design Team No. 5 led by Arkhangelsky at the Tupolev OKB began work on the ANT-40 (SB-1/ SB-2) high-speed bomber. The three-seat bomber, which in many respects was a new and innovative aircraft, was designed in just over six months, the prototype first flying on 7 October 1934. It was powered by two 560 kW (750 hp) VK-100 inline piston-engines, which in effect were Soviet copies of the Hispano-Suiza 12Y. Within a short while a second prototype was produced, and by the spring of 1935 the first SBs (fitted with M-100 engines) were leaving the production lines. The series SB-2 could attain a speed of 400 kph (250 mph) and carry a 500 kg (1,100 lb) bomb load over a range of up to 2,187 km (1,360 miles). Maximum bomb load was 600 kg (1,320 lb).

Roberto L. Bartini (Stal-)

Roberto L. Bartini was born on 14 May 1897 and trained in Italy as an engineer. In 1921, he became a founder of the Italian Communist Party, helping to organise workers' cells in Milan. When Mussolini banned the party in 1923, Bartini fled to the Soviet Union and joined the Red Army as an aviation engineer. Within seven years he was heading his own design bureau, Stal OKB, which, as the name suggests, was dedicated to concentrating on the use of steel in aircraft construction.

Before the Second World War he produced a number of designs, including the Stal-6, a fast, single-seat, low-wing monoplane which first flew in 1933. This was followed by the Stal-7, which was a light transport plane designed to meet an early Aeroflot requirement for a 12-seat airliner. Bartini had intended that his gull-wing transport and parallel bomber development should be constructed from fabric-covered steel tubing, but the steel tube design proved too complex and inefficient so the aircraft was redesigned with a light alloy structure. A major problem still remained in that the spars of the thick gull wing impinged into the cramped cabin area, making it unattractive as a transport. None the less, the basic design was sound and aerodynamically efficient and was to form the basis for the design of the Yermolayev Yer-2 (DB-240) heavy bomber. However, Bartini did not receive any credit for the design, as by the time the Yer-2 had evolved, the Stal-7 had crashed and Bartini had been arrested on Stalin's orders. Of course, with the advent of the Great Patriotic War, development of Soviet transports had ceased during the first half of 1940, the original requirement disappearing with the availability of large quantities of Lend-Lease Douglas C-47s and the DC-3 licensed-production agreement.

Throughout the war, Bartini led a special OKB in Siberia dedicated to designing military jet aircraft, but despite creating a series of advanced projects, including a twin-engined flying wing fighter and a vertically launched target defence interceptor, none gained official acceptance and, in 1948, the Siberian OKB was closed. However, Bartini returned to Siberia in 1952, to the SibNIA (Siberian Scientific Institute of Aerodynamics) in Novosibirsk as Chief of the Advanced Design Department, carrying out theoretical and experimental research in the T-203 wind tunnel. The conceptual work carried out by him in the early 1950s led to the design of two strategic aircraft: the A-55 bomber and the R-55 reconnaissance aircraft.

Bartini continued to work on a number of research projects, and in the late 1950s began working on the design of a large amphibious WIG (wing-in-ground) craft known as Project M and later as VVA-14 (vertical take-off amphibian No. 14). Along with a number of other designers associated with WIG craft, Bartini argued that flying boat operations at sea were often limited by wave height, and that the answer was to avoid conventional take-offs and use VTO instead, followed by transition to normal forward flight at low altitude, taking advantage of ground effect. He also stated that the craft should be capable at normal operating altitude of transiting at normal operating speeds to its destination. The initial design was designated M-62, and in 1967, having gained official interest in the project, Bartini approached Georgi Beriev with regard to initiating construction of the prototype at Taganrog with the assistance of Beriev engineers. However, realising that Bartini's ideas and designs were in direct competition Beriev refused permission for assistance, whereupon Bartini was assigned the use of Factory No. 31, also at Taganrog, and work began under the supervision of deputy designer Viktor Biryulin, who was later replaced by Nikolai Pogorelov. But, in June 1968, after it became apparent that Factory No. 31 lacked design expertise, the unit was immediately placed under the auspices of the Beriev OKB, which itself benefited as the bureau had very little other work at the time.

The VVA-14, or 14 MIP as it was also known, was a large machine, about 28.12 m (92 feet 3 inches) long, with triple-body configuration and two pontoon-like hulls under outrigger pylons with retractable floats, joined by a thick centre section that carried an aircraft-type centre fuselage. It had a conventional front crew cabin with extensive glazing where the pilot and co-pilot were seated on K-36L zero-zero ejection seats. The intention was that vertical lift should be provided by no fewer than twelve Kolesov RD-36-35PR engines mounted in the mid-wing section. Forward propulsion would be provided by two Soloviev D-30N turbofans installed on the rear upper fuselage and two further units fitted on the sides of the forward fuselage to generate the air cushion for wing-in-ground effect. The VVA-14 is reported to have weighed 36,000 kg (79,380 lb), with a span of 30 m (98 feet 4 inches).

After a number of years undergoing ground tests, the craft was prepared for its first flight in Aeroflot colours and with civil registration CCCP-19172. As the lift engines were not available (and indeed were never fitted), a temporary undercarriage was fitted for conventional take-off and landing. The craft had its first flight on 4 September 1972 in the hands of test pilot Yuri Kupriyanov and his co-pilot. Kupriyanov reported surprisingly good handling characteristics, and on a number of subsequent flights made towards the end of the year he again reported that there were no problems associated with longitudinal or directional stability. In 1975, sea trials were held which necessitated redesign of the floats a number of times, as the retracting gear gave problems. However, a top speed in level flight of 360 kph (223.5 mph) was attained and, once the float problem had been resolved, satisfactory taxiing at 40 kph (25 mph) was achieved.

Roberto Bartini died on 6 December 1974, aged 77, and his project died with him. Although Pogorelov endeavoured to carry on, the mounting complexity of the technical problems led to the final cancellation of the project in 1981. As mentioned previously, the Soviet Navy's interest in WIG craft had continued for almost twenty years, and whilst the VVA-14 itself was abandoned, valuable information was obtained for use in the development of the Ekranoplan sea-skimming vehicles designed for over-water operations.

Beriev (Be-)

Georgi Mikhailovich Beriashvili or Beriev was born on 13 February 1903 at Tiflis (now Tbilisi) in Georgia. He was accepted into the Leningrad Polytechnic Institute in 1919, and after graduating he joined Aviatrust. Later, in 1928, he was one of a group of twenty engineers assigned to the design of marine aircraft, from which time onwards Beriev, unlike many of his contemporaries, enjoyed a fairly straightforward and successful career.

In 1929, he was invited to form a design section for marine aircraft within the TsKB at Moscow. He later went to Taganrog to undertake design improvements to an Italian Savoia-Marchetti SM.62 flying boat, which was built in the Soviet Union as the MBR-4. Later Beriev received permission to build an improved replacement, the three-crew MBR-2. The aircraft made its first flight in May 1932, and 1,500 of these short-range reconnaissance flying boats were eventually built, including a large number of MBR-2*bis*, a much-improved version powered by a 641 kW (860 hp) M-34 engine. The MBR-2 was widely used throughout the Great Patriotic War, being able to carry up to 500 kg (1,100 lb) of bombs under the wings and armed with two DA-2 machine guns. Many survived well into the 1950s, still on active secondary duties. Some were also used as transport aircraft by Aeroflot.

On 6 August 1934, Beriev created his own OKB at Taganrog, which became the centre for all Soviet seaplane development and was where he built a series of aircraft: the KOR-1 ship-borne reconnaissance aircraft (later designated Be-2); the MDR-5 in 1937; the KOR-2 (Be-4); and the GST patrol bomber flying boat, a Soviet licence-built Consolidated Catalina PBY with modifications. Beriev was obliged to evacuate his OKB to Krasnoyarsk in 1941, where over the next four years 100 Be-4s were built. From 1947, he established a complete monopoly in the design and development of marine aircraft in the Soviet Union, designing and building Be-6, Be-8, R-1, Be-10 and

Be-12 naval aircraft. However, his landplane designs—the Be-30 and the later Be-32— were not so successful.

After Beriev died in July 1979 his OKB developed the famous A-40 followed by the Be-103 and Be-200 amphibians. There were more than 5,000 men working in design departments and the experimental plant at Taganrog and its test centre at Gelendzhik. In 1990, the Beriev OKB was redesignated as Taganrog Aviation Scientific Technical Complex (TANTK) and now includes the experimental OKB and experimental production facilities, financial and logistics support services with their test bases and proving grounds at the Black Sea and Sea of Azov. All aspects of the design, development, testing and production of amphibious designs are carried out, both conventional and unconventional. In addition, the training of personnel for the operation of seaplanes is undertaken using the Beriev Be-12 twin turboprop, the Be-200 twinjet and the Be-103 twin-piston-engined aircraft, pilots being able to obtain water check-outs and type ratings.

***

Distressed at the shortcomings of the KOR-1, Beriev was determined to create a first-class replacement. From the outset in August 1939, he decided that the new aircraft should be of stressed-skin construction. The hull, with an efficient planing bottom, was made entirely from aluminium. The go-ahead for the Be-4 project was given before the end of the year, and the aircraft was designed for a crew of three —pilot, navigator and radio operator—seated side by side in an enclosed cockpit. An observer gunner was accommodated in an enclosed glazed rear cockpit, with a pivoted hood fitted with one ShKAS machine gun. There was also provision for four FAB-100 bombs or an assortment of other stores on racks.

The prototype aircraft powered by a single 746 kW (1,000 hp) M-62 radial piston engine was built at the Beriev Taganrog OKB and flight tested in February 1941. In tests that included catapulting and armament trials it demonstrated excellent handling with no serious shortcomings. Flight tests were interrupted by evacuation of the Sevastopol test establishment in April 1942, but by this time the first two production aircraft were being tested by the GUSMP (Chief Administration of the Northern Sea Route) pilot Malkov. During the evacuation, components and parts sufficient for the production of thirty Be-4s were destroyed at GAZ-31, Taganrog, in 1941. Production restarted in 1943 at Krasnoyarsk (GAZ-4) in Siberia, although there were many problems, not least of which was an acute shortage of duralumin. This was the reason that only forty-five Be-4s were built at GAZ-4 before 1945. The production aircraft served operationally with Naval Aviation, including undertaking catapult operations on warships such as the cruiser *Molotov* in the Black Sea in 1944.

The Be-6 prototype, the LL-143, was launched and test-flown at Krasnoyarsk in September 1945, by which time the Beriev OKB had moved back to Taganrog after its wartime evacuation. Development and flight tests of the type continued from 1947 to

1949, and whilst still in Siberia the aircraft had undergone a full armament fit of six 12.7 mm UBT guns and under-wing racks to facilitate the carriage of various bomb loads ranging from 400 kg (normal) to 4,000 kg (overload).

The LL-143 had its first flight in February 1949, flown by M. I. Tsepilov, the Beriev OKB test pilot, and the NII state trials were completed in the same year. The prototype's outstanding performance led to plans for a major production programme to be centred at Taganrog, and 150 were built between 1951 and 1955 for service with Naval Aviation, with the designation Be-6. Twenty were later exported to China for use by the Chinese Navy. Production aircraft were fitted with slightly more powerful engines than the LL-143 prototype, using two 1,790 kW (2,400 hp) Shvetsov ASh-73 radial piston engines instead of the 1,678 kW (2,250 hp) ASh-72s. Production aircraft also had a slightly modified wing box and a redesigned bow with an extended nose to make room for an eighth crew member, interior provision for a complete relief crew, and balcony flight deck windows giving good downward vision. A retractable radar was fitted in the fuselage planing bottom, aft of the second step, and bow spray fences were featured to reduce propeller erosion. The aircraft was capable of carrying up to forty commandos.

In production aircraft the NR-23 nose cannon and the Ilyushin twin-tail cannon barbette were deleted to make way for two different nose radars for surveillance and missile guidance and a MAD (Magnetic Anomaly Detector) tail stinger respectively. The aircraft was similar in class to the American Martin Mariner and was used in the long-range maritime reconnaissance role from 1950 to 1967, when it was replaced by the turboprop Be-12. In the late 1950s, a number of aircraft were produced as dedicated utility transports for use by Aeroflot.

In 1946, following on from the Be-6, the Beriev design team carried out a considerable amount of research into jet-powered flying boats based on the earlier prototype design. The R-1 was slightly smaller than the LL-143 but retained its same gull wing to keep the engine nacelles as high as possible. The hull had a high length-to-beam ratio with a shallow front step and rear planing bottom tapered to a point near the stern. The wing utilised a number of features drawn from the American Boeing B-29 bomber designs with its machined skin and wing box forming integral tankage, and Fowler flaps inboard and outboard of the engines. Wing-tip floats on two struts retracted electrically to form the wing tips when airborne (as on the Catalina PBY). The wing with its two 2,740 kg (6,041 lb) VK-1 turbojets was positioned remarkably far back on the hull, and the fixed tailplane was mounted high on a large fin with a bullet tail fairing. The aircraft carried a crew of three in a non-pressurised compartment, the navigator/bomb-aimer entering through a door in the starboard side of the hull to his nose compartment with windows on both sides. The pilot was housed in a fighter-like cockpit on the top port side of the hull, with the rear gunner in the stern compartment with a sighting blister on each side to control the electrically driven twin NR-23 gun barbette.

The R-1 was flown for the first time by I. M. Sukhomlin on 30 May 1952. Valuable lessons learnt, especially with regard to integral tankage and hull stability at high planing speeds, combined with features from previous Beriev flying boat designs, gave rise to the Be-10 reconnaissance plane and torpedo carrier. The Be-10 was designed to combine a reasonable endurance with high subsonic dash speed and a limited capacity for operation in open waters. This latter consideration led to a tall hull, the turbojet nacelles set high on its sides underneath the shoulder-mounted wings. The location and high sweep of the wing combined to create a large dihedral effect, giving rise to a 'Dutch roll' problem at low airspeed, although this was corrected by the use of pronounced anhedral, which in turn permitted the tip floats to mount on relatively short pylons. Despite being protected to some extent by strakes on the sides of the hull, the intakes nevertheless still ingested a certain amount of water in high seas, inevitably causing corrosion and flame-out problems. In this respect, the American Martin P6M Master (the only other turbojet flying boat in the world at the time) was certainly a better aircraft, as the engines and intakes were set over the upper wing surfaces. However, the Beriev engine locations did make it relatively easy to change a powerplant at sea. The chosen powerplants were two 63.7 kN (14,330 lbf) Lyulka AL-7RV turbojets—actually un-reheated versions of the engines used on the Sukhoi Su-7 fighter.

The aircraft normally carried a crew of three: two in a pressurised drum in the upper bows and the gunner in a pressurised tail turret. The pilot was in a cockpit on the centreline fitted with a jettisonable canopy, with the navigator housed in the nose with a glazed visual bombing panel. Normal access was through a door in the right-hand side of the hull and then via steps in the interior. There was a communication tunnel between the front compartment and rear turret with its radar location and two 23 mm guns. The wing box sections formed internal tanking with additional overload tanks in the hull. The aircraft also had powered controls.

Twelve Be-10 prototype and pre-production aircraft were built, the first of which was flown on 20 June 1956 by test pilot V. Kuryachim. The aircraft entered series production at Taganrog, and remains the fastest maritime aircraft ever to have achieved operational status. It was first revealed to the rest of the world at the Soviet Aviation Day at Tushino on 9 July 1961 when a formation of four Be-10s (including aircraft coded Yellow 40 and 41) were followed by a single M-12 (Be-12) turboprop prototype. From August 1961 the Be-10 set a number of FAI-recognised speed, altitude and payload records for a jet-powered flying boat, including an altitude record of 12,733 m (41,775 feet) with a 10-tonne payload, these achievements further emphasising the aircraft's tremendous performance. An aircraft flown by N. Andryevski with two crew attained a maximum speed of 912 kph (567 mph) on 7 August 1961, and a further record was set on 3 September by G. Buryanov with two crew over a 1,000-km (621-mile) circuit with a 5-tonne payload at 876 kph (544 mph), attaining an altitude record of 14,962 m (49,087 feet). A total of 100 Be-10s were built at Taganrog from 1956 to 1961, but difficulties with the Lyulka jet engines in service led to a switch in production in 1963 to the turboprop-powered Be-12. The AV-MF had also discovered serious operational limitations in the Be-10's lack of a search radar or MAD probe. Moreover, it carried all of its weapons externally with the inevitable vulnerability to sea spray etc.

It was for these reasons that in the late 1960s the Beriev Be-12 replaced the Be-10 on front-line operational duties and remaining aircraft were used in the transport role, and by Aeroflot, as well as for training. The Be-10's operational duties were taken over by land-based Tupolev Tu-16s adapted for naval operations. Whilst in Naval Aviation service, the aircraft equipped eight naval squadrons, mainly in the Arctic (Atlantic) and Pacific fleets. In response to the announcement by the US that it was to develop Polaris nuclear missile submarines, Naval Aviation issued a requirement for an aircraft capable of detecting and attacking nuclear submarines in Soviet territorial waters.

Whilst the Be-6 had been progressively upgraded, Naval Aviation needed a larger aircraft capable of carrying an additional weapon load and fitted with advanced search radar and up-to-date sensors. In parallel with work on its jet-powered Be-10, the Beriev OKB began work on a completely new design for a Be-6 replacement, and in the late 1950s Beriev is thought to have flown a modified Be-6 fitted with turboprop engines, which explains the fact that the new aircraft retained the gull wing layout and tail configuration of the Be-6. The first Be-12 prototype flew from Taganrog on 18 October 1960. It was slightly smaller than the Be-10, with a similar shaped hull, but was much lighter. It is thought that two prototypes were built, of which the one that appeared at the Tushino Air Show was fitted with a prominent nose search radar, replacing the retractable 'dustbin' installation of the Be-6. The aircraft also featured a small internal weapons bay in the bottom of the hull, as well as external wing pylons.

It became obvious that the Be-12 Mail was well suited for maritime operations and ASW warfare in the conditions peculiar to the Soviet Union. With its excellent endurance of over 10 hours, permitting long-range operational maritime patrol up to 230 miles out from the coast, the aircraft was selected for Naval Aviation service as a replacement for the outdated Be-6. Series production started at GAZ-86 at Taganrog in 1964, production ceasing in 1973 after a total of 132 had been built, whereupon the plant was given over to Tupolev Tu-142 Bear F production. The Be-12 entered Naval Aviation service in late 1964 and was soon nicknamed 'Tchaika' (Seagull) on account of the shape of its wing. Its main role at this time was ASW patrol, operating up to 500 km (270 nm) from shore.

By 1970 the Be-12 had taken over all of Naval Aviation's front-line duties from the Be-6 and was beginning to carry out some of the secondary duties as well. Eventually the Naval Aviation aircraft were to undertake the full range of operational maritime duties, which included coastal surveillance, multi-sensor reconnaissance, anti-shipping patrol, photographic survey, naval co-operation, transport and SAR duties. The aircraft was powered by two 3,125 kW (4,190 shp) Ivchenko AI-20D turboprops and carried a crew of five or six in an unpressurised hull, depending on mission requirements. This included the pilot, co-pilot/radio operator, navigator, electronics operator and one or two ASW sensor operators, the pilot and co-pilot being in ejection seats. There was a glazed observation/weapon aiming and navigation station in the nose and an observation astrodome above the rear fuselage.

The aircraft featured a comprehensive electronics and operational equipment fit, which included communications and navigation equipment, Doppler navigation, a search radar with its antenna in the nose 'thimble' and MAD equipment in the tail stinger, with sonobuoys in a fuselage weapons bay and onboard tactical analysis equipment. Armaments were carried in the small fuselage bay and on four hard points (one large and one small under each wing) up to a maximum weight of 5,000 kg (11,023 lb). Weapons carried are believed to have included torpedoes and/or depth charges (in the weapons bay), bombs, missiles and rockets. Stores and weapons were replenished via side hatches in the rear hull when moored on water or land-based. Operationally the aircraft was highly regarded by its crews. It was reliable and manoeuvrable, with powerful responsive engines, although flying on long maritime patrol missions often became a test of endurance for the crews as engine noise and vibration were particularly penetrating.

Throughout its service life (it is still operational today) the Be-12 has been progressively upgraded. From the 1970s the ASW avionics suite was improved by the replacement of the original drum-shaped type A-304E nose ASW/nav radar with new radar housed in a radome flattened at the top and bottom, along with additional electronic support measures (ESM) receivers and a tail-mounted radar warning receiver (RWR) system. Some of the aircraft were fitted with new engines, the improved AI-20M, of the same power as the originals.

In the 1960s, the American SSBNs were progressively re-equipped with the improved Polaris A3 missile with its longer range and advanced efficiency. This meant that the American submarines could patrol at greater distances from the Soviet coastline. Thus it was that the Soviets decided to redeploy the Be-12s to secondary maritime operations, handing over the primary task of long-range patrol to the Ilyushin Il-38 and ASW duties to ship-borne Kamov Ka-25 and the later Ka-27 helicopters. As a result, from 1968 onwards, surplus Be-12s were converted and reassigned to a variety of other roles. Many had their weapons bay removed and a floor installed, and a large fuselage door in the hull beneath the starboard wing trailing edge and the MAD detector in the tail probe were also removed. It is thought that up to about thirty aircraft underwent modifications to the SAR role, receiving the designation Be-12PS.

As with the Be-6, the Be-12 was used in a number of many non-military tasks for the government, such as fishery protection, whaling patrols, Arctic base resupply, mapping, geophysical survey and utility transports, all using Naval Aviation crews and aircraft. Two aircraft were redesignated Be-12P and converted for operation as fire-bombers. Conversion to water tanker involved the fitting of twin water scoops mounted behind the hull step and the installation of three metal (1.5 tonne capacity) water tanks in the rear weapons bay. A further 3-tonne tank was fitted in the forward stores position, with extra drop doors in the planing hull below. Overflow portholes were fitted in the upper fuselage over the water tanks. The conversions were carried out at the Irkutsk factory in northern Siberia, near Lake Baikal, with flight and water-bombing tests carried out at Taganrog during 1992. Two Be-12P prototypes were available in the early 1990s, but with no orders received, the original aircraft converted (Yellow 40) was scrapped. In 1992, a further aircraft was converted into a utility freighter with an enlarged hatch in the fuselage and removal of all ASW avionics equipment. It is not known what has happened to this aircraft since.

At the peak of its activities the Be-12 was used by all four of Naval Aviation Fleets, each having four full aviation regiments (most with twelve squadrons of eight aircraft). Currently there are still in the region of fifty-five Be-12s in the Naval Aviation's inventory, twenty-four of which are in use with its Northern Naval Fleet based at Ostrov Kildin in the Barents Sea, the remainder being with the Black Sea Fleet and a squadron of Be-12SP SAR variants at Baku Kala in Azerbaijan on the Caspian Sea. These aircraft carry red tactical codes outlined in white; Northern Naval Fleet codes are in blue outlined in white. The Baltic Fleet now has only two ASW squadrons, based at Kronsztad near St Petersburg and at Baltiysk. The Pacific Fleet now operates about five Beriev aircraft alongside Ka-27 helicopters.

It is thought that in the late 1960s/early 1970s two or three standard Be-12s were covertly operated by Soviet Naval Aviation from Egyptian air bases, flying in Egyptian Air Force colours but operated by Naval Aviation crews tasked with surveillance of the US 16th Fleet. These aircraft ceased to operate in about 1972 when relations with President Anwar Sadat soured. Similarly, in the early 1980s, a number of Be-12s (between six and twelve) were deployed to Cam Ranh Bay in Vietnam for surveillance of the US 7th Fleet. They were flown by Soviet crews with the aircraft in the markings of the Vietnamese People's Army Air Force (VPAAF). Withdrawal of US forces from the country saw the aircraft handed over to the VPAAF. The sturdy and versatile Be-12 still remains in use with the AV-MF today, and with little or no funding available to carry on with the development of its successor, the Be-42/A-40 Mermaid, it is likely to remain in use well into the twenty-first century.

The Soviets traditionally used Antonov An-2s for spotting fires and followed up with tackling the outbreaks with Mil Mi-8 helicopters. To supplement existing equipment and assist with training, in 1993 the Beriev OKB provided the Irkutsk Forest Fire Service with a pair of Be-12 military amphibians fitted with scooping and discharge gear and tanks with a capacity of 6 tonnes. The Beriev Be-200 utility fire-fighting amphibian, an ongoing development of the Be-12 concept, was a joint venture known as Betair. It involved the Beriev OKB, Swiss marketing company ILTA, and the Irkutsk Aviation Production Association and produced four aircraft, including a full-scale mock-up in 1991. The first prototype flew in November 1995.

The amphibian's hull was designed for maximum aerodynamic and hydrodynamic efficiency, giving it a top speed of 700 kph (435 mph) and the ability to scoop up 12 tonnes out of a 1 km stretch of open water. The aircraft's high swept wing has winglets, leading-edge flaps and sectional trailing-edge flaps. Two Lotarev D-436TP turbofans are positioned above and behind the wing on extensions of the undercarriage fairings, thus avoiding ingestion of water and dirt, etc. The water for fire-fighting is carried in four tanks divided into eight sections and arranged fore and aft of the step, along with the two pairs of discharge hatches. Up to ten different drop patterns are available. The aircraft can handle waves up to 1.2m (4 feet) in height and was designed in close consultation with the Irkutsk Forest Fire Service, which has been collaborating with the US Forest Service since 1991.

Apart from increased speed, range and capacity, the Be-200 has an advanced avionics suite designed and manufactured by ARIA, a joint venture between Allied Signal and the Russian Avionics Research Institute (NIIAO). This is a basic Allied Signal avionics fit with some additional Russian elements and additional functions for fire-fighting and SAR purposes. Some mechanical features, and the HF radio and the transponder for the Russian version, are of Russian origin. The options requested by fire-fighters included water source/drop zone path memorisation by the FMS using GLONASS (Soviet GPS); automatic synthesizing of glide slope using GLONASS (these two functions reduce the pilot's workload in smoke); and hand-held GLONASS sets with VHF voice capability for ground personnel. These system capabilities feed digital information to the cockpit, allowing for FMS (flight management system) display to each crew position. The Russians were considering a FLIR option with head-up display presentation to enable accurate dropping over the target zone, and another possibility would be data-link capability between fire-fighting aircraft and spotters. The aircraft was to feature Allied Signal LCD cockpit displays, saving weight, power consumption, radiation and high voltages, and it was also necessary to develop a filtering system to compensate for problems arising with alignment of the attitude and heading reference system (AHRS) due to the aircraft bobbing on the water. It was hoped to sell fifty-four fire-fighting variants to the Russian State Forest Service and there were also high hopes for sales to the West, either in the fire-fighting configuration or as a passenger-or cargo-carrying aircraft. SAR, ambulance and maritime research versions are also available.

Ilyushin (Il-)

Born on 30 March 1894 at Dilyalevo, Sergey Vladimirovich Ilyushin was one of the Soviet Union's most successful aircraft designers. He began work in 1910 at St Petersburg and entered military service as a soldier in 1914, becoming a pilot two years later. In the summer of 1917 he was lucky to escape with his life, having been shot down. With his flying career ended, he became a technician in the Red Army in 1919, and three years later he was working as a student and glider designer at the Zhukovsky Aviation Academy. On graduating, his first appointment was at the Scientific and Technical Committee of the Administration of the Military Air Forces (NTK UVVS), which produced the specifications to which all Soviet aircraft were designed.

In 1933, Ilyushin joined the TsKB where he was put in charge of the Long-Range Bomber (No. 3) Design Brigade. Amongst the designs and projects initiated by the team before the war were the TsKB-32 (I-21) fighter, the TsKB-56 twin-engined bomber and the TsKB-57 Sturmovik long-range bomber. It was at this time that Ilyushin was badly injured in a crash when the Yakovlev-designed AIR-2 cabin monoplane he used to travel between his Moscow-based OKB and the factory (which at the time was producing Ilyushin DB-3 bombers) ran out of oil and his face struck the aircraft's instrument panel in the subsequent forced landing. Fortunately, the accident did not hold up work on the TsKB-57 prototype of the single-seat Il-2 ground attack or Sturmovik aircraft.

The Il-2 became renowned internationally and was one of the Soviet Union's decisive weapons of the Second World War. More were produced than any other type of Soviet aircraft at that time, and the aircraft achieved considerable success later when it was modified to accommodate a rear gunner (Il-2M3). The Il-2's successor was the Il-10, with a more powerful engine and increased armour protection for the crew. The Il-10 entered service in 1944 and remained in use until the late 1950s, with over 6,000 built.

The DB-3/Il-4 bomber, developed from the TsKB-26, of which 6,784 were built, was the mainstay of the Soviet long-range bomber force throughout the Second World War and was in continuous production between 1937 and 1944. In 1944, Ilyushin began design work again on airliners for use after the war. The first was the Il-12, which together with the Il-14 was used in the 1950s to build up a civil airline network that was virtually non-existent at the end of the war. The Il-12 was the first Soviet airliner to be exported, and 633 were built up until 1949. It was followed by the Il-16 in 1945 and the Il-22 in 1947.

The Ilyushin Il-28 Beagle light bomber, which first flew in 1948, was the backbone of the post-war Soviet bomber force until replaced by the Yak-28. The next designs to emerge from the Ilyushin OKB were the Il-46 in 1952 and the Il-54 in 1955. In 1959, the Il-18 became the first Soviet turboprop airliner to enter scheduled airline service with Aeroflot and was also widely exported, despite initial problems with the Ivchenko engines. More than 900 Il-18s were built, and it was the first Ilyushin aircraft in which machine panel construction was used. It also formed the basis for the Il-38 May maritime reconnaissance aircraft design.

A leading member of Ilyushin's design team was the first deputy Genrikh V. Novozhilov, who was responsible for the Il-62 development in 1962 and succeeded Sergey Ilyushin on his retirement in 1970. By late 1968, 57,000 Ilyushin aircraft had been built. Development of the Il-76 was started in 1969, with its first flight taking place in March 1971, work having started on the Il-86 wide-bodied airbus in 1970. It could carry up to 350 passengers and its maiden flight took place in December 1976. Sergey Ilyushin died in Moscow on 9 February 1977, aged 82. Much later, in July 1994, the GAZ-40 production plant at Voronezh was officially linked to the Ilyushin OKB, assuming the title of Ilyushin Aircraft Production Association.

***

The first attempt to produce an aircraft for direct support of ground troops had been made by the French aircraft designer Édouard Nieuport in 1913, when he attached armour plating to the pilot's seat and a fuel tank of one of his designs. In 1917, Junkers produced a D.I with an armoured fuselage, although this proved to be underpowered for its weight, and the same scenario occurred in 1918 with the Junkers J4. Thomas Sopwith in England was equally unsuccessful with his TF.2 Salamander, which had armour plates around its cabin and was armed with two downward-firing machine guns.

In the 1920s and 1930s, a number of ground attack aircraft were produced in various different countries but none were completely successful. The root cause of the failures was the attempt to use established design principles to create an entirely new aircraft, a concept which actually contained a number of contradicting requirements. What was normally needed was a balance of established and operational conceptual design requirements. Whilst the ground attack aircraft needed to be heavily armed, it also needed to produce the greatest firepower in the shortest possible time. Armour was necessary to protect the crew, engine, radiators and fuel tanks, as the reality was that low-flying ground attack aircraft were likely to be fired on by any weapon available. It also meant that the weight of the armour and armament must not adversely affect the aircraft's performance and handling characteristics in order that it might still effectively evade hostile fighters. Designers generally tended to sacrifice certain performance aspects in order to enhance others, but the key to finding a good compromise design for a ground attack aircraft was indeed elusive.

Tupolev created the twin-engined TShB-1 and TShB-2 heavily armoured ground attack aircraft based on the Polikarpov R-6 reconnaissance aircraft in 1930, but the weight of about 1,000 kg (2,205 lb) of armour still reduced overall performance considerably. Four years later, S. A. Kocherigin produced a TSh-3 monoplane with its front section covered by flat steel plates, which served only to worsen the aerodynamics and handling. In 1939, Kocherigin equipped his LBSh (light armoured attacker) with two cannon, a pair of machine guns and a 400 kg (882 lb) bomb load; protective armour was confined to the pilot's seat, although this proved to be insufficient. Attempts by other designers proved equally unfavourable, resulting in the aircraft being either underpowered or well armed but vulnerable to ground fire.

It was not until 1937 that a successful ground attack aircraft emerged. Sergey Ilyushin's Il-2 design blended optimal weight of armour and armament with manoeuvrability, speed, range and survivability. In particular, for the first time the protective armament was made an integral element of the airframe structure and as such provided protection of the vulnerable parts such as the pilot, engine, fuel tanks and radiator from flying bullets and shell fragments. As a result, this famous Soviet ground attack aircraft was built in greater numbers than any other aircraft in history.

In total, 36,163 were produced. The ungainly-looking Il-2 played as great a part in helping to win the Second World War for the Allies as any other type of weapon. From the time of the 1917 Revolution, the Soviet military were convinced that the aircraft had a role to play in support of ground troops, the role of the air force being seen as battlefield reconnaissance, ground attack and close support. For the Soviet aviation industry the greatest production effort was always focused on the dedicated armoured ground attack aircraft—the sturmoviks.

In the early 1930s a variety of design teams produced ground attack biplane prototypes, many of which were based on Polikarpov R-5 and R-Z designs. However, none were actually successful, as the weight of the armour severely curtailed the aircraft's performance and offensive capabilities. In 1938, Polikarpov himself produced a sophisticated and modern-looking twin-engined aircraft, the VIT, intended for both ground attack and conventional bombing. The VIT was powered by two M-105 engines and fitted with heavy cannon armament (four 37 mm cannon) but the design was never selected for production, probably because simpler and cheaper alternatives were also being developed at the same time. One of these was at the Ilyushin OKB, where, on the instructions of Stalin, they were investigating the use of armour plating to form part of the structural element of an aircraft's design, with the aim of building a well-protected ground attack aircraft without suffering too great a weight penalty. Considerable problems were encountered in forming, working and welding suitable armour plate, but eventually Ilyushin managed to find satisfactory solutions to these problems and approached Stalin and his government with his idea for what he termed a 'flying tank'—an armoured ground attack aircraft.

On 5 May 1938, the Soviet Air Force approved the Ilyushin design and the aircraft was included in the government's budget plans. The air force designated Ilyushin's project BSh-2 and the Central Design Bureau gave it the designation TsKB-55, which emerged in October 1939 as a large single-engine, two-seat aircraft in which the whole of the front fuselage was effectively an armoured shell enclosing the engine, cockpit and fuel tanks. The shell was made of 4.7 mm thick AB-1 armour plate, an alloy rich in nickel and molybdenum. The rear fuselage was a wooden monocoque, and the wings were of duralumin with a fabric-covered elevator.

The first of the two prototypes flew on 2 October 1939, powered by Alexander Mikulin's supercharged inline 895-1007 kW (1,220-1,350 hp) AM-35 engine (as used by the MiG-3) and piloted by Vladimir Kokkinaki. The second prototype flew a few weeks later and factory testing was completed by the end of March 1940. The state tests using the second prototype, which started on 1 April 1940, resulted in a number of recommendations being made. Visibility had to be improved, and it was also considered that the AM-35 supercharged engine, whilst excellent at high altitudes, did not appear to give enough power at the lower levels which the aircraft would be required to operate at. In addition, the authorities (the Soviet Government and Air Force) wanted a single-seater, not a two-seat aircraft. Ilyushin was aware of the first problem but not of the single-seat requirement, as in his opinion the aircraft needed a gunner to protect the tail because of the low operational altitude anticipated. However, he almost immediately set about making the necessary changes.

To improve visibility Ilyushin lowered the engine position by 175 mm (7 inches) and raised the pilot's seat by 50 mm (2 inches); he also redesigned the engine cowl and added a bulletproof canopy. In addition, he asked Mikulin to produce a new dedicated low-altitude non-supercharged version of the AM-35 engine. Elimination of the rear-facing gunner's position necessitated the repositioning of the wing forward, to correct the centre of gravity and compensate for the increased fuel capacity brought about by the additional space available. The replacement AM-38 low-altitude engine produced by Mikulin developed 1,213 kW (1,626 hp) for take-off and 1,119 kW (1,500 hp) at 1,650 m (5,413 feet). Whilst this was not enough to turn the TsKB-57, as the modified aircraft was redesignated, into a high-speed machine, it did achieve the aim of endowing it with sufficient power for its intended low-level operations. In reality, however, deletion of the supercharger was a retrograde step, as other designers were asking for bigger and better superchargers to permit their designs to fly higher and faster.

The redesigned aircraft made its maiden flight on 12 October 1940, again in the hands of Kokkinaki, who reported satisfactorily on its performance, and indeed the type was cleared for production in record time. Such was the urgency that three factories had been tooled up for production even before the state testing had started. However, the Soviet Air Force did not agree with the type entering production until all tests had been concluded, although Ilyushin was happy that after a number of design details had been completed the aircraft was ready for production. He informed Stalin of this in writing, whereupon Stalin ordered that production of the aircraft was to commence immediately, even if state tests had not been completed.

Production commenced at GAZ-1, GAZ-18 and GAZ-30 in the Moscow and Voronezh regions, but was slow. The aircraft that entered production as the Il-2 (the first to carry the Ilyushin name) was somewhat different to the TsKB-57 that had been accepted by the state test centre. It had reverted to the earlier-style cowling, windscreen and canopy, with a shorter (and glazed) fairing behind the pilot. The whole front fuselage (except for the top part of the engine cowling) was built from AB-1 armour, ending in a 7 mm plate behind the fuel tank aft of the pilot. The pilot was further protected by a 55 mm armour glass windscreen and similar rear windscreen, the canopy and side panels incorporating sections of 8 mm armour plate, which must have severely restricted the pilot's field of vision. As before, the rear fuselage was a wooden structure, and the wings were made of duralumin. All control surfaces were fabric-covered metal, except the all-metal flaps. Armament consisted of one 7.62 mm ShKAS machine gun and one ShVAK 20 mm cannon in each wing, with 750 and 200 rounds per gun respectively. Four small bomb bays were fitted in the wing centre section, capable of housing 100 kg (220 lb) bombs, and the outer wing panels could be fitted with racks for RS-82 or RS-132 unguided rocket projectiles or more bombs. This armament fit was not exactly an impressive war load for an aircraft of its size, and by western standards the Il-2 was grossly under-armed, although a lot of careful thought had gone into protecting vulnerable parts of the aircraft such as the engine, the radiator and the fuel tanks. In fact, the aircraft was almost totally immune to small-arms fire from the ground, even if it was vulnerable to flak.

However, what all the armour plating and careful design did not do was protect the Sturmovik from fighter attack. After initially treating the Il-2 with a great deal of respect, Luftwaffe pilots soon came to realise that this unwieldy aircraft was easy prey if attacked from behind. The combination of restricted rear vision, slow speed, poor acceleration and rather staid handling characteristics meant that the Il-2 pilot was a sitting duck, with little or no chance of escape if attacked by a prowling Messerschmitt Bf 109 or Bf 110. In fact, in the early stages of the aircraft's combat baptism, any pilot managing to survive ten sorties qualified for recognition as a 'Hero of the Soviet Union'.

The desperate need for aircraft meant that the Sturmovik entered series production simultaneously at three plants. In spite of this, output was extremely slow to gain momentum and only two aircraft were produced in March 1941, followed by twenty-four in April, seventy-four in May, 159 in June, and 310 in July, settling at an average of 215 per month from July to December. Stalin expressed his dissatisfaction at the low production output by awarding only a second class prize to Ilyushin for the design. In addition, he demanded an immediate explanation for the situation at GAZ-18 that had been expanded to increase capacity and output. The production plant explained that the problem was caused by lack of pre-formed armoured assemblies from the Kirov Works at Leningrad, whereupon the Director of the Kirov Works, Zazulski, blamed the problems on the drawings supplied by Ilyushin, claiming they were nothing more than 'doodles'. The result of these procrastinations was that Ilyushin, Zazulski, and the Director of GAZ-18 were summoned to Moscow for a long meeting with Stalin, in which the dictator flew into a rage and Zazulski was lucky to escape with his life. The situation was salvaged by the GAZ-18 team, and Zazulski returned to Leningrad to carry on with his job of ensuring that regular supplies of armoured assemblies were available.

In any event, so rapid was the German Army's advance by now that the Il-2 production lines were moved east to the Volga Region, as were so many of the Soviet armament production factories. The new factory produced its first aircraft by December 1941, having relocated only a month before, but it was not until the next spring that full production was restored. As mentioned earlier, Stalin had sent a telegram to all the factories involved in Il-2 production complaining about their low output and particularly berating the factory at Kuibyshev for producing only one aircraft a day. It responded by guaranteeing at least four a day from 5 January 1942, six from the 19th, and seven a day from the 26th, stating that the main reason for its poor output was that the production workers were still trying to complete the building of the factory. The factory was also devoid of an airstrip for several months, all of its output having to be delivered to Moscow by train. Eventually, after initial deferment to repair work, some of the evacuated factories were ordered to build Il-2s again.

At the time of Operation Barbarossa only about 100 Il-2s were in service out of a total of over 200 that had been built, so that although those available were used in the desperate battles that raged on the front, they initially had little impact. In the second half of 1941, despite the continued threat from advancing German forces, the operational strength of the Soviet ground attack units was building rapidly with the delivery of 1,293 Il-2s, although throughout the fierce fighting of the winter of 1941/42, replacements were hard pressed to keep pace with attrition as the relocated GAZs struggled to come fully on stream with output. The desperate need to produce as many Sturmoviks as possible caused another casualty for the Soviets—the loss of MiG-3 production—as the AM-35 engine production lines were given over to producing AM-38 power units for the Il-2.

As well as the evacuations and parts shortages, a number of other problems had further frustrated attempts to increase production. In the main, these were associated with welding of the AB-1 armour plate and weaknesses in the rear wooden fuselage. The latter problem was overcome by a redesign of the rear fuselage by the production engineers, although unfortunately this had led to increased weight and the inevitable reduction in performance. The performance of series aircraft was forever giving rise for concern, often compounded by poor quality manufacturing and the ever-increasing weight problem. Operational experience also showed the vulnerability of the aircraft, and the armament was of course found wanting: the 20 mm cannon could not deal with armoured vehicles, and the RS rockets were erratic and unreliable. Bomb-release mechanisms also gave trouble, to such an extent that the bravery of the Sturmovik pilots pressing home their attacks often went unrewarded. As a result of all these problems, as was normal with Soviet wartime production of aircraft, the operational and production problems were discussed at the highest level, the designers and factory managers having to answer directly to Stalin.

As the Il-2 was an important element in the Soviet Union's response to the German offensive on the homeland an urgent conference was called in February 1942, which brought engineers, designers and service personnel together in Stalin's presence to resolve the emerging problems with the aircraft. At the meeting Ilyushin reaffirmed that he had been strongly opposed to production of the single-seat Sturmovik and that he still considered that some rear defence was vital. Operations had confirmed his worse fears that the single-seat aircraft would be extremely vulnerable to attack from the rear, and consequently he was tasked with reintroducing a second crew member to the aircraft. Localised improvisations by operational units had proved mostly unsatisfactory, with the gunner placed behind the armoured shell becoming extremely vulnerable to enemy fire. In fact, the life expectancy of a rear gunner was extremely short whilst aircraft with these modifications were in use. Pending major redesign, the factory solution to the problem was to move the rear armoured bulkhead aft into the wooden monocoque, add extra side armour and mount a 12.7 mm machine gun on the bulkhead, with the gunner perched on a simple strap across the fuselage.

Other improvements were gradually introduced over a period of time as production continued, including the extension of the rear cockpit aft to accommodate the rear gunner. The opportunity was also taken to install an additional fuel tank between the pilot and the rear gunner, and the wing-mounted twin 20 mm cannon were replaced with 23 mm-calibre weapons offering greater armour penetration. Provision was also made for the eight 82 mm rockets to be replaced by four 132 mm weapons. As was only to be expected, these changes increased the aircraft's weight—4,525 kg (9,989 lb) empty; 6,060 kg (13,377 lb) fully loaded—again degrading its performance, but this was overcome by the introduction of the uprated AM-38 engine which produced 1,268 kW (1,700 hp) for take-off and a maximum continuous power of 1,119 kW (1,500 hp) at 750 m (2,460 feet). Other suggestions made to improve performance included more careful sealing of panel gaps, stronger springs to close the bomb bay doors to stop them falling open in flight, and a fairing ahead of the tail wheel. This interim two-seat model, designated Il-2M or Il-2 *tip* (type) 2, was placed in production, although not all aircraft produced had all the changes introduced at once.

An unforeseen problem now occurred, in that the modified aircraft's handling characteristics were barely acceptable due to the fact that the extra armour-plating for the gunner and the gun had inevitably moved the centre of gravity rearwards. Unfortunately such was the demand for aircraft that little could be done. The Il-2Ms were rushed into front-line service, the first flying operationally on 30 October 1942, and factory-built modification kits were supplied to operational units to permit the necessary changes to front-line aircraft. Initially the extra protection afforded the crew was extremely welcome and effective, but it was not long before Luftwaffe pilots learned to exploit a blind spot that existed behind the tail and began concentrating on taking out the gunner.

The barely acceptable handling characteristics of the Il-2M led Sergey Ilyushin to produce a redesigned two-seater as quickly as possible. The major change was to the wing, the outer panels being swept back by some 15 degrees. This had the effect of shifting the centre of aerodynamic lift relative to the centre of gravity, resulting in a marked improvement in handling. The overall length of the aircraft increased by 50 mm (2 inches), although where this small increase occurred is not clear. All the changes found in the Il-2M were included, along with the fitting of the AM-38F engine and a refined canopy, and faster actuation of the bomb bay doors and the bomb cells in the wings permitted quicker release of the 200 2.5 kg (5.51 lb) PTAB hollow-charge anti-tank bomblets that were often carried.

Production of the definitive Sturmovik, the Il-2M3, commenced in December 1942, and peaked in mid-1943, when it was sustained at close to 1,000 per month for most of the next year. Ultimately it was this variant that made up the great majority of the total Il-2 Sturmovik production. Also in 1943, the industry was at last to reap the benefits of a more stable production environment after the evacuations, the workforce having become more experienced, with the result that the average time needed to produce an Il-2 had dropped from 9,500 man-hours in 1941 to 5,900 man-hours in 1943. With both single-and two-seat versions now in production in reasonable numbers, Ilyushin and his team were able to concentrate on resolving production problems and further development of the aircraft, including the introduction of a number of variants, as shown in the table below:

Il-2 Variants	
Il-2M	Fitted with AM-38F engine with slightly increased power: 1,268-1,328 kW (1,700-1,780 hp) with lower compression ratio to permit it to run on petrol. Entered operational service in January 1943
Il-2i	Fitted with AM-38F engine, it was 760 kg (1,675 lb) lighter and carried two VYa-23 mm cannon. Only one produced, intended as a 'bomber exterminator'
Il-2	One two-seat Il-2 was modified with new wing featuring 15 degree mean chord sweep but not put into production
Il-2U	Trainer variant with dual controls, produced in small numbers between 1943 and 1945. Armament fit was halved and all-up weight reduced to 5,091 kg (11,220 lb). Full rear canopy covered instructor's position, and VYa cannon was deleted. Only limited production
Il-2KR	Reconnaissance variant, also made in small numbers. Some had oblique cameras in rear fuselage; others had cameras bulged in undercarriage fairings. (Photographic evidence exists of at least one aircraft fitted with large camera on machine-gun mount in rear cockpit)
Il-I	Fighter prototype built in 1944, powered by AM-42 engine with take-off power of 1,492 kW (2,000 hp). Featured wider chord wing with smaller wing area. Speed at 3,260 m (10,695 feet) was 525 kph (326 mph). Maiden flight on 19 May 1944, but production not continued
Il-2T	Torpedo-carrying aircraft developed for use by Naval Aviation in anti-shipping strike role.

Production of all Il-2 variants finally ceased in the autumn of 1945, in favour of the much-improved Il-10, but before concluding our brief look at the Il-2 Sturmovik we should examine why series aircraft appeared at times in what was on the surface a bewildering variety of different build standards.

The Soviet production plants—with Stalin constantly looking over their shoulders—were preoccupied with producing as many machines as possible. So it was often the case that design improvements and modifications based on operational use were incorporated on an 'as and when possible' basis. The general lack of co-ordination between what were supposed to be essentially the same aircraft and, particularly with reference to the Il-2, minimal use of jigs and employment of mostly semi-skilled labour, led to quite a degree of variation between individual aircraft. This is not, however, a phenomenon unique to the Soviets. The author is reliably informed that none of the supersonic English Electric Lightnings produced by BAC were exactly the same. Another example of this 'customisation' was on the Handley Page Victor aircraft produced at Radlett in Hertfordshire. When nearing the end of their operational life, the RAF could not find a spare door for an otherwise perfectly serviceable aircraft that had failed a pressurisation test from a number that had already been withdrawn from use, which meant that a recently serviced aircraft had to be prematurely scrapped.

We should also consider what the Il-2 was really like as a warplane. Stalin's propaganda machine naturally depicted the Sturmovik and its crews as conquering heroes, but truly objective summaries of the Il-2 are hard to find. When judged dispassionately, the reality was that the aircraft was slow, unwieldy, not particularly easy to fly and poorly armed when assessed against other strike aircraft of its day, such as the German Focke-Wulf Fw 190, the British Hawker Typhoon and the American Republic P-47 Thunderbolt. In fact, the Il-2 suffered quite astonishing losses in combat, losses that no other air force could or would have endured.

Such comparisons, however, are unrealistic. The Russian Front was quite different from any other theatre of war, fought with a savagery and disregard for casualties unmatched before or since. The Red Air Force did not have access to sophisticated fighter-bombers, but it is unlikely that they would have survived the harsh conditions and minimal maintenance typical of Eastern Front operations (the Soviets had a very low opinion of the 'delicate' Spitfire, for example). What the VVS needed was very large numbers of rugged aircraft that were simple to build and maintain, and the Il-2 was exactly such a machine. Thrown into battle in huge numbers, the Sturmoviks exacted a fearful toll on German armoured and ground forces, despite operating for much of the time without effective fighter cover or air superiority. Taking into account the fact that they were built by a largely unskilled workforce, flown by minimally trained pilots and serviced under appalling conditions by personnel with little technical background or mechanical aptitude, the results obtained were out of all proportion to the aircraft's apparent capabilities. In Soviet hands the Il-2 was a war winner and rates amongst the most significant of all Second World War aircraft. On an annual basis for comparison, in reality the operational losses were 15 per cent, but in only four months.

The DB-3 long-range bomber was a direct descendant of the TsKB-26. It was ordered into production in preference to the Sukhoi-designed DB-2 by Stalin after it had put on an impromptu air display by executing three successive loops over Moscow's Red Square at the May Day fly-past in 1936. Not only had the startling display thrilled the crowds, it had also gained the pilot, Vladimir Kokkinaki, and the designer, 42-year-old Sergey Ilyushin, an audience with Stalin in the Kremlin. The TsKB-26 had been designed by the Central Design Bureau to the requirements of a long-range bomber specification formulated in 1932, the same specification as the winner of the design competition, the ANT-37. This aircraft had been designed under the auspices of Andrei Tupolev by a team led by Pavel Sukhoi, who of course was already an experienced designer of combat aircraft, and was in reality the superior machine, being some 100 kph (62 mph) faster.

At the time that the ANT-37 was declared the winner of the contest the TsKB-26 had not even entered its flight test programme. The ANT-37 was planned to enter production as the DB-2 at GAZ-39, but immediately after Stalin had had his meeting with Ilyushin and his pilot the DB-2 programme was halted, in spite of protestations by General Yakov Alksnis and the Commissars for Heavy Industry and Defence, Sergo Ordzhonikidze and Kliment Voroshilov, that the availability of a modern long-range bomber to the Red Army Air Force would be seriously delayed, and that the DB-2 had already been 'tooled for'. However, the first production prototype, now designated DB-3 and painted in red, the CKB-30 'Moskva', was built at GAZ-1 at Moscow in 1936, the aircraft entering production at GAZ-18 at Voronezh and GAZ-39 at Moscow-Khodynka in February 1937. A total of twelve and thirty-three aircraft at the respective plants were built that year.

In 1938, GAZ-126 at Komsomolsk was also engaged in production of the aircraft, as the planned production output was well behind schedule. Also that year, the aircraft underwent a major redesign in order to simplify and speed up production. The redesigned aircraft was designated DB-3M and two new variants—the DB-3T (Torpedo) and DB-3PT—were introduced. By February 1940, a total of 1,528 aircraft had been produced, whilst in January a new model with a glazed nose had been introduced, the DB-3F, and was later redesignated as the Il-4. By June 1941, a total of 3,266 DB-3/Il-4s had been produced by the three factories, the bulk of which were DB-3M variants in use with the Long Range Bomber Force. At this time 34.8 per cent of the Red Air Force's bombers were DB-3s, many of which were lost in the war with Finland and Sweden as well as many in accidents.

When the Germans mounted Operation Barbarossa against the Soviet Union on 22 June 1941, the bulk of the Long Range Bomber Force was made up of DB-3M-equipped units, most of which had survived the pre-emptive strikes. Il-4s had entered service with the Black Sea Fleet Air Force, which used them operationally for the first time on 24 June when a small formation attacked Constanţa in Romania. By then Long Range Aviation had 1,148 Il-4s in the West and many more in the East, and Naval Aviation had more than 100. The heavy losses sustained by Frontal Aviation forced the Soviets to deploy their long-range DB-3/Il-4 bombers in the low-level strike role, but unfortunately this was a role they were totally unsuited to, as they possessed very little defensive armament, only basic crew protection, and had totally unprotected fuel tanks. Attrition losses were appalling and the success of the bombing missions on Berlin were minimal, the Germans claiming that of the many attacks launched by the Soviet long-range bombers, they were successful in reaching Berlin on only four occasions. The first of these occurred on the night of 8 August 1941, when fifteen DB-3Ts of the Baltic Fleet's Naval Air Force bombed the city, subsequent raids being made by the long-range VVS units.

In October 1941, GAZ-18 was evacuated to Kuibyshev to undertake Il-2 Sturmovik production. GAZ-39 was also evacuated, to Irkutsk, which inevitably led to a drop in production of the Il-4. By 1942, many wooden parts were incorporated in the

Il-4 to reduce the aluminium content and conserve stocks, which also reduced unit costs from 800,000 roubles to 468,000 roubles per aircraft. In May 1943, the Long Range Bomber Force comprised of eight corps with sixteen divisions and thirty-two regiments with thirty-two aircraft each. Many were Il-4s, although TB-3s, B-25s, Li-2 transports, Tu-2s and Yer-2s were also in use. By then, the unit cost of production had dropped to 380,000 roubles and the production time from 20,000 man-hours to 12,000 man-hours per aircraft. The following year unit costs dropped again, to 175,000 roubles, although production of the Il-4 ceased in 1944 after a total of 5,256 had been built, at one time at the rate of 200 per month. On 6 December 1944, the Long Range Bomber Force was disbanded and the bombers and transports were used to create the 18th Air Army. By 1947 the new Long Range Aviation Force had 1,839 aircraft, including thirty-two four-engined Pe-8s, some Boeing B-17s and Consolidated B-24 Liberators, a large number of Yer-4s and still some Il-4s, the remainder being North American B-25s and Li-2s transports, in a total of fifty-one regiments.

The Soviet Governmental Defence Committee invited Ilyushin and Sukhoi to submit proposals for a more modern sturmovik aircraft to replace the Il-2 with potential for further development. Ilyushin developed the Il-8, which was based on the Il-2, although slightly larger, and was fitted with the 1,492 kW (2,000 hp) AM-42 liquid-cooled engine driving a four-bladed propeller. In the event, the Il-8 offered little real improvement over the Il-2/Il-2M and consequently was very quickly abandoned. However, a number of its features were retained in the Il-10 design. Its basic layout had more in common with the Il-2 than the Il-8, and the airframe had a closer resemblance to the Il-1 than the Il-2. Ilyushin again used the Mikulin AM-42 engine, with a normal 1,305 kW (1,750 hp) output but with an emergency short-period capability of 1,492 kW (2,000 hp).

The Il-10 was constructed from modern pressed sheet and rolled sections in the centre, with improved weapons bays. Wing surface area was reduced from the 38.8 m² (418 square feet) of the Il-2 to 30 m². This meant that the weight increased only slightly with the introduction of the new armour, and the new aircraft was 100 kph (62 mph) faster than the earlier Il-2. The thickness of its armour was distributed in a rational manner to increase its combat survivability without any weight penalty, the 6-8 mm armour plate thickness for the rear gunner being increased to 13 mm. The new aerodynamics and uprated engine actually improved its performance and handling considerably, and a simplified, single-strut oleo leg allowed the main undercarriage to turn through 90 degrees and retract into the wings, thus avoiding the large drag-inducing pods of the Il-2. A more compact radiator was fitted, the carburettor air intakes were improved and the cockpit size reduced. Three prototypes were built in February 1944, the first of which took to the air, again in the hands of Kokkinaki, on 18 April. During testing the original armament was changed to two NR-23 cannon and two machine guns, followed by a further change to 37 mm cannon and two machine guns, or four NR-23 cannon. Factory tests were followed by official state tests, which were carried out and completed by Alexander Dolgov by 9 June 1944.

The aircraft proved outstanding and in all respects was vastly superior to the Il-2, the Il-8 and its Sukhoi competitor the Su-8. It was ordered into production on 23 August 1944, and both GAZ-1 and GAZ-18 at Kuibyshev started production in parallel with the Il-2, which was still being built at that time. Initial production was therefore low, although the first examples were delivered for training just two months later. Il-10s of the Rava-Ruski Regiment of the Aviation Assault Unit saw their first action on 2 February 1945 over the German Front near the Neisse River. Moderate numbers were used for attacks on other parts of the Third Reich, particularly Berlin.

On 1 May 1945, the Red Air Force had 630 Il-10s in service, and by August of that year was assisting the Allies in their war against Japan in an attack on the port of Rajin during which two Japanese freighters were sunk. Production of the Il-2 ceased after the Second World War, but the Il-10 continued in production at GAZ-18 until 1949, with GAZ-64 at Voronezh switching to Il-10 production from 1947 to 1949. GAZ-1 had ceased production of the Il-10 in 1946 to concentrate on jet fighter production. The last series variant was the Il-10M, which had a completely different wing to previous models. Trainer variants (Il-10UT/UIl-10) were produced in only very small numbers for the Soviet Air Force, although they did retain full armament. Total production of Il-10s amounted to 4,966 aircraft.

In 1949, the Soviet Union began to export Il-10s. Poland received forty aircraft from GAZ-64 and Hungary fifty, together with two UIl-10 training aircraft, others going to Czechoslovakia, Bulgaria and Romania. However, the most important export market was North Korea, which received sixty-five aircraft with which to launch the Korean War on 25 June 1950. China was sent 175 in 1950, which were also used in the Korean War. Massive supplies of Il-10s were later delivered to Asian and European countries, although the Soviets themselves were by now using the aircraft in much smaller numbers, even though the last Soviet Sturmovik Regiment (equipped with Il-10Ms produced from 1951 to 1954) was not retired from East Germany until 1956, a number of older base model Il-10s remaining in service as gunnery trainers for crews destined to fly the Il-28 twin-jet bomber.

Even when production ceased in the Soviet Union, the tooling was transferred to Czechoslovakia where the Avia plant at Letňany near Prague produced a further 1,200 Il-10s, including a number of VIl-10 training aircraft. Almost half of these aircraft were used by the Czechoslovak Air Force under the designation B-33. Of the balance of 504, from 1953 to 1957 Bulgaria received thirty-seven Il-10s plus three VIl-10 trainers, Poland 264 Il-10s plus twenty VIl-10s, and Romania 140 Il-10s plus sixteen VIl-10s. The final twenty-four Il-10s went to Yemen in 1957, where they remained in use for many years. With these final deliveries and cessation of production by the Czechs, the Sturmovik was dead. Later a few OKBs tried unsuccessfully to introduce a replacement until the Sukhoi Su-25 Frogfoot was used to such devastating effect in Chechnya.

The final Sturmovik in the Il-2 family was the Il-16. In essence it was a lighter Il-10, with an all-up weight of 6,180 kg (13,621 lb) as compared to the Il-10's 6,336 kg

(13,965 lb).Weight saving was achieved by the use of lighter armour plating, but its armament fit remained the same as that of the Il-10 and was also similar in size. The chosen powerplant was the 1,716 kW (2,300 hp) AM-43NV fitted with a four-bladed propeller, the extra power giving it a low-level top speed of 625 kph (388 mph). The type was ordered into production even before test flights began, and its maiden flight took place on 19 August 1944, again with Kokkinaki at the controls. However, the flight soon revealed that there were some inherent problems with the design, not least the fact that the new AM-43NV supercharged engine was unable to deliver the required power output. And it was this—together with high propeller speeds, tail surfaces that were too small, a narrow centre of gravity, and the fact that substantial buffeting was experienced—that revealed that a major redesign was required. The aerodynamic problems were overcome relatively easily by a fuselage stretch of some 0.5 m (1 foot 8 inches), but it was necessary to replace the AM-43NV engine by the tried and tested AM-42 on production aircraft. However, only fifty-three series production aircraft plus the prototype had been produced by the time the war ended, and in early 1946, with no further demand for the aircraft, the production line was closed. Total Sturmovik production throughout the Second World War amounted to 51,192 aircraft plus six prototypes—a record likely to stand for all time. The Ilyushin Sturmovik, rightly, is itself a 'Hero of the Soviet Union'.

The first prototype of the Il-18 transport aircraft, civil registration CCCP L 5811 (L for *Linyerny*—a liner) with 'MOSKVA' (Moscow) emblazoned on the top of its fuselage, made its maiden flight on 4 July 1957. A four-engined piston aircraft of the same name had seen brief service on a trial basis with Aeroflot during the late 1940s but had never entered series production. The more familiar variant was designed as a medium-capacity turboprop airliner for Aeroflot, for use on internal and European routes, and went into service with the airline on the Moscow–Adler route on 20 April 1959. At the time of its conception, Aeroflot had an urgent need for such an airliner and three of the first five aircraft produced for evaluation purposes were used for accelerated trials. It was of course eventually produced in a number of variants for both civil and military use.

Its development and construction was a matter of great urgency. It was for this reason that Sergey Ilyushin himself frequently visited the final assembly shop where a team of designers and production engineers were on hand to sort out any production problems. All of the 569 aircraft were manufactured exclusively at GAZ-30 at Khodynka between 1957 and 1969. The first twenty aircraft were fitted with either Kuznetsov NK-4 or Ivchenko AE-20 engines of 2,984 kW (4,000 hp) each, but unfortunately both types suffered from a number of teething troubles and frequent engine fires were encountered, a number in flight. Containment of these fires was achieved by the fitting of systems feeding an inert gas into vulnerable areas and by applying a titanium coating on the wing main spar. There were a number of instances where the offending engine had fallen from the aircraft, which fortunately was able to continue flying on just three engines. Eventually the engine problems were resolved, and from the 21st series aircraft onwards only the AI-20 powerplant was used. From 1958, the Il-18 was in sole production at GAZ-30, with four aircraft per month being produced up until 1960. By 1961, with ever-increasing demands by Aeroflot for more and more aircraft, output peaked at six per month, and some 450 Il-18s had been produced at the Khodynka factory in five different versions by 1967.

The Il-18A was the first production variant for Aeroflot and differed little from the original prototype, with accommodation for up to seventy-five passengers and a flight crew of five comprising two pilots, a navigator, a radio operator and an engineer. From the 21st aircraft onwards the type was designated Il-18B, having improved take-off weight, engines and capacity for eighty-four passengers, and was in production from 1959 to 1960. By 1961 the Il-18V, with its revised interior seating up to 110 passengers in a mixed tourist and economy class or ninety passengers in all-tourist seats, was available. This was the most prolific version for Aeroflot and was produced between up until 1965. The Il-18E, fitted with AI-20M engines, was an Il-18V with a communication equipment fit permitting its use on international routes. It had a variable passenger configuration from 110 to 112 seats, the additional capacity being obtained in summer in the Soviet Union by removing the 'winter coat' storage space otherwise demanded in a country with such rigorous winter conditions.

In 1964, the Il-18I (later the Il-18D) introduced the 3,170 kW (4,250 hp) AM-20K engine and an increased seating capacity of 122, obtained by moving the rear pressurised bulkhead back from frame 56 to 62 (eliminating the rear hold). Fuel capacity was increased by 32 per cent to more than 30,000 litres (6,600 gallons) by fitting four additional fuel cells in the wings and an underfloor tank. The Il-18D had a gross weight of 64,000 kg (141,096 lb) and a payload of up to 6,500 kg (14,330 lb) to be carried on flights of up to 6,500 km (4,040 miles). A pure freighter variant, the Il-18T was used by the Soviet Air Force in small numbers as transports, freighters and VIP aircraft. Total production is thought to have exceeded 700 aircraft, but an inherent defect with the type, which resulted in many being prematurely withdrawn from use, was fatigue damage to the tail sections. This also led to a lot of confusion among aviation enthusiasts with regard to serials as tail units (complete with c/n) were swapped between airworthy airframes to keep otherwise serviceable aircraft flying. Il-18s were used continuously throughout the 1960s, 1970s and 1980s by most Eastern European airlines and some politically friendly African countries. In the early 1990s, a number of Il-18s were still in limited use with Aeroflot and various CIS operators as well as with Cubana, Aerocarribean, Balkan, Air Koryo, Polnippon, Vietnam Airlines, China United Airlines, Tarom and Air Zory. Some fifty Il-18s were estimated to be in use worldwide in August 2000, of which thirty-seven were in Europe and the CIS.

Production of the Il-18 ceased in March 1969, but manufacture of specialised variants for the military continued in small batch production (between fifteen and twenty aircraft per year) until the mid-1970s. These included the dedicated ELINT reconnaissance derivative Il-20 Coot A, based on the Il-18D, the Il-22 long-range signals communications aircraft and airborne command post, and the Il-38 May, a maritime patrol and ASW aircraft (described in more detail later). In 1994, it was believed that the CIS Air Force still had around twenty Il-20/22s in service, whilst Naval Aviation had three Il-20s.

The Ilyushin OKB had begun work on a project designated the MSh aircraft in 1942. The engine was to be located inside the centre fuselage driving the airscrew via a long shaft (as per the Bell P-39 Airacobra fighter). Whilst the MSh failed to materialise, Ilyushin did not abandon the idea completely and a prototype Il-20 was built in 1947, intended as a successor to the Il-10 and based on the MSh. Of all-metal construction, its engine, cabin and fuel tanks were protected by an armoured shell and the forward section was designed so that it could be rapidly removed to facilitate replacement of the liquid-cooled engine that drove the four-blade variable-pitch airscrew. The crew cabin, with a 100 mm thick armoured windscreen, was positioned above the engine and allowed the pilot an excellent view forwards and downwards. Behind him, facing rearwards, was the wireless operator and the air gunner in a hydraulically operated barbette fitted with a NA-23 cannon. With a field of fire of 180 degree azimuth and 80 degree elevation, a system was devised to prevent firing onto the fuselage tail section or tailplane, offensive armament consisting of two wing-mounted NS-23 cannon. A second prototype was built with an installation of four downward-firing NA-23 cannon in a turret. The bombs were carried in four internal containers, and two racks for 500 kg (1,100 lb) bombs were provided under each wing. The first prototype was built without the fuselage-mounted cannon.

In December 1948, the Ilyushin OKB test pilot Kokkinaki began the flight development programme. In terms of speed and manoeuvrability the new aircraft was equal to its predecessors and in many respects superior. Kokkinaki noted that in attacks over the practice range the need for repeated passes was eliminated as the excellent field of vision afforded the pilot a full view of the target, permitting accurate strafing and bombing in a single pass. Unfortunately the future of the aircraft was marred by its unreliable engine and also by the notion emanating from leading aviation specialists at the time that the age of the piston-engined aircraft was dead and that any futuristic design should be fitted with a jet engine—the propulsion of the future. However, the Il-40 turbojet produced in 1953 also failed to enter series production, as it was felt that the need for a specialised ground attack aircraft to provide support for ground forces was, to say the least, rather outmoded with the possibility of nuclear warfare on the horizon. This was a mistake made not only by the Soviets but also by the Americans, who were basically pursuing the same policies and found themselves devoid of a good ground attack aircraft. Such aircraft were sorely needed in the Vietnam conflict, where the Americans discovered at first hand the deficiencies of trying to use modern fighter-bombers and helicopters in the ground attack role and were forced to press Second World War-type piston-engined training aircraft into the role.

Although the Il-20 did not enter service, the idea was put to good use by the British in 1949, when Fairey were tasked with providing the Fleet Air Arm with a carrier-borne ASW aircraft. It was realised by the Fairey design team that the concept of placing the cockpit above the engine did offer an excellent field of vision to the crew when landing on aircraft carriers as well as giving the aircraft a distinct advantage in the final stages of an attack on enemy submarines. As a result, the Fairey Gannet and the Douglas A-2D-1 Skyshark both made the most of Ilyushin's design concepts.

The three-seat Il-28 light bomber, like most early Soviet jets, was powered by two Rolls-Royce Nene turbojets. For its day it was a thoroughly modern aircraft: its straight-wing design drew comparisons with the English Electric Canberra and it carried radar bombing and navigation equipment, ejection seats for the pilot and navigator and a shielded bottom escape hatch for the rear gunner, with hot air de-icing for the wings and a swept tailplane with a manned twin-gun tail turret having two NR-23 cannon with 225 rounds per gun or two 12.7 mm machine guns, and two forward-firing 23 mm cannon with 100 rounds per gun in the nose. Disposable armament comprised a maximum of 3,000 kg (6,614 lb) or normal bomb load of four 500 kg (1,100 lb) or eight 250 kg (550 lb) free-fall bombs carried in a lower fuselage weapons bay. The first prototype flew on 8 August 1948 with its two Nene engines, later aircraft being fitted with two Soviet licence-built 26.5 kN (5,955 lbf) centrifugal-flow RD-45s (PP models) or non-afterburning Klimov VK-1A turbojets (series aircraft), giving a maximum speed of 900 kph (559 mph) at 4,500 m (14,765 feet) and a cruise speed of 770 kph (478 mph) at 10,000 m (32,810 feet). It could climb to that altitude in 18 minutes, and had a range of 2,180 km (1,350 miles) with maximum bomb load or 2,400 km (1,490 miles) with maximum fuel.

Deliveries of series production aircraft began in September 1950, aircraft entering service with Frontal Aviation the following year, replacing piston-engined Tupolev Tu-2s and Petlyakov Pe-2s. The Il-28 retained the glazed bombardier nose of the older piston-engined bombers, although fairly early in the production run the type was fitted with an all-weather bombing radar in a ventral fairing. Later aircraft carried tail-warning radar beneath the rear gun turret, although the rear guns still remained manually aimed. The bomber carried a crew of three—pilot, bomb-aimer/navigator and gunner. The Il-28 bears the distinction of being the first jet-powered aircraft operated by Aeroflot. A few aircraft, designated Il-20, were used by the airline in 1955 to carry high-priority freight and mail, and to give the airline experience of jet operation before the entry into service of its first passenger jet, the Tu-104.

Among Il-28 variants was the Il-28R, whose bomb bay had three or five cameras fitted, plus between twelve and eighteen photo-flash bombs. Some had an electronic reconnaissance package with a radome fitted under the rear fuselage. The Il-28T had a bomb bay adapted to carry one large or two small torpedoes, or mines in an alternative configuration, and the Il-28LL was a Soviet test aircraft in which the rear turret space was occupied by an experimental cabin for the testing of ejection seats, including the downward-firing seats fitted to the Tu-22 bomber.

Around 3,000 Il-28 of all variants were built in total, with hundreds produced in China as the Harbin H-5 and later the reverse-engineered Hong-5R before the

Sino-Soviet rift. The first Chinese copy flew on 25 September 1966, production being launched in April 1967 and continuing at Harbin until 1982, with 450 variants produced for the People's Liberation Army Air Force (PLAAF) and fifty for the CPNAA. It is believed that the CPNAA still operates at least fifty H-5s in the torpedo-bomber role for ASW operation over the Taiwan Strait. In 1985, the CPNAA had ordered a number of towed targets from the British Rushton Company for some of its H-5s to simulate sea-skimming anti-ship missiles.

The Harbin HZ-5 was a three-seat tactical reconnaissance version, similar to the Il-28R, fitted with wing-tip auxiliary tanks as standard and with its reconnaissance cameras and electronic sensor packs fitted in the weapons bay. The HJ-5 two-seat operational trainer, 186 of which were built, was based on the Il-28U Mascot, with all armament and the ventral ground-mapping radar fairing deleted. Instead a solid nose with a second 'stepped' cockpit (with dual controls) was fitted ahead of and below the instructor's cockpit. At the peak of its service with the PLAAF it is believed that each operational unit was supplied with two or three HJ-5s. A number of H-5s were exported to Romania, the last six being finally withdrawn from use with the Romanian Air Force in the summer of 2001. The type was also operated by Poland, Czechoslovakia, Hungary, East Germany, North Korea and Egypt among others.

The Ilyushin Il-38 May, a dedicated ASW long-range maritime patrol aircraft, was a fairly radical development of the Il-18D airliner. The amount of specialised equipment dictated considerable changes in the external fuselage shape and aircraft layout, the mainplane being moved forward by four bulkheads, although the wing, tail, engines, nose section and landing gear were all those of the Il-18D. Whilst the diameter of the fuselage remained the same, a fuselage plug increased the aircraft's overall length by 3.66 m (12 feet). The forward repositioning of the wing was necessary to maintain the centre of gravity with the installation of the heavy mission equipment in the forward fuselage, and to enable the aircraft to withstand the stresses and manoeuvres at low altitude in gusty weather a degree of fuselage strengthening was carried out. On either side of the fuselage, ahead of the wing, what appears as an air intake and outlet duct was fitted, presumably to provide cooling for the additional mission equipment fitted in the tactical control cabin above the wing. The aft fuselage, which was almost windowless, included galley facilities and sleeping accommodation for relief crews. The weapons bay was located well forward in the fuselage and housed the hydroacoustic sonobuoys, anti-submarine torpedoes and sea mines. The electronics and operational equipment comprised weather radar in the nose and ASW 'Wet Eye' radar with its under-nose radome for search and surveillance purposes, and the ASW aircraft's trademark MAD was installed in the long tail stinger.

A major difference compared to the Il-18D was the standard fitting of bag tanks to increase the Il-38's fuel capacity to 30,000 litres (6,600 gallons), giving a range of 7,200 km (3,888 nm) and a patrol endurance of some 12 hours. There was no provision for drop tanks or in-flight refuelling. A flight crew of three or four was carried, with a mission crew of eight or nine in the rear cabin. By western standards the Il-38 can be considered as a first-generation ASW type. Development began in 1962, with the first flight occurring two years later. Series production was undertaken at GAZ-30 'Znamya Truda' at Khodynka between 1964 and 1976, amounting to some 100 aircraft —one in 1964, one in 1965, three in 1967, one in 1968, twelve in 1969, eighteen in 1970, ten in 1971 and so on until 1976. The initial low-level production output meant deployment by Naval Aviation did not commence until 1970, and the aircraft was not known to the West until 1974. Throughout its long service life, based on external appearances, it appears that little or no updates or upgrades were carried out to its operational equipment. A new variant, thought to be designated Il-38 May B, was identified in 1984, fitted with a second large radome under the weapons bay. It was intended for mid-course missile guidance and therefore lacked ASW capability. Naval Aviation is thought to have had up to fifty-five Il-38s on inventory when the type's first overseas deployment was made in 1970. Aircraft in Egyptian markings were based at Mersa Matruh that year, and also in South Yemen (Al Anad near Aden) from 1978, and Libya from 1981, as well as in Syria.

In May 1984, two Naval Aviation Il-38s were destroyed by rebels at Asmara. By 1994, Naval Aviation's inventory had dropped to thirty-six aircraft in three squadrons of twelve with the Northern, Baltic and Pacific Fleets. At that time, the CIS Air Force had obtained sixteen Il-38s, although there use was unknown. Five aircraft are known to have been exported to India and were deployed at Dabolim in the Goa Region in 1977 by No. 315 Squadron of the Indian Air Force (serials IN301-IN305).

The Ilyushin OKB was led by its General Designer Genrikh Novozhilov in the mid-1960s when it set about designing the Soviet Union's first jet transport, the Il-76, to meet a joint civil/military requirement and as an Antonov An-12 replacement. The requirement called for an aircraft capable of carrying twice the maximum payload of the An-12 over greater distances but able to use the same short and semi-prepared airstrips. The aircraft was powered by four Soloviev D-30KP non-afterburning turbofans hung on low-drag pylons, the engines set well inboard on the wing as compared to western designs. The wing was fitted with extensive high-lift devices, including slats, triple slotted trailing-edge flaps and spoilers for low-speed roll control. A unique feature was the rough field landing gear, which was much more complex than that found on western aircraft. The main gear consisted of four units, each having a single axle fitted with four wheels abreast, giving the aircraft an exceptionally low 'footprint pressure'.

Internally the Il-76 was equipped with a cargo roller floor, 3,000 kg (6,614 lb) winches and two roof cranes with a total lift capacity of 10,000 kg (22,000 lb). Loading/unloading was facilitated by a rear ramp access with two hinged rear fuselage doors. The aircraft could accommodate a crew of seven made up of two pilots seated side by side, a flight engineer, a navigator, a radio operator, a loadmaster and a rear gunner in a barbette carrying the rather archaic armament of twin NR-23 cannon. The navigator occupied a cabin with a glazed nose below the flight deck. Production Il-76 aircraft have two radomes: the nose radome housing the weather radar, and the under-nose radome ground-mapping equipment. Three prototypes and two static test airframes were built at GAZ-30 at Khodynka, the prototype (SSSR-86712) flying on 25 March 1971 and appearing at the Paris Air Show two months later. Series production commenced in 1975, and from 1977 concentrated on the Il-76T, which had some 20 per cent more fuel capacity, giving the aircraft extra range.

The aircraft proved to be an excellent tactical transport with an impressive performance in the airlift role, and was destined to become the primary aircraft of the Soviet transport fleet for many years. Deliveries to Aeroflot commenced in 1978, and the airline is believed to have received more than 180 over a number of years, including 'T' and 'M' variants, thus forming a transport reserve for the VTA. The aircraft's versatility led to many different versions, which inevitably resulted in a number of major changes and modifications to the basic airframe. Among these were modifications to the cargo handling equipment to facilitate carriage of different types of loads, such as oversized and heavy equipment, standard containers and pallets, live animals, troops, paratroopers, passengers in special 'comfort' containers or in removable passenger seats, and even external loads carried on top of the fuselage (which included Tu-160 Blackjack tailplanes).

The Ilyushin OKB also developed a variety of 'air-drop' equipment for different modes of cargo weighing from as little as 20 kg (44 lb) to 45 tonnes. The equipment permitted easy discharge of loads at altitudes from 3 m (10 feet) to 16,000 m (52,500 feet). The Il-76 has been used in the evacuation role in combat and times of natural disaster, as flying hospitals and CASEVAC operations and as SAR aircraft capable of delivering a lifeboat and crew to aid stricken shipping or recovery of spacecraft and crew after splashdown.

The 1990s saw the Il-76 modified once again to fulfil a new and urgent requirement for a fire-fighter. The increase in forest fires over the recent decades in Russia and elsewhere has had a devastating effect on the environment and world economy. For example, during the last seven months of 1993, almost 20,000 forest fires were reported in Russia alone, destroying more than 1.5 million hectares (3.7 million acres) and causing damage estimated at 29 million roubles. Thousands of people and more than 150 aircraft, helicopters and specialist vehicles were involved in the battles to beat the flames. Il-76TD (serial RA-76835) was added to this inventory, having been fitted with the VAP-2 fire-fighting system which permitted it to discharge thousands of gallons of water via its rear loading ramp at airspeeds as low as 280 kph (174 mph).

By early 1994, more than 800 of these excellent transport aircraft had been produced at the Chkalov plant (GAZ-34) in Tashkent, Uzbekistan. It is thought that the VTA received some 450 Il-76s, and that around 296 were still in use, along with four Il-76MDs flying with the Algerian Air Force. Seven Il-76MDs and a further fifteen Il-76Ms obtained from Uzbekistan were in use in China, plus twenty Il-76MDs named 'Gajraj' with the Indian Air Force. In addition, there were commercial exports to a number of customers, with an estimated 294 aircraft in operation worldwide in August 2000, of which 241 were in Europe and the CIS.

In 1983, the Ilyushin OKB received a development contract for a regional airliner to replace the Antonov An-24 and An-26. The design of the Il-114 was completed by 1986, and the first prototype (CCCP-54000) made its maiden flight on 29 March 1990 at the Zhukovsky test centre. A twin turboprop fitted with two Klimov 1,864 kW (2,500 shp) TV7-117-3 engines, it was designed to carry up to sixty-four passengers and had a conventional low-wing structure with integral wing tanks. It had a circular fuselage 2.86 m (9 feet 4 inches) in diameter and a cabin 22.24 m (73 feet) long. Nominal cruising speed at 500 kph (310 mph) gave the aircraft a range of 1,000 km (621 miles) with a full passenger load, or 2,850 km (1,770 miles) with a 3.6-tonne payload. The airframe was fatigue-lifed at 30,000 hours. Three flight prototypes were built, plus two static and fatigue test airframes, and the production aircraft were fitted with western avionics, with further changes to export variants. Certification tests were successfully completed in 1993. The initial order was for 500 aircraft and fourteen different plants were earmarked for parts and sub-assembly production, although this number was later reduced, as was the planned production output of five aircraft per month.

By January 1994 a series run of 1,000 aircraft was envisaged, although eventually Aeroflot and its successors stated a requirement for only 350 aircraft. Similar in size and design to the BAe ATP (Advanced Turbo-Prop), one of the prototype aircraft (RA-54001) was destroyed during a test flight in July 1993. The main production plant was at Tashkent, where the first production aircraft was rolled out on 10 January 1994, with a second production line at MAPO, Moscow. By 1994 eight series aircraft had been built and had all flown by June 1995, with ten more on the Tashkent production line. At this time it was believed that the type was in limited service with Uzbekistan and Arkhangelsk Airlines. In late August 1995, two aircraft were spotted at the Zhukovsky test centre, serials RA-91002 'Il-OKB' (MAPO-line) and RA-54000 ('Il-OKB'), but by August 2000 only the two Uzbekistan aircraft appeared to be in use.

Kamov (Ka-)

Born on 14 September 1902 in Irkutsk, Prof. Dr-Ing. Nikolai Ilyich Kamov studied locomotive design at Tomsk Technical Institute during the 1920s before changing to aeronautics. At an early stage in his career Kamov worked under Dmitry Grigorovich on flying boat designs at the Department of Marine Experimental Aircraft Design (OMOS). In 1928, Kamov qualified as a pilot whilst working on the ROM-1 and other flying boat designs, and his work on rotary-wing aircraft dates from the Soviet KASKR-1 autogiro of 1929. From 1931 to 1940, as a member of the Special Design Department at TsAGI, he was in charge of Brigade No. 3 which had developed the A7 autogiro, but left the department to set up a factory for A7 production, and in 1941 he accompanied the autogiros on an expedition to the Tian Shan Mountains.

Kamov's AK autogiro design was under construction at the outbreak of the Second World War, but further development had to be abandoned and the design team was disbanded in 1943. It was after the war, in 1947, that the Kamov OKB was formed, Kamov having started the design of a new type of rotary-wing craft in 1945. Whilst his design was only an ultra-light helicopter, the twin contra-rotating coaxial basic layout used was to be developed for almost all of his subsequent designs. The coaxial layout was one of the first ever proposed for helicopters— Mikhail Lomonosov's experiment of 1754 was based on it. Sikorsky's first two designs were coaxials, and so were the Pescara, Ascanio, Breguet-Dorand, Asbóth and Hiller helicopters, as it was the easiest way of countering torque, albeit awkward to control. The contra-rotating coaxial transmission was complicated and heavy, and in the absence of a tail rotor, a conventional aircraft tail unit was required. Kamov, however, persevered with the coaxial concept, and with the help of turboshaft engines appears to have overcome most of the difficulties. Kamov claimed that the coaxial layout enjoyed great advantages over other types, its load-to-weight ratio, excellent manoeuvrability, minimal dimensions and a saving of 10 per cent on engine power being achieved through elimination of the tail rotor in a single-engine aircraft.

The Kamov design bureau is the only one in the world that constructs helicopters with coaxial rotors. This concept has some distinctive attributes over conventional helicopter design, including smaller dimensions and absence of power losses from the tail rotor etc. It should be noted that the Russian word for helicopter is *vertolet*, a word invented by Kamov. Early Kamov designs, all of which were one-to three-seaters, were produced only in small numbers, although having established a close working relationship with the Soviet Navy, all of the bureau designs (with the exception of the Ka-26) were accepted for use by the service. These included the Ka-8 in 1947, the Ka-10 in 1949, the Ka-15 in 1952, the Ka-18 in 1956, the Ka-25 in 1961, and more recently the Ka-27 and Ka-29 designs.

Ulan-Ude and Kazan are now the sole centres for the manufacture of Russian helicopters, the Kamov OKB being based at Ulan-Ude, together with Mil. Kamov, along with Tupolev, also produced at least two aerosleighs—the Ka-30 for eight passengers and the Ka-36 Veterok two-seater—both of which entered series production. Kamov's deputy was M. A. Kupfer, who won a DOSAAF competition in 1949 with a design for a kite-type autogiro named 'Smolensk'. He was later put in charge of the Ka-26 development.

Kamov died on 24 November 1973, aged 71, and among the new designs produced after his death were the Ka-27 in 1974, the Ka-50 attack helicopter in 1982, and the Ka-136 in 1983. Unlike all previous Kamov designs, the Ka-118 and the Ka-62 that were being developed in 1992 under the direction of Sergei Mikheyev had a single main rotor instead of the twin coaxial contra-rotating rotors. Design studies are continuing on tilt-rotor types.

***

In 1943, Kamov was the first Russian to begin work on a helicopter with the coaxial contra-rotating twin-rotor system. The result was the Kamov Ka-8, nicknamed the 'flying motorcycle', which had its first flight in 1948. The Soviet Navy had expressed an interest in the Ka-8, so Kamov submitted a proposal to the High Command for the development of a ship-borne single-seat liaison helicopter. This proposal met with a favourable response and a contract for the development and construction of such a machine was issued. After developing a refinement of the Ka-8, designated Ka-8M, with a service ceiling of 2,500 m (820 feet) and a top speed of 115 kph (71 mph), Kamov produced the improved Ka-10 Hat, retaining the coaxial contra-rotating rotors that made the tail boom and anti-torque tail rotor unnecessary.

The Ka-10 was ready for evaluation in 1949, and was first seen by the public at the 1951 Soviet Navy Day celebrations at Khimki. The aircraft lacked a fuselage, tail unit and undercarriage and was powered by an Ivchenko 41 kW (55 hp) AI-4V 4-cylinder engine that had been specially modified for helicopters. The transmission system had two reduction gearboxes, one directly attached to the engine to reduce the revolutions and the other directly attached to the contra-rotating coaxial rotors. The engine reductor gearbox included a clutch that acted as both a connecting and free-wheeling assembly. The vertical shaft drove the distribution redactor gear, which in turn drove the rotors. The wooden rotor blades were hinge-attached to their respective hubs, with their respective control systems included in an interlinked pitch control mechanism. The helicopter stood on a pair of inflatable pontoons made of a resin-coated fabric, and directional stability in level flight was provided by a pair of fins mounted on a light welded framework.

In September 1949, test pilot M. D. Gurov began the Ka-10's flight development programme. A total of four prototypes were built, all of which made a considerable number of test and demonstration flights before the aircraft was submitted for its NII acceptance tests. The Ka-10 was the first Soviet helicopter to take part in experiments to assess operational use from various naval vessels such as battleships, cruisers and fast armoured boats, and the sea trials were extremely successful. They demonstrated the helicopter's excellent manoeuvrability and control during landings and take-offs from vessels travelling at speeds up to 50 kph (31 mph). Throughout the winter of 1950/51 a Ka-10 was operated aboard the *Maxim Gorky* battleship in the Baltic Sea and was highly commended. The Ka-10 research programme provided the industry with valuable experience needed for the development of more advanced helicopters and was undoubtedly the progenitor of the family of Kamov helicopters that was to find such a wide use in both civilian and military service.

The Kamov Ka-15 was designed and developed to meet a specification issued by the Soviet Navy and was intended for use by naval and commercial vessels as well as for SAR duties and other roles. Kamov adopted the proven concept of coaxial contra-rotating rotors of its predecessors, but the Ka-15 was none the less an entirely new helicopter. It was powered by a 9-cylinder air-cooled 190 kW (255 hp) AI-14V radial piston engine with a top speed of 150 kph (93 mph). Maximum take-off weight was quadrupled over the Ka-8 and Ka-10, with a comparable increase in dimensions. The new helicopter now had a completely enclosed fuselage with extensive glazing for the pilot and observer seated side by side. The fuselage ended with paired tail fins at the end of the tailplane. The machine had a four-wheel undercarriage, which could be replaced by a pair of floating pontoons for maritime operations.

The Kamov OKB carried out extensive research to reduce the vibration levels to within acceptable limits. The vibration was caused by the need to finely balance the six rotor blades—a difficult problem to overcome—but it was resolved by D. K. Yefremov, the OKB test pilot, who devised a method of balancing the coaxial lifting rotors which proved to be extremely effective and helped reduce the level of vibrations of the Ka-15 to the lowest level of all contemporary Soviet helicopters. Yefremov had begun flight development of the Ka-15 in April 1953, series production commencing in the autumn of the same year.

Once the first series aircraft had been assembled it was decided to proceed with a comparative evaluation with the Mil Mi-1 for ship-borne naval operations. The smaller dimensions of the Ka-15 and the absence of a tail-boom rotor, as well its superior flight characteristics, led to the total acceptance of Kamov's helicopters for use by the Soviet Navy, and 100 machines were built at Ulan-Ude between 1957 and 1962. The first series helicopters to be delivered started their service lives on naval vessels operating with the Black Sea and Baltic Fleets and were fitted with RV-2 radio altimeters. In parallel with the service evaluation, the Kamov OKB sought to develop a civil utility version, designated Ka-15M and powered by a 205 kW (275 hp) AI-14VF engine. A passenger-mail variant could accommodate one passenger, with the mail in special containers, and the ambulance variant could carry two stretchers in nacelles attached to the fuselage sides, with the medical attendant seated in the main cabin alongside the pilot. Additional fuel tanks doubled the air ambulance's range. On 29 May 1958, test pilot V. V. Vinitsky, flying a Ka-15, established an international speed record over a 100-km (62-mile) circuit of 163 kph (100 mph), the same pilot flying a 500-km (310-mile) circuit at a top speed of 170 kph (105 mph) on 6 May the following year.

Two prototypes of the Ka-18 had been completed in 1956; a very early prototype was CCCP-L 0005. The Ka-18 was basically an improved and stretched Ka-15. It had an enlarged nose section, larger fins and an 81-cm (32-inch) fuselage stretch, providing space for the pilot and three passengers in two rows of two seats and permitting the carriage of a stretcher, the sliding doors of the Ka-15 being replaced by conventional doors. The two internal fuel tanks with a combined capacity of 176 litres could be supplemented by two additional 70-litre tanks, one mounted on each side of the fuselage. This permitted a maximum freight load of 300 kg (660 lb) to be carried over a distance of 300 km (186 miles). Along with its increased passenger load, the Ka-18's capabilities were further enhanced by the installation of a full cockpit instrument panel and rotor and windscreen de-icing. The Ka-18 used the same transmission, rotor pylon and rotors as the Ka-15 and also the same 190 kW (255 hp) AI-14V engine initially, although the slightly more powerful 205 kW (275 hp) powerplant was fitted when it became available in the late 1960s. Flight trials began in early 1957, and the aircraft entered production at Ulan-Ude (Zavod 99) the following year, 370 being built up until 1961.

In 1958, the Ka-18 was awarded a Gold Medal at the World's Fair in Brussels, and in the following year it raised the 500-km (310-mile) closed-circuit speed record for helicopters. It was used principally by Aeroflot, particularly in the Moldova and Ukraine districts, mainly on taxi services. In addition, many civil authorities used the type for medevac, crop spraying, aerial survey, and fishery and forestry patrols. Although ordered for service with Naval Aviation, only a small number were accepted for use on Soviet warships for experimental purposes. It was also evaluated by the Soviet Air Force but was never ordered for operational use. None were exported.

The Kamov Ka-25 Helix was the standard Soviet naval helicopter for over twenty years, its basic design having been established with the introduction of the piston-engined Ka-15 in 1952. In the early 1960s, Kamov flew a prototype Ka-20 helicopter fitted with two turboshaft engines which was displayed at the Tushino Air Show in July 1961, with NATO erroneously anticipating its entry into operational service. In the event, the Ka-20 did not enter series production but served instead as the basis for the Ka-25 prototype. This had smaller search radar in a chin radome, more pointed triple tail rudders and no aft sliding rear door on the port side, as compared to the production Ka-25s. Production commenced in 1966, the type being fitted with two 671 kW (900 shp) Glushenkov GTD-3F turboshaft engines mounted on the fuselage roof forward of the main gearbox and drive shaft. The Ka-25 featured folding three-blade coaxial rotors, which permitted the elimination of the tail rotor used in designs with the more conventional single-rotor assemblies. The rotor system also had full de-icing and automatic blade-folding, both of which were extremely important in ship-borne operations. The crew were accommodated in a side-by-side cabin and the main rear cabin could hold up to twelve passengers, although it was usually fitted to carry two or three ASW/missile-targeting system operators. Weapons included torpedoes and depth charges carried in a ventral bay between the four fixed undercarriage legs. It was believed that some Ka-25s with enlarged weapons bays extending into the sonar compartment were capable of carrying wire-guided torpedoes. Each of the three fins aft of the main fuselage had a large ventral area, and the two towed-in outer units had the rudder control surfaces embodied.

It is reported that there were as many as twenty-five Ka-25 versions, of which the three main variants were the basic ASW version known to NATO as Hormone-A; the special electronics variant with data-link facilities employed in the OTHT (Over-The-Horizon Targeting) and guidance and mid-course correction for the ship-launched SS-N missiles, known as Hormone-B; and the utility Hormone-C used in the SAR and transport roles by the Soviet Naval Aviation and Aeroflot. In total, 460 Ka-25s had been built when production ceased in 1975, which included a few that were exported to India, Syria and Yugoslavia.

The Kamov Ka-50 Hokum 'Black Shark' was the world's first single-seat combat helicopter conceived as a rival to the American Hughes AH-64A Apache. It retained the traditional Kamov tailless rotor and twin-coaxial main rotor configuration. Flight tests of the design started on 27 July 1982, and after almost ten years of development the Ka-50 won the day from the Mil Mi-28 Havoc (renamed Night Hunter in the new millennium) in a competitive fly-off in 1992. Optimised for ground attack, the helicopter carries a 500-round 30 mm cannon on the starboard fuselage as well sixteen tube-launched anti-tank missiles and eighty free-flight rockets on four pylons with twenty rounds each. As a single-seat machine a high degree of automation is assumed, with target acquisition and designation in all probability achieved by a support aircraft or by troops on the ground. The helicopter has been designed for high survivability on the battlefield, with 20 mm projectile-resistant armoured protection for the pilot, engines and transmission.

The aircraft is unique in rotary craft design in being fitted with an ejection seat system in which the rotor blades are detached explosively. When the ejection system is initiated, following release of the rotors, the hatch above the pilot opens and a rocket fires, extracting the pilot from the cockpit. On 17 June 1998, the first aircraft of the test batch of Ka-50 helicopter gunships crashed outside the town of Torzhok, a section of its rotor blades having broken off during a display routine. The aircraft was being flown at an altitude of about 50-100 m (165-330 feet) by Major-General Boris Vorobyov, Chief of the Torzhok Training Centre.

According to Russian sources, eight series Ka-50s had been produced at the Progress aircraft plant in the country's Far East, all having been delivered to Army Aviation units, with most based at Torzhok. It was also reported that a further thirteen unfinished 'Black Sharks' were on the Progress assembly lines, having been intended for delivery to Slovakia in lieu of bad debt. However, work was stopped when Slovakia refused the aircraft, preferring to purchase the S-300 PMU-1 anti-aircraft missile systems. Whether the recent renaissance in Russian military aviation will see the Ka-52 enter series production again remains to be seen, although the RFAF has selected the redesigned Mi-28 Night Hunter as its premier battlefield attack helicopter for the forthcoming decades of the new millennium.

Lavochkin (La-)

Semyon Alekseyevich Lavochkin was born on 11 September 1900 at Smolensk. He became a student at the Moscow Higher Technical School, during which time he worked at TsAGI on the ANT-3 and ANT-4. In 1918, he enlisted in the Red Army and served for nine years until 1927. Two years later Lavochkin joined the TsKB and became a member of Paul-Aimé Richard's design team at OPO-4. In June 1929, he was appointed Chief of the Aerodynamic Calculation Section working on the TOM-1. When Richard returned to France, on the abandonment of the TOM-1 project in 1931,

Igor Sikorsky, (1889-1972), with an assembly of senior Russian officials, who are being shown his proposed bomber prototype with a view to building the aircraft for official service. Sikorsky is the young man in the centre.

The Sikorsky Ilya Muromets large four-engine bomber was designed by Igor Sikorsky. The Ilya Muromets first appeared in 1913 and was a revolutionary design, intended for commercial service with its spacious fuselage incorporating a passenger saloon and washroom on board. During the War it became the first four-engine bomber to equip a dedicated strategic bombing unit and was unrivalled at the time. It was slow at just 68 mph but it could carry 12,000 lb (4,600 kg) of bombs.

Igor Sikorsky was not the only innovator in Russia, in 1913, Dmitry Grigorovich designed the world's first seaplane. The flying boat, called the M-1, participated in the Russian war effort. Dmitry Pavlovich Grigorovich, (1883-1938) was a Ukrainian, Russian and Soviet designer of a number of aircraft under the Grigorovich name.

Alexander Alexandrovich Kazakov, (1889-1919). Alexander Kazakov, the leading Russian air ace, was unofficially credited with a total of thirty-two victories and held sixteen decorations, including the British DSO, MC, and DFC, and the French *Légion d'honneur*. His official tally was 20 Victories. Kazakov initially flew a Russian-built Morane-Saulnier.

Tsar Nicholas II in the '*Russkiy Vityaz*', or 'Russian Knight', which was apparently intended as a transport for the Russian royal family, with the Royal Crest on the Bow. This aircraft led to the Ilya Muromets bomber.

Most of the aircraft used by the Imperial Russian Air Service were of French of other western designs such as the Farman F.30 and F.40 pusher two-seat biplanes. There were of both French and Russian build, and 400 of F.30 and F.30*bis* were built at the Dux factory in Moscow. They were armed with a machine gun and bombs, and used in reconnaissance and bomber roles in the War. This particular Farman with Bolshevik insignia came to an unfortunate end.

A Russian Polikarpov R-1 with officers and ground crew. The Polikarpov R-1 was an unlicensed version of the British Airco DH.9A, a single-engined light bomber designed and first used shortly before the end of the War. Over 2,400 examples of the pirated Polikarpov R-1 were built by the Bolsheviks and the star insignia on the uniforms shows this photograph to be after 1917.

The first international commercial air route was opened on 1 May 1922, Moscow to Königsberg and later this airline extended to Berlin. 'Dobrolet' was established as a company in the Russian Federation 17 March 1923 to facilitate the development of the nation's air fleet.

A Soviet R-1 fitted with a Wright Radial Engine. The R1 and R-2 were basically redesigned versions of the British Airco DH.9A. More than 2,400 were built between 1924 and 1934.

The Tupolev R-6 prototype ANT-7 first flew in 1929. It was designed as a twin-engine multi-role combat aircraft and some 407-411 (sources differ) were built in all variants between 1930 and 1932. It had a crew of four with a maximum speed in the region of 144 mph at 10,000 feet.

A close-up view of the R-6 ANT-7. The R-6 had five machine guns and carried 500 kg bombs. In later years it served as a trainer and also up to 1944 as a transport aircraft.

A Tupolev TB-3 bomber/mothership and three Polikarpov I-5 fighters.

Opposite below: A replacement aircraft, designated ANT-20*bis* had begun production the following year and first flew in 1938. It was largely identical in design but with six more-powerful engines instead of the previous eight. This aircraft, designated PS-124 and registered CCCP-L760, served with Aeroflot on transport routes in Russia and Uzbekistan. On 14 December 1942 it also crashed after the pilot allowed a passenger to take his seat momentarily and the passenger apparently disengaged the automatic pilot, sending the airplane into a nosedive from an altitude of 1,500 feet and killing all 36 on board.

The Tupolev ANT-20, the 'Maxim Gorky'. This was a huge aircraft. It was 112 feet long 22 feet high and had a wingspan of 206 feet. The 5,200 ft surface area resulted in it weighing some 59 tons. The plane's wings were so large they were fitted with bunk beds. When it was finished it was 11 feet more than the early Boeing 747 in its wingspan. It was equipped originally with eight engines. Its first flight was on 19 May 1934. The aircraft was destroyed on 18 May 1935 when an aerial stunt went badly wrong. One of the accompanying smaller aircraft collided with the Maxim Gorky and all aboard the aircraft were killed. The collision occurred while flying over the parade at Red Square. It was struck by a fighter plane trying to fly a loop around it. The crash occurred in a residential neighbourhood of Moscow killing some 41 people. At the time it was the worst disaster in aviation history.

The Polikarpov I-15 was a biplane fighter of the 1930s. Nicknamed *Chaika* (Seagull) because of its gulled upper wings, it was operated in large numbers by the Soviet Air Force, and 7,175 were built. Together with the Polikarpov I-16 monoplane, it was one of the standard fighters of the Spanish Republicans during the Spanish Civil War, where it was called *Chato* (snub-nose) in the Republican Air Force.

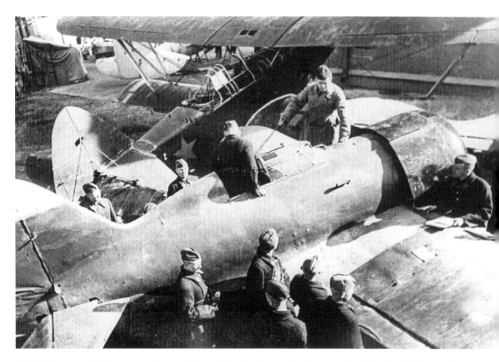

The Polikarpov I-16 was an advanced aircraft for its time when it made its debut in 1934, sporting retractable landing gear and a monoplane design. More than 9,000 I-16s were built and it served throughout the Second World War. This particular I-16 fighter is being used in the 'classroom' of the Soviet Army Air Force.

Sergey Vladimirovich Ilyushin, (1894-1977). Ilyushin (to the right in this 1933 photograph) was a Soviet aircraft designer who founded the Ilyushin aircraft design bureau. In 1933, Ilyushin became chief of TsKB at Moscow plant named after V. R. Menzhinski which later grew into the Ilyushin OKB in 1935. His Ilyushin Il-2 strike aircraft and Ilyushin Il-4 bomber were used extensively in the Second World War, with many thousands of aircraft produced.

The Ilyushin Il-2 Sturmovik was a ground-attack aircraft produced by the Soviet Union in large numbers during the Second World War. With some 36,163 examples of the Il-2 produced during and after the Second World War, it was the single most produced military aircraft design in aviation history. In this photograph: a line-up ready to attack, 1944. (*Via RART*)

Two-seater on the production line. Note the very prominent join lines on the armoured glass of the windscreen. The welding lines on the engine exhausts can also be clearly seen. This aircraft has a tall antenna mast indicating that it is either a late straight-winged two-seater or an arrow. (*Courtesy: G. F. Petrov photo archive*)

This is the crew of a straight-winged two-seater Il-2 Shturmovik of the 6th GvShAP, with the pilot Guards Junior Lieutenant V. A. Tarelkin and his gunner Guards Sergeant Aleksei Kaplin, taken on 21 July 1943. (*Via RART*)

Line up of brand new single-seater Il-2s at the factory in the summer of 1942. Note the three aiming lines on the upper cowling clearly seen on the nearest machine. (*Courtesy: Viktor Kulikov collection*)

This photograph, probably taken after the war, shows Sergey Ilyushin on the left, and the chief test pilot of the Ilyushin Design Bureau, Vladimir Kokkinaki, on the right. (*Courtesy: Viktor Kulikov collection*)

The Tupolev SB 'Katyusha' was in service from 1936 to 1944 with 6,656 having been built. Many Soviet SBs crashed or force-landed on Finnish soil during the Winter War against Russia, 30 November 1939–13 March 1940. The Finns salvaged as many aircraft as possible. This photograph shows salvaged SBs in Finnish service.

A closer look at a Tupolev SB in Finnish service.

After the Il-2 Shturmovik, the warplane built in most quantity was the Yakovlev series, Yak-1, (8,720 built), Yak-3, pictured here, (4,848 built) and the Yak 9 (below).

16,769 aircraft of the Yak 9 type were built between 1942 and 1948 including the variants Yak-9UV and Yak-9V trainers. The Yak-9 was the first Soviet aircraft to shoot down a Messerschmitt Me 262 jet.

Soviet Army officers interrogate a captured German soldier south of Voronezh, during the First Battle of Voronezh, 28 June - 24 July 1942. The Germans suffered 94,500 casualties including 19,000 KIA and MIA. The Russian losses were colossal, 290,522 killed, 80,000 captured and 197,825 wounded.

The Germans did not occupy Voronezh very long, for it was under the control of the Soviets again by 21 January 1943, albeit having suffered almost total destruction. The hard work of cleaning up the ruins of the plant, blown up by the Soviets themselves in July 1942, was started in earnest, and the new GAZ-64 repair plant was opened on 12 April 1943. In this photo Russian scouts reconnoitre for the counter-attack.

Opposite above: The aircraft factory at Voronezh was founded in 1932 as Voronezh Aviation Plant, branch registry number 18. In 2007, VASO became part of the Russian Federation state-owned United Aircraft Corporation (UAC). This Luftwaffe photograph of 19 May 1943 shows the plant from the height of 7,200 m after it had been repaired sufficiently to be back in action.

Il-2 Shturmovik assembly line at Kubyshev. Since 1992 Kuybyshev has been known as Samara. Kuybyshev was chosen to be the capital of the Soviet Union should Moscow fall to the Nazis. Kuybyshev played a major role in arming the country and from the very first months of the Second World War the city supplied the front with aircraft, firearms, and ammunition.

The Ilyushin Il-4 bomber had a long career. It came into service in 1941 and 5,256 were built. It served into the early 1950s and NATO gave it the reporting name '*Bob*'.

A torpedo being prepared for 'bombing up' an Ilyushin Il-4.

Soviet pilots and ground crew stand in front of a MiG-3 in what looks like a dug-out bunker hangar. The pilot in the front row, second from the right is Aleksandr Ivanovich Pokryshkin, the second-highest scoring ace in the Great Patriotic War, who flew the MiG-3 early in the war.

In what appears to be a posed propaganda photograph, aircrew stand at the tailplane of a Petlyakov Pe-2 'Peshka' bomber. Some 11,427 were built and it was in service from 1941 to the early 1950s. It had the NATO reporting name: 'Buck'.

MiG was formerly a Soviet design bureau, and was founded by Artem Mikoyan and Mikhail Gurevich as 'Mikoyan and Gurevich'. The first MiG fighter (MiG-1) appeared in 1940 and 3,120 MiG-3s were built between 1941 and 1945. This photograph shows a destroyed MiG-3 during *Operation Barbarossa*, 1941.

It was with the introduction of the jet engine in Russia that MiG came into their own. The first MiG-15 flew in 1949 and after that more than 12,000 were built. This particular MiG-15 was delivered to the US Air Force by a defecting North Korean pilot, September 1953.

The MiG-17 was introduced in 1952 and first saw combat in 1958 over the Straits of Taiwan. It was used as an effective threat against supersonic fighters of the United States in the Vietnam War. More than 11,000 were built and it was phased out in the 1970s. Its NATO reporting name was '*Fresco*'.

The MiG-17 was superseded by the MiG-19 and between 5,500 and 8,500 MiG-19s of all versions were produced, in the USSR, Czechoslovakia as the Avia S-105 and People's Republic of China as the Shenyang J-6. The aircraft saw service with a number of other national air forces, including those of Cuba, North Vietnam, Egypt, Pakistan, and North Korea. The aircraft saw combat during the Vietnam War, the 1967 Six Day War, and the 1971 Bangladesh War. All Soviet-built MiG-19 variants were single-seaters, but the Chinese developed a two-seat trainer version.

Perhaps the most important MiG fighter is the MiG-21, NATO reporting name '*Fishbed*'. It was in Russian service from 1959 to 1985 and it is the most volume-produced supersonic jet aircraft in aviation history with more than 11,000 having been built. It is still in service with some air forces more than 55 years after entering Soviet service. Photograph here, Batajnica Air Show 2009. *Courtesy Boksi*

From left to right: Mikhail Iosifovich Gurevich, (1893-1976) and Artem Mikoyan, (1905-1970). In 1937 Gurevich headed a designer team in the Polikarpov Design Bureau, where he met his future team partner Artem Mikoyan. In late 1939 they created the Mikoyan-Gurevich Design Bureau, with Gurevich in the position of Vice Chief Designer, and after 1957 as its Chief Designer. The last model Gurevich worked on was the MiG-25 interceptor, which is among the fastest military aircraft ever to enter service. From 1952 Mikoyan also designed missile systems to particularly suit their aircraft, such as the famous MiG-21. He continued to produce high performance fighters through the 1950s and 1960s.

The MiG-25, NATO reporting name '*Foxbat*'. The MiG-25 is a supersonic interceptor and reconnaissance aircraft that was among the fastest military aircraft to enter service. The prototype flew in 1964 and the aircraft entered service in 1970 with a top speed of Mach 2.83. The appearance of the MiG-25 sparked serious concern in the West and prompted dramatic increases in performance for the McDonnell Douglas F-15 Eagle then under development in the late 1960s. The capabilities of the MiG-25 were better understood in 1976 when Soviet pilot Viktor Belenko defected in a MiG-25 to the United States via Japan. *Courtesy: Leonid Faerberg (transport-photo.com)*

Production of the MiG-25 series ended in 1984 after completion of 1,190 aircraft. It is one of the highest-flying military aircraft, and the second fastest after the SR-71 reconnaissance aircraft. *Courtesy: Dmitry A. Mottl*

Andrei Nikolayevich Tupolev, (centre). On the extreme right is the future chief designer of the Tu-128, Iosif F. Nezpal; on the extreme left is the lead designer of the Tu-98 project, Dmitry S. Markov. During his career, Andrei Tupolev, (1888-1972), designed and oversaw the design of more than 100 types of aircraft, some of which set 78 world records. In 1937 Tupolev had been arrested on trumped up charges of sabotage, espionage and of aiding the Russian Fascist Party. He was tried and convicted in 1940 with a ten-year sentence. During this time he developed the Tupolev Tu-2. He was released in July 1941 'to conduct important defence work' but was not rehabilitated fully until two years after Stalin's death in 1953. *Courtesy OAO Tupolev*

Tupolev headed the major project of reverse engineering the American Boeing B-29 strategic bomber, which was the world's first nuclear delivery platform. The USSR had repeatedly asked unsuccessfully for lend-lease B-29s. Using three machines which landed in Siberia after bombing Japan in 1945, Tupolev succeeded in replicating them down to trivial detail. Moreover, he got it into volume production, with crews fully trained in time for the 1947 May Day parade. The copy was designated Tu-4, with many subsequent Tu aircraft having the number 4 in their designations. Photo: Tupolev Tu-4 at Monino, 2006. *Courtesy: Pavel Adzhigildaev*

Following on from the Tu-4 the Tupolev design bureau began work on the Tu-88, and the prototype first flew in 1952. After winning a competition against the Ilyushin Il-46, it was approved for production in December 1952. The first bombers entered service with Frontal Aviation in 1954, receiving the service designation Tu-16. It was given the NATO reporting name 'Badger-A'. Including variants, a total of 1,509 Tu-16 bombers were built and it remained in service until 1993. Photo: 1985, Soviet maritime reconnaissance variant, most likely Tu-16R (Badger E).

Tu-16s in the service of the Egyptian Air Force, 1980. *Courtesy: Donald Sutherland*

The Tupolev Tu-95, NATO reporting name 'Bear'. The Tu-95 is a large, four-engine turboprop-powered strategic bomber. The prototype first flew in 1952 and the Tu-95 entered service in 1956. More than 500 were built between 1956 and 1994. It is expected to remain in service until at least 2040. Photo: Tupolev Tu-95MS (28 RED) at Engels Air Force Base, Russia, 2006. *Courtesy: Marina Lystseva*

A Tu-95 Bear 'H' photographed from a RAF Typhoon Quick Reaction Alert aircraft (QRA) with 6 Squadron from RAF Leuchars in Scotland. RAF Typhoon Quick Reaction Alert aircraft were launched from RAF Leuchars to determine the identity of unknown aircraft that approached the NATO Air Policing Area north of Scotland and could not be identified by other means. The aircraft were subsequently identified as Russian military reconnaissance (Bears). The Bears remained in international airspace. Photo: 23 April 2014. *Courtesy: Ministry of Defence*

The Tupolev Tu-144 is one of only two SSTs to enter commercial service, the other being the Anglo-French Concorde. The design, publicly unveiled in January 1962, was constructed in the Soviet Union under the direction of the Tupolev design bureau, headed by Alexei Tupolev, (1925-2001), the son of Andrei. Photo 1977. *Courtesy: Christian Volpati*

The Tu-144 first went supersonic on 5 June 1969, and on 26 May 1970 became the first commercial transport to exceed Mach 2. A Tu-144 crashed in 1973 at the Paris Air Show, delaying its further development. The aircraft was introduced into passenger service on 1 November 1977, almost two years after Concorde, the delay being due to budget restrictions. The Tu-144 was later used by the Soviet space programme to train pilots of the Buran spacecraft, and by NASA for supersonic research. Photo MAKS-2007. *Courtesy: Elizeu Cardoso de Oliveira*

The Tupolev Tu-128, NATO reporting name: '*Fiddler*'. The Tu-128 was a long-range interceptor aircraft introduced by the Soviet Union in the 1960s. It was the largest and heaviest fighter ever in service. 198 were built and it entered service in 1966 and was retired in 1990. For many years this was the best photograph available of an operational Tu-128, taken by former USAF captain 'Zot' Barazzotto in June 1972. *Courtesy: 'Zot' Barazzotto*

An elegant study of the Tu-128 (here a Tu-128M) which emphasises the long wheelbase of this huge fighter. *Courtesy Nikolai Popov*

The Yakovlev Yak-38, NATO reporting name: '*Forger*'. The Yak-38 was the Soviet Navy's only operational VTOL strike fighter aircraft, in addition to being its first operational carrier-based fixed-wing aircraft. It was developed specifically for and served almost exclusively on the Kiev-class aircraft carriers. 231 were built and it entered service in 1976, but was retired by 1991. Photo: the right side view of a Soviet Yak-38 '*Forger*' aircraft on the deck of a Soviet aircraft carrier. *Courtesy U.S. Navy*

The Ilyushin Il-76, NATO reporting name: '*Candid*'. The Il-76 is a multi-purpose four-engine turbofan strategic transport aircraft designed for delivering heavy machinery to remote, poorly served areas of the USSR. Military versions of the Il-76 have seen widespread use in Europe, Asia and Africa, including use as an airborne refuelling tanker. More than 960 have been built since it entered service in 1974. Photo: 1 April 2010. *Courtesy: Igor Dvurekov*

The Mil Mi-17, NATO reporting name '*Hip*'. The Mi-17 was mass-produced with over 17,000 built between 1977 and the present day. In Russian service it is known as the Mi-8M, but it has been widely exported as the Mi-17. Photo: An Afghan Mi-17 helicopter flown takes off for an air-assault training flight, 29 May 2013 from Kabul International Airport. *Courtesy: Todd Pouliot*

The Mil Mi-24, NATO reporting name '*Hind*'. The Mi-24 is a large gunship attack helicopter and low-capacity troop transport with room for eight passengers. It has been operated since 1972 by the Soviet Air Force and the Russian Federation and remains in service. It is also in service with more than 30 other countries and it is estimated that about 2,300 have been built. Photo: 10 August 2012. *Courtesy: Dmitry Zherdin*

The Beriev A-50, NATO reporting name '*Mainstay*'. The A-50 is an Airborne early warning and control aircraft based on the design of the Ilyushin Il-76 transport. It entered service in 1984, with about 40 produced by 1992. It currently remains in service. The A-50 can control up to 10 fighter aircraft for either air-to-air intercept or air-to-ground attack missions. Photo: 2011. *Courtesy: Alex Beltyukov*

The Tupolev Tu-22M, NATO reporting name '*Backfire*'. The Tu-22M is a supersonic, variable-sweep wing, long-range strategic and maritime strike bomber. About 497 were built between 1967 and 1997 and more than 100 remain in service. The Tu-22M was first used in combat in Afghanistan, from 1987 to 1989. It is capable of dropping large tonnages of conventional ordnance. The Russian Federation used the Tu-22M3 in combat in Chechnya during 1995, performing strikes near Grozny. Photo: Russian Air Force Tupolev Tu-22M3 at Ryazan Dyagilevo. *Courtesy: Alex Beltyukov*

The Sukhoi Su-27, NATO reporting name '*Flanker*' is a twin-engine fighter designed by Sukhoi. It was intended as a direct competitor for the large United States fourth-generation fighters. The Su-27 entered service with the Soviet Air Force in 1985 and remains in service with the Russian Air Force. Photo: Sukhoi Su-27SKM multirole fighter at MAKS-2005 air show. *Courtesy: Dmitriy Pichugin*

A Russian Su-27 and a British Typhoon meet over the Baltic, 17 June 2014. RAF Typhoons were scrambled to intercept multiple Russian aircraft as part of NATO's ongoing mission to police Baltic airspace. The Typhoon aircraft, from 3 (Fighter) Squadron, were launched after four separate groups of aircraft were detected by NATO air defences in international airspace near to the Baltic States. Once airborne, the British jets identified the aircraft as a Russian Tupolev Tu22 '*Backfire*' bomber, four Sukhoi Su27 '*Flanker*' fighters, one Beriev A50 '*Mainstay*' early warning aircraft and an Antonov An26 '*Curl*' transport aircraft who appeared to be carrying out a variety of routine training. The Russian aircraft were monitored by the RAF Typhoons and escorted on their way. *Courtesy: Ministry of Defence*

The Tupolev Tu-160 'White Swan', NATO reporting name: '*Blackjack*'. The Tu-160 is the world's largest combat aircraft, largest supersonic aircraft and largest variable-sweep aircraft built. The Tu-160 has the heaviest take-off weight of any military aircraft apart from transports. Entering service in 1987, the Tu-160 was the last strategic bomber designed for the Soviet Union.

The Tu-160M modernisation programme has begun and the first new updated aircraft were delivered in December 2014. Newly built bombers will be fitted with new engines, new radars and new avionics. These future production aircraft are referred as Tu-160M2. Even though they will look similar they will, essentially, be a new aircraft.

On Thursday 10 September 2015 RAF Typhoon pilots were sent from RAF Lossiemouth in Scotland, spotted two Russian aircraft including this Tu-160 and escorted them while they were 'in the UK area of interest'. *Courtesy: Ministry of Defence*

The Sukhoi T-50 is the name of the prototype, a stealthy, single-seat, twin-engine jet fighter, and will be the first operational aircraft in Russian service to use stealth technology. It is a multirole fighter designed for air superiority and attack roles. The fighter is planned to have super-cruise, stealth, supermanoeuvrability, and advanced avionics to overcome the prior generation of fighter aircraft as well as ground and maritime defences. Photo: T-50 stealth multirole aircraft at MAKS-2011 air show *Courtesy: Alex Beltyukov*

The T-50 prototype first flew on 29 January 2010 and the first production aircraft is scheduled for delivery to the Russian Air Force starting in 2016 or 2017. It is intended to be the successor to the MiG-29 and Su-27 in the Russian Air Force and serve as the basis for the Fifth Generation Fighter Aircraft being co-developed by Sukhoi and Hindustan Aeronautics Limited for the Indian Air Force. The prototypes and initial production batch will be delivered with a highly upgraded variant of the AL-31F used by the Su-27 family as interim engines while newly designed engines are under development. The aircraft is expected to have a service life of up to 35 years. Photo: T-50 stealth multirole aircraft at MAKS-2011 air show. *Courtesy: Dmitry Zherdin*

Lavochkin joined another Frenchman, André Laville, at the Bureau of New Design (BNK) and was made responsible for aerodynamic and stress calculations for the DI-4 two-seat fighters. Working under him were former colleagues S. N. Lyushin, L. S. Kamennomostsky and E. S. Felsner. However, development of the DI-4 was abandoned and Lavochkin went to work at the Zhukovsky Aviation Academy, initially with Prof. S. G. Kozlov on the 'Gigant' (Giant) aircraft, but shortly afterwards joined V. A. Chizhevski at the Bureau of Special Design (BOK) to work on a project for a stratosphere fighter.

In 1935, Lavochkin joined the NKTP (People's Commissariat for Heavy Industry) where he worked with Lyushin under L. V. Kurchevsky on the LL (Lavochkin Lyushin) single-seat fighter, which was built during the winter of 1935/36 and was armed with a Kurchevsky APK heavy-calibre recoilless cannon. By then Lavochkin was a senior engineer in the Chief Administration of the Aviation Industry (GUAP), and in 1939 he joined with Vladimir Gorbunov and Mikhail Gudkov to design the I-22 (LaGG-1) single-seat fighter of all-wood construction. A new OKB to develop the project and build seven prototypes had been established at the end of 1938.

The LaGG-1 was the first of a series of fighters that remained in production from 1940 until 1950, of which a dozen or so prototypes were built. In production, large-scale use was made of Bakelite plywood and the majority of the aircraft were fitted with the M-82 radial engine. The production version of the LaGG-1, designated LaGG-3, was to become a highly successful wartime fighter, nearly 23,000 of which were built, despite being difficult to fly and unpopular with Soviet pilots. When the OKB was evacuated in 1941, Gudkov remained at the Moscow factory where he produced an M-82-powered LaGG-3 as the Gu-82 and the Gu-1, but the Gudkov OKB was closed down in 1943 after the loss of the Gu-1 prototype.

Gorbunov had been transferred to other work by the end of 1943 and, during a low period in the OKB's fortunes, Lavochkin was left with only a small nucleus of his design staff to develop the La-5 in secret. However, Lavochkin was awarded the State Prize for the La-5 design, which was powered by a radial rather than an inline engine. He continued at OKB-301 at Khimki near Moscow until the end of the war, to further the development of Lavochkin fighters, resulting in the all-metal La-9 in 1946 and the La-11 in 1947, Lavochkin winning State Prizes for both these designs. The La-11 was the last Soviet-designed piston-engined fighter.

Although the first Soviet jet fighters to fly were designed by the Mikoyan-Gurevich and Yakovlev design teams, the Lavochkin OKB also established a number of firsts in the Soviet Union associated with the development of gas turbine fighters. These included producing the first Soviet fighter equipped with reheat (La-150M), the first Soviet aircraft with a thin laminar wing section (La-152) and the first swept-wing Soviet fighter (La-160) as well as the La-190, La-200 and the La-250 in 1950. In 1951, the Lavochkin OKB worked on Object 201 (a drone La-17 series), followed by work on Objects 205, 207 and 400, produced respectively as the SA-1, SA-2 and SA-5 surface-to-air missiles (SAMs). Lavochkin started work in April 1953 on Object 350 or the La-Kh winged missile to attack the US, but the project was cancelled in 1957. Lavochkin died on 9 June 1960 at Moscow in an accident whilst testing the SA-5, and on 11 November 1962, under his successor M. M. Pashinin, the Lavochkin OKB became Chelomey's Filial No. 2 for missile development only.

***

In January 1939, Lavochkin attended the Kremlin conference called to discuss the strategy with regard to future Soviet combat aircraft and received permission to build a prototype fighter, the I-22. At the same time he was given approval to base his design bureau at Khimki. The I-22 was a standard fighter of conventional design and all-wood construction. It had a narrow oval fuselage section with integral fin. The wings were constructed of close-spaced ribs with two box spars and a Bakelite-ply skin of 3 mm thickness, with duralumin control surfaces with fabric covering. It had a hydraulically operated main landing gear and later a retractable tail wheel, and was powered by a 783 kW (1,050 hp) Klimov M-105P inline engine driving a three-bladed propeller. Armament comprised one ShVAK 20 mm cannon and two ShKAS 7.6 mm machine guns in the top decking.

Development of the I-22 began in May 1939, the aircraft making its first flight as the LaGG-1 on 30 March 1940 with pilot Nikashin, who found that the aircraft was short on range, had poor manoeuvrability and could be dangerous to the novice pilot. Immediately a programme was put in hand to rectify the faults, and after a number of structural and control refinements had been made, the improved I-301 prototype was produced and state tests started on 14 June 1940. The prototype was found to be a major all-round improvement on its predecessor and was ordered into series production on 29 July, at GAZ-21 at Gorky, GAZ-23 at Leningrad, GAZ-31 at Taganrog and GAZ-153 at Novosibirsk. To assist the series production 'start-up' Lavochkin was sent to Gorky, Gudkov to Leningrad and Gorbunov to Taganrog. In January 1941, the series aircraft were redesignated LaGG-3 and at the same time a production plan was established; 805 LaGG-3s were to be produced by 1 July, and 2,960 before 31 December 1941.

The first series aircraft was finished in January 1941 and the first batch of 100 were completed by early May. However, the quality of the production aircraft appeared to be very poor and it was for this reason that Stalin ordered on 31 May that the plant should concentrate on quality, not quantity. By 22 June, a total of 322 LaGG-3s had been completed, but the fatalities and write-offs in training were so high that morale among new LaGG-3 pilots had reached an all-time low. This was the reason why there were very few LaGG-3s based near the border at the time of the Wehrmacht attack on 22 June 1941. No. 6 Corps of the PVO in the Moscow area had only seventy-five new LaGG-3s out of a total inventory of 585 elderly fighters, but Batch 7 series aircraft had been completed by September 1941. Until this time the LaGG-3's armament was one ShVAK 20 mm cannon, one UBS 12.7 mm and two ShKAS 7.62 mm machine guns, but from Batch 8 onwards the ShKAS machine guns were deleted, in preference for eight RS-82 rockets or two FAB-50 bombs. It was at this time that both GAZ-23 and GAZ-31 were evacuated, the latter to Tbilisi. Even so, in the six months from July to December 1941, a total of 2,141 LaGG-3s were produced, many more than the Yak-1s in production at the same time. In early 1942, the LaGG-3 was an important fighter for the Red Air Force. For instance, on the Moscow front on 22 February it had eight LaGG-3 regiments out of a total of twenty-five (without the PVO).

An attempt was made to improve the aircraft's performance in April 1942, when two LaGG-3s were fitted with the more powerful 1,223 kW (1,640 hp) Shvetsov ASh-82 radial engines. GAZ-21 at Gorky also built a LaGG-3U prototype called 'Sparka', and in June 1942, LaGG-3s from Batch 29 were fitted with a 903 kW (1,210 hp) Klimov M-105PF engine to replace the earlier 820 kW (1,100 hp) M-105 fitted to early series aircraft. However, GAZ-21 ceased production of the LaGG-3 in August 1942 after producing 3,583 and GAZ-153 had already stopped production earlier in the year after producing only 330, leaving only GAZ-31 as the sole producer of the aircraft, where a number of new sub-types were introduced. Batch 34 had a 37 mm NS-37 cannon, and Batches 35 and 36 saw the introduction of the retractable rear wheel, although some aircraft of Batch 28 had already been built with this improvement (to reduce drag). In 1942, a total of 2,771 LaGG-3s were built, at which time many Soviet fighter regiments (e.g. 5 IAP, 88, 129, 131, 145, 156, 160, 162, 168, 172, 178, 182, 193, 234, 267, 297, 348, 413, 431, 435, 440, 513, etc.) were equipped with the type.

In 1943, GAZ-31 at Tbilisi built a further 1,065 LaGG-3s, and a further 229 up until March 1944. Total production was 6,528 aircraft in sixty-six batches, of which GAZ-31 built 2,550. On 1 October 1944, the Red Air Force still had 219 LaGG-3s in service on the German Front but the inventory was decreasing fast. Outside the Soviet Union, during the Second World War, Finland used three captured LaGG-3 aircraft, whilst Japan tested one in which a defecting Soviet pilot had landed at Manchukuo in 1942.

Instructions were sent to the Lavochkin, MiG and Yakovlev design bureaux in August 1941 to fit a recently qualified Shvetsov air-cooled M-82 engine to their fighters. The reason for this order was to safeguard the major fighter programmes against possible shortages or serious problems arising from existing engines. Gudkov had already undertaken this exercise independently with his Gu-82 design, albeit without success. Lavochkin received plenty of help from the Shvetsov engine team, and along with fellow designer Alekseyev endeavoured to ensure that the engine change was used to maximum advantage in the LaGG-3, work beginning at GAZ-31 in late September that year. The diameter of the new radial engine was 1.26 m (4 feet 2 inches) as compared to the 0.78m (2 feet 6 inches) of the M-105P already in use, and weighed 850 kg (1,875 lb) instead of the 600 kg (1,320 lb) of the earlier powerplant. Lavochkin's designers produced an outstanding installation with the new unit, with a tightly fitting cowling with a central fairing over the reduction gear, and radial controllable cooling air vanes were located behind the large spinner and exhaust pipes arranged to left and right. The supercharger was located on the top, and the oil cooler underneath. Seat armour was now 10 mm thick, with the cockpit and rear fuselage section remaining unchanged and an armament of two 20 mm ShVAK cannon. The changes were completed by December 1941, but the severe winter and various teething troubles delayed the first flight until March 1942, initial tests indicating that a further number of detailed changes were necessary. As a result, in late March 1942, NII VVS test pilots were extremely impressed with the fighter and Nikashin conveyed this to Stalin personally, and a crash programme of state trials was undertaken using two prototypes. In May, with the country in urgent need of a more powerful fighter and aware that at GAZ-19 at Perm there were at least 2,000 M-82 engines stockpiled, Stalin ordered the new fighter to be placed into production as the La-5 and that M-82 engines should be fitted to all other available production LaGG airframes. Control of GAZ-21 at Gorky was restored to Lavochkin. The first ten La-5s were completed in August 1942, and by the autumn several regiments near Stalingrad were already equipped with the type in readiness for the Battle of Stalingrad in October. Of simple design and rugged construction, the La-5 proved to be a perfect low-altitude fighter and was universally acclaimed, earning Lavochkin the title 'Hero of Socialist Labour'.

In 1942, 1,107 La-5s were built at GAZ-21, with a further twenty-two built at GAZ-31. On completion of the last La-5 based on the earlier LaGG-3 airframes, an improved rear canopy fitted with 75 mm bulletproof glazing was introduced to a cut-down rear fuselage in order to improve rearward vision and, in December 1942, the M-82F replaced the original engine. At the end of March 1943, the important direct-injection ASh-82FN engine became a standard, which when fitted to the standard La-5 gave rise to the La-5FN. In an effort to reduce training-familiarisation losses, a tandem dual-seat La-5UTI trainer variant was produced and tested in August and September 1943. Series production man-hours on the type were progressively reduced by up to 40 per cent, which had the effect of greatly increasing the output of what at the time was the best Soviet fighter. GAZ-21 built 619 in 1943, GAZ-31 only five, but two new production lines were established, at GAZ-99 at Ulan-Ude and GAZ-381 at Yaroslav, producing 184 and 240 aircraft respectively.

The first La-5FN regiments saw action in the Battle of Kursk in July 1943, with great success, although Soviet losses still remained extremely high. From 1-15 July, the Luftwaffe destroyed 907 Soviet fighters, among which were a large number of La-5s. Throughout 1943, the Soviet Air Force lost an average of 300 La-5s per month. In May 1944, a new wing with D1 duralumin spar webs and 30KhGSA booms was introduced to the sub-type La-5FN Type 41. The smaller spar dimensions saved 172 kg (380 lb) of structural weight, permitting an internal fuel increase of 560 litres (123 gallons). However, 1944 saw an overall reduction in output of the La-5—GAZ-21 built 3,503; GAZ-99, 102; and GAZ-301, 221—due to the series introduction of the La-7 aircraft, which used the new wing of the Type 41 matched to a new and improved fuselage. From 1942 to 1944, a total of 10,003 La-5s were built, 92.26 per cent of the output at the giant GAZ-21 plant at Gorky.

On 1 October 1944, the Soviet Air Force had a total of 2,417 La-5s, and the new La-7 with a maximum speed of 665 kph (413 mph) was in use on the German Front.

The La-5FN was supplied to the Guards Fighter Units and to others located at the most vital front-line sectors. The aircraft was often chosen as a 'personal mount' by Soviet fighter aces such as Ivan Kozhedub, 'Hero of the Soviet Union' with sixty-two kills between 26 March 1943 and 19 April 1945, all in Lavochkin fighters, while other La-5FNs were personal mounts of high-ranking officers commanding VVS units, which might be flying operationally outside the Soviet Union. In the spring of 1944, pilots of the newly formed 128th Independent Czechoslovak Fighter Squadron began conversion via the La-5UTI trainer to the La-5FN, a total of five La-5UTIs and twenty-four La-5FNs being received. Later the Czechoslovak Air Force received a further six La-5UTIs and twenty-eight La-5FNs, and still had a UTI trainer and twenty-three FN single-seat fighters in use on 1 July 1948.

By late 1943, the Soviet Union had received 145,000 tonnes of aluminium from Canada, the UK and the US to bolster the shortfall in its aircraft production. At the same time, the Lavochkin OKB proceeded with further development of the La-7 fighter, the most important difference from the La-5 being in its construction with replacement of the wooden box main spar by a new I-section spar with Chromansil steel flanges and duralumin web. Not only did this reduce the weight of the wing by 95 kg (210 lb), it also provided more space for fuel. A number of refinements were also made to fuselage aerodynamics, especially with regard to the engine installation. The two large air intakes on the cowling were combined in an undercarriage scoop situated level with the trailing edge of the wing, although wing-root intakes for the engine compressor were retained. On occasion a radio direction finding loop was fitted behind the cockpit. Various armament fits of either two or three ShVAK 20 mm cannon or, with later batches, two or three new 20 mm Berezin B-20 cannon were used.

The new La-120 prototype was built at Yaroslav and was flown for the first time on 19 November 1943 by Adamovich. It proved to be an outstanding aircraft, and NII VVS trials took place between January and April 1944. The La-7 entered VVS service in May 1944 after successful trials, but did not replace the La-5FNs. It appears to have been produced purely as an interceptor for use by the famous IAPs (fighter regiments) and a number of the top Soviet aces to try and catch the Focke-Wulf Fw 190 A-8. Some La-7s were fitted with small rocket booster engines to increase combat speed momentarily, receiving the designation La-7R, and a two-seat trainer/recce/liaison version was produced as the La-7UTI. A high-altitude variant, the La-7TK, was also tested in 1944. GAZ-21 at Gorky had built 1,588 La-7s, GAZ-99 at Ulan-Ude forty, and GAZ-381 at Yaroslav 638, giving a total of 2,266 in 1944. On 1 October that year, there were 2,417 La-5s and La-7s on the German Front.

In January 1945, an experimental La-7A with a 1,492 kW (2,000 hp) ASh-83 engine and two 23 mm NS-23 cannon made its maiden flight. It had a maximum speed of 725 kph (450 mph), but with the end of the war in Europe in sight, development was halted. Even so, in 1945, the La-7s were used extensively over Germany, Hungary and Poland. On 15 February 1945, flying a Lavochkin La-7, Ivan Kozhedub was the only

Soviet pilot in the Second World War to engage and destroy a Messerschmitt Me 262 jet aircraft. However, in general, losses of Lavochkin La-7s were heavy, with about 900 destroyed until 10 May 1945.

La-7 production still continued after the collapse of the Third Reich in 1945. In the same year, GAZ-21 built 2,799; GAZ-99, 210; and GAZ-381, 660: a total of 3,669 for 1945 alone. Both Ulan-Ude and Yaroslav had ceased production of the La-7 by VJ Day, but Gorky continued until early 1946, producing a further fifty-three. Total La-7 production was 5,988 in just two years, as opposed to 10,003 La-5s in three years. Czech fighter units based in the Soviet Union had also received La-7s from June 1944. After 1946, the new Czechoslovak Air Force received an additional sixty, which were eventually replaced in the 1950s by the MiG-15. Those La-5s that remained in Soviet service at the war's end were soon replaced by the La-7, although these were to be slowly replaced by the new La-9/11 escort fighters fitted with four 23 mm cannon, which remained in post-war Soviet Air Force service for many years, NATO code-named the 'Fin'.

Throughout the 1940s, with the advent of the jet engine, the Soviet physicist Vladimir Struminsky and aerodynamicist Sergey Hristianovich carried out a study involving a series of laboratory and wind tunnel tests examining the behaviour of different wings and other aerodynamic objects at near supersonic speeds. In 1944, the Lavochkin OKB requested permission to use the results of these investigations to help with its new aircraft designs, and over the next two years the design bureau developed a series of experimental aircraft. The first was the La-150 jet. The all-metal, high-wing aircraft received an RD-10 jet engine (a Soviet copy of the Junkers Jumo 004B turbojet) from the Kazan engine plant and featured a split-nose air intake with the jet flux (exhaust) leaving the engine at the bottom of the rear fuselage. The main undercarriage struts were spaced 1.82m (6 feet) apart and, along with the nose-wheel, could be fully retracted into the fuselage. Armament was provided by two 23 mm NS-23 guns located in the nose, each with a maximum of 150 shells. The prototype jet made its first flight in September 1946, flown by A. A. Popov five months after the Yak-15 had flown. During the test flights a series of shortcomings were observed, and for this reason the second prototype, marked '21', underwent a number of aerodynamic changes. Its vertical surfaces were increased by 24 per cent and larger fuel tanks were introduced, together with improved insulation for the jet engine and a flat windscreen to improve the pilot's vision. Unfortunately the improvements had an adverse effect on the aircraft's handling characteristics by virtue of the increased weight, but in spite of this, fifteen pre-series aircraft were built and used satisfactorily by the Soviet Air Force as the La-13 for a short period of time during the spring of 1947.

Lisunov (Li-2)

The engineer assigned to supervise the Soviet productionisation of the Douglas DC-3 was Boris Pavlovich Lisunov. When he was at the company's plant at Santa Monica in California between November 1936 and April 1939, he went over every part of the aircraft—its design, development, production jigs, tooling and in-service support. Despite his requests to avoid engineering changes, the Soviet Ministry of Aviation Industry ordered no fewer than 1,293 changes involving design, dimensions, materials and processing. The engines were also completely different, the original 895 kW (1,200 hp) Pratt & Whitney engines being replaced by the Soviet M-62IR, which in turn were replaced by the AV-7N in 1940. The aircraft was produced at Khimki (GAZ-84), and received the original designation PS-84. Soviet-built aircraft entered service with Aeroflot in June 1940, although only a few were delivered.

In January 1941, the type designation was revised to Li-2 and production concentrated on two military variants: Li-2D (airborne) and Li-2T (military transport). Again, only a handful of aircraft were built owing to the evacuation of the Khimki factory in October 1941 to Tashkent, where the plant was renumbered to GAZ-184, but production there was very slow due to a multitude of problems. Fortunately shipments of Douglas DC-3/C-47s from the US began in January 1943, and the 1st Detached Aviation Division received the first fourteen for operations on the Central Front in March 1943. Eventually the Red Air Force received a total of 707 C-47s directly from the US during the Second World War, and Soviet Transport Units such as the 1st Transport Division at Moscow-Vnukovo and a number of other Guards Transport Units were actually fully equipped with American aircraft. They undertook supply tasks to partisan units and evacuation of wounded troops and PoWs, and on a number of occasions were know to fly out agricultural produce from behind German lines. Prior to the arrival of the American DC-3s, the situation was particularly desperate for the Soviets on the transport front, which can be judged from the fact that in June 1942, eleven G-2s (transport TB-3s) were used to fly urgently needed ball-bearings and electrical assemblies and components to plants involved in army tank production.

Tashkent-built Li-2s were mostly the long-range bomber variant, designated Li-2DB. The aircraft was capable of carrying a payload of 1,000 kg (2,205 lb) and four machine guns were fitted. The Li-2R reconnaissance variant was also produced at the plant. In April 1943, Long Range Aviation II Corps was equipped entirely with Li-2DB aircraft and V Corps with a mixture of Li-2DB and Ilyushin DB-3 long-range bombers, and by 1945, Long Range Aviation had nineteen regiments equipped with 589 'bombers'. At this time the bomb load carried was often increased to 2,000 kg (4,409 lb).

During the Second World War, a total of 2,930 Li-2s were built, and GAZ-184 continued to build both military and civil variants after the war: Li-2P passenger aircraft and Li-2G freighters as well as Li-2D and Li-2T variants. Owing to the enormous needs of the Soviet Air Force, Aeroflot, the Soviet economy, and Soviet satellite states, a new production line was established at GAZ-126 in Komsomolsk, but this plant produced only a small quantity of Li-2s as it had already had been converted (in May 1949) for MiG-15 jet fighter production.

In 1952, the Tashkent plant, renamed GAZ-234, continuously increased Li-2 production as the Ilyushin Il-12 had ceased production in 1949, and the Li-2 and the smaller Antonov An-2 were the only Soviet transport aircraft available at this time. Despite all the production difficulties, the final total of Soviet-built Li-2s up until 1953 was 6,157, many of which remained in service in the Soviet Union and its many satellite and client countries long after production had ceased.

Mikoyan-Gurevich (MiG)

Artem Ivanovich Mikoyan was born on 5 August 1905 in Armenia. He was the brother of Stalin's former foreign minister Anastas Ivanovich Mikoyan and was admitted to the training school of a factory in Rostov in 1923. Two years later he was employed as a turner at the Dynamo Factory in Moscow, but in December 1928 he left to do his national service. Discharged two years later, he returned to Moscow to work as a draughtsman at the Kompressor Factory and it was here that he became interested in aviation. In 1931, he entered the Zhukovsky Aviation Academy where, with the assistance of two fellow students, he built himself an ultra-light aircraft named 'Oktyabronok'. In 1937, having obtained a first class diploma, he entered GAZ-1 as a military representative for the VVS controlling the preparation of I-153 production, where his position brought him into regular contact with the designer Polikarpov.

Mikhail Iosifovich Gurevich was born in 1893 near Kursk. After finishing high school he entered the advanced mathematics programme at Kharkov University and attended Montpellier University in France from 1913. He left Kharkov University Technological Institute in 1925 with a diploma and four years later entered Paul-Aimé Richard's OKB. He subsequently moved to the Kocherigin team, playing a leading part in the design of the TSh-3 (TsKB-4) armoured ground attack monoplane. When Mikoyan joined the Polikarpov OKB, Gurevich was a deputy chief designer at the TsKB, the two men becoming close friends.

In 1937, Gurevich was sent to the US to negotiate the Douglas DC-3 licence. On his return at the end of 1938, he also joined the Polikarpov OKB to take charge of the Projects Department. In October 1939, Stalin invited three men from the Polikarpov OKB to the Kremlin, and in the absence of Polikarpov, who was in Germany, he enquired as to the situation in respect of the 'Kh' interceptor project. When it was proposed that Artem Mikoyan should take charge of the project and manage a new OKB team, Stalin snarled and said, 'What! Anastas's brother! He has never even made a development!' before finally saying, 'OK, it's up to you.' The following day, Mikoyan, who was taken completely by surprise, agreed to the unexpected proposal only on condition that he could take his old friend Gurevich with him as his assistant. The new OKB was created towards the end of the year, and on 8 December, having attained full strength, it was appointed to develop the Polikarpov 'Kh' project, renamed I-200. In March 1940, Polikarpov was displaced to GAZ-51 and Mikoyan was appointed Chief Constructor at GAZ-1, with Gurevich as his deputy.

By December 1940 the aircraft had been redesignated MiG-1, and in the same month the first MiG-3 was produced. The MiG-3 was built in large quantities and was only taken out of production in 1942 when manufacture of the 1,007 kW (1,350 hp) Mikulin AM-35 engine ceased. From 1942, a new OKB was built at GAZ-155 in Moscow, and several experimental development aircraft using alternative engines were produced. Among these was the I-270, based on the Junkers Ju 248 (Me 263), a more advanced version of the Me 163 rocket plane. The I-270 was a new design, although its fuselage and landing gear bore a striking resemblance to the German designs. However, unlike the Me 263, it had a straight wing and a horizontal tail—the first T-tail used on any Soviet aircraft. The Soviet Dushkin-Glushko RD-2M-3W rocket engine gave the I-270 a more realistic endurance than that returned by the early German rocket fighters and was designed to achieve 1,000 kph (620 mph) at 17,600 m (57,750 feet). Two I-270s were built, the first of which flew in 1947, but both were destroyed in tests that year and no further work on operational rocket fighters was carried out in the Soviet Union.

It was not until 1946 that another MiG design was adopted for series production. This was the I-300/F (MiG-9), which shared with the Yak-15 the honour of being the first Soviet jet fighter, albeit powered by a Soviet copy of the German BMW 003A turbojet. The MiG-9 featured a new thin-wing section with increased relative thickness at the tips designed to improve aileron effectiveness and prevent tip stall. The new wing had first been introduced on the experimental I-250/N mixed powerplant interceptor in 1945. Only around 500 of the MiG-9 were built as it was not a particularly effective design, having been derived from the Me 262.

Ever since the introduction into service of the renowned swept-wing MiG-15 in 1947, believed by some to have been derived from the Focke-Wulf Ta 183 Huckebein X-plane, MiGs have dominated the Soviet Air Force's air defence fighter arm, along with the similar MiG-17, the MiG-19 and the delta-wing MiG-21, which has been the most widely exported Soviet aircraft of all types since the war. Around 2,000 MiG-21*bis* variants and upgrades (such as the Romanian Lancer) and its Chinese-built derivatives (1,161) remain in use, second in numbers only to the ubiquitous American F-16 Fighting Falcon.

In 1952, Mikoyan assumed responsibility for the design and production of cruise missiles from Chelomey, giving rise to a whole series based on MiG-15 aerodynamics. Later, in the early 1960s, following the dissolution of the Tsybin and Myasishchev OKBs, Korolev began discussing development of a winged space launcher with Mikoyan. Gleb Lozino-Lozinsky was placed in charge of development of the Spiral OS reusable space launch system, but Mikoyan did not live to see the test flights of the spacecraft that took place towards the end of the year—he died on 9 December 1970. Although failing health had caused Gurevich to leave the MiG OKB in the early 1960s, he actually outlived Mikoyan. However, contrary to tradition, Mikoyan had decided to retain Gurevich's name in the latest aircraft type designations in tribute to his former partner's contributions to their designs. On his death, Mikoyan was succeeded as Head of the Mikoyan OKB by Chief Designer R. A. Belyakov, who developed the

MiG-23, MiG-25, MiG-29, MiG-31 and MiG-33 aircraft, the latter being cancelled due to lack of funds.

In the early 1990s, the MiG OKB was also manufacturing horizontal tail surfaces for Dassault Falcon business jets. In 1995, the Russian Government approved the amalgamation of the Mikoyan OKB and MAPO to create the Moscow Aircraft Production Organisation-MiG (MAPO-MiG), which was subsequently renamed RSK MiG.

Mikoyan MiG-1/MiG-3

Work had started on the 'Kh' interceptor project at the Polikarpov Experimental Design Bureau, OKO-1, in October 1939 under the I-65 and I-61 design concepts. However, within two months, the project had been taken over by the new Mikoyan OKB under the designation I-200. The programme was of such urgency that only 100 days elapsed before production of the first set of drawings, and the maiden flight of the prototype took place on 5 April 1940. It was powered by a 895 kW (1,200 hp) Mikulin AM-35A water-cooled engine and attained a speed of 630 kph (391 mph), making it the world's fastest interceptor at the time. The I-200 was built with what materials were to hand, such as pine and birch plywood, fabric, and as little metal as possible. Two more prototypes were hastily assembled, the second making its maiden flight on 9 May, and the third on 6 June, and factory tests and NII VVS trials proceeded concurrently on all three prototypes. These were concluded on 12 September, and Stalin authorised an initial production run of 100 aircraft as the MiG-1, with an open cockpit or side-hinged canopy and an armament of one 12.7 mm and two 7.62 mm machine guns. However, with minimal range and poor longitudinal stability and an airframe structure apparently unable to sustain battle damage, the last MiG-1 rolled off the production line at Khodynka in December 1940. However, the new fighter did not reach the service units until April 1941, when even then it was considered totally unsuited for combat because of its extremely difficult handling characteristics. In fact, attrition rates were so high that very few of the 2,000 MiG-1s built remained in use to face the Germans in June 1941.

The MiG-3 was a much-improved MiG-1, which earned its designers a Stalin Prize. The first was completed at GAZ-1 in December 1940. The revised design had a rearward-sliding canopy, increased dihedral on the outer wing panels, greater fuel capacity, better armour protection and provision for weightier armament in the form of 200 kg (440 lb) of bombs or six 82-mm (3¼-inch) rockets under the wings. By the end of the month eleven MiG-3s had been built. With the production lines cleared of Yak-4s, the plant was now able to concentrate on MiG aircraft and production rose quickly, 140 fighters leaving the assembly lines in January 1941. The target was twenty-five per day, and 1,289 MiG-3s had been built before the German attack in June 1941. At the start of that month, thirteen regiments were equipped entirely and six partially with MiG-3s, and the type accounted for 37 per cent of the operational fighters at the start of Operation Barbarossa. Of the 980 new fighters in the Western Front MDs, 886 were MiG-3s, whilst the Byelorussian MD had only 233 MiG-3s and twenty Yak-1s out of a total of 1,012 fighter and ground attack aircraft. Many aircraft on the ground on this front were lost on 22 June, but ninety-nine MiG-3s arrived on the 23rd, and two new MiG-3 regiments—401 and 402 IAP, with experienced test pilots—arrived on the 30th. In spite of this, losses remained heavy, and only twenty-three MiG-3s remained on the Western Front by 10 July.

However, the big production effort enabled the Red Air Force to continue its modernisation. No. VI Fighter Corps of the PVO in the Moscow Region had 585 fighters on 22 July 1941: 170 MiG-3s; 75 LaGG-3s; 95 Yak-1s; 200 I-16s; and 45 I-153s. Only one month after the German attack 58 per cent of the fighters were modern. Furthermore, the Luftwaffe at this time had just 621 Messerschmitt Bf 109s for the entire Russian Front, equivalent to only one Soviet Fighter Corps. The evacuation of GAZ-1 to Kuibyshev meant that the Moscow factory was converted to Il-2 Sturmovik production and the MiG-3 programme was terminated on 23 December 1941. However within about ten months, 3,120 MiG-3s had been delivered from the new production line. By comparison, in Germany six well-established series production lines in six plants produced a total of 2,764 Messerschmitt Bf 109 fighters in the twelve months of 1941. Who would dare say that the Soviets were amateurs at aircraft building?

After the MiG OKB and a part of GAZ-1 had returned to Khodynka in March 1942 to form GAZ-30, fifty MiG-3s were assembled from components that had been hidden at the time of the evacuation. These aircraft were allotted to the Moscow PVO where many were even flown as night fighters. When production ceased in December 1941 due to a lack of AM-35 engines, the MiG OKB redesigned the MiG-3 to accept the M-82 radial engine and the aircraft was redesignated I-210. Despite poor performance, five I-210s designated MiG-5s were produced in November/December 1941 and tested on the Kalinin Front. The MiG-3 was also tested with the Mikulin AM-38 engine as fitted to the Il-2 Sturmovik, even though the engine was considered far from ideal for a fighter. However, when tested in August 1942, it produced quite positive results and five pre-production aircraft were delivered to 1 GvIAP where they were used quite successfully. Even so, by this time there was no capacity available to resume MiG-3 production.

Production totalled 3,322 aircraft, and forty MiG-3s were still in service on secondary tasks on the German Front on 1 October 1944! Many operational losses were actually due to the aircraft's poor manoeuvrability at low and medium altitude as a result of its heavy engine. Moreover, both the MiG-1 and the MiG-3 had an inherent design fault which was never addressed: namely, that they displayed poor longitudinal stability by virtue of the fact that the tail was located too close to the wings—i.e. the fuselage was too short.

Mikoyan MiG-9

The MiG-9 jet fighter was a unique design, its two engines mounted side by side in the fuselage directly under the wing and cockpit area, with their nozzles extending towards and under the fuselage tail section. Capable of a speed of 900 kph (560 mph) and attaining an altitude of 15,000m, it was armed with one N-37 cannon and two NS-23 machine guns.

Work on its design began in the autumn of 1945 as the I-300 with two BMW 003 engines. In January 1946, Order No. 156 was issued to build and test the aircraft, and the prototype (designed and built at GAZ-155) was completed on 6 March. The aircraft, designated F 1, was moved to Ramenskoye airfield for air tests on 23 March and made its maiden flight one month later, but it unfortunately crashed and was destroyed on 11 July. However, less than a month later, on 9 August, the third prototype, the F 3, was flown followed by the F 2 just two days later. On 28 August, the People's Commissariat for Aviation Industry ordered ten aircraft to be built within seventy days, and the FS-301s (MiG-9s), each fitted with two RD-20 engines built at Kazan, were completed by GAZ-1 at Kuibyshev by 22 October. In 1947/48, 594 were built there for the PVO, a number being used as development aircraft for the MiG-15 that followed. Around fifty MiG-9s were exported to China.

Mikoyan MiG-15

In January 1946, long before the first Soviet jet-powered aircraft flew, the State Defence Committee issued a specification for an advanced high-altitude day fighter-interceptor with a top speed of Mach 0.9 and a service ceiling of 10,000 m (32,810 feet) and endurance of at least one hour. The design bureaux of Lavochkin, MiG and Yakovlev were all issued with the specification and it was intended that all three would work closely with TsAGI, since many captured German reports had been evaluated there, especially with regard to the swept-wing concept, which it was assumed would be the wing plan used. As stated by the MiG design bureau, the programme was given the designation 'S' (*strelovidnostii* = swept) and Profs Savitsky and Sudez at TsAGI carefully analysed the aerodynamics of the swept-wing concept for the MiG OKB and models were tested in the modernised wind tunnel.

Aircraft 'S' was subsequently planned on the basis of a mid-mounted wing swept 35 degrees at quarter chord, on a short circular-section fuselage with a large swept vertical tail of 4 m² swept at 56 degrees carrying the 3 m² 35-degree swept tailplane set 1,582 mm (5 feet) above the fuselage with incidence ground-adjustable only. Each wing carried two fences from leading to trailing edge 100 mm (4 inches) high. A bold decision was made to make the fuselage in two parts, with the aft end quickly removed by four bolts at frame 13 for all-round access to the engine. A tricycle undercarriage was fitted, with levered-suspension legs throughout, the nose-wheel retracting forwards into the lower part of the inlet duct and main gear, with 660 x 160 mm tyres retracting inwards to lie entirely within the wing between spars. The aircraft featured a pressurised cockpit ahead of the wing, with a rear sliding canopy and an ejection seat.

The MiG OKB intended to use a progressive development of the RD-10 jet engine, but it soon became evident that an engine of sufficient power would not be available for some time in the Soviet Union. Therefore, when the decision was made to use the

Rolls-Royce Nene engine instead, a major redesign of the airframe became necessary. This meant further delays for project 'S', but work on the first prototype, S-01, began at Khodynka early in 1947. Rolled out on 27 November, S-01 was powered by a 1,820 kg (4,000 lb) Nene 1 engine and was sent to Ramenskoye airfield, where it flew for the first time on 30 December 1947, piloted by V. N. Yuganov. The second prototype, S-02, first flew on 27 May 1948 with Grigory Sedov at the controls, and S-03 followed on 5 July, flown by I. T. Ivashchyenko. Both S-02 and S-03 were built in March 1948 and were powered by the slightly more powerful 2,266 kg (5,000 lb) Nene 2.

S-02 had a small rocket added under each wing to assist recovery from spins, to which the aircraft was prone during stall tests, the tailplane sweep was increased to 40 degrees and slight modifications were made to the wing trailing edge and ailerons, all approved by the TsAGI team. S-03 incorporated a number of modifications, including a considerably strengthened wing structure. The flaps were increased in chord but reduced in span so that the ailerons could be enlarged, with each aileron made in two parts linked by a universal joint. Door-type airbrakes were installed, opening slightly downwards on each side of a strengthened rear fuselage, each driven by a hydraulic jack. The tailplane was moved 150 mm (6 inches) to the rear on a modified fin, and a bob weight was added to the elevator circuit. Provision was made for the fitting of 496-litre (109-gallon) non-jettisonable fuel tanks under each wing on hard points that could also take FAB-100 bombs. Among other changes was the fitting of a new canopy locking system and an engine bay fire-detection and extinguishing system, RSI-6M radio and an ASP-1N British gyro-type gunsight, and it was made easier to remove the gun pack.

OKB testing was undertaken by I. T. Ivashchyenko and S. N. Anokhin, with the new jet fighter attaining a top speed of Mach 0.934. Official NII VVS tests held at Saki in November 1948 were extremely successful but still revealed a tendency to spin in a tight turn, poor handling in high angles of attack and buzz/snaking. This resulted in a decision to redline for service use at a top speed of Mach 0.92, and later the airbrakes were triggered automatically at about Mach 0.91. Meanwhile, as the performance of the 'S' design already outstripped that of the rival OKBs by August 1948, Stalin had decided to produce the I-310 (military designation) in large quantities for the Soviet Air Force as the MiG-15, at the same time giving approval for a trainer version to be developed. However, the project was not given the official go-ahead until 13 April 1949, by which time the MiG OKB had completed the design.

GAZ-1 at Kuibyshev had begun making preparations for series production in March 1947, and the first series aircraft flew on 30 December 1948, exactly one year after the flight of the first prototype. At this time two other aircraft plants, Novosibirsk and Saratov, also started series production of the aircraft. So urgent was the Soviet Air Force's need for the aircraft that, on 20 May 1949, Stalin ordered that the production lines building the La-15, Li-2, Yak-17 and Yak-23 in four other plants should all now concentrate on MiG-15 production. The first PP models were delivered for NII VVS testing in the autumn of 1948, powered by a 21.5 kN (4,848 lbf) Klimov RD-45 engine, developed from the Nene engine, the MiG OKB having received accurate installation drawings in February 1947.

Initial production began at GAZ-1, with first deliveries to the AV-MF and newly formed IA-PVO on 8 October 1948, and, fitted with the revised RD-45F engine at an early stage, the new fighter returned a top speed of 1,050 kph (652 mph) at sea level and 983 kph (610 mph) at 10,000 m (32,810 feet), making it the world's lightest and fastest jet fighter at the time. Forty-five series production aircraft appeared at the May Day Air Show in 1949, ninety participated in an air display later that year, on 7 November, and 139 were observed at the May Day Air Show and fly-past in 1950.

The MiG-15SV became the main single-seat RD-45-powered MiG-15 variant. The *Samolyot Soldat* ('aircraft of the soldier') was born. It incorporated numerous modifications. The entire airframe was assessed to ensure its integrity at 8 g. Particular attention was paid to upper skinning, rear fuselage frames, airbrakes and the wing spar booms, which were enlarged and reshaped to eliminate nose-up pitch. New ailerons were fitted and a trim tab was added to the left aileron. Attention was also paid to the outer wing leading edges in respect of anti-flutter, the fuel system was revised, with the tanks pressurised by engine bleed, and the gun pack was modified to improve re-arming time further. The 37 mm N-37 cannon was replaced by the N-37D with new anti-vibration mounts, and the 23 mm NS-23 cannon by NR-23 revolving cannon with new mounts. All three guns were given larger link chutes (external blisters) to avoid blockage. There were new main oleo struts, and an electric starter supplied by a higher-capacity battery. The cockpit was improved, with rear-view periscope, a new ejection seat with triggers to jettison the one-piece canopy with hot bleed-air demisting and then fire the seat with different cartridges for summer and winter, and enhanced defensive armour protection. Among other improvements were the ASP-3N gunsight, a remote gyro compass sensing unit fitted near the starboard wing tip, and improved IFF (Identification Friend or Foe) (SRO-1). Ongoing modifications soon saw the introduction of a special tank to maintain fuel supply under negative-g, and the addition of 300-litre (66-gallon) under-wing drop tanks. The wing was further strengthened in torsion and many pipelines for fuel and hydraulics were replaced by steel assemblies with welded joints. The landing light was increased in power, an RSIU-3 VHF radio and new AGI-51 horizon were fitted, with EUP-46 standby, as well as an uprated RD-45F engine.

In September 1949, the 'SD' prototype was flown with the new 26.5 kN (5,950 lbf) Klimov VK-1 centrifugal-flow turbojet. Following successful trials during 1950, this version was ordered into production under the MiG-15*bis* designation. Associated with the '*bis*' development, tests were carried out in the summer of 1950 with new pressurised landing gear strut shock absorbers, which although effective were not fitted to production aircraft. Production aircraft had conventional main strut absorption and reduced-pressure nose strut absorbers. Soviet Air Force units reported that the aircraft sometimes bounced uncontrollably on rough landings, so the famous test pilot Stepan Suprun conducted all kinds of test landings in order to isolate the problem. Having worked on this over a period of time, he found that the instability was mainly apparent when high-speed landings were made. On his 25th landing, when greatly exceeding all normal recommended landing parameters, the aircraft came close to turning over and severe damage was caused to the nose and starboard struts. Suprun concluded that there was no fault with the aircraft but the problems were caused by poor landing technique. After this the absorber charging system and landing gear design were finalised for the '*bis*' variant.

The Soviet Air Force already had more than 1,200 MiG-15SVs in service by June 1950. In the autumn of the same year China and North Korea also received the aircraft, as did other communist satellites including Czechoslovakia, Hungary, Poland, Bulgaria and Romania. The demand for the aircraft was enormous: 6,000 for Soviet Frontal Aviation, 640 reconnaissance aircraft, 2,000 attack aircraft, 4,000 interceptors for the PVO, along with 2,000 for Soviet Naval Aviation and 2,000 for export. Eight plants produced the aircraft in the Soviet Union, one in Czechoslovakia, and one in Poland. A total of 13,129 were produced in the Soviet Union up until 1953, of which 3,380 were built at Zavod 1 'Stalin' at Kuibyshev. Czechoslovakia produced 853 between 1953 and 1964, and 620*bis* between 1955 and 1959. Of the latter, 251 were exported. Polish production amounted to 227 Lim-1s from 1952 to 1954 and 500 Lim-2*bis* between 1954 and 1956.

After the MiG-15 had entered series production the State Defence Committee requested the MiG OKB to develop a training variant within weeks. It was given the project code 'ST' and the military designation I-312. The first aircraft (c/n 10444), which was basically a two-seat conversion of the MiG-15, was designed, developed and readied for series production at GAZ-1 in record time. The instructor had a second seat, behind the pupil, in a pressurised and fully instrumented cabin to monitor performance and flying. The front canopy hinged to the right, the rear canopy sliding to the rear. The fitting of the rear cockpit reduced the capacity of the forward fuel tank, resulting in a total internal capacity of 1,120 litres (246 gallons), but there was provision for 280 (62) or 400 litre (88 gallon) under-wing tanks. Initially the full armament fit of a 23 mm NR-23 cannon and a 12.7 mm machine gun was retained, although after a small number of series aircraft the NR-23 cannon was deleted. However, the 'ST' could also carry a single 100 kg (220 lb) or two 50 kg bombs, thus retaining full combat capability.

The prototype, built using fighter components from Kuibyshev, made its first flight on 23 May 1949 from the MiG OKB airfield at Frunze, a further thirty-three test flights being made from the airfield up until 20 August. These were followed by fifty-eight other flights between 27 August and 25 September 1949 in connection with NII acceptance testing. A further 502 flights were made whilst attached to a Soviet Air Force fighter regiment at Kubinka. Finally the aircraft was returned to the MiG OKB plant to undergo a number of necessary modifications, followed by a further eight proving flights before being declared ready for series production at GAZ-1 (Kuibyshev) and GAZ-99 (Ulan-Ude) where preparations for production had already been made since 1949. For this reason the two plants were able to produce 100 aircraft in 1950. Production then increased rapidly, and by 1952 every MiG-15 regiment in the Soviet Union also had four MiG-15UTIs on strength. Production of the two-seat trainer ceased in 1959 after a total of 3,725 aircraft had been built, including a large number for export. In the Soviet Union this famous training aircraft (nicknamed by the Soviets *Babushka* (Grandmother) and *Matushka* (Good old woman) was used not only by the Soviet Air Force but also by DOSAAF from the early 1970s, when retired from the VVS, to train young civil pilots or provide military *ab initio* training. From 1954 to 1960, Czechoslovakia built another 2,012 MiG-15UTIs as CS-102s at the Aero Vodochody plant, and more than 1,200 were built in Poland as the Lim-3. Of these foreign-built aircraft, 1,864 were exported to ten different countries, including 1,418 to the Soviet Union and eighty-three to China. The last ten aircraft produced in Czechoslovakia were exported to Iraq.

The MiG-15UTI (there were also a number of variations of this designation: e.g. UTMiG-15, UMiG-15 and UTIMiG-15) was used by thirty-nine different air forces over a thirty-year period to train several tens of thousands of jet fighter pilots. Second-hand aircraft were sold from one country to another, as for example in Hungary, whose last five were sold to Bulgaria in 1975. Even in the early 1990s, some small air arms still had the MiG-15UTI in use. Others have long since found a resting place in the numerous aircraft museums and collectors' hangars around the world.

In the late 1990s, information from Russian sources revealed details regarding Soviet MiG-15 involvement in the Korean War, concerning the 29 AP and 151, 303 and 324 IADs. According to General Lobov, Soviet pilots brought down over 1,300 enemy aircraft in Korea for the loss of 345 MiG-15s. The Americans claim that they lost only fifty-eight F-86 Sabres in air battles, but a single squadron of the 196ºIAP claimed a total of twenty-eight F-86 fighters downed, in addition to other Soviet, Chinese and North Korean claims.

Polish MiG-15 production (UTMiG-5/SBLim-1/2)

The Polish Air Force received a number of Russian-built UTMiG-15 trainers in 1951, followed by a number of Czech-built CS-102s (known in Poland as CT). Poland received about eighty or ninety dual-seat UTMiG-15s, but by the early 1960s, with the trainers in ever-increasing demand, the Polish Military Aviation Works produced the SBLim-1 variant. This was achieved by taking the forward section of damaged BER (Beyond Economic Repair) Soviet UTMiG-15s and mating them with the rest of the airframe from Polish Lim-1s (licence-built MiG-15s). In 1965/66, at least forty were produced in this way and used for airborne observation/army co-operation duties, receiving the designation UTMiG-15Art (Artillery) and SBLim-1Art (or A). The control column in the rear cockpit was removed to make room for the navigator's equipment and the armament was changed, two 23 mm cannon replacing the single 12.7 mm machine gun. The modified aircraft were also used by the Polish Naval Air Arm's reconnaissance squadron and by two squadrons of tactical reconnaissance regiments of the air force based at Powidz and Sochaczew.

By the mid-1970s, the Polish Air Force again found itself extremely short of dual-seat aircraft for reconnaissance duties and advanced training. As a consequence, a similar exercise to that previously described was again implemented; a number of Lim-2s (Polish-built MiG-15*bis*) were modified and became known as SBLim-2s. Some of the existing UTMiG-15s or SBLim-1s were also upgraded, creating the SBLim-2Art variant. By the early 1980s, most of the remaining A/Art models had been changed into M (modified) variants—a training version with the flying controls reinstated in the rear cockpit, which differed from the standard SBLim-2 by retaining the modified armament fit.

Mikoyan MiG-17

The design of the MiG-15 restricted the aircraft to less than supersonic speed and limited its range. The challenge facing the MiG OKB was to increase the maximum speed of the jet fighter but only by improving its aerodynamic characteristics without adding additional thrust. The improved handling was also intended to eliminate the MiG-15's tendency to 'snap roll' into an uncontrollable spin during high-speed turns. For the projected I-330 (MiG-17) three prototypes were built: SI-1 for static tests, SI-2 and SI-3.

The prototypes appeared to be very similar to the MiG-15 and indeed used the same Klimov VK-1 engine. However, closer inspection revealed a number of differences. Compared to the MiG-15, the I-330 had a thinner and more sharply swept-back wing (approximately 45 degrees rather than the 35 degrees of the MiG-15), and the fuselage was lengthened by 900 mm (3 feet) to help reduce drag. The most characteristic features were the large central air intake and huge swept-back tail assembly. The enlarged wing area (by 2 m^2) was fitted with six wing fences (three per wing). Armament was identical to that of the MiG-15—one 37 mm N-37D cannon with forty rounds, and two 23 mm NR-23 machine guns with eighty rounds per gun—and wing hard points could carry drop tanks or 500 kg (1,100 lb) bombs. The SI-2 prototype was flight tested by Ivashchyenko and authorisation for series production was given in June 1951, full-scale production starting three months later.

The MiG OKB developed a full range of tactical fighters for specific missions, taking full advantage of the aircraft's greater versatility. It was also for this reason that the MiG-17s were used as test beds for a large number of systems for the next generation of fighters. The MiG-17PF model was the Soviet Union's first all-weather interceptor. An intercept radar was fitted in the upper-lip housing of the engine air intake (for scanning), with another (for ranging and fire control) housed in the air intake partition. Once the target was within 2 km (1¼ miles), the fire-control antenna activated automatically to sharpen the pilot's aim. In clear weather the radar was disconnected and the pilot used the gunsight. The radar antenna gave this model a distinctive silhouette.

Initial production aircraft were powered by the non-afterburning Klimov VK-1 engine, but from aircraft '850' the new 3,400 kg (7,500 lb) VK-IF afterburning engine was fitted, requiring a revised rear fuselage and featuring the now familiar exposed jet pipe. In addition, redesigned wider airbrakes were introduced (in September 1952) with a total area of 1.76 m^2 (19 square feet). Factory tests on the aircraft, designated MiG-17F (SF), had started on 29 September 1951 with A. N. Chernoburov at the controls. Other OKB pilots involved in the tests, which were concluded on 16 February 1952, were Grigory Sedov and Vladimir Kokkinaki. The SF was then sent for its NII VVS trials, entering series production in late 1952.

Poland produced a total of 730 MiG-17s at the Wytwórnia Sprzętu Komunikacyjnego (WSK) factory at Mielec between 1956 and 1964. Eight different versions, based on the MiG-17F and the radar-equipped all-weather MiG-17PF, were built for the Polish Air Force, where they served with Air Defence and Frontal Aviation regiments. Polish designations were Lim-5 and Lim-5P respectively, and both types remained in service use for nearly forty years. As the more advanced MiG-21 entered Polish Air Force service, many Lim 5s and Lim-5Ps were converted for ground attack and reconnaissance roles. Both Lim variants were exported to East Germany, Bulgaria and Indonesia, and some saw combat with the air forces of Syria and North Vietnam.

The radar-equipped MiG-17PF was the first all-weather interceptor to be deployed by the Polish Air Force. Twelve Soviet-built examples were received in 1955, the first batch of six in May of that year. They were operated by the Independent Fighter Aviation Flight at Bemowo, whose primary task was to defend the city of Warsaw. The eight survivors of this original delivery of MiG-17PFs were finally retired at Siemirowice in the mid-1980s.

The most prolific variant in Polish service was the Lim-5, of which 477 were built between October 1956 and June 1960 at Mielec. The decision to build the Lim-5 was taken in mid-1956, with the first aircraft rolled out just a month after Lim-2 (MiG-15*bis*) production had ended. The first four Lims were assembled from kits of parts supplied from Russia, large-scale Polish production starting in 1957. The first export customer was East Germany, a total of 120 being delivered between June 1957 and April 1958, and from April to July that year thirty-four aircraft were produced for export to an undisclosed overseas customer. On 22 January 1959, 34 PLM (Polish Naval Regiment) became the first such regiment to receive the Lim-5. Production of the Lim-5P (a licence-built variant of the MiG-17PF interceptor) followed, with the final delivery to the Polish Air Force made on 2 July 1961, after 125 Lim-5Ps had left the Mielec factory. Towards the end of the 1950s, the Polish Air Force's Scientific Institute converted a Lim-5 (c/n 1C-0201) for the reconnaissance role by installing a single AFA-39 camera in a fairing underneath the fuselage. Eventually thirty-six aircraft were converted and received the designation Lim-5R. In the early 1970s, as front-line units began equipping with the MiG-21 interceptor, Lim-5s were given over to the training units.

A decision had been made in the late 1950s to convert a number of Lim-5s for the ground attack role. One of the main requirements was that the aircraft would be able to operate from unprepared surfaces, and this was met by strengthening the main undercarriage and fitting dual wheels. Other changes included the addition of booster rockets to assist take-offs, and the fitting of a brake chute under the lower rear fuselage. Combat radius was increased by adding extra fuel in the enlarged wing roots. Tests were undertaken with two converted Lim-5s (c/n 1C-1030 and 1C-1601), flight trials beginning on 2 July 1959, with tests completed within the year. Series production began in the late 1960s, followed by delivery of the first four Lim-5Ms. However, the Lim-5M was not liked by pilots; ten aircraft were lost in accidents, most of which were attributed to its difficult handling characteristics.

As series production of the Lim-5 came to an end, Mielec engineers were studying ways of improving the aircraft's capabilities. Tests commenced in January 1961 with Lim-5 c/n 1C-1601 previously used on the ground attack trials, renumbered CM-1601. A number of modifications were made to the aircraft, but before proving tests could be completed, production of the new variant had commenced under the designation Lim-6. One Lim-6 joined CM-1601 on the test programme, which was ultimately halted in March 1962, with inconclusive results. Of more significance were the reports reaching the factory from operational units alarmed at the type's drastic reduction in speed and range caused by the fitting of enlarged fuel tanks in the wing roots. This modification had obviously had completely the opposite effect to that intended. On 8 April 1962, CM-1601 flew minus the wing root tanks and fitted with a standard undercarriage, the only changes retained being the new brake chute and improved armament. Subsequently full production of the new variant began after satisfactory proving in 1963. Along with a recce variant, Lim-6R, a batch of forty Lim-6s produced before the flight testing had been completed were converted to Lim-6*bis*. Deliveries of the Lim-6 to the Polish Air Force commenced on 25 March 1963, the final delivery being a Lim-6R on 30 September 1969, five years after production had finished. When the last aircraft retired from Polish Air Force service in February 1992, it ended a thirty-seven-year flying career of Polish-built MiG-17s.

Mikoyan MiG-19

Although fewer were built than the MiG-17 series, the MiG-19 represented a major advance in all respects. It was an outstanding combat aircraft—the first supersonic fighter to enter production anywhere in the world and the first Soviet aircraft to use a brake chute to reduce landing distance and brake wear.

Development of the MiG-19 started in the late 1940s with Stalin's request to Mikoyan, Yakovlev and Mikulin to join forces in order to develop a supersonic combat aircraft. A completely new aircraft was designed around the new Lyulka AL-5 gas turbine engine, but poor progress with the development of the AL-5 resulted in the newly developed AM-5 being used instead. The first aircraft, the I-360, distinguished by its T-tail, was destroyed whilst carrying out flight tests due to tailplane flutter. It was replaced by the I-350 (M), which first flew with a revised low-set tailplane on 18 September 1953, and was followed by the SM-9 prototype that flew on 5 January 1954. A month later, the Ministry of Aircraft Production issued order No. 286-133 to build the MiG-19 at GAZ-21 (Gorky) and GAZ-153 (Novosibirsk). Initial series aircraft were fitted with two afterburning AM-5F engines, and it was one of these aircraft that first went supersonic in level flight in 1953.

The MiG-19 entered service with the PVO in March 1955, and forty-eight were displayed at the Tushino Air Show on 3 July that year. However, upgraded MiG-19Fs and limited capability Izumrud radar-equipped all-weather MiG-19PFs proved less than successful, experiencing control problems, and were eventually withdrawn from use as a result of the high accident rate. The first major production version was the MiG-19S (later redesignated 'SF') with its all-moving slab tailplane, Tumansky RD-9B turbojets, revised control system and gun armament of three long-barrel 30 mm cannon in place of the mixed 23 mm and 37 mm battery in the earlier aircraft. Hard point mountings under the wings allowed carriage of a variety of rockets, and gravity bombs. Deliveries of the 'S' variant started in late 1955 and, from this time on, the aircraft continued almost unchanged for the whole of the series production, which saw some 2,500 produced between 1955 and 1957. A measure of the excellent basic handling of the redesigned aircraft can be gleaned from the fact that the two-seat MiG-19UTI trainer, although completed and flown, was never put into production in the Soviet Union as potential MiG-19 pilots found little difficulty in converting from the MiG-15UTI trainer to the supersonic fighter.

The MiG-19P version appeared in 1956, with its air-to-air Izumrud radar and receiving antenna in the intake bullet fairing and scanner in the inlet upper lip. Armed with AA-1 and AA-2 AAMs, it was the first Soviet missile-armed fighter. The rocket-carrying MiG-19PM variant suffered from engine problems due to rocket plume ingestion, but was none the less the primary interceptor with the PVO for many years.

Although Soviet production of the MiG-19 ended in 1960, Aero Vodochody continued to build the type in Czechoslovakia from 1958 to 1962. China produced the first of its unlicensed copies of the MiG-19S, designated Shenyang J-6, in 1961, and by the mid-1970s these were being produced at the rate of twenty-five per month. A total of around 2,000 were built, production still continuing at a rate of eight per month well into the 1980s. A large number of the Chinese J-6s were supplied to Pakistan in 1965/66 and again in 1972, where they were modified to accept American AIM-9L Sidewinder missiles, and also to North Vietnam from 1969 to 1972. A number were also supplied to Albania and Tanzania. China also used the MiG-19 as the basis for its J-6*bis* aircraft and its Q-5 Fantan strike fighter (also exported to Pakistan), which was an enlarged J-6 with side air intakes in place of the single nose intake.

Mikoyan MiG-21

Whilst the MiG-21 is probably not as famous as its predecessor, the ubiquitous MiG-15, it has its own claim to fame on several counts, not least that it has been manufactured in greater numbers than any other fighter since the Second World War and has had the longest operational life of any combat aircraft in history. It is still in operational service with a number of air arms and was the subject of a number of upgrade programmes that saw its operational life extended well into the new millennium.

The origins of the aircraft lie in the Korean War, when the Soviets along with their American counterparts realised that air superiority in any impending conflict would be of extreme importance and that there was a pressing need for a small, fast, agile combat aircraft with greater range and endurance than afforded by early-generation jet fighters. For the Soviets, the answer lay with the single-seat multi-role fighter from the Mikoyan design bureau. The question of size was addressed by the MiG OKB by designing the aircraft around a 7,500 kg (16,500 lb) Tumansky R-25 afterburning turbojet not much bigger than the two RD-9s that powered the earlier MiG-19, which in itself was not a large aircraft. Development undertaken in order to meet a Soviet specification issued in the autumn of 1953 led to the swept-wing Ye-2 (*Yedinitsa* = single unit) powered with an uprated AM 32 kN (7,194 lbf) RD-9Ye engine because the new Tumansky engine was not yet available. The MiG OKB had gained permission to produce two airframes in order to evaluate two different designs, the wing configuration not having been decided on, and it therefore produced the Ye-4 delta-wing prototype in parallel, also fitted with an uprated RD-9Ye engine. Of the two, the Ye-2 was the first aircraft to take to the air, although it is not clear when this took place. In an authoritative article by a Soviet engineer, V. Kondratyev, in 1986 it was stated that the Ye-2 flew on 14 February 1953, with the delta-configured aircraft flying two years later, whereas most aviation historians usual put the Ye-2's first flight in February 1955 (which seems more likely, as the requirement was not issued until the autumn of 1953—unless Mikoyan went ahead in anticipation and frustration at the earlier designs), followed four months later by the Ye-4.

As the new powerplant was still unavailable, permission was obtained to build a third prototype aircraft, the Ye-50, fitted with a ZhRD S-155 rocket engine to boost the performance of the small interim RD-9Ye so as to enable more meaningful comparisons to be made between the two wing types. It has been stated that a batch of twelve Ye-50As were built, but the reality is that there were only three, the first of which was flown in June 1955 by test pilot Valentin Mukhin. Later Mukhin was slightly injured when due to an engine flame-out on approach he was forced to make a crash landing short on the runway. Whilst he was recuperating, the second Ye-50A/2 was taken aloft by V. P. Vasin, who reached Mach 2.33 in level flight on 17 June 1957 and on another occasion attained an altitude of 25,600 m (83,990 feet). Vasin was made a 'Hero of the Soviet Union' when, on taking off in front of Marshal Zhukov in the winter of 1957, he activated the rocket booster normally only operated at 9,000 m (29,527 feet), thus providing a rather spectacular display for the visiting marshal. The Ye-50 programme was concluded in 1958, after the third Ye-50A/3 had undergone a number of tests with unspecified changes to the nose, rear fuselage and vertical tail.

The availability in early 1956 of the Tumansky R-11S engine led to a further rocket boosted series of prototype aircraft, designated Ye-6, of which more later. Immediately the new engine became available it was fitted to the original airframe that had been repaired subsequent to its crash landing. Designated Ye-2A, the aircraft was flown by test pilot Grigory Sedov on 22 March 1956. Like the Ye-2, it was fitted with a small swept-wing assembly similar to that used on the MiG-19, with two large ventral fins inclined at 45 degrees under the rear fuselage, two NR-30 cannon (at least one Ye-50 had three) and a novel one-piece Plexiglas canopy that hinged up at the front, with the rear of the canopy pivoted to the top of the ejection seat so that if the pilot ejected, the canopy would serve as a windbreak in front to protect him. The nose and forward fuselage were the same as the Ye-2, the two most obvious differences being the gigantic fence at mid-span on the wing, aligned with the inboard end of the ailerons, and projecting ram-air cooling inlets on the sides of the rear fuselage faired into the roots of the tailplane. The rear fuselage of the aircraft had also undergone a degree of redesign. In flight, the Ye-2A proved itself to be capable of Mach 1.9.

Also in 1956, the MiG OKB flew one of its delta-wing aircraft, the Ye-4/1, fitted with the new Tumansky engine. Apart from the wing, the aircraft was basically a Ye-2 and displayed rather disappointing performance, actually somewhat worse than series MiG-19s coming off the production line at the time and certainly not achieving the 2,000 kph (1,243 mph) that had been hoped for. For the next couple of years the OKB made a number of minor changes to the Ye-4/1 and Ye-4/2 in an effort to improve their performance, handling and top speeds. The most prolific changes were made to the wing fences, their size and shape being amended at least four times, and a number of modifications were eventually made to the rear fuselage section, especially around the jet nozzle. These had also been carried out on the Ye-2 and were found to have a dramatic effect in overcoming the inherent drag problem.

Almost coincidental with this discovery, an uprated 50 kN (11,240 lbf) R-11S engine was fitted to one of the Ye-4s, thus turning it into a Ye-5. Mikoyan engineers insisted that this was not a new aircraft, in spite of the fact that it had the revised wing tips of the Ye-4/1 and the definitive wing fences of the Ye-4/2. The Ye-5 (sometimes incorrectly designated I-500) actually topped the magical 2,000 kph and displayed its superiority over the Ye-2A with regard to manoeuvrability, climb and endurance. As a result, after almost four years of development, in early 1957 the NII VVS finally chose the delta-wing aircraft in preference to the traditional wing design to enter series production as the Soviet Union's premier fighter of the era.

It is interesting to note that concurrent with its quest for a MiG-19 replacement, the MiG OKB was working on a number of other prototype *istrebitel* (fighter) aircraft of similar shape, although all were much larger in size and were in fact members of different families of aircraft—as were the SM-12 prototypes, which despite resembling the Ye-2As were actually derived from the MiG-19 series. As already mentioned, in parallel with all the foregoing the MiG design bureau had produced the Ye-6, which incorporated all the changes and improvements embodied in the other prototypes but with a delta wing optimised at a 57 degree sweep and with Tumansky R-11 engines fitted. There were, however, some minor differences between the various Ye-6s. For example, the Ye-6/1 had very slightly clipped wing tips and the same fences as the Ye-5, the two inboard fences wrapping round the leading edge, with the outer being smaller and located entirely on the upper wing surface, and the two ventral inclined fins replaced by a single fin on the fuselage centreline. The Ye-6/1 was in fact a fully developed prototype, which when flown by test pilot Vladimir Nefedov soon achieved a top speed of Mach 2.05 at 12,000 m (39,370 feet). Unfortunately, on the seventh flight, on 28 May 1958, the engine exploded at a height of 18,000 m (59,055 feet) causing extensive damage that resulted in Nefedov progressively losing control and his life on the approach to land.

The MiG OKB was under great pressure to find the cause of the accident and implement any redesign that might be necessary to prevent a recurrence, and the man appointed for the task was Rostislav Belyakov, who would eventually succeed Mikoyan as General Constructor of the MiG OKB. Belyakov made a number of proposals, including complete duplication of a number of important hydraulic systems. He also incorporated a three-position centre body housing for ranging radar to improve the production fighter's combat capability, and auxiliary engine inlet doors under the wing-root leading edges. All these changes and a number of other minor ones, such as to the cockpit windows, the brake parachute housing and the fitting of clipped wing tips and the new wing fence configuration that had been flight tested on the Ye-6/2, were embodied on the Ye-6/3. This, in essence, was the aircraft that entered series production with its two NR-30 cannon after successful test flights in December 1958. The first batch of thirty MiG-21Fs were clear-weather, day-only fighter-interceptors and entered Soviet Air Force service in early 1959.

The first true series version was the MiG-21F-13 powered by a single R-11F-300 Tumansky engine. This was the productionised version of the Ye-6T, the 'T' standing for 'Trophy' in reference to the 'gift' from the Americans of an AIM-9B Sidewinder that had embedded itself in a Chinese fighter without exploding, thereby handing an up-to-date AAM for reverse-engineering on a plate to the Soviets. They produced their copy in double-quick time and immediately made provision for it on the new fighter-interceptor by way of two K-13 Atoll AAMs. The addition of these missiles on two simple under-wing pylons necessitated the deletion of the port side cannon and its 75-round ammunition box to provide a degree of weight compensation and space for additional missile control electrics. An opportunity was also taken to increase the chord (width) of the fin to improve yaw stability at high angles of attack.

Many thousands of the MiG-21F-13 were built, including the S-106 in Czechoslovakia and the J-7 unlicensed copy by Shenyang (later Chengdu) in Red China, which they accomplished in just four years. An inherent design fault with the MiG-21F-13 was that it was severely restricted in range, in that of the 2,470 litres (543 gallons) of fuel carried, not all could be used before the aircraft ran into instability problems. From the 115th aircraft, the first fitted with a broader fin, a radar warning receiver (RWR) was added.

By the time these had entered service, work was under way to upgrade and improve the aircraft's performance. An all-weather version, the MiG-21PF, was fitted with an uprated R-11F2-300 engine and upgraded air-search RP-21M Jay Bird radar with its antenna in an enlarged pointed cone centred in the engine air inlet and the cockpit faired into the fuselage, sacrificing rear vision for reduced drag. The single NR-30 cannon was deleted, reliance being placed on the two K-13 missiles for attack and defence. The new aircraft, variously designated in production as PF-1, PF-2 and PFV, began reaching Frontal Aviation regiments in 1963. The PFV was a high-altitude variant fitted with R2L radar, SRO-2M IFF and an improved Sirena passive RWR. The export version of this variant was designated MiG-21FL.

Throughout the 1960s, the MiG-21 family went from strength to strength with a proliferation of new and more capable variants all powered by the new engines from the Tumansky engine bureau, the first being the R-13 turbojet directly interchangeable with the R-11. The next variant to appear was the Type 92 MiG-21PFM, derived from the Ye-9 prototype with its F2S-300 engine and only one major difference from the preceding Ye-7 (PF and PFS series)—the fitting of the KM-1 ejection seat previously only fitted in trainers, which entered production in 1965. The first-generation MiG-21s were fighters with only modest capabilities, but with the introduction of the MiG-21PFMA this was about to change. The multi-role Type 94 MiG-21PFMA appeared from 1966 and was outwardly almost identical to the final Ye-9 prototype. The enlarged dorsal spine ran from the cockpit to the tail fin, and both wings were given two additional hard points to carry additional AAMs etc.

The Type 94R that followed was a reconnaissance development of the PFMA model. The MiG-21R was produced at the Gorky factory in parallel with the MiG-21S between 1965 and 1971, although the 'S' continued in production only until 1968 when the 'SMT' and third-generation '*bis*' variants entered production with their re-engineered airframes and greater fuel capacity. Powered by a single 60 kN (13,489 lbf) Tumansky R-11F2S-300 turbojet, the 'R' was fitted with the SPS (*Sduv Pogranichnogo Sloya*) boundary layer blowing system, with fuel capacity increased by 2,800 litres (616 gallons). As the aircraft was designed to carry a reconnaissance pod on its centreline station instead of a normal drop tank, the wing was strengthened and modified to accept two external wing tanks. However, the fitting of the reconnaissance pod and external tanks reduced the performance of the aircraft, it being some 530 kph (329 mph) slower than the MiG-21PF and MiG-21S. The 'R' could be armed if necessary, carrying UB-16 and UB-32 rocket pods, with S-24 rockets, bombs and the GP-9 gun pod if required. Two K-13T (R-3S) AAMs could also be carried for self-defence.

The only former Warsaw Pact countries to receive the 'R' were Poland and Czechoslovakia, the latter's twenty aircraft being split between the Czech (thirteen) and Slovak Republics (seven), although all were subsequently withdrawn in favour of the Sukhoi Su-22M4. In the 1970s, the original R-11F-300 engine was replaced by the more powerful R-13-300, giving rise to a new model: the Type 96 MiG-21MF. It carried the new Gryazev-Shipunov GSh-23 mm cannon internally and was probably made in greater numbers than any other Ye-9 derivative. The first, delivered in 1966, were produced with the original R-11F engine, but most series aircraft were fitted with the new powerplant. The aircraft also had as standard the GP-9 gun pack fitted with the powerful GSh-23L twin-barrelled guns. A reconnaissance variant of the MiG-21MF, designated the MiG-21RF, was built in two versions—one for the Soviet and Warsaw Pact air forces, and the other in small numbers for Egypt. Twenty-five MiG-21RFs were still in Polish Air Force service in the mid/late 1990s. In an effort to extend the MiG-21's range, the MiG-21SMB model was built with the large bulged dorsal hump running straight back from the cockpit to the fin, housing a large quantity of additional fuel and avionics, total internal capacity being 3,350 litres (737 gallons) as opposed to 2,762 litres (608 gallons) for the standard MF.

The final model in the third-generation Ye-9 family was the MiG-21*bis* powered by a 73.5kN (16,523 lbf) R-25-300 with reheat, having been preceded by a small number of interim MiG-21SMTs that, contrary to common belief, actually had less fuel in their dorsal spine than the SMB and the lower-profiled '*bis*' variant. The new Tumansky R-25 engine gave the aircraft a terrific boost in performance—it was less 'smoky' and provided much greater economy—along with improved avionics and provision for two radar homing AA-2C Atoll and two AA-8 Aphid AAMs, which gave rise to the MiG-21N (Nuclear).

When compared with later Soviet combat aircraft, the MiG-21 was limited in payload and range, but it was none the less widely used by the Soviet Air Force and was exported to some thirty-eight nations and air arms. It was thought that there were probably fewer than 500 still in use with Soviet front-line regiments in 1995, and three years later almost all of these had been withdrawn. Aerostar have updated about 100 Romanian Air Force MiG-21s, but in general it now appears that most air forces are not prepared to fund expensive refits and upgrades to an airframe that, even after a prolonged gestation period, appears to have a number of fundamental shortcomings in its basic design. (India is, of course, an exception and still has large numbers in use.)

In concluding this look at the MiG-21, mention should be made of the dual-seat trainers. The original MiG-21U was based on the MiG-21F, with armament removed and the original cockpit replaced by unstepped tandem cockpits with KM-1 ejection seats (ahead of the single-seat fighter), the two cockpit canopies hinging open to the right. Internal fuel at 2,400 litres (528 gallons) was only slightly less than the MiG-21F. By 1962, the standard trainer had become the Type 66, with the larger main gear of the MiG-21PF and the twin forward airbrakes replaced by a single assembly on the centreline, the pitot head boom having moved above the fuselage nose and the braking parachute above the jet pipe. In 1964, the Type 68 MiG-21US made its appearance with blown flaps and the broad vertical tail of the PFS along with many other changes including an extended dorsal spine. The following year the MiG-21US was succeeded by the Type 69 MiG-21UM, powered by the R-13-300. The aircraft was provided with a TS-27 periscope built into the canopy in the rear cockpit to give the instructor a better view on approach. This was also retrofitted to other variants. In addition, the UM had the small angle-of-attack sensor fitted on the port side of the nose.

Mikoyan MiG-23

The origins of the MiG-23 Flogger, the first Soviet fighter with variable-sweep wings, go back to the 1960s. Rostislav Belyakov was responsible for the project, 1-3/66, against an order from Minaviaprom in 1965. For a while the MiG OKB developed a swept-wing (Ye-231) and a delta wing (Ye-23DPD) aircraft to meet the requirement, both types powered by uprated Lyulka AL-7F engines. The two experimental fighters were first tested in late 1966, and after careful evaluation it was shown that the variable-geometry design was better suited for operational use, with the first of four '231' prototypes (as opposed to evaluation aircraft) flying on 10 June 1967.

The first production Flogger, designated MiG-23S, left the production lines at Samara for its maiden flight on 28 May 1969. That same month, the MiG-23UB two-seat trainer also had its first flight. Production aircraft were similar to the prototypes except they had four airbrakes on the tail, improved avionics and a GSh-23 two-barrelled gun on the centreline fuselage behind the nose-wheel bay. A centreline pylon was also fitted to carry a fuselage fuel tank. Two pylons for various external stores were fitted on both the fuselage and wings. An improved variant, the MiG-23SM, had further refinements but was externally similar to the MiG-23S, which was the last to use the Lyulka AL-7 powerplant. The -23S and -23SM Flogger-A variants were produced in only small numbers and saw limited use with the VVS. None of these early variants were exported. Subsequent variants were fitted with Tumansky R-27 engines with full reheat developing 100 kN (22,485 lbf), which involved the MiG OKB in a major redesign. The R-27 engine was placed slightly further forward than the AL-7F-1 but its supporting frames remained unaltered. The tail surfaces were moved aft and the nose was enlarged to accommodate the Jay Bird fire-control radar as well as additional avionics and electronic equipment. The MiG-23M retained the same wingspan of the earlier model but the wing area was increased and a 'dog-tooth' introduced at the intermediate sweep angle.

The first trials of the MiG-23M took place in 1969, and the type very quickly succeeded the -23SM on the production lines. It was soon followed by the MiG-23MS, which was externally quite similar. This was the first variant of the MiG-23 to see large-scale production and it was allocated in large numbers to the Frontal Aviation regiments. The MiG-23MS can be regarded as the base model for all other variants such as the MiG-23MF Flogger-B, the dual-seat MiG-23UM Flogger-C trainer and the ground attack MiG-27 Flogger-D.

Some MiG-23MS and many MiG-23MF variants were exported. The first were observed in operation with the Libyan Air Force, although these were in fact special downgraded export variants, designated Flogger-E, and actually carried the same radar and armament fit as the MiG-21*bis* Fishbed-N. Most of the Egyptian MFs and later BNs were given to the US to form a Top Secret 'Aggressor' training squadron at Nellis AFB in Nevada, and at least two Egyptian aircraft found their way to the People's Republic of China. In 1976, the ML variant emerged, with its enhanced electronics and avionics fit. The Jay Bird radar was replaced by the High Lark J Band fire-control radar. The High Lark was similar in size and had similar operation modes to the Westinghouse AWG-10 equipment fitted to McDonnell Douglas F-4 Phantoms. Its overall size called for a considerably enlarged plastic radome and the addition of a TP-23 IR (Infra Red) sensor in front of the nose-wheel bay, these changes providing the aircraft with full all-weather interceptor and stand-off kill capabilities. The MiG-23ML was series-produced from 1976 until 1981.

A new variant was observed in August 1978, when six MiG-23s from the air base at Kubinka near Moscow visited Rissala in Finland—the MiG-23ML Flogger-G. The aircraft was similar to the Flogger-B, but was powered by the Tumansky R-29 turbojet with a maximum rating of 122.3 kN (27,500 lbf) with afterburner. The Flogger-G also had a shorter and smaller dorsal fin and redesigned nose-wheel housing and a redesigned IR housing. The standard armament for the ML, which was essentially an interceptor variant, included AA-7 Apex long-range AAMs as well as AA-8 Aphid missiles for self-defence.

In 1986, the Flogger-K interceptor was observed, featuring pivoting weapon pylons under the outer wings which could also carry two 1,150-litre (253-gallon) fuel tanks if required, although these could only be carried with the wing sweep set at the minimum 16 degrees. The MiG-23UM trainer variant was developed from the downgraded MiG-23MS Flogger-E and retained the Jay Bird radar, although much of the avionics had been removed or moved forward in the nose to make space for the instructor's cockpit where forward vision was improved by fitting a retractable periscope. The aircraft also retained its GSh-23L centreline-mounted cannon and the same number of weapons carriage pylons as the Flogger-B and -G interceptor variants.

Mikoyan MiG-25 Foxbat

The MiG-25 was conceived to provide the Soviets with an interceptor capable of dealing primarily with the threat posed by the North American B-70 Valkyrie Mach 3 high-altitude strategic bomber and the Lockheed SR-71 Blackbird high-altitude reconnaissance aircraft. Despite cancellation of the B-70 Valkyrie, preliminary research work on project Ye-155 was started in 1958/59. In 1960, the basic layout was defined and, on 10 March 1961, the MiG OKB received instructions to proceed. Design bureau officials Valentin Stepanov and Lev Shengelaya were assigned to the project and a group of twelve project engineers was created; six months later they had produced the Ye-155 programme. The mock-up inspection commission was convened in 1962, and December 1963 saw the first prototype rolled out. Mikoyan's chief test pilot Alexander Fedotov made his first flight in the Ye-155R-1 on 6 March 1964, at which time the aircraft was unique in the world. The first flight of the second prototype, Ye-155-1P, followed later that year, on 9 September.

The Ye-155 (E-266) was designed for Mach 3 flight, and to deal with friction-generated heat at these high speeds the aircraft was built mainly of stainless steel and had titanium wing leading edges. On 30 October 1967, an attempt on the absolute World Air Speed record by Igor Lesnikov (an NII VVS test pilot) resulted in him losing his life in a crash caused by difficulties arising from aileron reversal, a defect that had also claimed the lives of a number of other test pilots. In order to overcome the problem the Mikoyan designers introduced all-moving stabilizers, although this modification in itself introduced fresh problems that resulted in an uncontrollable roll motion in certain flight conditions. Special flight tests were initiated to investigate the aircraft's behaviour in the roll, during which Oleg Gudkov, who was the leading test pilot at the Ministry of Aviation Industry Flight Research Institute, was killed. However, luckily for the project, only seconds before his death Gudkov had radioed the ground with some information that was to prove vital, leading ultimately to the redesign of the tailplane and the subsequent solving of the handling problems. By the end of 1968, after four prototypes had made a public demonstration on 9 July 1967 at Domodedovo, it was deemed that the aircraft had reached operational standard and consequently series production started at Gorky in 1969. Both versions of the aircraft—reconnaissance (1969) and interceptor (1970)—were accepted into Soviet Air Force service.

In 1971, unarmed reconnaissance versions of the aircraft were taking excellent photographs from altitudes of over 20 km (12 miles), although operational use was delayed following a fatal accident to the PVO C-in-C Anatoly Kadomtsev, who was killed as a result of an onboard fire. However, the interceptor variant did become operational on 25 May 1972 and the reconnaissance version in the December of that year. The interceptor variant entered VVS service with the designation MiG-25P and, at Mach 2.86, was the world's fastest interceptor, but at this speed it was restricted to non-manoeuvring flight. It had a valve technology radar that lacked the sophistication of western types but offered very high power and thus the ability to 'burn through' the defences presented by the enemy's countermeasures, although the UK's Panavia Tornado F.3 ADV with its GEC-Marconi AI.24 Foxhunter radar was specifically designed to intercept the Foxbat.

The MiG-25R was the basic operational reconnaissance version, with a maximum take-off weight of 33,400 kg (73,633 lb), unlinked wings reduced in span to 13.4 m (44 feet) and a combat radius of 1,117 km (694 miles). It carried a small SLAR (Side-Looking Airborne Radar) and five cameras in the nose (one vertical and four oblique) and a small Jay Bird radar in the nose forward of the SLAR installation, Doppler and ground-mapping radar in ventral radomes, and ECCM equipment. The MiG-25U was a two-seat operational conversion trainer using a new nose section with a separate trainee cockpit (overall length 23.82 m or 78 feet 2 inches) in place of the radar. The MiG-25RB Foxbat-D was an improved reconnaissance/attack version of the MiG-25R, with a larger SLAR but no nose cameras. However, it was fitted with ELINT equipment and could carry bombs for high-altitude strike missions.

In September 1976, Viktor Belenko flying a MiG-25P defected to Hakodate Air Base in Japan—the first time a Foxbat-A had been seen outside the Soviet Union. This resulted in the aircraft being carefully scrutinised by the USAF, and its secrets were revealed. As a result, the Soviets decided to release the aircraft for export. At the same time, following a government inquiry, a resolution to update the aircraft was made and within four weeks the technical details were defined and determined.

The MiG-25's first operational missions were flown outside the Soviet Union in the spring of 1971 by four MiG-25Rs in Egypt. From the autumn of 1971 and the spring of 1972, the aircraft flew in pairs from Cairo West Air Base to carry out high-speed reconnaissance missions over the Israeli-occupied Sinai Peninsula. Israeli IDF/AF McDonnell Douglas F-4 Phantoms sent up to intercept the MiGs failed to make contact. The idea of sending the MiG-25R to the Middle East for combat proving before its introduction into VVS service was that of Alexei Minoev, who had been promoted in 1970 to the position of Deputy Minister of Aviation Industry following his successful career as Deputy Chief Designer in the MiG OKB's Flight Control Systems Division. Early operational experience gained in the Middle East with the MiG-25 contributed significantly to the aircraft's rapid entry into both the VVS and the PVO, and to the development of new variants.

From 1980 to 1982 each VVS aircraft received new equipment and was converted to the new standard MiG-25MP, which resulted in limited look-down/shoot-down capability at lower altitude. The type was intended to deal with low-level intruders such as penetration bombers and cruise missiles and had new pulse-Doppler search-and-track radar and a new under-nose IR sensor blister. The engines were uprated R-31F units each with an afterburning thrust of 137.29 kN (30,864 lbf). An internal gun was fitted and the radar was matched to the six AA-9 AAM and the AA-11 missiles. The MiG-25BM Foxbat-F was another conversion designed for the air defence role, carrying AS-11 Kilter radar homing missiles launched on the basis of data provided by a specialised radar warning suite. This type first flew in prototype form in 1976, entering VVS service in 1988. In 1977, the MiG-25PD Foxbat-E was equipped with RP-25 Sapfir-25 radar and a small IR search-and-track sensor under the nose. The MiG-25PDs were fitted with two R-15BD-300 turbojets, each rated at 109.8 kN (24,690 lbf) with afterburner. Eventually over 300 operational MiG-25Ps of the PVO forces were upgraded to PD standard, receiving the MiG-25PDS designation. Production of the MiG-25 at the Gorky plant (now Nizhny Novgorod) on the Volga River was terminated in 1984.

Mikoyan MiG-27

The base model, the MiG-27 Flogger-D, was simply a MiG-23BM Flogger-F with a number of wing modifications and flap extension controls, whilst the MiG-27K was based on the MiG-23BK that was fitted with two small RWRs either side of the bottom fuselage forward of the nose-wheel doors. The entire nose section to the wings was completely rethought. The wedge-like shape of the nose earned the aircraft the nickname 'Utkanos' (Duckbill) by the Soviet pilots and ground crews, and the redesigned nose considerably improved the pilot's forward vision. The High Lark radar was replaced by a laser rangefinder and new Doppler navigation radar. In addition, titanium armour plates were fitted on both sides of the cockpit to protect the pilot from rifle fire and small anti-aircraft fire (lessons learned from Afghanistan). The MiG-23's variable-geometry engine inlets were replaced by smaller ones, and the Tumansky R-29-300 engine had a simpler afterburner extension and the same dry thrust rating as the previous R-29 powerplant used in the MiG-23 interceptor variants.

The first trials of the new MiG-27 ground attack aircraft were made in 1972, but it was not until three years later that the type was observed in East Germany in operational use with the Soviet 16th Air Army and the ASCC (NATO) name Flogger-D was annotated. It was observed that the GSh-23L cannon had been replaced by a 23 mm six-barrelled Gatling-type cannon. In 1981, a new variant of the Flogger-D was first seen in East Germany, the MiG-27M Flogger-J, which was also built under licence by HAL in India. Another ground attack variant was achieved by mating the MiG-23MS interceptor's rear fuselage with the nose section of the MiG-27 whilst retaining the two rear fuselage pylons of the latter, as well as the missile control directing antenna on the port wing glove. The resultant 'hybrid' aircraft, which used the same R-29-300 engine as the Flogger-D and –J, was designated MiG-23BN Flogger-H.

MiG-27 production started in 1973 at Irkutsk, where 560 MiG-27 Flogger-Ds were built. Later, around 500 were modified to MiG-27D standard. Production of the basic model ended at Irkutsk in 1977 when attention was switched to the next variant, the MiG-27K Flogger-J2. This variant, around 200 of which were built, has also been designated MiG-27KR by some users. The MiG-27K was equipped with the Kaira laser rangefinder and optical system, which replaced the Klen rangefinder fitted to the basic MiG-27. Before production of the MiG-27K had ended in 1979, a third variant had already entered production. Conceived in 1978, the MiG-27M (Modified) Flogger-J1 was initially produced in parallel with the MiG-27K, of which 150 were eventually built, manufacture of the MiG-27M ending in 1983. Production of the 150 MiG-25K aircraft had taken considerably longer than the 200 MiG-27Ms, although it is thought that embodiment of a certain number of modifications in production (not usual Soviet practice) had led to the increased timespan. The modified aircraft were designated MiG-27MD.

A major modernisation programme was carried out at Ulan-Ude between 1982 and 1985 in which 500 MiG-27s were brought up to a standard close to that of the MiG-27M and received the designation MiG-27D. The improvements included the fitting of the PrNK-23M nav/attack system to permit use of new stores in the form of a three-camera reconnaissance pod and 23 mm SPPU-22 gun pods each with 260 rounds, and twin gun barrels that could be depressed for ground attack. The MiG-27D and -27M types differed in that the former retained the RSBN-6S navigation approach and landing system, whereas the latter were fitted with the RSBN 'Korall-M' system, similar to that fitted to the MiG-27K. However, as this was an internal alteration it was not immediately obvious as to which were updated aircraft.

Mikoyan MiG-29 Fulcrum

Developed to meet a 1972 requirement to replace the ageing MiG-21, MiG-23 and Su-17, the first prototype of the superbly agile MiG-29A flew on 6 October 1977. This was the first of eleven prototypes given the provisional reporting name RAM-L, the first flight of the MiG-29UB operational conversion trainer following some years later, on 29 April 1981. Series production started at Znamya Truda, Khodynka and Gorky in June 1982. The first aircraft was delivered in 1984 and entered Soviet Air Force service the following year. By 1986, 150 aircraft were in PVO service, which included one regiment in East Germany.

A dual-role fighter optimised for air combat but with powerful attack capability, the aircraft possessed great agility and a genuine look-down/shoot-down capability offered by the NO-193 (often wrongly designated HO-93, confusion arising because the Cyrillic letter 'H' is in fact an English 'N') 'Slot Back' pulse-Doppler radar and the new snap-down AA-10 AAMs. The type underwent a number of changes whilst in production, and the first service model—seen at Kuopio and Rissala in Finland in July 1986—was without the small ventral fins of the first model. Extended dorsal fins and wider chord rudders were also observed on this aircraft. The MiG-29A had conventional instrumentation and flight controls. A unique feature are doors that are closed during take-off and landing that prevents foreign objects from entering the large engine air intake ducts whilst on the ground, the air at these times being passed to the engines through louvres in the wing extensions. In 1988, the aircraft appeared with an enlarged dorsal spine housing either more fuel or revised avionics.

The MiG-29UB was a two-seat combat-capable operational trainer derivative of the MiG-29A, with ranging radar in place of the pulse-Doppler unit of the single-seat aircraft and a slightly increased overall length of 17.4 m (57 feet). The trainer also featured a weapons system simulator allowing the instructor to generate HUD, IRST and radar symbology in the pupil's front cockpit. The navalised variant, designated MiG-29K, had its first flight in November 1989. This version featured folding wings, an arrester hook, provision for a 'buddy' refuelling pack, and a steerable IR sensor forward of the cockpit as well as a strengthened undercarriage for carrier operation. No air intake doors or top-of-wing louvres were fitted to this variant, although new avionics were provided.

A new variant, the MiG-29M, featuring an 'electronic' cockpit with flat HDD and fly-by-wire (FBW) controls has been flying since 25 April 1986, when the first of six prototypes flew at the Gromov Flight Research Institute at Zhukovsky. All six were 'new build' aircraft and received codes based on the OKB's internal 9-15 designations. The first prototype, 151, was used to prove the FBW control system; 152 was an aerodynamic and engine test bed; 153 was the radar development aircraft; 154 was the engine test bed; 155 served as a second radar/avionics integration airframe; and 156 was the ground attack avionics proving airframe. The final pair were used for air show display purposes (Farnborough, Paris, etc.).

In December 1990, the last MiG-29 for the Soviet Union was produced, some 800 having been delivered. However, an order for a further twenty-five aircraft was placed in 1992, and MiG-29M production restarted in 2000.

Mil (Mi-)

Mikhail Leontevich Mil was born on 22 November 1909 at Irkutsk. He attended the Siberian Technological Institute at Tomsk and later graduated from the Irkutsk Polytechnic Institute in 1931. He joined the Special Design Department at TsAGI, where he was involved in calculations relating to rotary-wing aircraft and also played a leading part in the design of the A-12 and A-15 autogiros in 1936, working as Kamov's deputy. Mil served at the front as an engineer with the Autogiro Artillery Communications Squadron, which was equipped with five A-7*bis* two-seat autogiros in the autumn of 1941. He returned to TsAGI in 1943 to work on problems of stability and control, and two years later became head of TsAGI's rotary wing brigade.

The Mil Experimental Design Bureau was established on 12 December 1947 to develop his GM-1 helicopter project. The Mil OKB was in fact the latest of the post-war helicopter design bureaux, and Ivan Bratukhin's OKB, which had spent many years trying to perfect the opposed twin-rotor system, was disbanded. Mil's former mentor Kamov was also working on the coaxial principle at this time. In spite of Igor Sikorsky's great success in the USA and Boris Yuryev's early pioneering work, along with the work done on the EA-1 and EA-3/5, Mil's GM-1 was the first Soviet helicopter to feature a single main rotor and a single anti-torque rotor. The main advantages of this system were the simplicity of the transmission coupled with a saving in weight as compared to the opposed twin rotor system. Like Sikorsky, Mil remained faithful to this system (with one exception, the Mi-12), which has proved so successful, and developed it over a wide range of helicopters, both with piston engines and turbine-powered designs. Improvements were made retrospectively and new designs were incorporated on older models as parts became due for renewal. A total of 3,525 were built in the Soviet Union, and 545 in China.

The Mi-4 helicopter was tested in the summer of 1952, and five years later the Mil OKB completed construction of what was then the largest helicopter in the world, the Mi-6. It was also the first helicopter to be powered by twin free turbines mounted on top of the fuselage. The engines were far enough forward for the centre of the cabin to be immediately below the helicopter's main shaft (i.e. centre of gravity) and the whole of the cabin space was available for payload. With the free turbine, rotor revolutions could change without affecting engine speed, maintaining constant revolutions up to its rated altitude. The gas turbine was also lighter per horsepower than the piston engine. This can be seen by examining the development of the Mi-2 and Mi-8 from the Mi-1 and Mi-4 respectively. For example, while using (initially) the same rotors, transmission, tail booms and undercarriage, their payloads doubled and performance was dramatically improved.

The prototype for the Mi-10 crane helicopter, the V-7, flew in 1959. It was fitted with two 42 kW (56 hp) engines, and the Mi-10 made its first flight in June 1960. In September 1961, the V-2 prototype of the Mi-2 to be produced in Poland was revealed. A further prototype to be given a 'V' designation was the V-8, the prototype of the

Mi-8, which was also unveiled in 1961. Since 1963, 8,800 Mi-8s have been built and it is still in production today. Deputy Chief Designer A. V. Nekrasov stated that more helicopters had been built by Mil than any other organisation in the world.

The maiden flight of the Soviet Union's first combat helicopter, the Mi-24, took place during a press conference at London's Gatwick Airport in March 1967, and in the July of the following year the Mi-6 was replaced as the world's largest helicopter by the Mil-12. This giant twin-rotor helicopter had more than double the carrying capacity of the Mi-6 and quickly established several international records. It departed from the traditional formula, reverting to the Bratukhin layout of the late 1940s of horizontally opposed rotors, but in this case the Mi-6 powerplants and rotor units were mounted at the ends of stub wings.

Mikhail Mil died on 31 January 1970, aged 60, and on the same day his deputy, Marat N. Tishchenko, a previously little known figure, was appointed to take over responsibility for a number of new designs such as the Mi-14, Mi-17, Mi-26 and Mi-28. The Mil OKB employed more than 4,000 people (50,000 including the three production plants), and 95 per cent of Soviet helicopters were designed and produced by Mil, compared with only 5 per cent by Kamov. Mil helicopters are probably the most widely used make throughout the world, more than 25,000 in eleven different variants having been produced since 1947. Over 10,000 of these were the popular Mi-8/17 series, which included some 2,800 for export and currently make up some 95 per cent of the CIS helicopter fleet.

In 1993, Mil helicopters, products and services comprised six different organisations headed by the Mil Moscow Helicopter Plant with its OKB and the Mil Helicopter Co. along with the Kazan Helicopter Plant, the Rostov Helicopter Production Enterprise (Rostvertol), the Ulan-Ude Aviation Plant, the US-based joint venture Mil-Brooke spares and technical support supply company, and subsidiaries Mil Light Helicopters Ltd and the MilAvia Company. The largest of the production plants are at Kazan and Ulan-Ude, with some 30,000 workers between them, and are each capable of producing two Mi-8Ts or export Mi-17s per week. The Rostov plant, which also employs some 15,000 workers, can similarly produce at least two Mi-26 Halos per week and is to manufacture the Mi-28 Night Hunter attack helicopter.

With more than 50 per cent of the current CIS helicopter fleet due for retirement by the end of the century and no light helicopters in production to replace more than 4,000 of the 5,500 Mi-2s variants produced in Poland by PZl-Świdnik, the potential production requirements for both civil and military helicopters are enormous. With well over 300 56-tonne Mi-26MK heavy lift helicopters having been built, the Moscow Helicopter Plant under Deputy General Designer Alexei Samusenko developed an uprated Mi-26M with a much-improved payload capability for 'hot & high' operations. It is fitted with new Ivchenko/Lotarev D-127 turboshafts developing 10,444 kW (14,000 hp), all-composite main rotor blades with revised aerodynamics, and an updated integrated flight control/navigation system. Maximum slung payload is 25 tonnes. The Mi-26 is the first helicopter to operate successfully with an eight-bladed rotor, enabling it to hover at 1,000 m (3,280 feet) with a 12,300 kg (27,117 lb) payload. Further developments planned for the Mi-26M are FBW controls that will probably be fitted to the Mi-26K flying crane version to replace the Mi-6s and Mi-10Ks, 80 per cent of which had come to the end of their useful lives by the end of the twentieth century.

Although a small number of pre-series aircraft were produced by Rostvertol at Rostov, the future of the Mi-28 two-seat twin turbine combat helicopter with all-weather night capability had been in doubt following a decision by the Russian Army to deploy the Kamov Ka-50 and Ka-52 as its attack helicopters. However, this was subsequently reversed in favour of the Mi-28 Night Hunter now in production.

Mikhail Mil was well rewarded for his contribution to Soviet helicopter design and development, having received the Order of Lenin three times and also the Orders of the Great Patriotic War, the Red Banner and the Red Star. As well as being a brilliant designer, Mil was adept at dealing with the worst of Soviet bureaucracy and on numerous occasions was able to side-step pressures from the Soviet High Command to produce bigger and better weapons of war. Realising the helicopter's long-term potential as a means of transport, he sought, as did his Soviet-born American counterpart Sikorsky, to develop the helicopter as a general-purpose aircraft for the benefit of mankind as a whole.

Mil Mi-1 (GM-1)

The Mi-1, originally designated GM-1, was designed by a team that included N. G. Rusanovich, G. V. Kozelkov, A. K. Kotikov and A. E. Malakovski, the first aircraft being completed in September 1948. It was a single-engined, single-rotor helicopter with an anti-torque tail rotor, and the basic design was as used by Yuryev in 1911 and by Sikorsky and others in the US and by Hafner in the UK.

The aircraft was powered by an AI-26V 7-cylinder radial engine with fan-assisted cooling specially developed for helicopters by Ivchenko and was first used on the Bratukhin G-4. Take-off power at sea-level was 429 kW (575 hp) and rated power up to 2,000 m (6,560 feet) was 343 kW (460 hp). Cruising power was 241 kW (323 hp) at 1,860 rpm. Early in the test programme the first prototype, flown by test pilot M. K. Baikalov (formerly with the Bratukhin OKB), got out of control at 5,000 m (16,400 feet) and crashed. Baikalov baled out and was lucky to escape with his life, but was unfortunately killed during the 105th flight of the second prototype whilst carrying out tolerance parameter tests. Although these tests were unpopular with test pilots, this crash was due to failure of the anti-torque tail rotor due to poor welding. Test pilots M. L. Gallai and V. V. Vinitsky continued with the test flying of the second and third prototypes, undertaking ninety-three test flights, and during factory tests a maximum speed of 118 kph (73 mph) was achieved. However, on completion of the NII acceptance tests in September 1949, test pilots G. A. Tinyakov and S. G. Brovtsev recommended that the maximum permissible speed should be limited to 170 kph (105 mph) in order to minimise the possibility of retreating blade stall at higher speeds. Later, maximum permissible speed was raised to 207 kph (128 mph).

On completion of state acceptance testing, production commenced almost immediately. Eight pre-production machines took part in the Tushino Air Show in 1951, and by the end of that year the Mi-1 had entered Soviet Air Force service. The Mi-1 was the first Soviet helicopter to enter quantity production, and it remained in production in the Soviet Union and Poland until 1965, some 1,845 Soviet examples being built. The aircraft represented a major advance in Soviet helicopter design philosophy and enabled the country to catch up with contemporary western helicopters of similar size and power. Between 1957 and 1968, the Mi-1 and the Polish built variant, the SM-1, set twenty-four world records, including six set by female crews.

The Mi-1 was capable of undertaking a wide variety of civil and military tasks, although usually unarmed. Modifications and improvements were incorporated over the years, and two major variants were built: the dual-control trainer with side-by-side seating, which was variously designated as Mi-1U (Instructional), Mi-1T (Training) or Mi-1UT (Instructional Training); and a Mi-1NKh (National Economy) all-weather, multi-purpose civil model, used for crop spraying, forestry and fishery patrol. Less successful was the Mi-1S (Ambulance) version, which at one time was thought (wrongly) to be a Mi-3 due to the fact it was fitted with a four-bladed rotor to cope with the extra weight of the externally attached panniers. In 1958, pontoons were made available for the Mi-1 and this version were then designated the Mi-1P, sometimes being used on whaling ships. Finally the Mi-1 Moskvich was developed in limited quantities in 1961 for Aeroflot as a VIP transport. This variant, which could carry three passengers, had all-metal rotor blades, better soundproofing, hydraulic controls and more comprehensive instrumentation.

Production of the Mi-1 was transferred to the WSK-PZL factory at Świdnik, Poland, in 1955. The principal reason for this move was to free Soviet factories for the production of the larger Mi-4 and Yak-24 helicopters. Now redesignated the SM-1, the aircraft incorporated a licence-built AI-26V engine that was given the designation LiT-3. During the course of the next ten years over 1,680 aircraft were built in Poland, of which 250 were exported to the Soviet Union. The Poles built a variety of types, such as the SM-1W with metal rotors; the SM-1WS ambulance version with two external stretcher pods; the SM-1SZ dual-control trainer; and the SM-2 five-seater that entered production in 1961. They also experimented with the Mi-1 by adding stub wings with a span of 7.8 m (25 feet 7 inches), a length equivalent to 54 per cent of the rotor diameter.

In 1988, the Mi-1 celebrated its 40th birthday. At that time many were still in use in both military and civil roles in Eastern Europe and the Middle East and in some Third World countries. This was in direct contrast to contemporary western helicopters, only a few of which of the same era then remained in service.

Mil Mi-8/17

In developing the medium general-purpose Mi-8 helicopter the Mil OKB used the same basic premise as employed earlier in 1961, when the Mi-1 was mated to new turboshaft engines and given a larger fuselage to produce the Mi-2. As such, a Mi-4 was fitted with a 2,013 kW (2,700 shp) Soloviev engine and given an enlarged main fuselage, the aircraft retaining the tail boom, tail rotor and four-bladed main rotor of the Mi-4. The new helicopter (Hip-A) was designated Mi-8 and first appeared on 3 July 1961 when flight trials began. However, early tests soon found it to be dangerously underpowered and, in September 1962, a second prototype (Hip-B) appeared that was fitted with two smaller 1,119 kW (1,500 shp) Izotov TV2-117 turboshaft engines in place of the single powerplant but which only limited operational improvement. In the meantime the first prototype was fitted with a five-bladed main rotor and two uprated TV2-117 engines, and it was this design that entered series production in 1964. Substantial deliveries were made to the Soviet and Warsaw Pact forces as the Hip-C assault/transport, which had a capacity for up to thirty-two assault troops who could leave the aircraft through the rear clamshell doors. The Mi-8 helicopter appeared in a number of versions, including the Hip-D, -G, -J and -K transport, communication and electronic warfare variants, the Hip-E with its 12.7 mm machine gun on a flexible mount in the nose, and the Hip-F anti-tank variant with its six Sagger missiles, as well as a SAR variant.

In 1966, the aircraft was fitted with uprated 1,268 kW (1,700 shp) TV2-117A engines, and a civil variant, the Mi-8P, entered service with a maximum passenger load of twenty-eight and a toilet, coat cupboard and luggage rack incorporated into the design. With the seats folded, the 23m^3 (248 square feet) cabin could accept up to 4,000 kg (8,820 lb) of freight through the rear doors. A VIP variant offered accommodation in comfortable seating for around ten passengers, the cabin being fitted with a galley and tables. Hungary was the recipient of a number of specially configured military variants for use in the control and command role and as ECM jammers. To date, in excess of 8,000 Mi-8s have been built and at least 1,300 are still in use with the Russian Federation Air Force, as well as many of the 1,500 sold to foreign operators that are still in use with other air arms worldwide.

Mil introduced an upgraded variant of the Mi-8 in 1981. Designated the Mi-17 Hip-H, it was powered by two 1,417 kW (1,900 shp) Izotov TV3-117MT turboshafts, either one being able to develop 1,640 kW (2,200 shp) in the event of the other's failure. The Mi-17, which is 30 per cent more powerful than the Mi-8 and enjoys greater fuel economy, can be readily distinguished from its famous counterpart by its repositioned tail rotor and shorter engine nacelles. Currently the Mi-17 is still in production at Kazan, having found a number of new markets, including South America and Europe. A number of new variants have been produced, including an NVG-capable aircraft.

Mil Mi-24 Hind

Development of the Mi-24 assault helicopter began in the late 1960s, and it is thought that the prototypes were flying in 1971. A number of Hind-B (PP models) are believed to have been delivered to two units of the VVS in East Germany for evaluation in 1972. What is certain, however, is that by early 1973, series Hind-As with a 16-degree anhedral to the stub wings and additional weapons pylons fitted were in service in East Germany alongside the earlier Hind-B (PP) models.

The Hind-A armament consisted of four AT-2 Swatter anti-tank missiles on rails under the wing-tip endplate pylons, four under-wing pylons for rocket pods, bombs or other stores. The aircraft was later fitted with more powerful 1,640 kW (2,200 shp) TV3-117 engines and the tail rotor was moved from the starboard side to the port side of the tail fin, a modification also embodied on late series production -A models. The Hind-C, as the uprated model was known, was developed by Mil into a new gunship variant featuring a completely new nose section, with stepped tandem cockpits for the pilot and weapons operator as opposed to the earlier configuration of the weapons operator being housed slightly forward of the pilot. A single 12.7 mm DShK machine gun in the nose was slaved to a chin-mounted IR sighting system. In addition, under-nose radar was fitted, and armour plating protection was introduced for the crew and critical components, as well as glass fibre skinned rotor blades instead of the original metal ones. Unusually for a helicopter gunship, the aircraft could accommodate up to eight fully armed troops in the main cabin aft of the flight deck.

Eventually the Hind-D, -E and -F variants followed the earlier models into production at the Arsenyev and Rostov series production plants, the type being operated by the Soviet forces in Afghanistan. More than 1,000 had been delivered by 1985. Some export Hind-E variants, designated Mi-25, were fitted with modified wing-tip launchers for four AT-6 Spiral anti-tank missiles and an enlarged sensor pod, the under-nose gun turret being replaced with a twin-barrel cannon mounted in a semi-cylindrical fairing on the starboard side of the front fuselage. Mi-24 Hind-D/E production continued into the early 1990s at a rate of fifteen per month for both the domestic and export markets, with exports going to a number of former Warsaw Pact countries in addition to Algeria, Iraq, Libya, Cuba and India. In excess of 3,000 were delivered.

Myasishchev (Mya-)

Vladimir Mikhailovich Myasishchev was born on 28 September 1902 at Yefremov. He was a pupil of Zhukovsky at the Moscow Higher Technical School from 1918 to 1921, and two years later he joined the Central Institute of Aviation Motors, where he worked with Klimov on aero-engine design and development. At TsAGI from 1925, he was to be assigned increasingly important roles in various Tupolev ANT designs, including the flush radiators of the R-6, the rear fuselage of the TB-3 and TB-4, and the entire design of the DIP (ANT-29).

In August 1934, Myasishchev began work on the ANT-41 (T-1). An accomplished designer of metal structures, he led moves away from the traditional Tupolev truss-corrugation to smooth, stressed-skin construction, and in 1936 went to America to help translate the DC-3 drawings at Douglas for its licensed production in the Soviet Union. Arrested in 1938 and imprisoned in GAZ-156 at Moscow, he assisted the Chief of the NKVD (Secret Police) to run the Special Brigade KB-102 responsible for developing the DVB-102 long-range, high-altitude bomber. Design started in early 1940 and prototype construction in April of that year, with the airframe in static test in the summer of 1941. However, the KB-102 Brigade was evacuated to Omsk in August 1941, which resulted in the DVB-102 prototypes being seriously delayed.

Myasishchev was made Major General Engineer in 1944, and was Chief Constructor for the development and series production of the Pe-2 bomber from 25 June 1945. He supervised eight modifications to the aircraft, of which 11,426 were built in different variants. He was working on several projects at that time, including the four-engined jet bomber WM-24, but the OKB was closed in January 1946 and Myasishchev became a lecturer at the Moscow Aviation Institute. However, in 1949, he was called back by Stalin to develop a new intercontinental jet bomber, the M-4, and his new OKB was formed on 24 March 1951 at the Moscow-Fili factory (GAZ-23) with 1,100 engineers. The last drawings were sent to production on 1 May 1952, the prototype of the M-4 strategic bomber making its first flight on 20 January 1953 and the aircraft entering series production in 1955. At the NATO aviation meeting of 1 May 1954, the bomber's existence came as a big surprise to the West. Myasishchev won the Lenin Prize for 1957 for this design.

The M-50 supersonic bomber was Myasishchev's next work, although the designer was actually Georgi Nazarov. The aircraft, which was flight tested by Nikolai Goriaynov on 27 October 1959, was considered only as a technology demonstrator for the M-52 and Khrushchev closed the Myasishchev OKB once again in 1960. Myasishchev was appointed Director of TsAGI, but in 1967 he received a new OKB mainly for the development of a supersonic transport aircraft and missiles, although it was to be the Tupolev OKB that designed the Tu-144 SST, the chosen Soviet aircraft for production in this field.

Myasishchev died on 14 October 1978, aged 76, and responsibility for the OKB and the Experimental Machine Factory 'Sickle and Hammer' that produced the Myasishchev designs was ultimately taken over by the Molniya Scientific and Industrial Enterprise. Later designs to come out of the Myasishchev OKB were the single-engined M-17 Mystic-A and the development of the twin-engined M-55 super high altitude atmospheric and reconnaissance aircraft (equivalent to the Lockheed U-2 spy plane), which was shown at the Farnborough Air Show in 1994.

Myasishchev strategic long-range bombers

The Soviets' first strategic long-range bomber was conceived as early as 1951, along with a passenger derivative the M-6P. The first example from Myasishchev was the SDB strategic bomber powered by four 8,250 kg (18,188 lb) AM-TKRD-03 engines with a maximum speed of 700 kph (435 mph). It was slightly faster than the M-4

Bison that followed and its range was estimated at over 12,000 km (7,456 miles). The SDB was superseded at the Myasishchev OKB by the 1M (customer designation) M-2 (OKB designation), which had the outer engines moved symmetrically inboard, necessitating the addition of small pods to house the outrigger landing gear. This variant was powered by four 8,500 kg (18,739 lb) AM-TKRD-03 engines with a maximum speed of 930 kph (578 mph) at an altitude of 12,000 m (39,370 feet). There appears to have been considerable confusion over this version's designation. Initially the first version built was designated M-4 by the OKB, but 2M by the customer, with a 3M variant subsequently. The final model in this series was a passenger variant designated M-29 (or M-28?) or M-6P, itself a derivative of the M-6 bomber. The M-4 Bison-B was a direct descendant of these early versions.

As already mentioned, Myasishchev was working at the Moscow Aviation Institute following the closure of his OKB. However, he was keen to return to aircraft design and indicated to Stalin that he was interested in submitting a design to meet the Soviet requirement for a long-range strategic bomber. Stalin instructed that he should submit his designs and aspirations in writing, being, as they were, in direct competition with Tupolev. This he did, and on 24 March 1951, within days of copies of his letter having been placed before the Soviet Council of Ministers, the Minister of Aircraft Production was authorised to reopen the Myasishchev OKB in order to produce a flying strategic bomber prototype. The bureau was called OKB-23, as it was located at GAZ-23, which although originally in Leningrad was then at the new Fili factory on the famous Junkers site of some twenty years earlier. Virtually all Myasishchev's bombers were built at GAZ-23, although later many were rebuilt for other roles at Ryazan.

Myasishchev DVB-102

While interned in Moscow in 1938, Myasishchev started work on a design for a high-altitude, long-range, twin-engined bomber. The proposed aircraft was to have a range of 4,000 km (2,485 miles), a speed of over 500 kph (310 mph) and a service ceiling of 3,048 m (10,000 feet) and was to be powered by the newly developed 1,342 kW (1,800 hp) M-120TK engines fitted with turbo superchargers. Construction of the prototype began in May 1940, but release from internment in the summer of 1941, with the subsequent reinstatement of Myasishchev and his team at Omsk, caused a temporary halt in progress.

The DVB-102 was an all-metal cantilever high-wing monoplane with a twinned tailplane and retractable tricycle nose-wheel undercarriage. The wing, of unusually high aspect ratio, appeared to be too slender for such a heavy aircraft. Its spacious bomb bay could accommodate a single 2,000 kg (4,409 lb) bomb. The bomb bay doors were hydraulically operated and were retracted inwards to reduce drag. Many variations of its offensive load were proposed, and the internal bomb load could be augmented by an external load of 2,000 kg. Defensive armament consisted of a flexible-mounted 20 mm ShVAK cannon in the nose and two turrets in the rear section of the fuselage (upper and lower). The upper turret included a 12.7 mm UBK and 7.62 mm ShKAS machine gun on a common mounting, the lower turret carrying a single UBK gun. It was also planned that the aircraft would carry an RSB-BIS transceiver and AFA-6 camera.

Amongst the innovations introduced in the DVB-102 airframe was the installation of two separate pressurised cabins, allowing the crew to carry out their duties without the need for oxygen masks at all altitudes up to its service ceiling. The construction of these pressurised cabins and the extensive research and design work undertaken by Myasishchev and his team strongly influenced the work that followed by other OKB design teams. Another major innovation was the tricycle nose-wheel undercarriage designed to make take-off and landing easier, the DVB-102 being the first Soviet aircraft fitted with such an undercarriage. The nose-wheel retracted into the fuselage; the main wheels into the engine nacelles. Another important improvement was the use of a remotely operated, hydraulically controlled gun turret.

On 17 February 1942, test pilot V. Zhdanov flew the DVB-102 on its maiden flight, later flights being made by test pilot F. Opsdchi. Flights were made with and without the use of the engine supercharger, and this stage of the flight development was concluded by 2 September 1942, although it had been somewhat adversely affected by the poor reliability of the M-120 engines. Only eleven flights were made at normal take-off weight, and just a further nineteen at reduced flight weight. At the end of May the first set of M-120 engines had been replaced by another set and in July the turbochargers had been deleted, which led to modification of the exhaust and the inlet ducting and changes to the shape of the engine cowlings and to the fuel system. Removal of the turbochargers was made for two reasons: their poor performance and the need for greater take-off power. The revised engine worked satisfactorily at all altitudes up to 8,000 m (26,246 feet). The final test report stated that the performance of the DVB-102 was equal to the best foreign aircraft of this class, and that its speed was better than that of contemporary Soviet and foreign long-range bombers and very close to many medium- and short-range bombers of this period. However, whilst the flight characteristics of the DVB-102 were very good, its M-120 engines were still very unreliable. An alternative source of power was found in the form of two 1,567 kW (2,100 hp) M-71 radial engines, which necessitated a redesign of the engine nacelles and mountings. Initially the engines were fitted with superchargers, and later with TK-3 turbo-superchargers.

Flight development of the revised DB-102 continued in May 1943, although the events of the summer of that year severely affected its further development, in particular the appointment of Myasishchev to the post of Chief Designer to one of the Pe-2 production works. He had been entrusted with the development and production of the Pe-2 after Petlyakov was killed in an air crash, leaving only Myasishchev's design team to continue the work on the DVB-102. In August 1943, test pilot Zhdanov flew the DVB-102 on the Omsk–Kazan–Moscow route, demonstrating its excellent flight characteristics. However, its new M-71 engines appeared to be as unreliable as the original M-120s and were replaced with the M-71F, but the unreliability remained. The main source of the problem proved to be the turbochargers that had also adversely affected development of the M-71-powered I-185 fighter aircraft designed by Polikarpov.

Flight development of the DVB-102 continued and did not conclude until 1946. The M-71F variant had a maximum take-off weight of 15,500 kg (34,172 lb) and a maximum speed of 570 kph (354 mph) at 8,500 m (27,887 feet), with a service ceiling of 10,750 m (35,269 feet). Range when fully laden with maximum fuel was 3,740 km (2,324 miles). Eventually the DVB-102 shared the fate of numerous wartime developments and failed to enter series production, due mainly to the unreliability of its engines. It should be noted that a number of alternative engines (MB-100, M-82, ASh-73 and M-20) were proposed but not used. Also at this time, Stalin demanded all efforts be applied to copying the captured Boeing B-29 bomber aircraft, eventually leading to the production of the Tupolev Tu-4.

Petlyakov (Pe-)

Born on 15 June 1891 at Sambek near Rostov, Vladimir Mikhailovich Petlyakov was a graduate of Taganrog Technical School. From 1911 he was a student of Zhukovsky at the Moscow Higher Technical School, and on graduating in 1920 he joined the Hydro-Aviation and Experimental Construction Section of TsAGI. Here he worked on the ANT-1 hydroplane boat and torpedo boats and airships (first flight, June 1926) as well as early Tupolev aircraft and aerosleighs. He was head of the TsAGI First Design Brigade from 1925 until 1926, working on the TB-1 (ANT-4) and TB-3, and was also responsible for the ANT-20 'Maksim Gorky' while Tupolev was abroad visiting the US aircraft industry.

The TB-1 prototype twin-engined monoplane bomber first flew on 24 November 1925, production aircraft entering service as the first Soviet heavy bombers in 1929. In 1936, Petlyakov was appointed Chief Designer at the Experimental Design factory and became responsible for the design and development of the TB-7 (ANT-42) heavy long-range bomber, which was later designated as Pe-8 in January 1941.

After his arrest in 1938 he was incarcerated in the TsKB-29 Special Prison, set up at GAZ-156, where he was placed in charge of KB-100, from which the number of his next project was derived. Project 100 was designated Pe-2 in January 1941. Subsequently the Pe-3 interceptor was derived from Project 100 (or Samolet 100). During the early development of the Pe-2 the design team were transferred to the infamous Menzhinsky Factory No. 39, the aircraft being introduced into production there and at Factory No. 22. Following the evacuation of both factories to Kazan in 1941, Petlyakov was appointed Chief Designer at the Kazan factory, Pe-2 production continuing at a rate of approximately thirteen per day during the peak period from 1942 to 1944.

Vladimir Petlyakov was killed on 12 January 1942 whilst flying in the second series Pe-2 aircraft from Kazan to Moscow. His death was followed by arrests and a full investigation personally ordered by Stalin into the cause of death of his talented designer and patriot. A. M. Izakson, who had been a fellow prisoner and one of Petlyakov's closest associates, took over direction of the design bureau. However, shortly afterwards he was replaced by A. I. Putilov, who was in turn replaced by Vladimir Myasishchev in 1943. The OKB was finally closed down in 1946.

Petlyakov Pe-2

Late in 1939, a decision was made to build the VI-100 high-altitude bomber designed by Petlyakov. It was a complex and expensive three-seat bomber with heavy armament, and Arkhangelsky, Ilyushin and Yakovlev OKBs made a number of engineers available to KB-100 to increase the total workforce to 300 personnel. The new aircraft was designated PB-100, with a crew of three rather than the original two. The final crew cabin arrangements resulted in the pilot being seated ahead of the wing, the navigator/bomb-aimer prone beneath the floor, and the radio operator/gunner aft of the wing. The type, of all-metal construction, was a thoroughly modern concept with a cantilever low-set wing, endplate vertical tail surfaces, a circular-section fuselage and retractable tail-wheel landing gear. There were two armament schemes: one with four ShKAS machine guns in the nose and two pairs (above/below) at the rear; the other with two ShKAS guns on the left and two ShVAKs on the right, all located under the fuselage in a shallow box on pivots to angle all four downwards in the attack profile. The aircraft's bomb load was 1,000 kg (2,205 lb), of which 600 kg (1,320 lb) was carried internally, and five rubberised fabric fuel tanks were rendered inert by the application of cooled exhaust gases. The design was rationalised to reduce production man-hours.

A single PB-100 produced by modification of the second prototype VI-100 completed NII acceptance tests in early June 1940, the aircraft proving to be an outstanding tactical bomber. On 23 June, a decision was made to mass-produce it with a number of small modifications without producing a further prototype. Production was to take place at GAZ-22 (Fili) and GAZ-39 (Khodynka). GAZ-22 received the first modified example on 7 July and the first series production aircraft was flown just four months later, on 18 November. In the spring of 1941, two new plants, GAZ-124 at Kazan and GAZ-125 at Irkutsk, began tooling up for Pe-2 bomber production, the aircraft having received its new designation in January that year. Up until 22 June 1941, a total of 460 Pe-2s were built, mostly at Fili. At that time, 437 were in service with the Soviet Air Force, but only ninety-two were in service with the units in the five military districts lying on the western border. The Byelorussian MD alone had forty-two of these. The remainder were with Nos 5, 6, 18 and 95 Training Regiments. Initially Pe-2 losses were low, and on the other hand production was increasing, with 1,405 built between July and December 1941. For this reason, more Pe-2s units were formed. On 7 July 1941, 410 BAP (Bomber Aviation Regiment) was created and three days later the ex-Byelorussian MD—now Western Front—had already received sixty additional Pe-2s to replace the original forty-two aircraft it had received at the start of the war. However, from 20 August new regiments received only twenty aircraft each. In October 1941, both GAZ-22 and GAZ-39 were evacuated from Moscow, GAZ-22 to Kazan and GAZ-39 to Irkutsk. Because of problems with metal supplies, in late 1941 GAZ-22 produced the fuselage rear section from wood. This also changed the aircraft's external appearance, and gradually the glazed area was reduced and the small glass windows at the extreme end of the tail disappeared completely.

On 22 February 1942, the VVS had six Pe-2 regiments on the Moscow Front, and by April the Pe-2 was already the main Soviet tactical bomber. Production of the type increased quickly, GAZ-22 alone increasing its output from 108 aircraft in March to 210 in December 1942. The construction man-hours were reduced from 25,300 in 1941 to only 13,200 in 1942, and the cost also decreased from 420,000 roubles in 1941 to 353,000 in 1942, and to 265,000 in 1943 and 1944. Unfortunately the performance of the later aircraft did not match that of the earlier ones, due to an increase in weight (armour and armament) and poorer quality production. In the factories in the East, women, old people and juveniles worked in very bad conditions—12 hours a day on very small rations—and the skill levels were too low to permit production of bombers without many shortcomings. Only the fitting of more powerful engines could increase the type's performance, the 179A series receiving the 947 kW (1,270 hp) M-105PF. The change of engine was in fact partially forced on the production plants, as the earlier M-105R engine was withdrawn from production in order to increase output of the M-105P variant needed for fighter aircraft.

Conceived as a light bomber, the PB-100 (Pe-2) performed a wide range of duties with great success and rightly achieved a reputation for its ruggedness and adaptability, doubling as a dive bomber and tactical level reconnaissance bomber and eventually serving as a long-range night fighter as well. Its design bore some resemblance to and influence from the Junkers Ju 88. Bomb load varied between 600 kg (1,320 lb) and an overload of 1,000 kg (2,205 lb) carried in small bays in the fuselage and the rear of the engine nacelles, and also on external racks beneath the inner wings. The aircraft was reported to be steady in a dive, and a stable bombing platform. Large numbers were used by the Soviet Air Force during the war, and post-war it equipped many of the Soviet satellite air arms. Some with modified noses were fitted with a single forward machine gun and two guns in a turret at the rear of the cockpit canopy.

The Pe-2U, a dual-controlled trainer with a second cockpit in the place of the turret and No. 2 fuel tank, was built in 1943. The instructor sat in a slightly elevated position compared to the student, providing better forward vision. Many other versions of the Pe-2 were built, such as reconnaissance and ground attack aircraft, torpedo bombers, etc., although the main variant was always the tactical bomber, in which role very heavy losses were experienced. From 1-15 July 1943, for example, during the Battle of Kursk a total of 207 Pe-2s were destroyed.

From the 205th series aircraft, 100 production aircraft received new individual exhaust pipes (reactive) resulting in an increase in speed. On the 271st series aircraft the bomb racks were moved inside and VISh-61P propellers were fitted. In general, aircraft produced in 1944 were heavier (normal weight was now 8,000 kg (17,637 lb) as opposed to 7,700 kg (16,975 lb), although the overall speed increased by between 5 and 30 kph (3 and 18.6 mph) over the earlier aircraft of 1943. Also in 1943, a radial engined variant was introduced and in the spring of the following year 135 bombers were produced with 1,149 kW (1,540 hp) M-82FN engines. Many of these aircraft were delivered to reconnaissance units, each receiving between three and five aircraft.

The Pe-2I was a rather radical transformation of the original design. Firstly it was equipped with 1,230 kW (1,650 hp) M-107 engines. Engine nacelles were lengthened and the wing had a new profile and was placed directly in the middle of the fuselage. The fuselage itself was widened to permit carriage of a new bomb type, being fatter and shorter. Bomb load was increased to 3,000 kg (6,614 lb)—1,000 kg (2,205 lb) on earlier versions only. The aircraft had a crew of two and the defensive armament of a UBT MG, and a remotely controlled UBT in the tail was operated by the navigator. Other changes occurred to the equipment fit and the undercarriage. The Pe-2K that followed was in reality a new aircraft designed by Myasishchev. It passed its NII VVS trials in May and June 1944 and was accepted for series production. A transition series variant incorporated the wings, nacelles and undercarriage of the Pe-2I with other parts from the earlier Pe-2, including the M-105PF engines. A small number of series Pe-2Is and Pe-2Ks were produced in 1945. However, many M-107A engines failed to attain anticipated performance so were changed to M-105PF standard. Pe-2 production was finally halted during the winter of 1945/46 after a total production run of 11,427 had been built, making it the most prolific Soviet bomber design of the Second World War.

On 1 October 1944, the Red Air Force had 1,766 Pe-2 bombers with sixty regiments on the German Front alone. The type saw considerable post-war use, although from 1947 it began to be replaced by the Tupolev Tu-2. However, the Pe-2 did not finally leave Soviet Air Force service until 1951. The Finnish Air Force's PLeLv 48 (48th Bomber Squadron) had used three captured Pe-2s as reconnaissance aircraft during the Second World War. In May 1945, the Polish Air Force had 107 Pe-2s in service. Also in 1945, Bulgaria received ninety-eight Pe-2s and Czechoslovakia had about twenty (designated B-32), and Yugoslavia also received a large number post-war. The last Pe-2s to be exported in 1950 went to China and Hungary. Hungary received three, but all were destroyed whilst on acceptance flights. A further development of the Pe-2 was the Pe-3, which was produced specifically for night fighting and reconnaissance. Entering service in mid-1943, it was powered by two 977 kW (1,310 hp) M-105PF engines and featured a 'solid' nose and a shorter cockpit enclosure with a dorsal turret to the rear.

Petlyakov Pe-8

Although the Soviet authorities did not seriously support the concept of heavy strategic bombers in the Second World War, design of the ANT-42 had been started in

September 1934. The aircraft was intended as the successor to the TB-3 heavy bomber. In October 1934, the Soviet Air Force issued specifications for a new heavy bomber with a maximum speed of 600 kph (373 mph), a 15,000 m (49,212 feet) ceiling and a range of 2,000 km (1,243 miles). The following year the specification was revised for the aircraft to be configured as a troop transport for up to fifty troops or a heavy bomber with a maximum speed of 400 kph (248 mph), an operational ceiling of 12,000 m (39,370 feet) and a range of 3,800 km (2,361 miles) with a 2,000 kg (4,409 lb) bomb load. The prototype ANT-42 was powered by an ATsN unit comprising a 634 kW (850 hp) M-100 and four 694 kW (930 hp) AM-34FRNB propulsion engines. The aircraft was designed for a maximum crew of eleven.

The Petlyakov Brigade was chosen for the design, and the prototype (c/n 4201), built at GAZ-156, was rolled out on 9 November 1936. Flight trials started on 27 December, the aircraft being piloted by Mikhail Gromov. Despite the aircraft being damaged in a heavy landing incident (with a different pilot) GAZ tests were completed on 20 March 1937 and NII VVS testing was carried out between 11 August and 28 October 1937, a second series of joint GAZ/NII VVS tests being undertaken between 6 March and 30 April 1938. As a result of these tests a number of changes were carried out. At this time the programme was managed by Josef Nezval as Petlyakov had been interned. In addition, the two senior VVS proponents of the project had been removed: Marshal Mikhail Tukhachevsky was executed and General Yakov Alksnis died in prison. Nevertheless, in early 1936 a second ANT-42 prototype (c/n 4202) was authorised. Completed in May 1938, it was first flown on 26 July that year.

The second prototype embodied a number of improvements, including the fitting of four FRNV-type engines with all four radiators inboard and the ATsN driven by an M-100A engine instead of the M-100. The aircraft's normal bomb load was now six FAB-100s or four FAB-250s with full fuel (two FAB-2000s if less than a full load). Amongst the crew of eleven were five gunners. Five PP aircraft had been authorised in April 1937, but increasing disinterest in heavy bombers culminated in the cancellation of these aircraft at a Kremlin meeting that called a halt to the programme in early 1939. However, A. I. Filin, head of the NII VVS, eventually succeeded in reversing this decision and production of the pre-series aircraft was authorised at GAZ-124 at Kazan under the Red Air Force designation TB-7. The main influence in this decision was the selection of the supercharged AM-35 radials as the main engines in place of the ATsN installation. The AM-35 was itself superseded by the AM-35A high-altitude engine, developing 895 kW (1,200 hp).

Initial aircraft suffered severe engine problems in operational service and Nezval desperately sought alternative engines. A number of aircraft were built with a variety of engines (M-30, M-40, M-82) until 7 December 1940, when it was decided to standardise on the M-40F inline diesel engine without changing the type's designation. Seventeen aircraft were produced with the 1,119 kW (1,500 hp) M-40, although the fitting of diesel engines was abandoned after only six of the aircraft returned to base at Pushkino following a bombing raid on Berlin. Of the eighteen aircraft prepared for the raid, one crashed from engine failure on take-off, one was shot down by friendly fire (flak) and at least three suffered engine failure prior to reaching the target. Of the eleven that reached Berlin, excepting the six that returned to base, all but one made forced landings due to engine failure. Consequently the diesel engine conversion programme was terminated. In 1941, the type was redesignated Pe-8 and variants produced in 1943/44 returned to the 1,268 kW (1,700 hp) ASh-82 (M-82) radial engines, although the last four aircraft produced in 1944 were fitted with ACh-30B diesels.

The Pe-8 was the only modern four-engined Soviet heavy bomber to see service in the Second World War, holding the distinction of being the world's first bomber to drop 5-tonne bombs. A number of Pe-8s were used during the war and afterwards as engine test beds and several were used on transport duties. One was used to fly Vyacheslav Molotov to RAF Tealing in Scotland for a meeting on 20 May 1942. Two civil-registered aircraft (CCCP-H395 and CCCP-H419) helped in setting up the Nordpol Arctic Station. CCCP-H395 was lost in the Arctic on 7 June 1947, whilst CCCP-H419 was instrumental in the expedition's withdrawal in 1952, undertaking the 5,000-km (3,106-mile) flight to Moscow non-stop.

Polikarpov (Po-)

Born on 8 July 1892, Nikolai Nikolaevich Polikarpov was one of the main pioneers of Soviet aviation. In twenty-two years he was responsible for the design of no fewer than forty different aircraft and hundreds of modifications. More Polikarpov-designed aircraft were built in the Soviet Union before the Second World War than the total of all the other types. However, by 1940, the virtual monopoly that Polikarpov had enjoyed in fighter, reconnaissance and trainer aircraft design was coming to an end as a number of new Soviet designers entered the field.

Polikarpov had graduated from St Petersburg Polytechnic Institute in January 1916 and first worked under Igor Sikorsky at the Russo-Baltic Wagon Works where he helped to prepare the S-16 escort fighter for production and worked on the later models of the great four-engined Sikorsky Ilya Muromets bombers. After the revolution he went to the Directorate of the VVF and from there was sent to the Duks Works in Moscow, which was about the only pre-revolution aircraft factory still in production in 1918. Under Polikarpov's direction the SPAD S.VII was put into production, and later, when the factory had become GAZ-1, the Aviakhim, DH.4, DH.9, and DH.9A were manufactured there. Between 1923 and 1930, 2,800 R-1s (DH.9s) were built. Polikarpov also designed a twin-float undercarriage for a seaplane version of the DH.9A.

Polikarpov was appointed Director of the OSS Department of Landplane Construction, based at Factory No. 25, in 1925. His first fighter, the cantilevered low-wing monoplane Il-400 powered by an American Liberty engine, was apparently an extremely tricky aircraft to fly and only thirty-three were built. However, this was the first series production of a Soviet designed fighter aircraft and it was followed by a series of biplanes of mixed construction. The U-2 trainer, which Polikarpov designed in 1928, was still flying in the Soviet Union in the 1960s, and nearly 40,000 of the type were built between 1928 and 1953. Later redesignated as the Po-2, the aircraft saw action in the Second World War as a light night bomber and for agent-dropping. It was still in use in the early 1950s, serving in Korea as a night nuisance raider.

Polikarpov and Dmitry Grigorovich, who had been Director of the Department of Experimental Marine Aircraft Design, were placed in detention in 1930, along with their staff, at Menzhinsky Factory No. 39 and were thus 'pioneers' of the Soviet Special Prison system. They earned their release by designing the single-seat I-5 biplane fighter, 803 of which were built between 1931 and 1934, and the I-Z cannon monoplane fighter, seventy-one of which were built between 1933 and 1935. Polikarpov went to Factory No. 36 as Chief Designer following his release from detention and enjoyed a brief spell as one of the Soviet Union's most successful aircraft designers. A number of his designs entered series production, notably the R-5 aircraft (4,914 being produced from 1930 to 1935), the R-5SSS (620 from 1935 to 1937) and the R-7 (1,031 during the same period).

The success Polikarpov enjoyed with these designs probably saved him from the Communist Party's pre-war purges. The I-15, I-15*bis* and I-16 series of biplane and monoplane fighters established a reputation for themselves during the early part of the Spanish Civil War, the first I-15s arriving at Cartagena on 13 October 1936. Subsequent Soviet deliveries to the Republicans totalled over 1,400 military aircraft, paid for by Spanish gold reserves.

Polikarpov designs monopolised the Red Air Force fighter arm during the 1930s, and it was this reputation that probably stood him in good stead when new prototypes from the Polikarpov Brigade started to suffer accidents. Towards the end of the 1930s, the brigade turned out an impressive number of prototypes and production aircraft ranging from single-seat fighters to heavy bombers. These included the I-16, (9,450 built from 1934 to 1941), the I-15 (384 built from 1934 to 1936), the I-152 (2,408 built in 1938/39) and the I-153 (3,437 built from 1939 to 1941). Unfortunately they were all plagued with a series of mishaps, many of which were fatal. These started with the I-17 undercarriage failures and included the break-up of the VIT-2 (which resulted in the temporary imprisonment of Polikarpov's assistant Zhemchuzin) and the I-180 losses that caused the deaths of famous test pilots V. P. Chkalov, on 15 December 1938, and A. G. Proshakov and Tomas Suzi (although the cause appeared to be engine failure) for which Chief Designer Dmitry Tomashevich was held responsible. Another development aircraft, the I-185, also suffered from engine failure, killing test pilot V. A. Stepanchenok.

In 1941, the Polikarpov OKB was evacuated to Novosibirsk where development of the I-185 and work on the BDP assault glider was continued, the OKB returning to Moscow with the other design bureaux in 1941/42. Following Polikarpov's death on

30 July 1944, work on the rocket-powered Malyutka fighter and the VP high-altitude fighter was abandoned. Of the dozen or so prototypes completed by the OKB between 1938 and 1943, only the BDP glider reached production status.

Polikarpov U-2/Po-2

A simple but effective wooden, fabric-covered training biplane, the U-2 made its first flight on 7 January 1928. It was ordered into production at GAZ-23 (Leningrad) and GAZ-387 (Stalingrad) in 1930, production continuing throughout the war. In 1941, 1,245 U-2s were built at Stalingrad alone, and by the December of that year some 13,700 U-2 biplane trainers had been built, the plant being evacuated to Kazan in August 1942.

In June 1941, about 7,500 U-2s were in service with the Soviet Air Force and DOSAAF, as well as with Aeroflot for agricultural purposes. From October to December 1941, the VVS formed seventy-one LNB (light night bomber) regiments with 1,500 U-2s acquired from DOSAAF. Pilots were recruited from VVS instructors and DOSAAF students. The LNB regiments became expert at night harassment of German troops, although losses were still very heavy, only 375 LNB U-2s remaining in service on 1 May 1942. The type was redesignated Po-2 in July 1944 as a night harassment bomber.

Use of the type as a light night bomber resulted in production of the U-2WS (military variant) at GAZ-387 and in a number of small factories normally involved in furniture making, such as Zavod 494 in late 1942 and Zavods 464 and 471 in 1943. Between July 1941 and May 1945, 15,500 U-2s were built, mainly as LNBs capable of carrying a 200-300 kg (440-660 lb) bomb load, but also as ambulance, liaison, trainers and three-seat transport aircraft. From May 1942, ten LNB divisions were formed— Nos 208, 213, 218, 242, 262, 271, 272, 312, 313 and 314—each with ninety-eight U-2 LNBs, and there were also many U-2 LNB regiments in bomber and other mixed divisions. Over a three-year period production of the U-2 increased constantly: 2,243 in 1942; 3,127 in 1943; and 5,133 in 1944. A total of 17,140 aircraft were built between 1941 and 1945.

The U-2 was used to carry out harassing attacks against Axis troop concentrations and lines of communication behind the front using small fragmentation bombs. The German troops referred to these antiquated aircraft, which were often flown by women pilots, as 'sewing machines'. But the constant presence of these nuisance raids caused considerable discomfort and resulted in many losses in concentration of troops who were not as yet used to air attacks. By the autumn of 1942 the raids had become a source of inspiration to the Soviets, as well as an extreme annoyance to the German Air Force. As a result, the Luftwaffe started to use obsolete but more powerful aircraft in its own newly formed harassment units. However, the number of aircraft available to the Germans was only a fraction of the Soviet U-2 inventory and was therefore much less effective. For this reason night harassment raids remained a speciality of the Soviets throughout the Second World War. When Polikarpov died in July 1944, the U-2 was renamed Po-2 in his memory. In October that year the VVS had 1,500 ambulance, liaison and transport Po-2s on the German Front as well as more than 2,000 LNBs and 5,000 training aircraft.

On 10 May 1945, the new Polish Air Force had 215 Po-2s out of a total inventory of 751 aircraft (28.63 per cent). After the war, GAZ-387 at Kazan continued to build civil Po-2 aircraft for DOSAAF, as trainers and for Aeroflot as ambulances, liaison and transport aircraft etc. A further 7,200 were produced up until 1953, when large supplies of Antonov An-2 and Yakovlev Yak-18 aircraft began to replace them, giving a total build of some 40,000 aircraft. Between 1948 and 1955, 550 other Po-2s were built in Poland, designated CSS-13: WSK Okęcie built 311 CSS-13s and fifty-nine S-13 ambulance aircraft, and PZL Mielec built 180 CSS-13s. The type was finally withdrawn from use in 1962.

Polikarpov I-16
The I-16 was the first low-wing fighter monoplane to enter service fitted with fully retractable landing gear. It had a cantilevered metal wing matched to a monocoque wooden fuselage fitted with a manually retracted main undercarriage, and had long-span split ailerons that doubled as flaps. The I-16 was truly the world's first 'modern' monoplane fighter.

The type first flew as the TsKB-12 on 31 December 1933, fitted with a 358 kW (480 hp) M-22 radial engine. Two months later the TsKB*bis* was flown, with an imported 529 kW (710 hp) Wright SR-1820-F3 Cyclone radial, offering better performance although not overcoming the type's shortcomings in handling, probably caused by its short and portly fuselage which reduced its longitudinal stability. With a wingspan of 9 m (30 feet), an overall length of 6 m (20 feet) and its blunt nose and cockpit set well back on its short, stubby fuselage, it became known as Polikarpov's *yastrebok* or 'little hawk'. An initial production batch of ten was ordered, fitted with the M-22 engine in view of its speed and good rate of climb. A fast and rugged little aircraft, it attracted much foreign interest before the war and was widely employed by the Soviets in Spain and Finland. Normal armament was two 20 mm ShVAK and two 7.62 mm ShKAS machine guns, as well as provision for small bombs or six rocket projectiles under-wing. Although obsolete by the beginning of the Second World War, the aircraft continued to render the Soviets valuable service until more modern machines replaced it in 1943.

From 1934 until 1940 production totalled 6,554 aircraft of varying types that were progressively better powered and better armed. In June 1941, it bore the brunt of the German attacks, even though Red Air Force fighter pilots used to the more docile I-5 and I-7 biplanes and the I-4 sesquiplane fighters found its much faster landing and take-off speeds somewhat disconcerting. Pilots often misjudged landing speeds and stalled on approach and underestimated take-off runs and careered off the runway, and when they put the little fighter into a tight turn they were alarmed by its tendency to fall into a vicious spin. They disliked its cramped, enclosed cockpit and the high level of concentration needed to fly it successfully in combat. As aversion to the aircraft grew and the accident rate escalated, a programme to lengthen fighter airfield runways was put in hand and Polikarpov was instructed to produce a two-seat fighter variant (UTI-4) to permit conversion training. As a concession to grant the fighter pilots better all-round visibility, permission was given for the inferior Plexiglas canopy to be removed—in the absence of airborne radios this also permitted them to communicate by hand signals—and pilots continued to fly throughout the 1930s with open cockpits. NII VVS test pilots carried out exhaustive trials on spin recovery, and a manual was issued to all combat units on the handling of the new fighters.

In late 1935, senior NII VVS pilots toured the fighter units, instructing, advising, demonstrating and displaying the aircraft in order to instil confidence in those who were destined to fly the I-16 in combat. To some degree these measures worked and the airframe, which lent itself to easy and continued modification, was continually upgraded to meet the pressing need of the Soviet Air Force to replace fighter losses in 1941/42. Production of the type was reinstated using the M-63 radial engine under the designations Type 28 and Type 30, with a further 450 produced. There was also a dive bomber variant, designated SPB, and a dual-control trainer, designated I-16UTI. The I-16 was the last Polikarpov design to be produced, and the OKB was disbanded following his death in 1944.

Shcherbakov (Shche-)

Alexei Shcherbakov was the Chief Engineer and Director of GAZ-45 at Chkalov. In July 1942, a design designated TS-1 was started to meet an urgent requirement for a utility transport to carry items to front-line areas and various factories and repair facilities. Needed as a replacement for the U-2 and R-5, the aircraft was required to have the capability to carry loads weighing up to 1 tonne and have the ability to be converted for use in the CASEVAC and passenger transport roles. Finance for the project was obtained from Naval Aviation in September 1942 and design work was completed in six weeks, work starting on the prototype TS-1 before the end of the year. As far as possible non-strategic materials were to be used for its construction and the airframe was designed for lightness even at the cost of labour-intensive construction. Because the intended engine, the MG-31, was no longer available, the much less powerful M-11 was used, which despite lacking in performance was judged not to be dangerous and adequate for the job.

The aircraft was a twin-engined, high-wing design with a light boxed section fuselage. The airframe was fabric-covered and spray-doped, and there was a single loading door on the port side of the fuselage. The first flight is often reported as occurring sometime in 1942, although it is now thought that this did not actually take place until the flight testing programme started on 17 April 1943, with immediate progression to NII VVS testing and a decision to start series production in August 1943. With the start of series production, the aircraft received the designation Shche-2.

The first series aircraft flew on 1 August 1944 and between 1944 and 1948, 550 Shche-2 aircraft were produced at Chkalov. The first production aircraft made twenty full load flights on the Chalov–Kuibyshev–Moscow route, thereby demonstrating an expected in-service life of 1,000 hours. Series aircraft were also used as sixteen-seat passenger transports, air ambulances with eleven stretchers, assault transports to carry nine paratroopers, or as five-pupil navigation trainers.

There were a number of experimental models, which included a lighter variant with the same tail but the wing cut down to 55 m² (592 square feet) and another variant fitted with General Motors diesel engines developed for US armoured vehicles. Although OKB Deputy Chief M. V. Iyapin suggested a twin-boom version with a third M-11D engine at the rear of the cargo nacelle, this was never built. The final model built was the Shche-2SKh, which had main-gear landing legs that were 450 mm longer and 800 x 260 mm tyres. However, this model was never accepted into series production due to its extremely poor performance. By western standards the basic aircraft was grossly underpowered, but none the less it was an easy aircraft to fly and could even remain above the stall on one engine at about 80 kph (50 mph).

Sikorsky (S-)

Igor Ivanovich Sikorsky was born in Kiev on 25 May 1889. Renowned worldwide as the father of the helicopter, Sikorsky's interest in aviation and science in general began whilst he was still a schoolboy making model aeroplanes and small rubber-band-powered helicopters. His interest was bolstered further after accompanying his father on a trip to Germany, where he met the Wright brothers and Count von Zeppelin. In 1903, Sikorsky entered the naval academy in St Petersburg with the intention of becoming a career officer in the Imperial Russian Navy. However, he resigned three years later to concentrate on engineering, going to Paris to further his studies. After returning to Kiev he entered the Mechanical Engineering College of the Polytechnic Institute in 1907, but within two years he had returned to Paris, which was then the Mecca of pioneering aviation, to further his learning in this field.

Whilst in the French capital he became acquainted with Louis Blériot, Ferdinand Ferber and many other famous names. Suitably impressed, he returned to Kiev to put his theories into practice, and having borrowed some money from his sister he set about designing his first helicopter, which actually failed to lift his own weight—as did his second design a year later. Disappointed but not disillusioned, he turned his attention to more conventional fixed-wing flight, designing his first aircraft, the S-1 biplane, which he tested in 1910. The biplane's 11 kW (15 hp) engine proved inadequate, and it was to suffer the same fate as his first helicopters. However, a swift redesign and a larger engine produced the S-2 that did actually convey him on his first short flight. His S-3 and S-4 models followed in quick succession, with each aircraft adding to his piloting skills and experience. By the summer of 1911, Sikorsky had built his S-5, fitted with a 37 kW (50 hp) engine, with which he could stay aloft for up to an hour attaining altitudes of 450 m (1,476 feet) and with which he could make short cross-country flights.

Within a year Sikorsky had gained his International Pilot's Licence (No. 64) and a year later his S-6A won him the highest award at the Moscow Aviation Exhibition of 1912 and first prize at a military aviation competition in St Petersburg. In recognition of these awards, Sikorsky was appointed as head of the aviation subsidiary of the Russo-Baltic Wagon Works (RBVZ), where he was to produce the world's first four-engined aircraft ever to fly. The twin-engined Grand Bolshoi Baltisky (The Great Baltic) or Grand RBVZ biplane appeared early in 1913 and was an immediate success. It featured an enclosed cabin, a lavatory, upholstered seats and even an outside walkway in the nose section where a limited number of passengers could take turns to view in the air. The 'Russky Vityaz' (Russian Knight) that followed flew on 13 May 1913. It had a long, thin fuselage and also had a fully enclosed cockpit, but was powered by four engines in tandem pairs (tractor-pusher configuration). Its first flight lasted 10 minutes, but the engine arrangement proved less than satisfactory.

Ilya Muromets

In June 1913, Sikorsky produced his modified Ilya Muromets (named after a hero of Russian folklore). It was the world's first strategic bomber, with four 75 kW (100 hp) German Argus engines mounted in 'normal' tractor configuration. On 12 February 1914, it climbed to a height of 2,000 m (6,560 feet)—a record at the time—with sixteen passengers and a dog on board, remaining aloft over Moscow for 5 hours flying at speeds in excess of 100 kph (62 mph). For the more daring passengers an observation platform was provided on the fuselage top behind the wings. The aircraft had a peculiar snub-nosed 'cut off' appearance, as the enclosed cabin protruded only slightly in front of the wings, giving it a tail-heavy look.

In May 1914, ten Ilya Muromets (IMs) were ordered from the Russo-Baltic Wagon Works, followed by orders for a further thirty-two for the Imperial Russian Air Service after war broke out. As well as their name, these aircraft received type designations, such as IM III, IM IV, IM V, etc. It appears that the first two Type A IMs delivered to the Imperial Russian Air Service at the front gave a great deal of consternation, having obviously been mishandled by their poorly trained crews. General Helgard, Chief of the Central Military Technical Board, issued instructions that production should cease, but the RBVZ chairman, Mikhail Shidlovsky, protested and persuaded the Secretary of War to rescind the order. On 10 December 1914, Shidlovsky himself was appointed as commander of the new EVK (*Eskadra Vozdushnykh Korablei*) or 'Squadron of Flying Ships' with the rank of major-general. He soon developed the new squadron, equipped with the Type B IM, into an efficient and creditable bomber force with its own flying school and ground support echelon, with its own workshops, laboratory, garages, meteorological station and anti-aircraft defences. Powered by four Salmson engines and with a wingspan of 31 m (101 feet 6 inches), the Type B IM was capable of carrying up to 508 kg (1,120 lb) of bombs, with two machine guns and a carbine for defensive purposes.

The new squadron commenced operations from Jabłonna in Poland in February 1915, making regular daylight raids on German targets in Poland and East Prussia. As more aircraft became available, more units were formed and moved around the battlefront as required. The EVK became the élite of the Imperial Russian Air Service and 2,300 bombs were dropped on the enemy, the IMs appearing apparently indestructible. Only one aircraft, an IM XVI, was shot down by a fighter attack on 12 September 1916, and then only after it had destroyed three and damaged a fourth of its seven attackers. As production of the IM increased, a chronic shortage of engines arose, which led to the installation of a vast array of different powerplants: the German Argus (see *German Aircraft Industry and Production 1933-1945* by this author, KDP), the French Salmson and Renault, the British Sunbeam and Beardmore, and Russian-produced RBVZs. It is interesting to note that four Argus engines obtained and fitted in 1914 were installed in no fewer than four different IMs over a period of two years and five months, logging a total of 700 flying hours.

As the aircraft continued in production, a number of variants emerged. The Type B, which had narrower-chord wings and a more pointed nose than the two Type As, was followed by the Type V, the E-1, the G-2 and the G-3. The largest of the series was the E-1, which used four 164 kW (220 hp) Renault engines and had a wingspan of 32.2 m (105 feet 8 inches), carrying a crew of two pilots, a navigator, a mechanic, and three gunners to operate the seven machine guns. A few aircraft had 50 mm cannon fitted and carried 10 mm armour plating for self-defence, and fireproof fuel tanks. On the IM IX, a trolley car was provided to enable the tail gunner to reach his seat without interfering with the interior fuselage cross-bracing. It is believed that total IM production amounted to eighty aircraft, all of which were constructed by RBVZ. The EVK had five IM squadrons in operation by 1917 and carried out some 400 raids before production was halted by the Kerensky government in 1917, and the Russian Revolution and German invasion led to the end of the 'Squadron of Flying Ships'. It is reported that some thirty aircraft were destroyed by their own crews on 17 February 1918 when the aerodrome at Vinnitsa was overrun by the Germans.

Operation of these giant strategic bombers was no mean feat. They were not easy to fly or land, the pressure required on the control column being extremely high. When landing, it was normal practice to send the entire crew into the rear of the fuselage in order to help the pilot to get the stick pulled back. The engines required regular overhauls, and careful maintenance was needed to keep the IMs serviceable and flying. However, despite all of the above, three Sikorsky Type G-4s inaugurated the first passenger and freight service in Russia in 1921.

Sukhoi (Su-)

Pavel Osipovich Sukhoi was born on 22 July 1895 at Glubokoye in Byelorussia. After finishing his schooling at Gomel Gymnasium he joined the Physics-Mathematics

Faculty at Moscow University in 1914, but then decided to switch to Prof. Zhukovsky's aerodynamics course at the Moscow Higher Technical School. Called up in 1916 and commissioned in February 1917, he joined the Bolshevik Army and completed his aeronautical training after the Civil War in 1920 on his return to High School. After his diploma project, Sukhoi became a member of the Tupolev team at the Aviation, Hydro-aviation and Experimental Construction Section (AGOS) of TsAGI. Under Tupolev's direction he designed a single-seat biplane fighter, although his very first task was to design a tail skid for the ANT-4 heavy bomber. Following completion of this first small task, Sukhoi was made responsible for the design of the ANT-5 (I-4) single-seat sesquiplane fighter. He finished this in July 1927, and 349 were constructed up until 1931. Subsequently, from 1932 to 1934, Sukhoi's team designed the ANT-25 (RD) and the ANT-37 (DB-2) long-range, record-breaking aircraft and the all-metal, low-wing monoplane single-seat fighter the ANT-31 (I-14) with a retractable undercarriage and enclosed cockpit. In 1936, he was put in charge of the design department at GAZ-126 at Komsomol and started work on the design of the ANT-51 'Ivanov' attack aircraft, which later received the designation Su-2. Sukhoi set up his own OKB in 1938.

Apart from the Su-2, only 600 of which were produced up until 1942, no other Sukhoi designs entered series production during the Second World War. Nevertheless, Sukhoi did receive a Stalin Prize (first class) for the Su-6 ground attack aircraft developed from the Su-2, but which did not go into production, initially due to engine problems followed by a decision to concentrate on Il-2 production rather than change over to an entirely new design. However, Sukhoi did produce a number of experimental designs during the war, including interceptors and mixed powerplant fighters. These included the Su-1, Su-3, Su-5 and Su-7. None of these progressed beyond the prototype stage, although the Sukhoi OKB did develop the UTB bomber trainer from the Tupolev Tu-2.

After the war, Sukhoi was a pioneer in the jet aircraft field. Amongst the experimental aircraft produced by his OKB was the Su-10 four-engined bomber in 1947, the Su-12 reconnaissance aircraft in 1946/47 and the Su-17 single-seat swept-wing fighter with ejection capsule that was never completed owing to the closure of the Sukhoi OKB in 1949. From December 1949, Sukhoi and about half of his design team were assigned to the Tupolev OKB-1, Sukhoi himself concentrating on the design of a supersonic fighter. He spent most of 1950 in aerodynamic and structural research in close collaboration with TsAGI, and whilst Tupolev had every right to expect Sukhoi to apply himself to Tupolev projects, he did allow him to concentrate on his own fighter project studies that had no relevance to the Tupolev programmes.

Immediately on Stalin's death Sukhoi applied for permission to reopen his own design bureau and was given permission to pursue work, in direct competition with the MiG OKB, on two experimental fighter prototypes—the S-1 swept-wing fighter and the T-3 delta-wing interceptor. These aircraft were later designated as the Su-7 and Su-9, both types being produced in quantity for the Soviet Air Force with its

Frontal Aviation (PVO) regiments. They were also exported to many of the Soviet satellites and other communist countries and were followed by the Su-11 and Su-15 interceptors. On 5 September 1955, the S-1 fighter fitted with a 63.7 kN (14,320 lbf) AL-7F engine was at the Zhukovsky test centre and made its first flight three days later with Andrey G. Kochetkov at the controls. In all there were five S-1 prototypes to permit investigation of various airframe configurations and armament fits. In 1956, the S-1s were fitted with afterburning engines, and at the conclusion of the test programme in 1957, one aircraft fitted with a special AL-7F-1 engine and piloted by Nikolai Korovushkin attained a record speed of Mach 2.05. Unfortunately the S-1 prototype was destroyed on 21 November 1956.

At the 1967 Soviet Aviation Day a new Sukhoi single-seat fighter was shown in conventional and STOL versions, along with a variable-geometry version of the Su-7. In addition to Warsaw Pact countries, the Su-7 was operated by the Indian Air Force against Pakistan in 1971, and Egypt flew the type in the Arab-Israeli War of 1973. The Su-17 with its variable-geometry outer wing panels, and the Su-20 and Su-22, developed from the Su-7, were produced at Moscow in large numbers up until September 1975.

Until his death in 1975, Sukhoi had been responsible for the design of fifty different aircraft types, of which thirty-four were built either as prototypes or series production. The Sukhoi OKB was to continue to design and develop a series of modern aircraft, all seeing quantity service with the Soviet Air Force, including the Su-24M Fencer, the excellent Su-25 Frogfoot sturmovik aircraft, whose field trials and development were completed by a task team in quite austere conditions in Afghanistan in 1982, and the Su-27 Flanker, with its quite breathtaking manoeuvrability with the use of thrust vectoring, oft demonstrated at the Paris and Farnborough air shows.

Sukhoi Su-2

The idea of a Soviet frontal multi-role aircraft was put forward by Stalin, who issued a directive for a new aircraft that could serve as a ground attack aircraft, a reconnaissance aircraft and as a short-range bomber and escort fighter when required. The competition for the new design was entered by the OKB of the TsAGI Experimental Design factory and by Nikolai Polikarpov, by Josef Neman (at Kharkov Aviation Institute) and by Dmitry Grigorovich. The aircraft not only needed to meet high specification requirements but also had to be easy to manufacture. In Stalin's words, 'The aircraft must be very simple to produce so that we can make as many as there are people called Ivanov in our country.' In 1936, the project received the designation ANT-51 or SZ (Stalin's task). A year later the Tupolev OKB was reorganised, and KB-3 under the direction of Sukhoi also worked on the 'Ivanov' project. Sukhoi was to emerge as the winner of the design competition, as Polikarpov and Neman lagged behind and Grigorovich withdrew.

The ANT-51 was designed as a two-seat all-metal monoplane powered by an M-62 radial engine and with an armament of six ShKAS machine guns and 200 kg (440 lb) of bombs. Production was achieved using the most modern techniques available, with pressed and cast assemblies and components making it simple to assemble and suitable for mass-production. The first prototype was flown by test pilot Mikhail Gromov on 25 August 1937, Gromov finding the aircraft stable and responsive and reporting favourably on its overall performance. Successful NII VVS tests were held from January to March 1938, although metal shortages prevented the 'Ivanov' from entering immediate production. As a consequence, it had to be changed to mixed fabrication, with a wooden fuselage, plywood covering and duralumin wings and fin. With its designation changed to SZ-2, the new prototype was tested in February 1938. Several engines were tried in an effort to obtain more power and finally the 709 kW (950 hp) M-87A radial engine was selected for the SZ-3 flown in November 1938, although further trials were held in January 1940 with an M-88 radial. State tests were again successful and the SZ-2 was ordered into production at GAZ-135 at Kharkov as the BB-1 in August 1938. However, the plant was fully occupied at the time with series production of the R-10 reconnaissance aircraft, but a group of Sukhoi's designers left for Kharkov in the summer of 1939 to supervise the introduction of the type into production.

The new variant was a semi-monocoque fuselage of wooden construction with a stressed Bakelite ply skin, two-spar duralumin wings, dural-framed and fabric-covered rudder and elevators, a retractable undercarriage and tail wheel, a gun turret for the navigator/rear gunner and 9 mm armour for both crew members. It had a 435-litre (96-gallon) main fuel tank in the fuselage and two 70-litre (15-gallon) tanks in the wings. The aircraft was armed with four 7.62 mm ShKAS machine guns in the wings, turret and ventral position, with a maximum bomb load of 500 kg (two 250 kg bombs).

Early in 1940, Sukhoi began work on a modified BB-1 fitted with a 820 kW (1,100 hp) M-88B radial engine that would enable it to carry 600 kg (1,320 lb) of bombs. The aircraft subsequently passed its NII VVS tests and entered production at four factories: GAZ-18 at Voronezh, GAZ-31 at Taganrog, GAZ-135 at Kharkov, and GAZ-207 at Moscow. Both GAZ-18 and GAZ-31 were busy factories, with more than one production line, and GAZ-31 was also producing the BB-1 on two production lines by the end of 1940. In January 1941, the aircraft received the new designation Su-2, and the order was now to build 2,040 aircraft for thirty-four Bomber Aviation Regiments (BAPs)—one bomber regiment of Su-2s for each of the thirty-four mixed aviation divisions. By 22 June 1941, the VVS had a total of 445 Su-2s, mainly in the Western Front MDs: the Byelorussian MD had seventy-five in service, the Odessa MD another sixty, but 211 BAP at Kotovsk in Bessarabia did not have enough to replace the older R-Zs.

Production of the Su-2 at GAZ-31 was terminated in June 1941, and GAZ-18 was then concentrating on Il-2 Sturmovik production. The only production line still building Su-2s was GAZ-135, where 640 were produced by 1 September 1941 at a rate of six aircraft per day. This was sufficient to equip many new regiments (e.g. 135 BAP and 210 BAP) with Su-2s, but due to the heavy losses of June 1941, new regiments were equipped with only twenty aircraft each from 20 August. The following month GAZ-135 was evacuated to Perm, where Su-2s were assembled and fitted with M-82 engines, but early in 1942 the supply of parts from the Kharkov factory ran out, bringing the manufacture of the Su-2 to an abrupt end. GAZ-135 had produced 785 aircraft in total (110 in 1940, 635 in 1941 and forty in 1942) and GAZ-207 had built ninety-two (three in 1940 and eighty-nine in 1941). Although production figures for Taganrog are not available, it should be assumed that in the region of 2,000 Su-2s and Su-4s (Su-2 variant) were produced in total.

In October 1941, the all-female 587 BAP was created, and at about this time each Il-2 ShAP (Ground Attack Regiment) received three Su-2 aircraft to be used as fighters. During 1942, the Su-2s were deployed in relatively large numbers and in the November of that year 52 NBAP at Stalingrad was still using the type as a night bomber. In 1943, the remaining aircraft were sent to the Far East or used for various second-line duties.

Sukhoi Su-7

The Su-7, one of the most important Soviet tactical fighter-bombers, began as a production offspring of the S-1 development aircraft. Whilst the Su-7 lacked internal fuel capacity, this was compensated for by its superb handling and general robust simplicity, the aircraft possessing high penetration speed and low-level stability. Prototypes of the Su-7 family, designated S-2, introduced slab tailplanes with anti-flutter rods. All pre-production Su-7B aircraft (about twenty), designated S-22, had airframes derived from the S-1. The first S-22 flew in April 1957. Contrary to common belief, only a small number (120) of series Su-7 fighters were delivered, seeing only limited use, as a decision was made in 1958 to use the Su-7 as a Frontal Aviation attack fighter-bomber.

The initial fighter interceptor batches (1-12) were produced at Novosibirsk, the rest being built in eighty-one batches at Komsomolsk between 1957 and 1971. Series Su-7s used the 88.25 kN (19,840 lbf) Lyulka AL-7F turbojet engine. The Su-7B was produced in a number of sub-variants, starting with batches 13-45, producing 660 fighter-bombers. From the combined total of 780 initial series aircraft, twenty-eight were destroyed completely and, from late 1965 until 1974, 418 were transformed to Su-7BMK standard, fitted with AL-7F-1 turbojets with reheat. Some export variants were fitted with British (Smiths/Ferranti) nav/attack systems, and up until 1973, 334 were transformed to tandem dual-seat models U/UM/UKL and UMK, all of which were produced in parallel with the single-seaters with the same suffix letters. From mid-1963, batches 46-56 produced 320 Su-7BMs, and from January 1966 batches 57-81 produced 1,000 Su-7BKL aircraft, giving a total build of 2,100 aircraft.

By July 1968, the Soviet Union had received orders for 300 Su-7s, and 150 were exported that year. Before the Six-Day War of June 1967, the Soviets had delivered twenty-five Su-7s to Egypt, six to Iraq and five to Syria. Deliveries continued after the war, a further twenty-five going to Egypt, twenty to Iraq and forty to Syria, with Czechoslovakia receiving eighteen and Poland twelve. Su-7B fighter-bombers were finally retired from VVS service in 1986.

Sukhoi Su-15 Flagon

On 1 September 1983, a Korean Airlines Boeing 747 (flight KL007) en route from Anchorage to Seoul was shot out of the skies by a Soviet Air Force Su-15TM Flagon-F, having strayed into Soviet airspace. Prior to this incident, outside of the Soviet Union little was known of this aircraft. However, it was in fact the Soviets' premier front-line, all-weather, short-range supersonic interceptor until its replacement by the Su-27 Flanker began in 1985. All 269 passengers aboard the Korean airliner were killed, and questions that remain to this day are why the airliner was so far off course, why the Soviets failed to recognise it as a civil airliner, and why the Korean crew failed to respond to the Su-15 pilot's challenges and requests to change course. (It has been alleged that the aircraft was mistaken by the Soviets as a surveillance aircraft such as those used by the USAF, the Boeing E-4 Command Posts.) A similar incident involving another Korean airliner had taken place on 20 April 1978, when an Su-15 interceptor had forced the airliner to land on a frozen lake, killing two passengers.

The Su-15 is unique in the annals of Soviet jets, as although some 1,400 were built, none were ever exported and indeed few were ever seen outside the Soviet Union. The first prototype T-58D-1 (Flagon-A) flew without radar fitted on 30 May 1962, to be followed almost a year later, on 4 May 1963, by T-58D-2 fitted with Oryol-D58 radar in a conical nose radome. Whilst the second prototype had twin nose-wheels, these were not used on series aircraft until the heavier Taifun radar was introduced. On completion of the test programme, the second prototype (T-58D-2) was used for trials employing a variation of skid undercarriages, under the designation T-58L. The third aircraft (T-58D-3), which was the production prototype, flew on 2 October 1963, with a new non-waisted rear fuselage producing less drag and capable of carrying more fuel. Series aircraft (T-58-98) were manufactured at GAZ-153 at Novosibirsk from early 1966, entering PVO service as the Su-15 in 1967.

Like the Su-9 and Su-11 that preceded it, the Su-15 was of tailed delta configuration, but was fitted with two Tumansky R-11F2S-300 engines positioned side by side instead of a single Lyulka AL-7F. The wings had a straight leading edge and were swept back at 60 degrees until Batch 11, when they were given a compound delta shape with the leading-edge outer panel sweep-back reduced to 45 degrees from the wing fence, from where it drooped, giving a slightly twisted look. The overall span was increased slightly, and this wing configuration became known as 'compound delta 1'. Although it is known that an improved Oryol-D58M radar was fitted sometime later, the outward appearance of the aircraft remained unchanged.

Armament usually consisted of two medium-range R-98 AAM missiles (AA-3 Anab), in either the R-98TM form with passive IR or the R-98M with semi-active radar homing. The missiles, known as R-98 by the military but as K-98 by the designers, were carried on under-wing pylons later supplemented by smaller pylons for R-60 (AA-8 Aphid) short-range IR homing missiles and pylons for two 600-litre (132-gallon) drop tanks. On fitting the more powerful Tumansky R-13-300 engines in the Su-58T (T-58T) in 1969, boundary layer control on the flaps was introduced. The 'T' suffix indicated that the aircraft was fitted with the new heavier Taifun radar, necessitating the use of twin nose-wheels. In the event, the new radar was unsuccessful and only about twelve Su-58Ts were built. With the introduction of the more successful Taifun-M radar the aircraft designation changed to Su-15M, and this was to prove the most important variant, which although a big improvement on previous types still lacked look-down/shoot-down capability. To simplify manufacture, the previously mentioned leading-edge wing droop on the outer wing panels was eliminated to give the 'compound delta 2' configuration.

The Su-58TM (T-58M) variant was produced from 1971 to 1974. Accommodation of the new radar was facilitated by the fitting of an ogival nose radome used to reduce internal reflection of radar waves. It is not known whether earlier conical radomes were replaced with ogival types. Use of the R-13-300 engines permitted the replacement of the long air intakes either side of the vertical tail by shorter intakes in the fuselage nearer the wing. In 1975, the Su-15-98M, with its improved R-98M missile, was introduced. This aircraft was part of the Soviet Vozdukh-1M ground-controlled interceptor system that permitted semi- or, more usually, fully automatic vectoring of the fighter by the ground station to targets detected by its more powerful radar. The Su-15-98M had two extra pylons for R-60 (AA-8 Aphid) short-range missiles, and two UPK-23-250 gun pods carrying twin-barrelled GSh-23L cannon each with 250 rounds on modified under-fuselage pylons, once an attempt to introduce an internal cannon had proved unsuccessful.

In 1970, the Su-15UT (U-58T) training version entered service, the prototype having first flown the previous year. The aircraft did not carry radar or live weapons but could carry dummy missiles and simulation of firing could be undertaken. The trainer's fuselage was lengthened by 4.5 m (14 feet 9 inches) and the aircraft could be identified externally by the long intakes of the R-13F2S-300 engine and the longer canopy, slightly humped at the rear. The first batch of aircraft had wings with straight leading edges, but subsequent aircraft used the compound delta wings with drooped outer panels. A training variant of the Su-15TM was built in small numbers in 1976, after production of the fighter aircraft had ceased. It was designated U-58M by the Sukhoi OKB, receiving the service designation Su-15UM, and did not carry radar, although weapons could be fired. The aircraft's fuselage was the same length as the Su-15TM fighter but could be distinguished from the Su-15UT by the ogival nose, shorter fuselage and new flatter canopy, with a rear-view mirror over the front seat, and the absence of long fuselage air intakes. Later, a Su-15UM trainer was produced with radar fitted and full weapons fit, redesignated U-58UB, but only one was built as the design proved too heavy and unstable.

Sukhoi Su-17/20/22

The Sukhoi OKB led by Nikolai Zyrin gradually transformed a basic Su-7BMK into the formidable variable-geometry Su-17/20/22 models that were in production for some twenty-seven years. The prototype aircraft was designated S-22I (service designation Su-7IG), and the first example flew on 2 August 1966. The following year it was displayed to the public at Domodedovo Airport during the Soviet Aviation Day, flown by Vladimir Ilyushin, the son of the founder of the Ilyushin OKB. Detailed tests that followed revealed that the S-22I possessed improved take-off performance and range over the Su-7 with its wings in the forward position, and with its wings folded back it was a true fast combat jet. The outer wing panels could be swept back from 28 degrees to 45 or 62 degrees.

The Soviet Air Force decided that the Su-17 should enter full series production, but as a ground attack fighter rather than the air superiority fighter originally intended. Carrying the Sukhoi OKB designation S-32, production began in 1971, with the addition of an improved and more powerful engine, the 98 kN (22,046 lbf) AL-7F-1 and later, in 1972, the Su-17M was fitted with the 109.8 kN (24,690 lbf) AL-21F-3. The resultant series production Su-17 was a very economical solution to producing a superior and up-to-date variable-geometry combat aircraft from the earlier Su-7B with the majority of jigs and tools readily available.

The swing-wing Su-17 entered VVS service in 1971 as a ground attack/close support aircraft despite its fighter designation. The aircraft had the same profile as the S-22I prototype (developed from the Su-7B), having a semi-monocoque construction with the fuselage of circular section with a ram-air intake in the nose fitted with a variable shock cone centre-body. Four door-type airbrakes were fitted to each side of the rear fuselage at the top and base of the tail area. A distinctive feature of the Su-17 was the spine fairing, which was used to accommodate extra fuel, increasing capacity to 4,550 litres (1,000 gallons). External tanks could also be carried on the outer wing and on under-fuselage pylons. Updated avionics included the SRD-5M 'High Fix' radar, which was an I-Band ranging radar in the intake centre-body. It included an ASP-5ND fire-control system, the 360-degree Sirena 3 homing and warning system with its associated aerials at the base of the rudder, above the brake chute container and in each of the wing leading edges between the fences, and SRO-2M IFF, R5B-70 HF and RSIU-5/R-831 VHF/UHF radio. Weapons included the standard NR-30 cannon with seventy rounds each. In addition to the gun, eight pylons were fitted and two tandem points on the fuselage, one each under the main wing fence and one under the centre section of the wing. The Su-17 inboard pylons were moved forward so as not to interfere with the main wheel wells. Later VVS aircraft could carry the AS-7 Kerry ASM, rocket pods (UV-16-57 and UV-32-57) with sixteen or thirty-two 57 mm S-5 or 240 S-24 rockets, and 3,200 kg (7,055 lb) of bombs, including nuclear devices.

In addition to Soviet Air Force use, the new aircraft was deployed by Naval Aviation as an anti-shipping strike and amphibious support aircraft in the Pacific and Baltic regions. The Su-17 was eventually offered for export under the new designation Su-20 (Su-17MK) with the Sukhoi OKB designation S-32MK. Export variants were to a lower specification than VVS aircraft (not strictly a Soviet phenomenon, of course), and it is thought that a number of export aircraft were even powered by the older AL-7F-1 engine originally fitted to the Su-7.

The Su-17 received its baptism of fire in Afghanistan in the early and mid-1980s, and it was not long before a number of deficiencies were revealed. Subsequent investigations showed that combat losses were in the main the result of system failures (engines, gearbox, fuel tanks, control and hydraulic systems) due to penetration of bullets and other small-calibre projectiles, including fragments from high-velocity SAMs (exploding warheads). As a consequence, urgent improvements were made to Su-17M3/M4 aircraft already in use or still on the production line to improve the type's survivability in combat. Those aircraft already in operation in Afghanistan received additional armour to the lower fuselage to provide protection for the gearbox, electrical generator and fuel pump, and the fuel tanks were filled with protective self-sealing foam. Increased protection from man-portable, shoulder-launched SAMs was provided by fitting four additional 32-round ASO-2V chaff/flare dispensers ' scabbed' on to the upper fuselage. Later, eight or even twelve were fitted. These were subsequently provided as standard to series Su-17M4s and Su-22M4s built in the mid- to late 1980s. The first country to receive the export Su-20 was Poland, the type later being exported to Algeria, Czechoslovakia, Egypt, Iraq, North Korea and Vietnam.

In 1976, a new variant appeared—the Su-17M2 Fitter-D (OKB designation S-32M). The aircraft had an improved avionics suite, including a laser rangefinder and a marked target-seeker in the inlet centre-body. Terrain-avoidance Doppler radar was also fitted in the new nose pod. The new radar and avionics equipment necessitated a 38-cm (15-inch) extension of the nose ahead of the cockpit. Unfortunately, with no compensatory alterations in the tail area, a certain amount of directional instability was introduced. Following the Su-17M was the two-seat variant designated Su-17UM Fitter-E (OKB designation U-32). A distinctive feature of this aircraft was that the whole fuselage forward of the wing was drooped slightly to give an improved overall view from the cockpit. The 'H' variant that followed had an enlarged dorsal fin with a square top and resulted in a rationalisation of the design. This materialised in the reduction of the multitude of small ram-air inlets at the rear of the fuselage around the engine area to just two. In addition, the rear fuselage diameter was increased and an expanded fairing was added behind the cockpit to hold more fuel and/or equipment. Two further weapons pylons were added along with a deepened nose into which was fitted a terrain-avoidance radar, the aircraft's primary role now being tactical reconnaissance. A two-seat variant of the 'H' also appeared, the Su-17 Fitter-G, which was similar in most respects to the 'E'. As with most two-seat variants, the port gun was omitted. The 'H' variant was exported to Algeria, Egypt, Iraq and Vietnam.

The Su-17 Fitter-K appeared in 1984, with its improved ECM fit and fuselage fin root intakes to cool the additional internal avionics. Poland often referred to this variant as the Su-22. In reality it was a greatly revised export model for countries such as North and South Yemen, Libya, Peru, North and South Vietnam. In 1976, thirty-six aircraft (thirty-two Fitter-Fs and four Fitter-Es) had been offered to Peru, as the US had refused to sell it the Northrop F-5 Tiger II aircraft. The total cost of the programme was £140.5 million, payable over ten years. Conversion training for the Peruvian pilots was provided by the Cuban Air Force at Santa Clara and Camagüey. Cuba also loaned twelve MiG-21s to Peru to help its pilots familiarise themselves with Soviet equipment, and 100 Cuban and seventy-five Soviet technicians assisted with the construction of a new airbase at La Joya in southern Peru. Subsequently Peru received a number of Antonov transports as well as twenty-four Su-24s in 1996, and twenty Mi-24 Hind helicopters.

From 1984, problems with communications and radars led to the whole fleet of Peruvian Su-22s being subject to a degree of updating of the avionics with equipment supplied from western sources. The same applies to more recent Soviet types delivered, most being retrofitted with US-manufactured avionics equipment, some only spec'd to civil standards (equipment manufactured for the general aviation field). Further Su-22 Fitters were produced with the Tumansky R-29B-300 engine, such as the Su-22M4 Fitter-G as used by the former East German Air Force and, finally, the Su-22 Fitter-J single-seater (there was also a two-seat Fitter-J), an export variant of the 'H' with a Tumansky engine, internal fuel tank of 6,270 litres (1,380 gallons) and a more angular dorsal fin.

The Su-22M-3 Fitter-J was supplied to Hungary in 1981 to replace earlier Su-7Bs. Libya also received Fitter-Js, which although purchased as ground attack aircraft were used in the air defence role when the famous encounter with the US Navy took place on 19 August 1981 over the Gulf of Sidra. Prior to their 'shoot down' by the Navy's Grumman F-14 Tomcats, the Libyan Su-22s were seen to be carrying two Atolls on inboard wing pylons and two external tanks on the outboard wing pylons. The encounter was an important one in the history of aviation as it was the first time that two variable-geometry (VG) aircraft had locked in combat. In some ways the engagement did not determine relative superiority between the two aircraft types, as the Libyan pilots did not exploit their aircraft's VG characteristics and indeed flew them in a very negative manner. For the US, however, it did prove the advantages to be gained in an aerial dogfight when using a variable-geometry aircraft in terms of increased combat manoeuvrability rather than a one-shot, high-speed pass, as was the only option with earlier types such as the Lockheed F-104 Starfighter, for example.

Whilst the Su-17 was by no means state-of-the-art, it did provide the Soviets with a highly capable series of swing-wing aircraft based on the earlier short-range Su-7, and it is true to say that these ground attack aircraft were well liked by the majority of combat pilots who flew them. For an aircraft that was originally conceived as part of a research and development programme into swept-wing (or delta) configuration, with the eventual adoption to swing-wing technology, it can be said to have been one of the most cost-effective developments of any combat aircraft ever. A total of 2,200 aircraft were built in 110 batches of twenty (including two-seat training variants) at Komsomolsk from 1970 to 1984, and a further 800 (forty batches of twenty) were built at Irkutsk, giving a total build of 3,000. Most VVS Su-17M3/M4 aircraft were withdrawn from use in the early to mid-1990s and stored, although around seventy were converted to Su-17M3R/M4R reconnaissance variants for use in the First Chechen War from 1994 to 1996. Early export variants (Su-20s) for Egypt, Syria, etc. cost around $2 million, with late series Su-24M4s delivered to three Warsaw Pact members in the late 1980s costing around $6-7 million.

In the 1980s, Poland became the largest Su-22M4 user outside of the Soviet Union, the first aircraft from Block 23 entering service with the 7th Bomber-Reconnaissance Regiment's 3rd Flight at Powidz. The Su-22M4s produced at that time had an all-weather, low-level precision tactical nuclear bombing capability, and it was reported that the first batch delivered to the Powidz and Piła 3rd and 6th Fighter-Bomber Regiments were fitted with the special (nuclear) stores cockpit panel along with the special ejection racks (*specbelki*) adapters and electronic interfaces necessary for the aircraft's nuclear role. Later, as the likelihood of nuclear war in Europe diminished, series aircraft from Block 30 were optimised for conventional strike missions with the more sophisticated ground attack missiles and weapons. Aircraft previously supplied with the nuclear weapons cockpit panel could be retrofitted with a monitor for the Kh-29T TV-guided missile installation. About 150 Su-22Ms and fifteen Su-22UM3s were supplied to Poland from Blocks 23, 24, 27, 28, 29, 30, 37 and 38.

The Polish Air Force proposed a programme of upgrades in 1994 to prolong the operational life of the Su-22 until 2015. The upgrade was to include the fitting of western avionics and radar, HUD, navigation and weapons aiming systems along with weapon adapters to carry western 'smart' weapons. The modernisation cost per aircraft was estimated at $2.3-2.5 million, but after a series of crashes in 1995 these plans were shelved and moves were made to purchase F-16 Fighting Falcons from the US. In addition, a number of Su-22Ms will be optimised for the reconnaissance role, equipped with a KKR-1 recce pod.

Sukhoi Su-24 Fencer

In 1964, the Soviet Air Force requested a modern swing-wing bomber as a replacement for the Ilyushin Il-28, the Yakovlev Yak-28 and the Tupolev Tu-16 and Tu-22. The experience gained by Sukhoi with the Su-7 and later the Su-17/22 variable-geometry series resulted in initial design studies under the direction of Pavel Sukhoi together with Chief Designer Evgeny Felsner, starting in 1965. An initial prototype designated T6-1 ('61') flew in June 1967, although in fact this aircraft bore little resemblance to the eventual Su-24 swing-wing strike fighter as it was a small delta incorporating four lift engines. However, what it did do was define the basic twin-jet fuselage and single swept tail of the Su-24, the two-seat side-by-side seating as used in the American GD F-111 Aardvark and the rectangular non-variable ramp lateral intakes mounted slightly proud of the flat-sided centre-fuselage for boundary layer bleed.

After a number of problems were encountered in respect of control and stability at high speed and low altitude, Sukhoi embarked on a major redesign incorporating variable geometry through variable wing sweep. Preliminary swing-wing experience had been gained by the Sukhoi OKB with the Su-17, first shown as a converted Su-17IG in July 1967, although with the T6-2 ('62') full-span variable sweep from triangular inner glove strakes was achieved to a maximum of 69 degrees (slightly less than the 72.5 degrees of the F-111), the full-span retractable leading-edge slats and double-slotted flaps for short take-off and landing, with the wing swept fully forward (16 degrees) as with the F-111, giving an approach speed of only 230 kph (145 mph). The prototype swing-wing Su-24, the T6-2IG, retained the sharp-cornered rectangular fuselage cross-section and twin ventral under-fins of its immediate predecessor, as well as a similar tail assembly and forward-retracting twin low-pressure main-wheel units stowed in the lower aft intake ducts. To meet standard Soviet Air Force combat aircraft requirement for grass-field operational capability, the aircraft was fitted with large stone and debris guards, as well as the usual Soviet nose-wheel braking system.

For the first time the Sukhoi design team were faced with the intricacies of developing a navigation system that would fly the aircraft to the target area along a pre-programmed route under full automatic or manual control, with an interlinked weapons delivery system. The elements of the system, known as PNS-24MK, comprised an Orion-A pulse-Doppler search and mapping radar and relief terrain-following radar, believed to be linked for the first time in the Su-24M with the flight control system and integrated with a Kaira-24 laser and TV sighting system and a Fantasmagoriya forward-looking LO-80 or LO-81 passive radar receiver pod. Navigation and weapons delivery data was also derived from the TsVU-10-058K onboard digital computers and MIS-P Series 2 inertial gyro platforms, with a DNM-T6M command link and SAU-6M1 automatic flight control system, plus a PPV twin-combiner HUD, RV-21 Mk A1 radio altimeter, SUO-1-6M armament control system and Tecon-1SM video monitoring link. Other vital elements included an SVS-PN-5-3A Series 3 air data system and a UUAP-72M-13 angle-of-attack and load factor indicator, SRZO IFF, SKIP-2 long-range navigation equipment, a Klystron homing and landing system, ARK-15M automatic direction finder, SO-69 transponder, MRP-56P marker beacon receiver, R-862/R-864G VHF/UHF nav/comms and SPU-9 intercom.

The Su-24 was the first of the Soviet Air Force's combat aircraft to incorporate integrated and automatic defensive aids in its 1975 upgrade programme. Like the American F-111, the Su-24 was designed to accommodate rapid firing six-barrelled rotary cannon as standard fixed armament, with provision for up to three twin-barrelled 23 mm GSh-23L-2 cannon in SPPU-6 pods on fuselage and wing pylons as alternatives to other weapons and stores, some of which were specifically designed for the aircraft. Apart from nuclear weapons, primary armament normally comprised stand-off AAMs.

Following the initial flight trials of the T6-2IG in 1970, further development of the first Su-24s was undertaken by a test team led by the General Designer Mikhail

Simonov, who had replaced J. A. Ivanov as head of the OKB, and Vladimir Ilyushin as chief test pilot. The development programme was not without incident, resulting in the loss of test pilot S. Lavrentyev, although other crew members (including pilots V. Krechetov, Evgeny Soloviev and N. Rukhlyado, together with navigators N. Alferov, V. Belykh, L. Smyshlyaev and L. Rudenko) successfully concluded the programme after a number of minor modifications had been made to aircraft and systems. Series production started in 1972, and about forty-eight aircraft were built at GAZ-153 at Novosibirsk. All but the first few aircraft were powered by two Lyulka AL-21F-3A turbojets similar to those used in the single-engined Su-17s.

The first fifteen production Su-24 Fencer-As retained the slab-sided rear-fuselage cross-section of the prototypes and were used mainly by the Soviet Air Force's Operational Trials Regiment from November 1974 at Chernyakhovsk (Baltic MD), entering regular service units in 1975. From 1976, production output increased to over seventy-five per year, and the Su-24M Fencer-D was introduced in 1978, entering service with the test unit at Templin (Berlin) the following year, with some 250 in service by the late 1980s. In 1980, GAZ-146 at Komsomolsk became the second production plant to produce the Su-24, Frontal Aviation's tactical strike element having doubled its inventory to some 550 aircraft by 1982.

In 1984, the Su-24 underwent its operational baptism of fire in Afghanistan, where from 21 April twenty-four aircraft joined with Tu-16s in the carpet-bombing of Mujahideen tribesmen in the Panjshir Valley north of Kabul, although both types were based on Soviet territory at Termez and elsewhere, just across the northern border of Afghanistan. Both operated for several months without losses, albeit with inconclusive results against the guerrilla targets. Soviet Air Force reorganisation in 1987 resulted in the Su-24 entering service with the Attack Regiment of the 24th Air Army, with its HQ at Legnica in Poland, and with the 4th Air Army at Vinnitsa in Ukraine. By the late 1980s, these two air armies alone controlled some 220 Su-24Ms. However, by September 1991, with a total of 1,085 Su-24s in service use, production was halved to between thirty and thirty-five per year. In 1992, the total Soviet Su-24 inventory comprised 840 bombers, 235 reconnaissance and ECM types and ten naval reconnaissance types. Production of the Su-24 ceased in 1993, being replaced on the production lines by the Su-27IB Flanker. GAZ-153 had produced more than 1,000 Su-24s between 1974 and 1992, with production peaking at some 200 aircraft built from 1979 to 1982.

The Pentagon's annual review of Soviet air power in 1987 credited the VVS with almost 800 Su-24s in use, but it appears that these estimates were somewhat overstated. It was acknowledged that deliveries of the navalised Su-24MR Fencer-E had commenced, with initial deliveries having been made to the Baltic Fleet of the Soviet Naval Aviation. Also according to Pentagon sources, by 1989 some 250 Fencer-Cs/Ds had been transferred from the Soviet Air Force to replace the 480 Su-17 Fitter-K fighter-bombers of the Soviet Pacific Fleet, as well as others with the Black Sea and Northern Fleets. In 1990, US Navy Intelligence Chief Rear Admiral Thomas

A. Brooks claimed that the Soviet Naval Aviation was considering a ship-borne Su-24 variant for carrier operations, that the type would supplement the lighter navalised Su-25K Frogfoot in the anti-shipping role, and that a cadre of about 100 aircraft was already available to train Soviet naval pilots for carrier operations. Carrier suitability trials were reportedly undertaken at Saki naval experimental airfield in Crimea, with a 300 m (984 feet) dummy deck with arrester wires and twin ski-ramps. In the event, Rear Admiral Brooks' claims appeared to be premature, as the Soviets switched their interest to the navalised Su-27 Flanker for their new ship-borne strike fighter.

Specialised Su-24s comprised Su-24MR Fencer-Es equipped for reconnaissance, and the electronic warfare-dedicated Su-24MP, known as the Fencer-F. Only twelve Su-24MP variants were built. A development of the standard Su-24M (Modified), the Fencer-E has daylight and IR cameras, TV and a range of pods, one of which contains a line scan system, while another has ELINT equipment fitted. The pods also have a wide-band transmitter for data-linking reconnaissance information to the ground in real time. The weapon targeting radar in the nose is replaced by a SLAR, and a further identifying feature is the large-capacity bulged heat exchanger intake above the centre fuselage. Fencer-F features include a large hockey-stick antenna angled from each intake flank, plus a prominent aerial beneath the nose radome. With no attack radar, neither the 'E' nor the 'F' has offensive capabilities, although self-defence provision is catered for by carrying two R-60 AA-8 Aphids or other defensive AAMs on the under-wing pylons. Unconfirmed reports indicate that only sixty-five Fencer-Es may have been built, as Tu-16 Badger and Yak-28 Brewer ECM replacements were used instead. Around thirty are reported as having been operated by the 11th Reconnaissance Regiment from Welzow in East Germany until mid-1991.

Libya was one of the first countries to take delivery of the Su-24MK export variant, the first six of its order of fifteen being delivered by An-22s to Umm Aitiqah Air Base in March 1989. Payment problems due to reduced oil sales and a cooling of relations between the Soviet Union and President Gaddafi curtailed any further deliveries to Libya. Syria had started negotiations with the Soviet Union in late 1987 for twenty-two Su-24MKs, as well as up to forty-eight MiG-29s, and despite strong US objections due to the potential threat to Israel, had reached an agreement in principle. However, delivery was delayed due to funding problems until 1990, when only twenty aircraft were delivered. In 1989/90, the Iraqi Air Force took delivery of an initial batch of ten, which was soon followed by a further fourteen, together with appropriate weapons including AS-14 Kedge (X-29) and Maverick-type ASMs. Nine of these were amongst the 115 Iraqi Air Force aircraft that defected to Iran in January 1991 during the First Gulf War. Other countries taking delivery of the Su-24MK included Iran, which received twenty-four, and Algeria with twelve. —

Sukhoi Su-25 Frogfoot
Development of the Soviet Union's most capable close support aircraft began in 1968. However, the design and definition phase proceeded slowly and the first flight of

the prototype (T8-1) was not until 22 July 1975, using the by then out-of-production Tumansky RD-9, the same engine that had been used in the MiG-19. It was eventually replaced by the non-afterburning Tumansky R-13, as used in the MiG-21, which was fitted to the T8-3 prototype flown in 1978. This engine, designated R-95Sh, was later replaced by the R-195, which was introduced in 1987.

Great care was taken in the development phase to take into account the anticipated operational requirements of the type. The Su-25 accommodated the pilot in a titanium-bath cockpit with armoured glass, the engines being located in a stainless steel protective box and the fuel tanks and fuel lines encased in protective foam. Since the aircraft was intended to operate at low levels during combat, with the possibility of extreme vulnerability to portable IR heat-seeking anti-aircraft missiles, it carried 256 decoy flares in containers above the engines and tail which could be ejected singly, in pairs, or in any sequence selected by the pilot. The aircraft was capable of operating from unprepared airstrips of under 1,200 m (3,940 feet) in length with a full weapons load. The cockpit instrumentation was of conventional design (dials and switches) representing technology from the 1960s, although a radar warning system and IFF was available. For greater off-field operability the aircraft could use a variety of fuels, including diesel oils and petrol, and particular attention during the design and development of the Su-25 was paid to reducing maintenance and routine servicing requirements. When deployed to forward operating areas, the aircraft could carry enough spares and support equipment in four pods on the under-wing pylons to keep it flying for nearly two weeks.

The initial production variant of the Su-25 was operated by Soviet forces in Afghanistan in 1982. Two years later it became fully operational with the rest of the Soviet Air Force, with the introduction of an upgraded version fitted with a more capable cannon installation and improved flight and mission electronics, with two AAMs on the outermost pair of under-wing hard points for self-defence. The Su-25UB was a two-seat trainer version, with an additional cockpit for the pupil situated in the humped fuselage, the subsequent Su-25UBK being a two-seat operational trainer with a longer fuselage, increased to 15.4 m (50 feet 5 inches). The tail-fin height was also increased and an arrester hook fitted. These trainers were intended to train Naval Aviation pilots to operate from carriers and were not earmarked for use in the operational combat role. In 1988, a two-seat trainer with the designation Su-25UT was introduced. Intended for the export trainer market, with much of the original protective armament removed, it was subsequently given the designation Su-28. However, the aircraft proved to be very expensive to produce and no orders were received. In 1992, the Su-25TK variant was introduced, followed by the Su-25TM in 1998. The latest version is the Su-25TM (Su-39), a development of the Su-25T, and some twelve prototypes were completed. These aircraft are believed to be modified Su-25Ts. One Su-25TM prototype has been used for Kopyo-25 radar trials at the Akhtubinsk test centre, the radar being carried in a pod under the fuselage centreline, although Sukhoi considered modifying the nose to accommodate the radar. In 1998, the Su-25TM became the first new combat aircraft to be ordered for the Russian Air Force for several years, an initial batch of six all-weather, day/night ground attack aircraft being produced at the Ulan-Ude plant. As the Su-39 'Strike Shield', the aircraft has been offered for export by Sturmovik Sukhego (Sukhoi Attack Aircraft).

Su-25 Frogfoot development and combat testing—Operation Rhombus, Afghanistan
The Afghan Rhombus test team came into being in 1979, when Soviet Air Force Commander Pavel Kutakhov was in discussion with Soviet Minister of Defence Dmitry Ustinov regarding results of tests of the new Su-25 Frogfoot. It is reported that Ustinov declared, 'Why should combat aircraft iron the skies over the Volga when there is an ideal testing ground with severe environmental and real combat conditions?'—the Afghan War. As a result of the Defence Minister's remarks, it was decided to send two Su-25s, the second prototype (T8-1D) and the PP model (T8-3) to Afghanistan for development flight trials. However, prior to the test team's departure, the Sukhoi OKB needed to address a number of problems.

Of utmost importance was the development of the T8-3's weapon control system, and all unnecessary test and recording equipment was to be removed from the T8-1D. In addition, the fuel tanks were to be filled with polyurethane foam to prevent explosion if the aircraft was hit. This included the 800-litre (176-gallon) external tanks which were standard to all Sukhoi combat aircraft. All electronic wiring for weapon types not to be used in the Afghan tests was 'capped off' and the associated cockpit switches disconnected. The test programme was devised jointly by the Sukhoi OKB and GNIKI VVS (State Research Test Institute of the Soviet Air Force) under the command of Major-General Vladimir Alferov, Deputy Chief of GNIKI VVS research.

The Rhombus team consisted of specialists who had worked at the Sukhoi OKB Flight Test and Development Facility at Zhukovsky and personnel from the OKB affiliate in Akhtubinsk where the tests had been carried out. Departure for Afghanistan was scheduled for 16 April 1980, and the party was to include two test pilots from the Sukhoi OKB, Nikolai Sadovnikov and Anatoly Ivanov, plus two from GNIKI VVS, Vyacheslav Soloviev and Valery Muzyka. In addition to the Sukhoi staff, the Rhombus team included nav/attack specialists from the Kiev Arsenal Plant and an air data recorder specialist, Timofey Klimenko, who was to rewrite, decode and analyse the flight recorder information. In total there were forty-six civilian Su-25 maintenance specialists in addition to aerodynamicists, weapons specialists and bomb sight specialists, the VVS supplying about fifteen military engineers and about 100 maintenance staff. The Commander of the Air Division in Afghanistan was informed that whilst the team's primary mission was to undertake combat testing, if it should become necessary he could use the aircraft for combat missions.

Whilst in Afghanistan, the Rhombus team were based at Shindand airfield at an altitude of 1,140 m (3,740 feet) above sea level with a continental-type climate. Daytime highs of 30° C were followed by night chills that at least afforded the test team the opportunity of restful sleep. The first flight took place only two days after arrival at Shindand. Former pilot instructor and 'Hero of the Soviet Union' Dmitry Smirnov warned the young test pilots not to be taken in by the beauty of the mountains in the immediate area of the base, as the changing light conditions and reflections from the mountains could at times make navigation difficult. However, the team were extremely fortunate with their 50-day stay in Afghanistan, the weather remaining good with only occasional cloud cover over the base. At first air-firing and bombing trials were inhibited, as it was often difficult to check the accuracy of the attacks due to the absence of a dedicated test range, but once a properly dedicated unused tank practice firing range was allowed to be used for the tests this problem was overcome. As the range was only 9 km (5.5 miles) from the base, the tests proceeded to schedule, and although no Mujahideen activity was observed near or around the range, Rhombus team members who went to the range always travelled in armoured personnel carriers and were escorted by Soviet ground forces.

In addition to weapons testing on the range, there were a number of other tests carried out in relation to radio altimeter capabilities, radio communications and laser rangefinding in mountainous areas. However, the most complex testing involved developing methods of attacking targets in such terrain. Test pilots studied ways of breaking off attacks in valleys without turning away whilst pulling 5 g. The two Tumansky R-195 non-afterburning turbojets (derivatives of the MiG-21's R-13-300) performed well in the 'hot & high' conditions. The aircraft's wing design, with its aspect ratio of 6.5 and thickness-to-chord ratio of 10.5 per cent, created sufficient lift which was increased by the leading-edge flaps, while the distinctive wing-tip split airbrakes added to the machine's manoeuvrability.

After only a week in theatre, the local Air Commander was exercising his prerogative to make use of the aircraft in the combat scenario. In the event, the Su-25's combat baptism of fire turned out to be a severe trial for the military, and even more so for the civilian test pilots, who were not comfortable attacking 'real' targets. However, a bonus for which the Commander was extremely grateful came when it was found that a bomb had hit a Mujahideen ammunition depot as a result of one of the test aircraft's ground attacks. One of the Su-25's most important operational combat missions at this time was carried out in early May 1980, after Soviet land forces had found an Afghan stronghold in a gorge 120 km (75 miles) south of the base at Shindand in the Farakh area. Following an unsuccessful attempt by Soviet ground forces with armoured personnel carriers to enter the area, the Frogfoots were called upon to tackle the problem. The heavily fortified area, which had numerous permanent gun emplacements at every twist and turn in the narrow canyon, was an idea target for the Su-25. As the area was relatively close to where the aircraft were based they did not require external fuel tanks, so all the under-wing pylons could carry stores. The weapons racks were borrowed from an adjacent Su-17 unit as the trials team did not have any of their own, one aircraft being loaded with its full combat load of eight 500 kg (1,100 lb) bombs and the other with thirty-two 100 kg (220 lb) bombs on multiple under-wing racks.

This was the first time that Su-25 Frogfoots had taken off with a full operational bomb load and there was a degree of apprehension amongst the Rhombus test team, as it was well known that the Su-17s carrying similar armaments often only just managed to scramble into the air after traversing the length of the 2,300 m (7,545 feet) runway, especially in the high midday temperatures often encountered. However, much to the team's surprise, the two aircraft lifted off the runway about midway along and climbed away easily. The Soviet ground forces in the area were not concerned at their own safety, having observed the aircraft on a number of its earlier flights and being aware that it could fly lower and approach the target with much greater accuracy than some of the earlier types called on to support operations. The highly manoeuvrable Frogfoot with its excellent sighting system allowed the pilots to attack with a great degree of accuracy, even when the targets were obscured by boulders and concrete emplacements. Following the successful attack, the GNIKI VVS moved into the gorge to conduct experiments with regard to the acoustic effects of exploding ordnance in confined spaces.

The first Su-25 Frogfoot operational unit, the 200th Independent Air Attack Squadron, was formed at Sitalchay Air Base in Azerbaijan, the squadron of twelve aircraft arriving at Shindand on 19 June 1981. Although Soviet leaders had indicated that operations in Afghanistan would be on a 'limited military contingent' basis, in 1984, with combat operations continuing to escalate, it was decided to add three more squadrons of Frogfoots to the Afghan establishment—two at Bagram and one at Kandahar. In the same year, the Afghan guerrillas obtained American portable Redeye SAMs for the first time, the Soviets recording sixty launches that year and 140 in 1985. In order to afford the Su-25s a degree of protection from the Redeye missiles, the Soviets devised an automatic-release flare decoy system (previously it had relied on the pilot to activate release), and the number of decoys carried was doubled from 128 to 256. This contingency worked well until the Mujahideen began to receive shoulder-launched Stinger SAMs in 1986, with total SAM launches for that year recorded at around 600.

Unfortunately this time there was no easy solution, as the Stinger proved to be deadly accurate and the Su-25's thermal emissions too difficult to mask with decoys. The only answer was to increase the aircraft's survivability coefficient. This was done by redesigning the fire protection system, strengthening the control rods and, most importantly, the two engines were shielded from the fuselage by two 5-mm thick steel and glass fibre armoured plates. The first of these modified aircraft arrived in Afghanistan in August 1987. Whilst there, the Frogfoot proved itself an equal to its indomitable Second World War counterpart the Ilyushin Il-2 Sturmovik, rightly earning its accolade of 'the modern-day Sturmovik'. It was perfect for the needs of the Afghan War—easy to fly, effective in combat and possessing great survivability.

During its time in Afghanistan the Su-25 carried out attacks using mainly free-fall bombs and unguided rockets, but it could also carry AS-10 Karen and AS-14 Kedge laser-guided missiles. According to the Sukhoi OKB, of 139 missile launches made after 1986, all but two successfully hit the target. During the eight years of the war, the Frogfoot made some 60,000 sorties; twenty-three aircraft were lost and eight pilots killed. With regard to survivability, it was reported that at least one aircraft suffered between eighty and ninety combat hits yet still returned safely to base. This contrasts markedly with the possible fifteen to twenty hits sufficient to completely destroy the earlier more lightly armoured Su-17. Interestingly, throughout the conflict from the early 1980s a number of young Afghan pilots deserted, landing their aircraft in Pakistan. Moreover, according to reports in the Pakistani press at the time, a number of Soviet pilots also landed in Pakistan by mistake! One such event occurred on 16 August 1988, when Colonel Alexander Vladimirovich Rudskoi, a Soviet Su-25 pilot, landed at Miranshah but was quickly handed over to the Soviet Embassy in Islamabad.

During their stay in Afghanistan the Su-25s carried out some 100 flying missions, including forty operational combat sorties, although initially only sixty-eight trial flights had been planned. Deemed a resounding success, the test flights were highly praised by the Ministry of Defence, the General Staff and VVS HQ, and it is true to say that the activities of the Rhombus team greatly contributed to the aircraft's successful development and subsequent wide use not only in Afghanistan but also at Grozny in Chechnya. Subsequent to the withdrawal of Soviet forces from Afghanistan, developed Su-25 variants were used in the conflict in Chechnya in support of Russian ground forces, with a navalised training variant developed for onboard flying training for pilots flying the Su-34 Fullback from the only nuclear-powered Soviet aircraft carrier *Admiral Kuznetsov*.

Sukhoi Su-27 Flanker

The origins of the Su-27 Flanker go back to 1969, when work began on a new interceptor to replace the Tupolev Tu-28P under the direction of Pavel Sukhoi. Control of the project passed to Mikhail Simonov in 1974, the first of ten prototypes, the T-10-1, flying on 22 May 1977 piloted by Vladimir Ilyushin. The first prototype was a very different aircraft to the Su-27 Flanker-B (T-10S-1) that made its first flight on 20 April 1981, which was in effect a production-standard T-10P interceptor variant intended for the PVO. The T-10-1 had curved wing tips, a rearward-retracting nose-wheel, with the tail fins mounted centrally above the engine housings.

The flight test programme soon encountered a number of problems as the development aircraft displayed inadequate directional stability at speeds above Mach 2.0. Operational studies revealed the aircraft to be considerably inferior to the McDonnell Douglas F-15 Eagle, having less than 75 per cent of the American aircraft's capability. There were also a number of faults with the FBW software, which resulted in the death of at least two Sukhoi test pilots, one being Evgeny Soloviev. Because mass-production of a fighter with a known performance considerably inferior to that of its well-established main adversary, the F-15, was far from desirable, the Kremlin ordered the project to undergo a major overall. This resulted in the appearance of the Flanker-B, a production-standard aircraft that was obviously very different from the original. Although the centre section of the aircraft was basically the same as the original design, the cockpit was enlarged and raised and given a semi-bubble canopy for good all-round vision.

The Flanker-B was powered by two AL-31F augmented turbofans in place of the Tumansky R-32s fitted to the Flanker-A, the new engines being spaced slightly further apart and the wedge type intakes having changed slightly. The wings were also altered considerably, the original straight-edged strakes having been replaced by ogival leading-edge root extensions very similar to those on the F-16 Fighting Falcon, and the fences deleted. Full-span flaps appeared on the formerly fixed leading edge to augment the half-span flaperons on the trailing edge, with both surfaces capable of manual control for take-off and landing and with in-flight computer control to give a degree of variable camber. The previously rounded wing tips were now square, permitting the fitting of extra missiles, the rails acting as endplates to prevent span-wise flow. This modification also brought the AAM count carried by the aircraft to ten. The main missile carried was the AA-10 Alamo, in the semi-active radar and IR homing versions, with a range of about 45 km (24 nm). The outboard pylons and wing-tip rails carried the AA-11 Archer IR homing missiles or the AA-8 Aphid with a range of about 8 km (4.3 nm) for aerial dogfighting. These were supplemented by a 30 mm GSh-301 cannon (1,500 rpm) armed with 150 rounds. The enormous 10-tonne internal fuel load gave the aircraft outstanding range without tanks.

The previously stalky rearward-retracting nose-wheel situated immediately beneath the cockpit was moved to a position aft of the cockpit and made to retract forward, which also greatly improved ground handling of the aircraft. The main gear retracted forward into the wing roots and the main gear doors ceased to double as airbrakes as there was now a dorsal unit located behind the cockpit as on the F-15. The angular vertical tail surfaces had a broader chord, with a correspondingly lower aspect ratio with raked tops. The tail surfaces were now mounted on shelves outboard of the engines instead of on top of the engine cowlings, thus overcoming instability problems at high Mach numbers. In addition, two ventral fins were added on the undersides to improve stability at high alpha. These changes, along with a number of other detailed improvements, such as the AL-31F turbofans and the exceptionally reliable FBW control systems, transformed the aircraft into a truly potent interceptor with superb handling characteristics and potential for ongoing development, as evidenced by the subsequent proliferation of new models. Series production of the Su-27 started at Komsomolsk in 1982, whilst the dual-seat trainer Su-27UB, first flown on 7 March 1985, was built at Irkutsk from 1986.

The first series aircraft were completed in October 1984, the first four being delivered to the training base at Lipetsk the following month. Despite the first fighter regiment deliveries occurring in December 1984, and with only fifteen series aircraft produced in 1986 due to a number of technical problems, mainly with the fuel system and with the radar, it was not until 1987 that 831°IAP at Mirgorod in Ukraine was declared operational. At one time it was reported that several dozen Flankers were parked outside the factory at Komsomolsk awaiting radars (not a uniquely Soviet problem, of course; RAF Panavia Tornado F2s originally flew without their AI.24 Foxhunter radars). Production was halted until the backlog was cleared, only thirty-five aircraft being produced in 1987, this figure rising to sixty in 1988, and reaching the planned production capacity of 100 per year in 1989, with some 500 completed by 1 January 1992. By 1993, it was reported that the PVO had 200 aircraft in service, Frontal Aviation had 150, and Naval Aviation had twenty Su-33s (Su-27Ks). The first export Flankers were ordered by China in mid-1991: forty-two Su-27SKs and eight two-seater UBKs. Subsequently China signed to manufacture up to 200 air defence fighters under licence. In addition, fifty long-range, multi-role Su-30MKs were purchased by China. In 1996, Vietnam took delivery of ten Su-27SKs and subsequently placed an order for a further two, plus four Su-27UBKs in 1997.

Sukhoi Su-27IB (Su-34)

In 1986, a requirement was issued in respect of two aerodynamic prototypes for a dedicated ship-borne fighter trainer. These were completed by Sukhoi in 1988 and 1989, designated Su-27KU, and were intended to prove the aerodynamics of a radically new forward fuselage matched to the airframe of the standard Su-27 interceptor. The aircraft featured a broader forward fuselage with movable canard foreplanes and embodied a cockpit accommodating staggered and splayed side-by-side ejection seats for two occupants, with access to the cockpit via the nose-wheel bay. The shape of the nose led the Russians to nickname the aircraft 'Platypus'. A retractable in-flight refuelling probe was provided, together with a strengthened undercarriage and a twin nose-wheel similar to the Su-27K, although it did not possess wing and tail folding and other features generally associated with ship-borne naval aircraft.

The first 'TASS' photographs of the aircraft appeared in 1991, but following the demise of the Soviet Union and the dramatic reduction in demand for ship-borne fighter aircraft, the official requirement for the carrier trainer was cancelled. Consequently the Sukhoi OKB proposed the adaptation of the two-seater as a fighter-bomber and one of the Su-27KU aerodynamic prototypes was mocked up with weaponry, although not a genuine combat prototype. It was flown in 1991, being displayed to CIS leaders at Machulische airfield, Minsk, in February 1992, as the proposed Su-27IB and offered to the RFAF as a replacement for the Su-24. Two aircraft—originally laid down as fully navalised Su-27KU prototypes—were rebuilt as Su-27IB prototypes and the OKB redesignated the aircraft Su-34. The first Su-34 prototype was flown on 18 December 1993, and the first pre-series aircraft flew a year later, on 28 December 1994, from the Chkalov plant at Novosibirsk.

Intended primarily for strike missions with a secondary air-to-air capability, the Su-34 was dedicated to making pin-point strikes against heavily defended targets, day and night and in all weathers, the avionics enabling the aircraft to perform low-level terrain-following flights. The new aircraft was of integrated aerodynamic configuration with a foreplane, strengthened undercarriage main-wheel members and a twin nose-wheel configuration. The under-fuselage strakes on the standard Su-27 were deleted. The cabin was a self-contained armoured capsule, making considerable use of titanium alloys and armoured glass panels, entry being by way of a hatch in the nose-wheel well. The cabin (cockpit) was fully equipped with multi-mode display units, whilst the crew seats were devised with improved ergonomics.

The Su-34 could carry Kh-31 anti-radar homing missiles on racks located below the air intakes, along with laser-guided bombs up to 500 kg (1,100 lb) on its under-wing inner racks. TV-guided Kh-29T ASMs (which could be used with a helmet-mounted sighting system), laser-guided Kh-29L ASMs or medium-range R-77 AAMs were carried on the outer wing racks, and close-range IR homing R-73 AAMs on the wing-tip pylons. The KAB-1500 or KAB-500 (laser- or TV-guided versions) bombs could also be carried. At the starboard leading-edge extension was a 30 mm GSh-301 cannon, with a retractable in-flight refuelling probe in the port, and the flattened radome blending into the wing leading-edge extensions embraced Leninets phased-array radar.

According to Sukhoi officials, flight testing commenced in early 1997, with the 'second production aircraft' based at Pushkino near St Petersburg where the Leninets design bureau is based. The 'third series production' Su-34 (Su-27IB—T-10V-4) was flown from the Novosibirsk production plant shortly before the end of 1996. It is claimed that it carried a full avionics and weapons systems suite, with the exception of the electronic warfare fit that had suffered extreme delays. In late 1996, it was reported that four more Su-27IB aircraft were in various stages of assembly at Novosibirsk.

The Su-27IB (Su-34) was viewed as a priority programme by the RFAF, as the aircraft was destined to replace the Su-24 Fencer in the strike role, with reconnaissance and electronic warfare variants to follow. The Su-27IB programme, unlike many other air force projects, continues to receive Russian state funding, signalling its importance to the RFAF in service or development. Russian air superiority fighters and interceptors are given odd-number designations, whereas attack and strike aircraft are given even numbers.

Other Su-27 variants

Su-27 Flanker-B/Su-27UB Flanker-C

The Su-27 Flanker-B was a single-seat, all-weather, air-superiority fighter, more than fifty early versions of which are operated by the Ukrainian Air Force at Kirovskye. A single-seat land-based version for the PVO, the Su-27P, made its maiden flight on 20 April 1981. The Su-27S, similar to the 'P' but specifically dual-roled for air combat/ground attack operations, was distinguished by Sorbtsiya active ECM jammer pods on each wing tip. The Su-27SK was an export variant fitted with upgraded radar, and the Su-27PD was a basic single-seat version specially prepared for demonstration flying by Anatoly Kvochur. It was fitted with an in-flight refuelling probe on the port side of the windscreen.

The Su-27UB Flanker-C was a combat-capable, dual-seat trainer, more than fifty of which were built at Irkutsk. A modified version, the Su-27LL-PS (T-10-16), underwent thrust vectoring development trials at the Zhukovsky test centre under the direction of TsIAM and the Saturn-Lyulka engine design bureau.

Su-32FN

First flown on 28 December 1994, the Su-32FN is a production development of the Su-34 optimised for long-range maritime and anti-shipping operations with terrain-following capabilities and a high level of automatic operation. The aircraft can carry up to three Alfa anti-shipping missiles. The Alfa, which can be launched at high altitude, is powered by an afterburning turbojet and cruises at 20,000 m (65,620 feet) at Mach 2.5/3 before diving for a sea-skimming terminal homing phase. The aircraft's maximum range is 300 km (162 nm) carrying a massive 300 kg (660 lb) warhead. Mid-course guidance is carried out by an INS/GPS combination. Twelve Su-32FNs were scheduled for delivery by 1998, with an electronic warfare variant under development.

Su-27K (Su-33) Flanker-D

Development of a single-seat ship-based interceptor began in 1976, based on a production Su-27 but embodying movable foreplanes, folding wings and other features for ship-borne operations. The navalised Su-27 (T-10-25) with arrester hook flew in 1984, whilst the first Su-27K-1 (T-10K-1 '29') prototype flew on 17 August 1987, and on 1 November 1989 the second prototype Su-27K-2 (T-10K-2) made the first conventional (non-V/STOL) landing on the aircraft carrier *Admiral Kuznetsov* (then *Tbilisi*) as well as a take-off with the use of the ski-jump ramp. Designated Su-33 (T-10K-3), the aircraft entered production at Komsomolsk in 1990, deliveries commencing the following year. State acceptance evaluation was concluded in July 1992, and initial declaration of operational capability was made in 1992. Twenty aircraft were delivered to the Kola Peninsula in mid-1994, and in the second half of that year a number of aircraft embarked on the *Admiral Kuznetsov* for extensive operational trials prior to the carrier's first operational tour in the Adriatic enforcing UN embargoes in connection with the Balkan conflict.

Su-30 (T-10P U) (Su-27PU)

Design of a two-seat long-range combat trainer began in 1986, construction of two prototypes beginning at Irkutsk the following year as the Su-27PU, which made its first flight in 1988. It was based more closely on the earlier Su-27UB airframe, with no canards, the original 'Slot Back' radar and the standard flight control system. With a small number of pre-series aircraft built, the type was redesignated Su-30 (probably in an attempt to obtain funding from the Kremlin). It was developed into a multi-role fighter-bomber as the Su-30M and the subsequent Su-30MK export variant when it became clear that the PVO was not interested in procuring the type. Two Su-27PUs were used by the test pilots' aerobatic display team at the Zhukovsky test centre.

Su-30MK (T-10PMK)

Design work started in 1991 and work began on converting an Su-27UB ('603', an Su-27UB prototype) for demonstration and development work in 1993. Two other Su-27UBs, '321' and '56', were also used. The conversion contained extra navigation equipment and a tactical data exchange kit that allowed it to operate as a 'command' aircraft, with the commander able to hand off targets to other group mission aircraft.

Another variant of the Su-30MK also appeared. Referred to as the 'controller' aircraft, it has no air-to-ground capability but is fitted with air interception radar (Phazotron Topaz coherent pulse-Doppler) and extra avionics, its function appearing to be to hand off airborne targets to other intercepts or via data link. Forty of the most recent version Su-30MKIs were ordered by the Indian Air Force for delivery between 1997 and 2001, eight Su-30MKs being delivered to No. 24 'Hunting Hawks' Squadron at Ambala. The Su-30MKI differs from the Su-30MK in having canard foreplanes, the latest Phazotron phased-array radar and thrust vectoring nozzles to the Saturn AL-31 engines, for which the rear fuselage has been strengthened. The developed Su-30MKI was reported to have first flown in early July 1997 when still under development, and it was also reported that the tail stinger had been lengthened and modified in shape.

Su-35

The Su-35 is a single-seat advanced air-superiority fighter, distinguished externally by moving canard foreplanes, wing-tip pods and square-tipped fins. The first experimental version Su-27 (T-10-24) flew in May 1985, and the first of six converted Su-27M prototypes (T-10S-70) was flown on 28 June 1988. In 1992, the Sukhoi OKB assigned the new aircraft the designation Su-35. It is reported that eleven prototype and production aircraft (701-711) had been built by September 1994, 711 having been modified for thrust vectoring experiments whilst in production at Komsomolsk.

The Su-35 is fitted with the Phazotron N011 Zhuk 27 multi-mode, low-altitude, terrain-following/avoidance radar with ground-mapping/attack mode and a phased-array antenna. The radar has a maximum search range of 400 km (216 nm) and can track fifteen targets and engage six simultaneously. A short-range rear-looking radar is carried in the tail-boom extension. Production aircraft have a 'glass' cockpit, a side-stick controller replacing the orthodox central control column. It was reported that one of the prototype aircraft came close to disaster in April 1997 when the flight control system suffered a double malfunction. The test pilot Oleg Tsoi nursed the aircraft back to the Akhtubinsk test centre in Kazakhstan, only to have the main gear collapse after landing. Fortunately Tsoi was unhurt.

Sukhoi T-4 Sotka ('100')

As the mechanical control systems for this supersonic strategic bomber became more and more complex, after many disputes Sukhoi decided to apply an active (FBW) control system. The T-4 Sotka was therefore the world's first aircraft purpose-built for fly-by-wire. Previously such systems had only been air tested with flying test beds developed in existing aircraft, such as the American F-4 Phantom II and F-8 Crusader and the Soviet 100LDU (Su-7U).

The origin of the Sotka (the '100') was quite dramatic. A requirement was issued to the OKBs of Myasishchev, Yakovlev and Sukhoi for a supersonic bomber/rocket launcher dedicated to the interception and destruction of launchers of winged missiles (such as Hound Dog—Rockwell B-1; Blue Steel—Avro Vulcan). Of these projects, the proposal put forward by the Sukhoi OKB was chosen for development. The project called for the aircraft to fly at speeds approaching Mach 3, a proposed performance considered to be unique. A number of doubts about the feasibility of the project were voiced, principally by Andrei Tupolev, who said, 'Sukhoi is unable to cope with this machine. I am able to emphasise this because he was my pupil.' Pavel Sukhoi replied, 'Exactly! Because I was your pupil, I will cope with this.'

The decision for the requirement reached by the Scientific and Technical Committee of the Ministry of Aviation Industry was subject to the approval of the Soviet Government, but it was considered doubtful that such a government directive would be signed. In 1962, an American newspaper commented that despite all the current ideological differences between the then US Defense Secretary Robert MacNamara and the Soviet leader Nikita Khrushchev, both agreed on one thing: they did not favour the bomber or, more correctly, new development of such types of aircraft. Khrushchev during a session of the Soviet Supreme Council had made a memorable speech announcing that thanks to Soviet successes in missile and space technology, all other types of weapons, particularly heavy bombers, could be discarded. Government agencies attempted to enforce a missile culture on almost all the design bureaux, with even Sukhoi designing a three-stage strategic ballistic missile, and several Soviet aircraft factories were subsequently assigned to the missile/space industry.

However, the personal role of Khrushchev in the cessation of work on strategic bombers should not be overestimated. Although important, there were a number of other factors favouring this trend. It was a fact that at this time the conventional heavy bomber had been rendered almost defenceless against improved air defences now equipped with powerful ground surveillance radars and guided surface-to-air missiles. Airborne stand-off missiles developed for carriage by the heavy bombers in the early 1950s were inadequate and did not address the problem. In essence they were too heavy (one bomber could only carry up to three missiles) and the main problem was their lack of accuracy. Nevertheless, after several years of Khrushchev's 'pause', the subject of the heavy bomber was raised again, partially forced onto the agenda by the Americans, who in 1965 had formulated new requirements for a new AMSA (Advanced Manned Strategic Aircraft), the Rockwell B-1A.

In 1967, the Soviets announced a competition to find a design for a multi-mode intercontinental strike/reconnaissance aircraft with advanced parameters. Sukhoi submitted his T-4M and T-4MS projects, and after top-level support from the First Deputy Chairman of Gosplan (the state planning administration), the Central Committee of the Communist Party and the Council of Ministers of the Soviet Union agreed that construction of the T-4 should be proceeded with. The government decree placed responsibility for the detailed design and construction on the Sukhoi OKB and directed that production should fall under the control of the plant named after S. A. Lavochkin. However, once Sukhoi's advisers set out to decide how the work was to be co-ordinated, the Lavochkin factory facilities were suddenly switched to other work. To replace them, the government designated the Tushino engineering works and the Burevestnik design office to the role of a deputising agency for the Sukhoi OKB.

The relationship between the Tushino works and the design office was, to say the least, fragile. The works management approached all new tasks from the Sukhoi OKB with reluctance. This was understandable, as the Tushino works at this time was heavily involved in a series programme that had been proven using considerable conventional technology. The management tried to rescind the programme by constantly criticising the design, picking on the most complex details. Its Directors even approached the Communist Party Central Committee, but this proved to be a waste of time and gradually the management and engineering staff proceeded with the project, once it was realised that the new work had aroused considerable interest and that the project carried considerable future benefits for the factory. Entirely new technological processes were to be introduced during the construction of the aircraft, especially in the field of welding of non-conventional materials. The Chief Designer of the T-4, Naum Chernyakov, had stated, 'Its range and speed are determined by the weight of the aircraft,' and according to preliminary estimates the weight of the proposed machine was to be 100 tonnes, which led to the nickname 'Sotka' ('100').

The T-4's design, development and construction period lasted nine years. This might appear to be excessive when compared to a comparable project in the West, where a similar project would normally be brought to fruition in five to seven years. The overrun can best be explained when it is understood that many of the problems were being tackled by the Soviet designers for the first time. The Sotka was a highly innovative programme and represented 100 per cent risk. New conventional aircraft designs usually represent only 50 per cent risk; that is, 50 per cent is of proven design, components, methods and materials. For the T-4, entirely new materials (heat-resistant alloys, non-metallic materials, special rubber products and new plastics) were devised. In fact, it was revealed at a symposium in London in 1967 that the Soviet Union, driven by the T-4 project requirements, had become leaders in the processing (rolling) of titanium. All production processes on the T-4 were to be automated, as were 95 per cent of the welding processes. The coefficient of use of materials was far higher than in previous types of aircraft. The number of welded plates with profiles reduced a great deal of the machining, but the complexity of the construction was such that it would have been more difficult if it had been constructed of easily machined light alloys. Eventually, on 22 August 1972, the T-4 prototype with its RD-36-41 engines, but without a complete equipment and armament fit, was flight tested for the first time by pilot Vladimir Ilyushin and navigator Nikolai Alferov. The aircraft actually made only ten flights (the last being on 22 January 1974) and only once achieved supersonic flight at Mach 1.3.

In 1975, Sukhoi decided to stop work on the T-4. The first prototype, 101, was handed over to the Soviet Air Force Museum at Monino, while successive prototypes 102, 103 and 104 (in various stages of construction) were scrapped. Sukhoi had always been faced by a great deal of prejudice against the T-4, and the delays and extremely long gestation period had meant that by the mid-1970s there was no longer a need for the aircraft; its tasks could be performed by more conventional and less troublesome machines such as the Tu-22M Backfire. None the less, Sukhoi's Sotka could rightly take its place in the annals of Soviet aviation as a highly sophisticated experimental design, forcing the industry into the use of a whole range of new materials that are now commonplace in modern civil and military aircraft designs.

Sukhoi prototype aircraft

During the Great Patriotic War each OKB Chief Designer tried to produce new designs or improve on the designs of existing aircraft to please Stalin, thus ensuring that they kept their own positions and design bureaux together and avoided the real possibility of being sent to the concentration camps in Siberia. For the Sukhoi OKB, however, the problem was more complicated. In 1942, its sole series aircraft, the Su-2, was withdrawn from production. The OKB tried without success to produce other designs for series production, most of the new prototypes being technically excellent, but Pavel Sukhoi was not a member of the Communist Party and did not therefore have high-level associates to recommend his designs for series production. It was for this reason that Stalin closed the Sukhoi OKB in 1949. It is prudent at this point therefore to examine briefly the Sukhoi prototype designs that did not enter series production.

ShB: This was a single ground attack design, modified from a Sukhoi 'Ivanov' in the spring of 1940. It was armoured and carried a 600 kg (1,320 lb) bomb load but was inferior to Ilyushin's Il-2 Sturmovik.

Su-1: A mixed-construction high-altitude fighter similar to the Su-2 but with an 820 kW (1,100 hp) M-105P engine. Its first flight took place in October 1940, the prototype (I-330) showing considerable promise. However, when the OKB was evacuated in October 1941 the programme was halted.

Su-3: Development started in parallel with the Su-1, and the almost completed prototype (I-360) was evacuated to Novosibirsk and flown in 1942. However, the turbos were found to be unreliable and the programme was halted in late 1942.

Su-4: The vulnerability of the Su-2 had been its lack of power. First flown in December 1941, the Su-4 light bomber was powered by a 1,567 kW (2,100 hp) M-90 engine and had an internal bomb load. The aircraft displayed good performance, but the M-90 engine went out of production. Re-engined with a 932 kW (1,250 hp) ASh-62, a small series batch was produced in 1942.

Su-5: This was an experimental interceptor and had a compressor driven by a shaft from the engine installed in the rear fuselage. The compressor fed a combustor and variable exhaust nozzle. Known as the VRDK, this booster was also used on the MiG-13 or I-250. The idea was more practical than a rocket booster or pulsejet and boosted the Su-5 to more than 800 kph (500 mph), but the development was overtaken by the turbojet engine. The prototype (I-107) was authorised in early 1944, powered by a 1,230 kW (1,650 hp) modified VK-107A engine and with an all-metal airframe. Company tests were carried out between April and June 1945, during which the prototype attained 815 kph (506 mph) at 7,800 m (25,590 feet). Although the Su-5 was a satisfactory design, its production came too late to compete with the early jet fighters.

Su-6: Started in June 1940 as an armoured attack aircraft, prototype construction was rapid and the first flight took place in April 1941. Of mixed construction, it was powered by a 1,492 kW (2,000 hp) M-17 engine. Prior to evacuation of the OKB a second aircraft was also tested, and in early 1942 the OKB was instructed to prepare a two-seat variant. In many respects the Su-6 was superior to the Il-2, being smaller, faster and more agile, and NII VVS evaluation engineers and pilots strongly recommended its series production in place of the Sturmovik. However, Stalin did not want to disrupt production. The Su-6 (S2A) two-seater was developed and tested at Novosibirsk in September 1943. It was also a much better aircraft than the Il-2 and won a State Prize for its design, but Stalin still maintained his objection to disruption of Il-2 production.

Tsybin (Ts-)

Colonel of Aviation Engineering Services, Pavel Vladimirovich Tsybin was a designer of gliders, beginning his career with the UL-1 training glider in 1928. Subsequently he collaborated with Oleg Antonov in the design of early examples of gliders in the 'Standard' series, and in 1944, with D. N. Kolesnikov, he designed the KTs-20 heavy cargo glider. From 1940 to 1946, with his close associate Sergei Korolev, he was responsible for development and construction of Soviet transport gliders.

The period from 1955 to 1959 saw Tsybin leading an OKB entrusted with development of a Mach 3 reconnaissance aircraft. Concurrently he worked on a project with Korolev for a recoverable piloted space glider vehicle. Both these projects were way ahead of their time. In 1961, Tsybin transferred to the S. P. Korolev OKB, where he directed the construction of the versions of Vostok spacecraft requiring fewer pilots, the Molniya communications satellite and Soyuz spacecraft. He became Deputy Chief

Designer in 1974 and was later a scientific consultant to the Buran spacecraft project. In his later years Tsybin directed the scientific research programme for development of a recoverable space vehicle. Tsybin died on 4 February 1992, aged 87.

Tsybin Ts-25

From a specification issued in early 1944, Tsybin produced a new assault glider two years later, the Ts-25, designed to carry twenty-five fully armed troops and two pilots. With a maximum towing speed of 250 kph (155 mph), the aircraft was a braced high-wing monoplane with a span of 25.2 m (82 feet 8 inches) and a length of 16.5 m (54 feet 1½ inches). The flight deck was situated above the slab-sided cabin, which had a hinged nose for rapid loading and unloading. Empty weight was 2,320 kg (5,115 lb) and maximum take-off weight 4,500 kg (9,920 lb). The aircraft, fitted with wheels and skids, was of mixed construction, mainly of wood, with steel tube bracing and a fabric-covered nose, and was originally designed for a load comprising a 57 mm anti-tank gun plus a jeep.

The Ts-25 went into production in 1948 at the Chkalov (Orenburg) aircraft plant, and 480 were built there for airborne troops up until 1954. A prototype powered version, designated Ts-25M, had been built in 1946. In 1952, Ts-25 gliders were handed over to the Czechoslovak Air Force (one was the D-41), where they were given the designation NK-25.

Tsybin RS/RSR

In March 1954, Tsybin proposed the ultra-modern strategic RS bomber, capable of carrying a nuclear bomb 14,000 km (7,560 nm). The RS was unusually small for an intercontinental bomber, with a take-off weight of 22,000 kg (48,488 lb) and measuring 30 m (98 feet) in length with a wingspan of 10 m (33 feet). It was to have extremely thin trapezoid wings and two ramjet engines of 49.03 kN (11,020 lbf) of thrust each installed at the wing tips. The aircraft was the most unusual ever built in the Soviet Union, yet built it was, and full-scale piloted models also flew successfully, although ultimately everything was abandoned and forgotten.

At a time when jet aircraft were just starting to fly at supersonic speeds, Tsybin submitted a proposal to build a new type of experimental aircraft with unprecedented performance: a speed of 3,000 kph (1,865 mph), a ceiling of 30 km (98,425 feet) and a range of 14,000 km (7,560 nm). The project evoked great interest. The latest achievements in supersonic aerodynamics were to be applied and totally new engines were to be used. The proposal was deliberated in the Ministry of Aircraft Production and a commission was formed under N. N. Tsebrikov from the Sukhoi OKB. An analysis of the proposal showed that many of the project's parameters were obviously excessive, although it was acknowledged that the very thin wing profile clearly held the promise of attaining high speeds.

In spite of Tupolev's reservations about forming a new design bureau, on 23 May 1955, a decree of official approval signed by Khrushchev, Bulganin, Malenkov,

Kaganovich, Voroshilov, Mikoyan, Suslov and other party and government leaders was given for the organisation of OKB-256 and the initiation of the RS project. The sum of 224,115,000 roubles was allocated for the construction of two prototypes, the first to be completed by 1 February and the second by 1 April 1957. At the same time all the major established design bureaux were directed to make a certain number of their personnel available for secondment to the OKB. Naturally, none of them released their best people and therefore the composition of the OKB-256 design team was not of the highest calibre. However, as many new design concepts needed examination and much experimental work was necessary, this was not too serious a constraint. In the first place, no final overall design or layout could be arrived at. There were frequent consultations with TsAGI. At first a canard layout was decided upon and the whole rear section with the main wing was to be detachable, to glide down on its target like a 'winged torpedo' whilst the remaining 'canard' returned home independently. However, this idea was soon abandoned and a normal layout with a tailplane was envisaged. The bomb load too was rejected, and the RS was now seen as a photo-reconnaissance aircraft with the revised designation RSR, denoting 'jet reconnaissance aircraft'. The difficult task of designing the new engines was undertaken by the P. A. Soloviev OKB.

The project took a new twist in 1955, when the idea arose of mounting the RSR under a Tupolev Tu-95 strategic bomber, which could carry it to the necessary operational region up to a distance of 4,000 km (2,160 nm) from base. After release, the RSR pilot would switch on his main and auxiliary booster rocket engines and release them after attaining the requisite height, continuing the flight using two standard gas turbine engines. However, work on modifying a Tu-95 bomber as a carrier was never completed.

On 31 August 1956, a resolution was issued by the Council of Ministers for completion of the first RSR fitted with D-21 engines in the first quarter of 1958. The aircraft's requirements were modified to provide a speed of 2,500 kph (1,553 mph) and a ceiling of 25 km (82,020 feet). In fact, the project was kept alive by relaxation of these requirements and the initial proposal to build scale models which had actually already started. However, the viability of the idea for such an unusual and revolutionary aircraft had to be tested to examine how it behaved in the air, so work began in 1956 on the NM-1 piloted aircraft that incorporated virtually all the basic elements of the RSR design, airframe, control systems, etc. The NM-1 was therefore the RSR on a smaller scale, with two 19.6 kN (4,410 lbf) AM-5 gas turbine engines. Construction was completed in July 1958, although it had been rolled out quite some time before—to show that the date for the plan had been met.

The NM-1 carried out taxiing tests and made its first hop on 1 October 1958, remaining airborne for some 17 seconds, but doubts about the strength of the undercarriage and the looming Soviet winter delayed permission for flight tests until the following spring. Taxiing tests began again on 18 March 1959, the NM-1 making its first circuit flight of 11 minutes' duration on 7 April, with twice 'Hero of the Soviet

Union' Amet-Khan Sultan at the controls. Five further flights followed, and seven more were made by Radi Zakharov. Altogether thirty-two satisfactory flights of the NM-1 were made in 1959/60, although performance was limited by the inadequate thrust of the AM-5 engines.

Rework and production of the RSR prototypes was slow. In the course of two years, five sets of general arrangement drawings were done, all bearing the signature of the Chief Designer, although they only partly met the requirements for a detailed revision of the design. Continual 'improvements' meant that not a single problem was thought through to conclusion; there was no proper focus of attention, and the major questions remained unsolved. It was therefore almost impossible to gain a proper picture of the RSR variants (2RS and 3RS) under construction, except that the basic geometry of the wing and tail assembly and part of the fuselage remained as for the NM-1 technology demonstrator.

The layout of the RSR was that of a single-seat mid-wing monoplane with a trapezoidal wing planform and a similar all-moving tailplane. The profile of all the surfaces was 2.5 per cent and symmetrical, constructed of flat panels, and the fuselage had a basic section diameter of 1,500 mm (5 feet). The vertical middle section was triple-faceted with a pressurised section housing photo and radio equipment, this feature being incorporated only in later design work. The engines were mounted on the wing tips and construction was of duralumin and other aluminium alloys. The attempt to use beryllium proved premature due to its inadequate purity and the lack of expertise in employing it. The task of overcoming the thermal and sound barrier had not at this time been effectively accomplished. The wing, of an unusual thin profile, was developed with five spars for a period of three years, before the Chief Designer, on the advice of the head of the wing design team Yu. I. Belkov, decided to use sixteen spars and at the same time modify the design of the fuselage. It was no easy task to mount the engines, each weighing a tonne, on wing tips whose thickness did not exceed 86 mm (3½ inches). It was under this guise that the construction of several examples of the RSR began at Ulan-Ude in late 1959. On 1 October 1959, OKB-256 was amalgamated with the staff of Myasishchev's OKB-23 and moved to the latter's premises. The still unperfected RSR was transported to the LII on 29 September 1960, and the following year saw the closure of OKB-256 and the termination of the project.

In the spring of 1961, the building of RSR airframes at Ulan-Ude was abandoned. Tsybin's protests to the VVS were to no avail, and he was first posted to Vladimir Chelomey's OKB-52 and soon afterwards to Sergei Korolev's OKB-1. The LII handed over the RSR to the Moscow Aviation Institute where it was used as a teaching aid before being scrapped. 'The Great Leap Forward' to attain speeds in excess of 3,000 kph (1,865 mph) in the 1950s had been well ahead of its time, but was constrained by the lack of advanced aerodynamic technology and composite materials and by insufficient knowledge to integrate available flight/propulsion and control technologies.

Tupolev (Tu-)

Born on 10 November 1888 at Pustomasovo, Andrei Nikolayevich Tupolev lent his name to more than sixty Soviet designs. He was the senior designer in the Soviet Union and managed the largest OKB, which from 1922 until his death in December 1972 created more diverse types of aircraft (129) than any other designer or company.

A design engineer at the Duks Works at Moscow-Khodynka, he was co-founder with Zhukovsky of TsAGI in 1918. As a member of the Commission for Heavy Aviation (KOMTA), he headed the State Commission on metal construction in October 1922, building the ANT-1 and ANT-2 cantilever monoplanes using corrugated Kolchug skin, the first flights of these aircraft taking place on 26 May 1924. Metal construction proven, Tupolev formed AGOS (Aviation, Hydro-aviation and Experimental Construction Section) and, as head of TsAGI's Construction Bureau, produced the ANT-3 biplane designated R-3 and first flown on 6 August 1925, of which 101 were built with an imported Lorraine engine. Following on from the R-3 he produced an amazing succession of large and challenging monoplanes, often with major parts or complete designs carried out by Petlyakov, Myasishchev or Sukhoi.

When the Junkers concession in Russia expired, the factory at Fili was taken over by Tupolev. It was there, at GAZ-22, that aircraft such as the ANT-4 (TB-1) were built. Designed by Petlyakov, it was the world's first all-metal heavy bomber with two M-17 (licence-built BMW VI) wing-mounted engines. The R-6, KR-6 and TB-3 were also produced there, some partly, other plants also being involved in the building of these aircraft. A total of 216 TB-1 bombers were produced, together with 136 R-6s, 270 KR-6s and some TB-1P seaplane bombers. The outstanding ANT-6 four-engined heavy bomber, whose maiden flight took place on 22 December 1930, led to production of 819 TB-3s as well as sixty-six ANT-9/PS-9s and the ANT-20 'Maksim Gorky' which in 1934 was the largest aircraft in the world, equipped with eight 671 kW (900 hp) engines and a crew of eight.

The ANT-20 was an incredible aircraft with numerous cabins and compartments and seating for seventy-two passengers. It had radio studios, printing machinery, film projection facilities, its own powerplant, a public address system (the 'Voice from Heaven') and an automatic telephone exchange (shades of the Airbus A380 Superjumbo). However, the aircraft crashed on 18 May 1935, when an escorting I-5 fighter struck and smashed the wing of the 'Maksim Gorky' when doing unauthorised aerobatics. Only one smaller six-engined ANT-20*bis* was built and operated by Aeroflot between 1939 and 1942. The ANT-25 long-distance bomber and the ANT-40 modern bomber, designed by Arkhangelsky, led to the production of 6,831 SB-2s and the ANT-42 high-altitude bomber.

Tupolev was Chief Engineer in the Chief Administration of the Aviation Industry (GUAP) from 1931 to 1936. However, he was arrested on 27 October 1937 by the NKVD (Secret Police) and interned in Butyrka prison and later in GAZ-156 Special Prison. Then, with the Soviet Government conscious of impending war, NKVD prisoners with suitable backgrounds (R. Bartini, J. Neman, K. Kalinin, and B. Chizhevsky) were joined together to form Central Design Bureau TsKB-29. Personnel from GAZ-156 joined TsKB-29 and soon several different design bureaux were formed, including those of Tupolev, Myasishchev, Petlyakov and Tomashevich. It was under these most extraordinary circumstances that Tupolev designed the ANT-58/Tu-2 bomber, which led to the ANT-61 and the subsequent production of 1,111 Tu-2s.

In January 1941, on the orders of Stalin, Tupolev began the largest 'copying' exercise ever, when he was tasked with producing a direct copy of the captured American B-29 Superfortress bomber. Later that year, in July, Tupolev and most of his team were released from prison and his bureau was relocated to Omsk, where work also continued on the improvement and production of the Tu-2, which was to equip two Soviet bomber regiments by the end of 1942. From this exercise the Tu-70/75 transports were produced, followed by the Tu-4 bomber, which via the piston-engined Tu-80/85 led to the giant swept-wing turboprop Tu-95 (initially designated Tu-20) and the Tu-142 Bear. The aircraft and its variants were produced over a period of thirty-eight years.

Tupolev won the State Prize for his Tu-2 design in 1943, and again in 1948 for his work on the Tu-4 design. The Tu-88, which first flew on 27 April 1952, led to the production of 1,500 Tu-16 Badgers, the first Soviet jet bomber in over twenty-five versions, plus 220 Tu-104 passenger transports, for which Tupolev won the Lenin Prize in 1957. Bomber development led to the Tu-22 supersonic bomber, the Tu-22M swing-wing bomber and missile launcher and the Tu-128 long-range interceptor. Transport development led to the turbofan-engined Tu-124 and the aft-engined Tu-134, as well as to the world's first supersonic airliner to begin flight tests, the Tu-144, and the Tu-154/164 passenger jets. For all these achievements Tupolev was made an Honorary Fellow of the Royal Aeronautical Society.

Following Andrei Tupolev's death on 23 December 1972, aged 84, the OKB continued to bear his name, its Chief Designer now being his son Alexei Andreyevich Tupolev, with Andrei Kanalov as his deputy. By this time most military aircraft production was centred at the vast Kazan complex, where the Tu-160 bomber was produced from 1981 until 1992. The notable exception to this was the Tu-95, which was built at Kuibyshev. Civil teams under Lev Lanovski developed aircraft for production at Kharkov and Ulyanovsk, notably the Tu-204, which had British engines. The Tu-334 flew in 1993 with turbofans and in 1994 with propfans. Also in 1993, the OKB decided to diversify into the design and manufacture of smaller aircraft.

Tupolev ANT-40 (SB-1/2)

In response to an official NII VVS request in October 1934 for a modern bomber, Tupolev saw the need for a fresh design of the simplest possible nature and chose a development of the ANT-21, ANT-29 and ANT-38 designs from the KOSOS Brigade led by Arkhangelsky. The overall layout was that of a twin-engined monoplane, with the main undercarriage retracting in the engine nacelles. The fuselage was made as slim as possible, the wing resembling that of the Arkhangelsky ANT-29 but of simpler construction.

Designed by the Tupolev OKB, the prototype of the ANT-40 (SB), later designated SB-1, was powered by two 530 kW (710 hp) Wright Cyclone F-3 air-cooled radials and first flew on 7 October 1934, with test pilot K. K. Popov at the controls. Early tests identified the need for numerous modifications to all the flight controls as well as a number of other changes. A particular problem was unacceptable elevator control, which appeared to cause spontaneous soaring or diving with very little pressure on the control wheel. As a result of the poor handling, on the ninth flight, on 31 October 1934, the first prototype was seriously damaged but rebuilt with a considerably lengthened fuselage and new outer wing panels. The engines were also replaced with 597 kW (800 hp) M-85 two-row radials installed as in the ANT-37*bis*. The rebuilt aircraft was company tested between 5 February and 31 July 1935. However, it was eventually abandoned as the second prototype, completed in December 1934 and making its first flight on 16 February 1935, displayed much-improved handling and performance.

In spite of a number of faults remaining, instructions were received from the NII VVS to organise series production of the type, and this was done at GAZ-22 (Fili) and at the new GAZ-125 (Irkutsk). The third prototype (ANT-40 No. 2) incorporated a number of major aerodynamic changes to improve stability and control, and the entire flight control system was redesigned with the assistance of the TsAGI Experimental Aerodynamics Section led by Ye. P. Grossman and M. V. Keldysh. The aircraft was tested between September 1935 and April 1936, at which time Commissar Ordzhonikidze was investigating the bomber's problems. NII VVS engineers covered the aircraft in placards pointing to the numerous defects that existed. Tupolev became incensed and began tearing down the placards, shouting 'Hooligans!', although the incident led to a meeting with Stalin, who proclaimed, 'There are no trivialities in aviation,' which resulted in many modifications to the design, a number of which were embodied on series aircraft. Stalin was not pleased that, with over thirty aircraft on the GAZ-22 assembly lines and GAZ-125 already tooled for production, major changes should be needed to the aircraft's design. So, with the type still under development, aircraft began leaving the GAZ-22 SB production line in June 1936. This resulted in any number of versions and sub-types being produced in any particular month. Annual production from Fili was 268 in 1936, 853 in 1937, 1,250 in 1938, 1,435 in 1939, 1,820 in 1940 (an average of five per day, including Sundays) and 69 in 1941. Production at Irkutsk started in May 1937, with 73 in 1937, 177 in 1938, 343 in 1939, 375 in 1940 and 168 in 1941.

The SB had first seen service in the Spanish Civil War in October 1936, much to the surprise of the Nationalists, who initially mistook it for the Martin 139W bomber. Of all-metal, stressed-skin construction, it was powered by two 560 kW (750 hp) VK-100 inline piston engines (effectively Soviet copies of the Hispano-Suiza 12Y). The Spanish Government had paid the equivalent of £63 million in gold to the Soviets for assistance. The first Soviet unit to receive the type was *Grupo 12*, which until late 1936 lost only six aircraft, two of which were lost to aerial fighter interception. This was rather surprising, as later during Operation Barbarossa, much to the Red Air Force's cost, the aircraft's large size and almost total lack of defensive armour and armament rendered it extremely vulnerable to German fighter aircraft. For this reason, the few bombers that survived the Luftwaffe fighters' initial onslaughts were relegated to night-time operations only. At the start of Operation Barbarossa 47.2 per cent of the Red Air Force's bombers were SB-2s. Later *Grupo 24* also flew the SB-2 in Spain, operations continuing until 1939. After the war the Nationalists used the type under the designation B.5 and for several years operated sixteen captured from the Republican Air Force. Later, in 1943, the last eight still in use were replaced with Junkers Ju 88As.

The first exports (B.71s) to Czechoslovakia had commenced in April 1937 (serials 1-61), with the Czechs then acquiring a licence for local production by Letov (serials 62-101), Aero (serials 102-151) and Avia (serials 152-222). The licence also included authority for the production of sixty reconnaissance variants. With the German occupation of the Czech-Moravia Protectorate, the aircraft continued to be built under German supervision, with forty-two delivered to Bulgaria for service with the 5th Bomber Wing at Plovdiv, six to Hungary for target-towing duties, and others to the Luftwaffe for the same use. One was delivered to the Slovak Air Force, which initially escaped to Turkey, but later, in August 1944, arrived in the UK. Delivery from Irkutsk to Wuhan, China, of sixty-two SB-2s was undertaken in September and October 1937; ten were for a Soviet conversion unit which already had the SB-2, the remainder being for Chinese Government Air Force's 2nd Bomber Group, as well as a Soviet VVS squadron which had begun operations against Japanese shipping in December 1937. Later, on 23 February 1938, to celebrate Red Army Day, twelve Soviet Air Force SB-2s bombed Taiwan.

In the Winter War of 1939/40 with Finland, two Finnish Air Force units, LeLv 6 (six aircraft) and 2/LeLv 6 (eight aircraft), destroyed a number of Soviet submarines using the SB-2. As the war continued, the Finns shot down more than 200 Soviet SB-2s, which included ninety-two by fighters, a further fifty having crashed on Finnish territory. A number of these were recovered and operated by the Finnish Air Force. However, by this time the obsolete SB-2s, and particularly their liquid-cooled piston engines, were being gravely affected by the extremely harsh winter conditions. This led to the appearance, in 1939, of the SB-2*bis* with its two 820 kW (1,100 hp) M-100A engines and later with the uprated M-103 inline engines, increasing the aircraft's top speed to 451 kph (280 mph). However, from 1941 to 1944, a further sixty-nine Soviet SB-2s were downed by Finnish fighters, and eighty-eight by anti-aircraft fire. Throughout this period of almost four years not one Finnish SB-2 was lost in combat, although seven were destroyed in accidents. It was later revealed that Finnish SB-2 aircraft had flown a total of 4,460 hours in the war.

Despite being seriously under-gunned and suffering heavy losses in the opening months of Operation Barbarossa, the SB-2 served with the Soviet Air Force throughout the duration of the Second World War, finally in the last two years of the conflict being employed as a night fighter. In 1946, the remaining Soviet Air Force aircraft were scrapped. The SB was built in greater numbers than any comparable light bomber of the era, total production of all types amounting to 6,831 aircraft, with the most produced in 1941/42. A number of aircraft that survived the war against Japan were used to defend the Chinese city of Paotao when it was besieged by Communist forces from 8 November to 3 December 1945. However, early in 1946, the North-West Composite Squadron (Soviet SB-2s joined with Curtiss P-40 Warhawks) based at Tihua was disbanded, bringing to an end the Chinese chapter of the SB-2's career.

Tupolev Tu-2

Project ANT-58 (Samolet 103) was started at GAZ-156 on 1 March 1940, and the mock-up was built and preliminary estimates completed by 21 April. The aircraft was to be fitted with two M-120TK-2 engines and would carry a crew of three. On 1 July, the State Defence Committee issued detailed requirements for three prototypes of the aircraft. One was to be powered by AM-37 engines and the other two by M-120TK-2s. Project definition was completed by 3 October, the first prototype making its maiden flight on 29 January 1941, but unfortunately the aircraft crashed and was destroyed.

The second aircraft, 103U, built simultaneously with the first prototype, made its maiden flight on 18 May 1941. The 103U incorporated additional requirements as specified by the Soviet Air Force, flight development and state evaluation continuing until June 1941. Already, even in these early days, it was clear that a unique aircraft had been created—an aircraft that was urgently needed by the VVS. For these reasons, even though the evaluations had not been concluded, preparations for series production were being made. The speed of the aircraft would permit its use without the need of a fighter escort, and its range would allow it to be used for special missions. The crew were protected by armour, with the pilot and navigator seated in the front cabin and the air gunner in a dorsal turret.

Construction of the third prototype was resumed after Tupolev and his team had been evacuated following the first German raids on Moscow in July 1941. It was to be powered by M-120 engines fitted with TK-2 turbochargers, but as these engines were now cancelled and production of the AM-37 engines had been terminated, the future of the aircraft was in real peril. However, it was decided to adopt the M-82 air-cooled radial engines (later redesignated ASh-82), the change in engine type necessitating the production of some 1,500 new drawings and requiring engineers to work 10-12 hours a day without rest. Tupolev visited the assembly hall daily to oversee progress, and in spite of all the problems the 103V third prototype made its first flight on 15 December 1941, with test pilot M. Vasyakin at the controls. Vasyakin was later to become Commander of a Tu-2 bomber regiment.

Tupolev appointed leading engineers from his design group as workshop superintendents' assistants in order to minimise production problems. New manufacturing techniques were introduced, such as production of the airframe in numerous sub-assemblies, reducing the number of production cycles, and the fitting of complex electrical and hydraulic systems as separate modules, along with numerous other measures. Having overcome all these difficulties, the first production 103V was taken to the airfield at the end of February 1942. In spite of the fact that the aircraft's maximum speed was reduced by 100 kph (62 mph) due to the enforced engine change, flight development and acceptance evaluation progressed well, and it was at this time that the 103 was redesignated Tu-2.

In April 1942, the Tu-2 was sent for front-line operational evaluation in the Kalinin Sector with the 2nd Air Army commanded by Mikhail Gromov. The aircraft was supported by a number of OKB technicians and engineers led by Dmitry Markov, and service pilots reported favourably on the aircraft's tactical and operational ability as a contemporary bomber. Excellent flight characteristics, an effective bomb load of three 1,000 kg (2,205 lb) weapons, well-arranged defensive armament, good power-to-weight characteristics and apparent ease of crew conversion were all highly appreciated. However, a number of design changes were introduced in 1945.

The fuselage nose section was of all-metal construction and rounded, the glazing being increased by 50 mm (2 inches) from series c/n 48 onwards. The upper section was straighter, and the navigator's turret was replaced by a VUS-1 turret. Four-bladed feathering airscrews were introduced and engine air intakes were enlarged with dust filters added. In addition, there were a number of production changes. The VUB-2M turret in the wireless operator/air gunner's position was replaced by a VUB-68 (series c/n 44 onwards) and the moving canopy section was replaced by a fixed screen (series c/n 50 onwards). The Lu turret taken unchanged from the Pe-2 aircraft was modified and designated Lu-68, and the adjacent panels were armoured. Wing tips originally made of wood were made of metal from c/n 52 onwards and were of various shapes. Those from GAZ-166 were slightly pointed. Aircraft from c/n 59 onwards were fitted with mechanical de-icing equipment on the wings, tailplanes and tail fins, and the size of the tail fin was increased. From 1947 onwards, the photo-reconnaissance versions of the Tu-2 were redesignated Tu-6, the main distinguishing feature being the blister fairing of the AK AFU-156L camera mounted in the rear section of the bomb bay.

The Tupolev Tu-2D, a long-range version of the 103D, was conceived in the summer of 1941, but construction was not proceeded with until 1944. Flight development of aircraft No. 718 began on 17 June 1944, followed by No. 714 on 20 October. They were recorded as ANT-62 and Tu-2D respectively. The wingspan of the Tu-2D was increased from 18.86 m (62 feet) to 22.06 m (72 feet 5 inches), and additional fuel tanks were fitted in the outer wing panels, increasing the range by 800-900 km (500-560 miles). According to the project specifications, a bomb load of 4,000 kg (8,820 lb) was planned, which subsequently demanded undercarriage strengthening.

Tupolev Tu-4 Bull

In December 1943, the Shvetsov OKB started to prepare plans for production of the Wright Cyclone R-3350 engine (Soviet designation ASh-73TK) as a licence was held to produce it in the USSR. Stalin had made three requests to the Allies for the B-29 Superfortress strategic bomber without success. However, the first of three B-29s made forced landings near Vladivostok on 29 July 1944, the second and third aircraft landing on 20 August and 21 November respectively, and work started in January 1945 on copying the aircraft and its systems. At the time it was the biggest reverse-engineering project ever undertaken anywhere in the world. However, the project was bedevilled with problems, mainly caused by the necessity to convert US measurements to metric. Technicians were retrained in great secrecy to work in inches, feet, pounds and foot pounds. Even so, few parts of the copy were identical to the original US components once the processes were complete, and consequently the first of twenty pre-production aircraft, which flew on 3 July 1947, experienced severe and prolonged problems with all of its systems. As a result, despite three aircraft appearing at the Aviation Day parade at Tushino on 3 August 1947, it was not until two years later that the twentieth prototype (pre-production) aircraft, built at GAZ-22 at Kazan, finally flew. At the height of the problems with the aircraft and its systems, Soviet agents tried unsuccessfully to purchase quantities of tyres and landing gear in the US, but after two years of development several plants (such as Severomorsk, Omsk and Stalinsk) began delivery of parts. By January 1950, 400 aircraft had been built, mainly at Kazan, although the aircraft was produced at other plants, Kazan alone producing 1,345 bombers up until 1953.

Design work on the Tu-70 passenger aircraft with a pressurised cabin—the first Soviet airliner to be so equipped—ran in parallel with the work on the Tu-4 bomber. The first flight of the Tu-70 was on 27 November 1946, six months earlier than the first production Tu-4, a B-29 wing having been mated to a newly designed fuselage. Experience gained on the Tu-70 was later employed in the design of the Tu-104. However, the Tu-70 did not enter series production.

Tu-4 variants and derivatives

Tu-4LI: An engine flying test bed on which the AI-5, AI-7, AM-3, AM-5, NK-4, NK-12, AI-20 and VD-7 turbojet and turboprop engines were test flown, either installed in the wings or in the bomb bay.

Tu-75: A military transport version of the Tu-70, fitted with a tail turret and a rear loading ramp and with a strengthened fuselage floor. The type did not enter series production.

Tu-80: Although a direct derivative of the Tu-4, it had little commonality with the B-29. The fuselage outlines were revised, the flush glazing of the pilot's cabin was replaced by a stepped windscreen, a radar radome was located in the nose, the outer wing panels had no dihedral and the gunner's observation blisters were semi-recessed into the fuselage. The Tu-80 was an interim development aircraft, part of the progress towards the Tu-85, and made its first flight in November 1949. The Tu-85's maiden flight took place in January 1950.

Series production Tu-4 Bulls saw service with Long Range Aviation where they replaced earlier twin-engined bombers. The fleet increased from 300 in 1950 to

1,100 in 1955. Long Range Aviation had thirty-four regiments in 1954, including six in the Far East. At the peak of Tu-4 deployment, Long Range Aviation had three air armies, two in the western Soviet Union and one in the Far East. The first regiment was created in 1949, at the same time that the Soviet atomic bomb was developed, both of the first Soviet A- and H-bombs being dropped from Tu-4s. The aircraft did not possess sufficient range to embark on round-trip attacks on the US, but could reach most points in the US on one-way missions with a 5-tonne payload (one A- or H-bomb). Even in 1960, 375 remained in service, despite the availability of the more capable Tu-16. The last fifty Tu-4s were retired from Long Range Aviation use in 1964, although the type was still used for many years in the training and transport roles and as an experimental aircraft for various test flights.

In February 1952, the Soviet Union sent ten Tu-4A bombers to China. They were used by the 4th Independent Regiment of the People's Liberation Army Air Force near Beijing, which was the main Chinese strategic strike force in the 1960s. Three additional Tu-4As were received by China in 1959/60 to make up for attrition losses. From 1947 until 1953, a total of 1,795 Tu-4 bombers were built by GAZ-18 and GAZ-22.

Tupolev Tu-14 Bosun and variants

Design and production of the prototype Tu-14 started in 1946, after the Soviet Air Force had requested a jet bomber capable of carrying a 3,000 kg (6,614 lb) bomb load. The original prototype was actually a Tu-2 fitted with two Rolls-Royce Nene engines and a tricycle undercarriage. Designated RD-Tu-2, it had its first flight on 27 July 1947, and was followed by the Tu-72, which was a project design of Arkhangelsky using two Nene engines in response to a Soviet requirement for a naval bomber with a crew of four. However, Tupolev soon realised that this aircraft was underpowered and it therefore remained only a development project. For this reason, work started on a new prototype, the Tu-73, in March 1947. Fitted with a Rolls-Royce Derwent and two Nene engines, it made its first flight on 29 December 1947. State acceptance tests commenced on 14 June 1948, and four months later the Tu-73R, which became the Tu-74, was evaluated against the Ilyushin Il-28. The Il-28 actually came out the winner.

In 1948, a development of the Tu-74, the Tu-78, fitted with two RD-45s and a RD-500 engine had its first flight on 17 April, and NII VVS testing started on 28 December 1948. The Tu-78 gave rise to the Tu-78R reconnaissance variant, but this also only remained a project and did not enter series production. This was followed by a proposal for a Tu-79, using two Klimov VK-1s and a tail-mounted RD-500. However, this was never built and the project was later abandoned.

The Tu-81 was a development of the Tu-72, powered by two VK-1 engines. First flown and tested in 1948, it was accepted for Naval Aviation service in June 1949. Whilst the Tu-81 carried a crew of five, the production variant, the Tu-89, had a crew of only three. The aircraft, redesignated Tu-14 by the military, was the first jet bomber to enter Soviet Naval Aviation service, in 1951, and remained in use for almost ten years. GAZ-39 at Irkutsk built ten Tu-14s in 1950, 110 in 1951, and a total of 360 by 1953. Production peaked at ten aircraft per month, but the plant switched to production of the Il-28 in 1953. China received sixty Tu-14 bombers in the 1950s.

Two other variants of the Tu-14 were produced: a reconnaissance version, the Tu-14R (Tu-81R), and the Tu-14T (Tu-89T) torpedo variant fitted with two 23 mm cannon, state trials having been held between September and December 1951. A swept-wing variant had also been produced, making its first flight in February 1949 as the Tu-83. In 1951, a slightly enlarged version of this was proposed and given the designation Tu-86, but this was never built and the project was subsequently cancelled due to the development of the Tu-88.

Tupolev Tu-16 Badger

Following the first flight of the Boeing B-47 Stratojet bomber on 17 December 1947, the Soviet administration pressed Tupolev to speed up work on several new jet bomber projects to counter the threat. During 1949, preliminary sketches of various designs (Tu-86, Tu-88 and Tu-89) appeared on Tupolev's drawing board, differing mainly in the engine fit. Tupolev preferred the Tu-88 (which for security reasons was also referred to simply as 'N'). The Tu-88 design used the powerful 85.8 kN (19,290 lbf) AM-3 jet engines developed by the Mikulin OKB, and the airframe, designed by Tupolev's Chief Engineer Markov, had a wide cross-section. However, Tupolev himself was not satisfied with the design and using the area rule, redesigned the airframe in the form of a narrow-diameter cylindrical-shaped fuselage with the engines semi-recessed along the fuselage sides. The Tu-88 was capable of carrying a FAB-9000 weapon in its bomb bay.

In July 1950, three prototypes were ordered, wind tunnel tests subsequently revealing that the aircraft was of clean design with low drag. The four-bogie main-wheel landing gear was housed in wing pods extending back past the wing trailing edge. This unique aircraft, with its engines attached to the fuselage at the thickest section of the wing root, was handed over for its final works and acceptance testing programme at the end of 1951. The first prototype was flown on 27 April 1952 by test pilot Nikolai Rybko. State acceptance tests took six months, during which a top speed of 1,012 kph (629 mph) was achieved, exceeding specification requirements. However, only average speeds of 945 kph (587 mph) were obtained and range requirements did not meet specifications as the airframe was too heavy. Tupolev and Markov immediately set about reassessing the airframe design, imposing a strict weight-saving campaign, but Stalin had already ordered the aircraft into series production in December 1952, and the plant at Kazan began preparing to series-produce the aircraft based on the design of the prototype. When MAP became aware of the airframe reconstruction programme Markov was severely reprimanded, in spite of the fact that the second prototype, fitted with uprated AM-3A turbojets, now exceeded the specified range requirements whilst still attaining a maximum speed of 992 kph (616 mph).

Full-scale series production of the twin-jet aircraft, now designated Tu-16, began at Kazan in early 1954, and at Kuibyshev a year later, with the first nine aircraft revealed to the public on the May Day fly-past in 1954. Already by 1954 the two plants between them had produced a total of 105 Tu-16s, most of which were the Badger-A bomber variant. In 1955, GAZ-64 at Voronezh also started production of the type, building a total of 435 in that year alone. The last twenty Tu-16s were produced at Kuibyshev in 1959, a total of 1,490 eventually being built.

The Tu-16 was introduced into Soviet service extremely quickly, the first series aircraft entering operational service with the Long Range Bomber Force in early 1954, with fifty-four bombers appearing in the Aviation Day fly-past over Moscow on 16 August 1955. The following year, 370 were in service, with 665 in 1957, 970 in 1958, and 1,030 in 1959. The peak was reached in 1961, with a total of 1,100 in service with the Long Range Bomber Force and Soviet Naval Aviation. To meet the needs of the Soviet Navy, the Tu-16KS missile carrier (for KS-1 cruise missiles) was built in 1960, over 100 of which eventually operated from Naval Aviation's shore bases. The missiles were directed by a Kobalt-N transmitter as used in the Tu-4K aircraft. The operational range of the Tu-16KS was 1,800 km (1,120 miles), with the effective range of the KS-1 missile being 90 km (55 miles). In the mid-1950s, the Tu-16T torpedo bomber was produced, which could also carry sea mines as well as torpedoes.

Later, in 1965, all Tu-16Ts were converted to SAR variants (Tu-16S) with a range of 2,000 km (1,243 miles). Fregat boats carried below the bomb bay were released in the direction of those to be rescued and then remotely controlled by the Rech transmitter. To increase the Tu-16's effective range, a system of in-flight refuelling was devised, developed from the system tested on the Tu-4. The fuel was provided by attaching the hose to the wing tip of the receiving aircraft, and after successful evaluation in 1955, the Tu-16Z entered series production with extra tankage in the bomb bay. When required, the additional tanks and refuelling equipment could be quickly removed to allow the aircraft to be operated as a conventional bomber. Tu-16Z tankers were later used to refuel Tu-22 aircraft etc.

The Tu-16R (Project 92), a reconnaissance variant, began its state acceptance evaluation in 1955. It was produced in two day and night photo-reconnaissance versions, and in the same year the new cruise missile K-10S developed by Mikoyan became available, the intention being to use the Tu-16K-10 aircraft as its launcher. The aircraft's fuselage nose section was revised to accommodate the YeN search and tracking radar, the guidance radar being located below the flight deck. The bomb bay contained the rack for the missile, and there was a fuel tank for the missile and a pressurised cabin for the YeN radar operator. The K-10S missile was semi-recessed in the bomb bay, from which it was dropped prior to its engines being started. The prototype Tu-16K-10 was built in 1958, and series production began a year later. The aircraft made its first public appearance at the 1961 Tushino Air Show, at which time K-10S missile trials were under way, being successfully concluded in the October of that year.

In 1959, the Tu-16 was fitted with the PBR-4 Rubin I mapping radar. Concurrently the OKB led by Mikoyan and Bereznyak developed a new type of cruise missile, the

KR-11-16, which was accepted into service use in 1962. The carriers, the Tu-16K-11-16s, were converted from the earlier Tu-16, the Tu-16Z and Tu-16KS, which could carry two KSR-2 (K-16) or KSR-11 (K-11) missiles on under-wing racks. In 1962, a new weapons system—the K-26, based on the KSR-5—was developed. All entered service in the second half of the 1960s. The advantage of the K-11-16 and K-26 missiles was that no special launch equipment was required, so they could therefore be carried by conventional bombers, this operational flexibility also being extended to the K-10 missile. The Tu-16K-10-26 could carry the KSR-5 on its wing pylons in addition to the K-10S under the fuselage. The KSR-5 could be supplemented by the KSR-2 or similar.

From 1963 onwards, a number of Tu-16 bombers were converted into Tu-16N tankers with the probe and drogue refuelling system for the Tu-22 aircraft. Tu-16s were also used for ECM operations, the first versions appearing at the end of the 1950s, and in the early 1960s the Tu-16P and Tu-16E emerged. Later, the ECM equipment was fitted to all strike and reconnaissance versions of the Tu-16. In the late 1960s, a certain number of Tu-16K-10s were converted to a maritime reconnaissance version, the Tu-16RM, and a few of these were modified to target rocket drone carriers, Tu-16KRMs, for the PVO. As these aircraft ran out of airframe hours they were converted to radio-controlled drones.

Tu-16s were also used as test beds for development of the AL-7F-1, VD-7 and other engines, the bomb bay being fitted with retractable engine framework. During take-off, landing and taxiing, the carriage and engine under test were partly recessed in the fuselage (bomb bay) and at altitude were extended for tests. Various test beds of the Tu-16LL were used not only for engine testing but also for aerodynamic tests of other types of aircraft. One of these test beds flew with a zero-track undercarriage. It also carried various containers with chemicals for cloud dispersal.

The aircraft was also operated abroad. In the summer of 1961, twenty-five Tu-16KS aircraft and KS-1 missiles were exported to Indonesia. Libya also received eight Tu-16s in 1974 for use as trainers for the Tu-22 bombers it had received. Deliveries to China had commenced in 1958, four aircraft having been received by May 1959. However, deliveries were halted following a deterioration in the relationship between the Soviet Union and China, and the Xian Aircraft Company began production of the aircraft under the designation H-6. Between 1968 and 1987, about 120 were produced. In addition, China produced an updated variant, the H-6D, which carried two C-601 cruise missiles and was equipped with more advanced avionics, including an onboard computer and new mapping radar. Four H-6Ds were also sold to Iraq.

The Tu-16 saw combat in several wars, the Soviet Air Force using the aircraft to carry out medium-level bombing attacks against targets in Afghanistan from its bases across the border in Uzbekistan. At the outbreak of the Six-Day War in June 1967, Egypt operated about twenty Tu-16s, but all were destroyed on the ground by the Israeli Air Force in the early hours of the conflict. Later, Egypt received a further twenty-four Tu-16K-11-16s, which were used in the 1973 Yom Kippur War to launch several AS-5 missile attacks against Israeli radars and other targets. Two radar stations were destroyed, with only one Tu-16 lost. The Iraqi Air Force operated eight Tu-16s in the war against Iran in the 1980s, twelve aircraft having been delivered in 1964. Bombers conducted at least one raid against Tehran Airport as well as several missile attacks against other Iranian targets.

Only the US, with its Boeing B-52, could match the Tu-16's longevity in operational service, its flying career extending over more than forty years. It is a truly unique aircraft, not only in Soviet terms but on a world scale, having been produced in more than fifty versions and modifications, and is a credit to its creators and designers. Many of the structural concepts and elements became classic techniques for the construction of heavy Soviet combat aircraft. The Tu-16 was used in the development of new Soviet aviation materials, including light, high-strength alloys, and means of countering corrosion, and contributed to the development of newer types of missiles and other types of armament. As late as 1993, the Russian Air Force still had thirty Tu-16 missile carriers, seventy reconnaissance aircraft and twenty tankers in operational use, and the Russian Navy had fifteen missile carriers, twenty-four reconnaissance aircraft and six tankers. Ukraine had fifty-three Tu-16s and Belarus eighteen. Out of the total build of 1,490, the CIS had 236 aircraft still in use in 1993, 113 had been exported and the remainder had been destroyed or retired in thirty-eight years of service, an average of thirty per year.

In addition to its operational combat role, the Tu-16 proved to be a good training machine for generations of Soviet airmen. Many learned to fly the more advance bombers and missile carriers that followed, and after leaving the Soviet Air Force found it easy to adapt to a number of Tupolev airliner designs that had been based on the original Tu-88 (Tu-16) concepts.

Tupolev Tu-20, Tu-95 Bear, Tu-142 Bear F

The Soviet Union tested its first atomic bomb on 2 August 1949. A few days later Stalin ordered a jet bomber capable of flying with the A-bomb to the US and back (a range of 16,000 km or 9,940 miles). Knowing that suitable engines were not available in the Soviet Union, Tupolev opted for a turboprop design, although Stalin accepted both the Myasishchev M-4 four-jet bomber project and the Tupolev Tu-95 turbine bomber project for development. An 8,950 kW (12,000 hp) NK-12 engine was developed by a team of Germans (in reality, the Junkers team), led by Ferdinand Brandner at Kuibyshev, and was tested in 1953. The NK-12 engines with electronic variable-pitch propellers formed the heart of the aircraft. The Tu-95 design was initiated in 1951, and, the prototype made its first flight in the late summer of 1954, entering service in April 1956. The Tu-20 designation was dropped in favour of Tu-95 and series production was ordered at GAZ-18 at Kuibyshev in 1954. A year later, in July 1955, five new Tu-20s (Tu-95s) made an appearance over Tushino and deliveries to the Soviet Air Force began during the second half of the year. The Bear A, with a glazed nose, was the original bomber version received. During the late-1950s, seventy-five aircraft were produced—enough for two strategic bomber regiments of the VVS.

The aircraft had its roots back in Seattle, where Boeing engineers had developed the Model 345, which had entered USAAF service as the B-29. As mentioned earlier, with the three forced landings of the B-29s in the USSR the design was pirated by the Soviets. The resulting Tu-4, identical except for the fuel tanks, engines and armament, was subsequently enlarged and developed into the Tu-80, which with uprated 3,208 kW (4,300 hp) engines and a span of 56 m (183 feet 6 inches) was to become the Tu-85. However, it soon became clear that turboprops could enable engine power to be doubled, trebled and even quadrupled, and as an engine of such power was already well ahead in development, the Tu-85, a superb aircraft, was cancelled. The power of the turboprop engines was coupled through a complex power-dividing gearbox to tandem coaxial propellers. The huge AV-60 series propeller had two units each with four blades with a diameter of 5.59 m (18 feet 4 inches). Each propeller was independent of its partner and the electronic pitch control permitted slow rotating speeds, allowing the aircraft to fly at near jet speeds without the propeller tips exceeding the speed of sound.

The fuselage of the bomber fitted with the new powerful engines and propellers was that of the Tu-85 with a slight stretch, designated Tu-95/I. It flew in late 1952, when it was in direct competition with the Myasishchev 103 (M-4 Bison) long-range jet bomber project. However, on the Tu-95/I's 17th flight the intermediate gearbox of one of the eight engines failed, resulting in a fire which led to the loss of the aircraft and three of its test crew. Tupolev was forced into using four of the more powerful TV-12 (later NK-12) engines, but the setback was to delay the whole Tu-95 programme for several years. The Tu-95/II did not fly until February 1955, and in 1960, due to the new American fighters and anti-aircraft missiles, the Bear A became obsolete. For this reason Tupolev developed the radar-nosed Bear B. The revised nose accommodated the 'Crown Drum' high-definition search radar and A-336Z missile guidance system for the new AS-3 Kangaroo missile carried by the aircraft in a semi-recessed position under the fuselage. At the Soviet Aviation Day in July 1961, fifteen Bear B aircraft were seen flying over Moscow, and the following year seventy-five of these, fitted with in-flight refuelling probes, were produced for two strategic bomber regiments. Some aircraft were subsequently modified for the strategic reconnaissance role with a blister fairing on the starboard side of the rear fuselage.

September 1964 saw the first appearance of the Bear C. This was a dedicated maritime reconnaissance and ELINT-gathering derivative of the Bear B with six cameras but retaining missile capability, radar and an in-flight refuelling probe. The weapons bays were reworked for an additional 19,000 litres (4,179 gallons) of fuel and EW equipment characterised by two lateral blister fairings on the rear fuselage and a number of ventral radomes. However, only fifteen of this type were produced, the Soviet Navy preferring the Bear D support variant produced by the conversion of Bear A aircraft. There were a number of detailed differences between the aircraft, but most had the 'Short Horn' radar in a chin radome, 'Big Bulge' surface search radar in a ventral radome, blister fairings on both sides of the rear fuselage, pods on the tip of the tailplane, anti-flutter masses (probably containing antennae for the Sirena RWR) and a longer in-flight refuelling probe and 'Box Tail' rear-warning and tail turret fire-control radar. For the missile support role the Bear D carried A-346Z digital data-link equipment used in association with the 'Short Horn' under-nose navigation and weapon delivery radar. In the mid-1970s, some Bear Ds were revised with a long fairing, containing four aerials, in place of the tail turret. Fifty Bear D aircraft were produced up until 1970, when Tu-95 production ceased with the 217th aircraft.

Retirement of the Bear A from Soviet Air Force service began in 1966. Forty Bear As were converted to Bear Es, retaining the AS-3 missile and in-flight refuelling capability, plus (in the rear weapons bay) additional fuel tankage and a conformal pallet for six or seven cameras and other sensors (probably SLAR and IR line scan equipment) and in the forward weapons bay electronic equipment characterised by two external blister fairings. The type also had the lateral rear fuselage blister strakes of the Bear C and D and retained the glazed nose.

Fifteen other Bear As were modified to Bear F anti-submarine aircraft for the Soviet Navy and given the new designation Tu-142. These 'new build' long-range maritime anti-submarine aircraft were produced in the late 1960s in response to a continuing demand for the type and began entering AV-MF service in 1972. The Tu-142 had a number of design, engineering and equipment improvements compared to the original series aircraft. These included more highly cambered wings and a longer fuselage forward of the wings, which allowed for a higher maximum take-off weight of 188,000 kg (414,470 lb) attributable in part to the considerable greater fuel capacity of 95,000 litres (20,897 gallons). Fuselage length was increased to 49.5 m (162 feet 5 inches). The protruding flaps of the earlier variants were replaced by narrow-chord units in a completely re-stressed wing, with stronger landing gear units and larger tyres. The rear fuselage accommodated a crew rest area, with galley and toilet, as well as stowage and launchers for sonobuoys/MAD housed in a pod at the top of the fin (on later aircraft only). Gun armament was reduced to a two-gun rear turret, and small ventral radar was fitted along with provision for small chin radar.

Tu-142 variants

Bear F Model 1: With original type of small engine nacelles, no chin radar and fewer fuselage protrusions.

Bear F Model 2: With nose lengthened by 230 mm (9 inches), the angle of the in-flight refuelling probe was lowered and the height of the flight deck roof increased.

Bear F Model 3: With MAD sensor projecting rearwards from the top of the fin, tailplane tip fairings removed and rear weapons bay made longer and narrower.

Bear F Model 4: With chin radar restored and ECM added in nose-mounted 'thimble' radome. Designation Tu-142M was applied to model operated by Indian Navy in long-range maritime reconnaissance role (with secondary heavy bombing capability). Although details of this aircraft are uncertain, it is thought to be the export sub-variant of the Bear F Model 2 with a range capability of 8,300 km (5,158 miles).

During the 1980s the Tu-95 Bear G and H variants made their appearance. These were reworked Bear B and C aircraft for ELINT and launch platforms for the two AS-4 Kitchen missiles carried under the wings. The type also had an ECM 'thimble' under the in-flight refuelling probe, ECM fairings on each side of the centre and rear fuselage, and a solid tail cone resembling that of the Bear D. Only fifteen were made. In 1982, twelve years after cessation of production, a 'new build' variant was put into production, the type entering service in late 1984. The Bear H was based on the Bear F but featured a shorter fuselage, having been designed as a launch platform for the subsonic 3,000-km (1,865-mile) range AS-15 Kent cruise missile. The Bear H carried at least four AS-15s, two under each inboard wing section, and possibly six more internally. It was originally intended that it would carry the more advanced long-range AS-X-19 cruise missiles, although this programme was cancelled. The aircraft had a considerably refined fuselage, the ventral barbette having been eliminated to leave only the tail turret (sometimes fitted with twin-barrel cannon rather than two separate cannon) and external ECM and ESM equipment replaced by external units. The type had a maximum take-off weight of 154,000 kg (339,512 lb) and an unrefuelled range of 8,285 km (5,148 miles). Total Bear H production amounted to thirty aircraft. The Bear J was an older, reworked Bear F airframe designed for the VLF (Very Low Frequency) communications role, with a long trailing antenna allowing communication with submerged nuclear submarines. A small number are in use with the CIS Navy.

Tupolev Tu-22 Blinder, Tu-22M Backfire

Failure of the Tu-105 as a strategic supersonic bomber due to its inadequate range required the Tupolev OKB to try again, and from the Tu-22 a new generation of swing-wing bombers of greatly increased capabilities was developed. The original design, begun in 1966 under OKB designation Tu-136, incorporated many of the parts of the Tu-22. Two prototypes (rebuilt Tu-22s) were constructed at Kazan in 1968. The only new design features were the horizontal tail, the outer wing panels with synchronised hydraulic drive to alter the sweep from 20 to 55 degrees, and the position of the new 196.13 kN (44,092 lbf) Kuznetsov NK-144 afterburning turbofans. The first prototype flew in March 1969, but this aircraft was also unable to achieve the required mission extended range. However, this was soon remedied by a redesign (Tu-153) that amounted to increasing the wingspan and deleting the large main landing gear pods on the inner wings. It is thought that there were twelve Tu-22M development aircraft in existence by 1973 (all ex-Tu-22 airframes), which later were said to be equipping a long-range operational VVS bomber unit.

Production aircraft (Tu-26s) were very different. The requisite range of 5,500 km (3,418 miles)—to obviate the need for in-flight refuelling—was finally obtained, whilst intercontinental range was possible with aerial refuelling. Maximum speed was reported as some 1,800 kph (1,118 mph). However, initial production output was low, with only one aircraft per month being produced, and the aircraft slowly entered service with Long Range Bomber Force and Naval Aviation in 1974. Production at Kazan increased in 1978 (due only to the extension of the factory) to twenty aircraft, and by 1979 some thirty aircraft a year were being produced in a number of new sub-variants. In early 1980, the newly reorganised Soviet Strategic Aviation had fifty Tu-26s in service with two air armies at Smolensk and Irkutsk (one regiment in each). At the same time Naval Aviation also had fifty Tu-26s in two regiments. By 1985, Strategic Aviation had a total of 130 Tu-26s and Naval Aviation had 110, and three years later this had increased to a total of 321 aircraft, of which 178 were with Strategic Aviation. The Smolensk and Irkutsk air armies had three regiments each, with thirty Tu-26 aircraft per regiment. Naval Aviation also had 143 Tu-26 bombers: one regiment (thirty aircraft) in the Baltic Fleet, two regiments (sixty aircraft) in the Black Sea Fleet, and two regiments (fifty-three aircraft) in the Pacific Fleet.

Tupolev Tu-104

The Soviet Union's first jet airliner design was approved by Stalin in February 1953, only a few weeks before his death. The prototype Tu-104 (CCCP-L5400) took to the air at Vnukovo on 14 June 1955, piloted by Yuri Alasheev, and for a period of twenty years from September 1956, some 200 of these first-generation 100/115-seat passenger jets carried over 100 million passengers.

The Tu-104 airliner was actually a development of the Tu-16 bomber, itself a re-fuselaged and uprated Tu-88, the wings, landing gear and engines of the Tu-16 being married to a passenger-carrying fuselage. As with later versions of the Tu-16, the Tu-104 used two Mikulin AM-35-500 turbojets of 95.1 kN (21,385 lbf) thrust each. Five prototypes, built at GAZ-400 at the Bykovo repair plant using Tu-16 parts and components, were consecutively numbered 25 L5400, 26, 27 L5413, 28, and 29 L5412. Work began on the flight development of the Tu-104 on 17 July 1955, and NII acceptance trials took place in the October of that year. The type entered Aeroflot service on 15 September 1956 on the Moscow–Irkutsk route, crew training having been carried out on demilitarised Tu-16s (designated Tu-104Gs), nine of which were used for this purpose from May 1956. Tu-104Gs were also used as freight carriers for Aeroflot express mail deliveries.

The first series production aircraft that entered Aeroflot service carried only fifty passengers with 1,200 kg (2,646 lb) of baggage in a series of compartments with a total volume of 13m³ (459 cubic feet). The maximum payload was 5,200 kg (11,464 lb) and the maximum range with one hour's fuel reserve was 2,650 km (1,647 miles) at a maximum speed of 950 kph (590 mph) at 10,000 m (32,810 feet). However, the rapid increase in domestic air travel in the Soviet Union soon called for an increase in seating capacity. This gave rise to the Tu-104A, which was first revealed in July 1957 and entered service the following year with seating for seventy passengers (sixteen first class and fifty-four tourist class). The passenger cabin was 16.11 m (52 feet 10 inches) long out of an overall fuselage length of 38.85 m (127 feet 6 inches), with a width of 3.2 m (10 feet 6 inches) and a height of 1.95 m (6 feet 5 inches). In 1962, some Tu-104As were converted to 100-seat aircraft and redesignated Tu-104V. The series 100-seat Tu-104B that had entered service in 1959 was distinguishable from the Tu-104A by virtue of its lengthened fuselage, which was 1.21 m (4 feet) longer, and increased flap area, the passenger cabin now being 20.12 m (66 feet) long, with the maximum internal height increased to 1.97 m (6 feet 6 inches). All Tu-104 airliners had a crew of five, comprising two pilots, a navigator, a radio operator and a flight engineer.

The Tu-104 established a number of international speed and load-to-altitude records for an airliner: eleven in 1957, five in 1958, and six in 1960. In the late 1950s, an attempt was made to adapt the aircraft to a military transport, designated Tu-107. A loading ramp with a powered hoist mechanism was installed in the rear fuselage, together with a retractable strut to prevent the aircraft sitting on its tail as heavy loads were moved towards the rear of the hold. Although a Tu-107 (c/n 76600302) did fly in 1957, the Antonov An-12 was found to be a much more efficient STOL military freighter, so further work on the Tu-107 was abandoned. The Tu-104 airliner was finally withdrawn from Aeroflot service in 1981.

Tupolev Tu-110

The arrival of the Tu-104 turbojet airliner on a proving flight at London's Heathrow Airport on 22 March 1956 had created a sensation in the world of aviation, its appearance having revealed to the West just how quickly Soviet post-war aviation had developed. The pages of the aviation press were full of praise for the 'great success of the Russians, who had overtaken the British and the Americans'. The de Havilland Comet had experienced severe setbacks in the form of a number of fatal crashes, and the Boeing 707 had yet to be cleared for airline use. Inspired by the success of the Tu-104, Tupolev determined that his OKB should proceed with a developed version that would meet the West's airworthiness standards.

The need for sustained flight over water dictated a four-engined design to enhance flight safety margins, and taking this requirement into account, the OKB design team under Dmitry Markov's leadership began work in 1956 on an uprated version of the Tu-104, designated Tu-110. The OKB chose four 53.9 kN (12,100 lbf) AL-7 Lyulka engines, which were located in the wing roots in a similar fashion to the M-4 bombers designed by the Myasishchev OKB. To accommodate the increased number of passengers, the fuselage was slightly increased in length and the arrangement of the cabins was altered, but in other aspects the Tu-110 differed little from the Tu-104. Consequently only minor alterations were needed before series production of the type could proceed.

On 11 March 1957, a crew led by test pilot D. V. Zyuzin began flight test development of the Tu-110. Both company flight development and state acceptance evaluation were cleared without any difficulties, but the four engines of the Tu-110 at cruise speed had greater fuel consumption than the twice as powerful RD-3M engines of the Tu-104A, and were also less reliable. Tu-110 CCCP-5600 was shown publicly for the first time on 10 July 1957 at Vnukovo, carrying air force insignia. However, by the end of the 1950s, with the Boeing 707 entering service and the Comet resuming airline use in the West, closely followed by the Douglas DC-8 and the French Caravelle, it was no surprise that the interest initially shown by western airlines vanished. This was instrumental in the decision of the Soviets not to place the Tu-110 into series production, the three prototypes later being passed to the Soviet Air Force for use as staff transports and for other special transport duties. However, the experience gained by the development of the Tu-110 was not wasted. Its stretched fuselage was used in the construction of the Tu-104B, which began scheduled Aeroflot flights early in April 1959.

Tupolev Tu-114

Developed from the Tu-95 long-range bomber, the Tu-114 first flew on 15 October 1957, with A. Yakimov at the controls. It operated principally on Aeroflot's long-distance routes to Montreal, Havana, Delhi and Accra as well as on domestic routes, which commenced from Moscow to Khabarovsk on 24 April 1961. The Tu-114's route took it over the Arctic and Atlantic Oceans and covered a length of 11,000 km (6,835 miles).

From the mid-1950s, Soviet airliner design had begun to change as the new types incorporated the latest technologies, and it was decided in March 1955 to build a new turboprop airliner for non-stop, long-distance services. The Tu-114 test brigade was headed by engineer A. Ter-Akopyan, with A. Yakimov and I. Sukhomlin as test pilots. In 1958, even before NII VVS trials had taken place, Tupolev received the FAI Gold Medal for the design of the Tu-104 and Tu-114. State evaluation trials were completed in 1960.

The Tu-114 attracted the elite among engineering and flight crews, about thirty meritorious pilots and navigators working on the project. The OKB worked to develop the aircraft's systems and powerplant and managed to lengthen airframe and engine life significantly, to improve landing gear design, and to perfect control and navigation systems. There were very few technical problems, but Tupolev wasted no time in finding solutions when these did occur, even enlisting the help of the Soviet leader Nikita Khrushchev. Thirty-six Tu-114s were built at GAZ-27 at Kuibyshev between 1957 and 1961. In 1959, on Tupolev's initiative, demonstration flights from Moscow to Khabarovsk, Tehran, Budapest, Paris and New York were organised, the first international flights being flown by the Tupolev OKB crew comprising A. Yakimov, M. Nyuhtikov, K. Malkhasyan, L. Zabaluev and N. Mayorov. A civil crew, including Captain K. Sapelkin, co-pilot N. Shapkin and navigator N. Solyanov also took part. Non-stop passenger flights began in April 1961. Tupolev OKB designers S. Gorbunov, M. Tuger, O. Arkhangelsky, G. Tarasov, A. Ganushkin, L. Zimin amongst others undertook much work to organise production and train Aeroflot personnel in the new skills needed in connection with the operation of a modern airliner.

The aircraft was fitted with four 11,190 kW (15,000 hp) NK-12MV turboprop engines, capable of 750-800 kph (465-500 mph) at 8,000-11,000 m altitude, and unique contra-rotating eight-blade AV-60 propellers. TsAGI and TsIAM helped to resolve a series of challenging problems relating to powerplant operation and reliability. Automatic feathering was employed and airscrew effectiveness at speeds beyond 800 kph (500 mph) was attained. The Tu-114 was a massive machine, measuring 54 m (177 feet) long and 15.5 m (50 feet 10 inches) high, with a wingspan of 51 m (feet) and a fuselage diameter of 4.2 m (feet), an airscrew diameter of 5.6 m (18 feet 4 inches) and a wing area of 311 m² (3,348 square feet). It could carry 84 tonnes of fuel and had a payload of 22.5 tonnes. The roomy fuselage had two decks, with the cabin, sleeping quarters and pantries above, and the freight holds and galley below.

It is interesting to consider some early Aeroflot flight reports. As early as the summer of 1958, the type made an unprecedented non-stop flight from Moscow to New York, prompting the *News Chronicle* headline 'Russian Air Giant Shakes New York'. The opening of the Cuba route was an important event in the development of the Soviet international flight network. On 10 July 1962, a route-proving flight to Havana (with a technical stop at Conakry) took 21 hours and 16 minutes. However, flights to Cuba via Africa had to stop for a number of reasons, chief among them the desire of the US to blockade the country, which led to the decision to fly via the North Atlantic and down the eastern coast of Canada and the US. This was preceded by a maximum air range test flight cycle to determine fuel needs.

On 22 December, the aircraft, piloted by H. Tskhovrebov, took off from Murmansk and flew non-stop for 14-15 hours, during which best speeds and altitudes were assessed, climatic conditions were carefully studied and navigational charts were corrected. The route was the longest and most difficult ever flown by Aeroflot crews. With the flight originating north of the Arctic Circle and ending in the Tropics, the aircraft encountered extreme climatic conditions, radio links were often cut by magnetic storms, and there were no diversion airfields en route. In the case of an emergency, the aircraft would either have turned back or flown on to Havana non-stop. The return proving flight, on 29 December, took somewhat longer due to variable headwinds and unexpected external air temperature fluctuations, reducing speed and complicating optimum cruising height selections. Scheduled passenger flights between Moscow and Havana commenced on 7 January 1963, using a Tu-114D aircraft, and Tu-114s would fly the Murmansk–Havana route non-stop over 1,400 times without any incidents.

Prior to the Tu-114 entering service a long-range airliner was needed to fly Khrushchev to a UN meeting in New York, and a standard Tu-95 bomber was converted by installing a 35-seat passenger compartment. It was designated Tu-116 by the Tupolev OKB and, perhaps more correctly, Tu-114D by Aeroflot. Only one Tu-114D ever flew with Aeroflot, although it is believed that at least two others were observed in Soviet Air Force colours. The VVS also flew the Tu-126 Moss, which was an AWACS variant of the Tu-114.

The proving flight to Tokyo in 1966 was another great event. It too was preceded by flight tests and trials. Two options were explored: a great-circle route or an airways route with alternative airfields available en route. Test flights developed techniques for a maximum-weight take-off followed by a turn from runway heading while still at low speeds, and provided practice in attaining certain minimum altitudes to cope with the peculiarities of Tokyo's Haneda Airport. Landings there were made difficult by the sheer-sided artificial peninsula runway jutting into the ocean, the slightest imprecision being fraught with danger, not to mention the impossibility of landing alongside such a runway. Take-off at Haneda was equally hair-raising and was executed either towards the city or over the ocean. However, the former was not an option for the Tu-114 due to obstacles such as the city's television mast and the Imperial Palace. Moreover, take-off runs could often be considerably lengthened due to high temperatures and humidity. Nevertheless, on 17 April 1967, joint Aeroflot and JAL services commenced on the Moscow–Tokyo route, both airlines having a changeover of cabin crew on this service.

In sixteen years of accident-free and reliable operation the Tu-114 performed about 50,000 flights and carried 6 million passengers. For over six years it was Aeroflot's only long-range aircraft. However, in 1974, the airline began to withdraw aircraft reaching 14,000 airframe hours in favour of the new Ilyushin Il-62. All who flew the Tu-114 remarked on its 'flyability', the aircraft remaining stable in all flight phases. Its great distinction was its economy due both to the use of efficient turboprop engines and to the generally sound aerodynamics of the design. Despite its prodigious size, great weight and large capacity, its fuel usage per hour averaged just 6 tonnes, which allowed it to fly ultra-long stages of some 14-15 hours at a time. Undoubtedly the Tu-114 was iconic in the annals of Soviet civil aviation and was another fitting epitaph to the Tupolev OKB and its General Designer Andrei Tupolev.

Tupolev Tu-124

The Tu-124 was a twin-jet airliner intended to replace the old piston-engined Ilyushin Il-14. Slightly smaller than the Tu-104 from which it was derived, the first prototype flew in March 1960. The aircraft was the first turbofan-powered short/medium-range airliner in commercial service. It was particularly suited to Aeroflot's need for an airliner with the performance capability to operate from less developed airfields within an hour's flight of Moscow. The high-lift wing system and an excellent thrust-to-weight ratio enabled the Tu-124 to operate from grass strips if necessary. The wing had double-slotted flaps (30 degree maximum deflection) and lift bumpers on the upper surface of the wing. (52 degree maximum), and a special flap located beneath the fuselage used only during landing (40 degree maximum deflection) served to increase the approach angle for difficult airfields. Powered by two 53 kN (11,905 lbf) Soloviev D-20P turbofans, the Tu-124 was capable of 970 kph (603 mph) and its maximum cruising speed was 870 kph (541 mph) at 8,000-11,000 m (26,247-36,090 feet). Range was 2,100 km (1,134 nm) at 36,500 kg (80,470 lb) with an hour's fuel reserve and a 6,000 kg (13,228 lb) payload. The crew normally consisted of three members, two pilots and a navigator, whilst space was provided for a second navigator on international routes.

Operational service with Aeroflot began on 2 October 1962, although it was not until two months later that the aircraft entered regular service on the Moscow–Tallinn route. The aircraft was available in four versions. The basic 44-seat airliner had three separate cabins (12 + 8 + 24), two tables being provided in each cabin between pairs of seats. The Tu-124V, the most prolific variant, carried fifty-six passengers seated in three cabins (12 + 12+ 32) with two tables in the forward cabin between the pairs of seats; seat pitch was 750 mm (30 inches). The Tu-124K was a 36-passenger variant with one salon and two cabins (4 +8 + 24), and the Tu-124K2 was a 22-seat variant with two salons and one cabin (4 + 2 + 16). Total production at GAZ-135 at Kharkov between 1960 and 1966 is believed to have been 112 aircraft, a few having been sold abroad to Interflug of East Germany and CSA of Czechoslovakia as well as to Iraq. The type was withdrawn from Aeroflot service on 21 January 1980.

Tupolev Tu-128

The first Soviet attempt to produce a long-range interceptor was made by the S. A. Lavochkin OKB in 1956, when the prototype of the La-250 K-15 aircraft was built. However, the many difficulties encountered during the project and its flight development stages prevented the successful conclusion of the programme. As the Soviet Union became more aware of its vulnerability to Boeing B-52 bombers and Snark cruise missiles, a new set of technical specifications for an aircraft to counter this threat were drawn up, and the Tupolev OKB was entrusted with the task of producing it. This appeared unusual even to observers in the Soviet Union, as the Tupolev OKB had previously specialised in the development of heavy bombers and passenger aircraft. Intended to replace the Yak-25, the new aircraft was to intercept airborne targets flying at altitudes up to 21,000 m (feet), at speeds up to 2,000 kph (1,243 mph) and with a flight endurance time of two hours.

Project development of the Tu-128 did not start without prior work on a similar type of aircraft. In 1956, Tupolev had started prototype flight development work using a Tu-98 supersonic medium-range bomber, with test pilot V. Kovalev at the controls. Tupolev himself organised and led a research programme into the study of aerodynamics of highly swept-back wing high-speed airflow sections, and the theory of power-booster controls and use of afterburners in turbojet engines. The outline of the new interceptor was devised in the Configuration Department under the direction of Sergei Yeger, with Josef Nezval as the chief project designer.

A full-scale mock-up was built in 1960, and test pilot M. Kozlov and test navigator K. Malkhasyan began company flight development of the Tu-28-80 prototype on 18 March 1961. Originally the aircraft was to be powered by VD-19 engines developed by the V. Dobrynin engine OKB, but as the development of these was delayed it was decided to adopt engines produced by the A. Lyulka OKB, with only prototype and early series aircraft to be fitted with these engines. However, series aircraft actually differed little from the prototype—only in wing geometry and the number of missile racks, which in the production aircraft was raised from two to four. Below the rear fuselage section were two strakes to enhance directional stability and to compensate for the increased cross-section area caused by the added under-fuselage pod fairing. NII acceptance tests and evaluation began on 20 March 1962, the tests revealing a number of deficiencies. These problems, together with work associated with the weapons system avionics, were to lead to a considerable delay in the Tu-128's entry into operational service. Production ceased in 1970, by which time a total of 198 had been built, including a number of trainer variants fitted with a second cockpit for training flight crews in low-level manoeuvres.

Tupolev Tu-134

The Tu-134 was essentially a Tu-124 stretched to seat 64/72 passengers but with the engines mounted at the tail in order to reduce cabin noise. The aircraft made its first flight in July 1963, entering Aeroflot service in August 1965. Some 700 were built over the next twenty years, making it the most prolific type ever used by Aeroflot, although by August 2000 only six Tu-134As remained in use with the state airline. Others saw service in East Germany, Poland, Czechoslovakia, Bulgaria, Hungary, Syria, Turkey, Vietnam and Kampuchea (Cambodia), a total of 328 being in use in August 2000, of which 321 were in Europe and the CIS.

The Tu-134UBL and Tu-134BSh Blackjack trainers were conversions of Tu-134B airliners used to train Strategic Aviation pilots and navigators. Conversions produced by the Kharkov factory were delivered to the 184th Guards Heavy Bomber Regiment at Engels Air Base in southern Russia for training Tu-160 Blackjack strategic bomber crews. The Tu-134UBL had a new nose containing a Tu-160 radar, increasing the overall length by nearly 5 m (16 feet 5 inches) to 41.92 m (137 feet 6½ inches), although the aircraft's handling characteristics remained unchanged. The Tu-134BSh differed from the Tu-134UBL only in respect of the Tu-22M radar in the nose for training fourth year student navigators at the military school at Tambov, the cabin consoles containing bomb-sight displays for up to twelve pupils, and under-wing racks fitted for the carriage of training bombs.

Tupolev Tu-144 SST

The Tu-144 SST (SuperSonic Transport) first flew on 31 December 1968, piloted by E. V. Elyan, a few months before Concorde's maiden flight, and made its first appearance in the West at the Paris Air Show in June 1971. Two years later, on 3 June 1973, an early production aircraft was destroyed at Le Bourget Airport after breaking up in mid-air, the pilot possibly having over-stressed the aircraft when taking evasive action to avoid colliding with a French Air Force Mirage that had been set up to 'shadow' and take photographs of the demonstration flight of the 'Concordski'. The French authorities have always denied this allegation, stressing that no records exist of any authorisation of such a flight by the French military, in spite of the fact that a French Air Force Dassault Mirage 5R reconnaissance aircraft was observed taking off at Le Bourget just prior to the Tu-144 starting its display sequence over the airfield.

Further evidence that the French Mirage was the reason for the catastrophic accident is that the Soviet crew had allowed a TV reporter who wished to make a video recording of the flight on board the flight deck with his camera. It is thought likely that the reporter stood beside the pilot whilst taking pictures and that during the avoidance action by the Soviet crew, the reporter's camera may have fallen onto the flight deck floor. This could have jammed the rudder pedals, causing the resultant 'dive' until the offending object could be removed, by which time it was too late and the pilot's valiant attempt to recover the aircraft ultimately led to it breaking up in the air. The accident dealt a devastating blow to the Soviet aviation industry and to the country's prestige. However, production did continue at Voronezh and the type entered service with Aeroflot on freight flights to Alma-Ata (Almaty) in Kazakhstan on 26 December 1975, limited internal passenger services beginning on 1 November 1977 from Moscow to Alma-Ata.

The second fatal accident of the Tu-144 involved a prototype development aircraft (CCCP-77111) on a test flight on 23 May 1978, testing engines developed by the P. A. Kolesov aero-engine OKB as possible alternatives to the NK-144s already in use. The cause of the accident was the failure of a section of the fuel system feed to the engines under test. A temporary ban on Tu-144 flights was enforced whilst the necessary corrective actions were to be determined, services finally being withdrawn on 1 June 1978 after only 102 passenger flights, not only as a result of the crash but also for economic reasons (Aeroflot found the aircraft too expensive and complex to operate). Total production amounted to twenty aircraft, of which only sixteen flew. Not all of the airframes were scrapped; a number were sent to be displayed at aviation museums, four were sent to Zhukovsky for research purposes and another to the Samara Research Institute. The first prototype (CCCP-68001) was unfortunately amongst those airframes scrapped.

The surviving airframes were used to educate student aviation specialists at the Kazan and Kuibyshev Institutes of Civilian Aviation, acquainting them with the most advanced aviation systems including hydraulics, large components made of titanium composites, and onboard analogue computers. Those based at Zhukovsky were flown as experimental aircraft and as airborne multi-aspect research laboratories, carrying equipment for the study of the higher layers of the atmosphere and in searches for gaps in the ozone layer. The Tu-144 was also used by the future crews of the Soviet space shuttle vehicle to practise high-speed landing techniques. Having been deemed a failure by the West, it is rather ironic that from mid-1997 a refurbished Tu-144L SST was leased to the US for development flying with regard to the production of a second generation of SSTs. The cost of the refurbishment and the flight development programme is to be met by the US and all development flying is to be undertaken in the former Soviet Union.

Tupolev Tu-154 Careless
The Tu-154 three-engined airliner first flew in 1964, and over 1,050 of all variants were produced until mid-1993. A 160-plus seat airliner, the base model appeared in 1966

to replace the Tu-104, the Il-18 and the An-10 on Aeroflot's medium- and long-range routes of up to 6,000 km (3,725 miles). The first of six prototype/PP models flew on 4 October 1968, and regular Aeroflot services started on 9 February 1972. By 1985, 606 prototype and production Tu-154s, Tu-154As, Tu-154Bs and Tu-154B-2s with uprated turbofans and other refinements were delivered, of which over 500 went to Aeroflot. The prototype Tu-154M (SSSR-85317) was a converted Tu-154B-2 configured to carry 180 passengers and first flew in 1982, the first production aircraft being delivered from GAZ-27 at Kuibyshev in December 1984. Almost 290 had been built by March 1995. Aeroflot used the Tu-154M as a light freighter with all the passenger seats removed. In 1990, almost 75 per cent of all Aeroflot's passenger-kilometres were flown by the Tu-134 and Tu-154, and the type was used by some sixty-six other operators. In August 2000, some 570 Tu-154B and Tu-154M variants were still in use, almost 500 of them in Europe and the CIS.

Tupolev Tu-160 Blackjack

Development of the Tu-160 strategic bomber was given the go-ahead in 1974, the same year as the American Rockwell B-1A, which had its first flight on 23 December 1974. Similarly configured to the B-1, the Tu-160 variable-geometry long-range supersonic penetration and missile-carrying bomber was actually the world's largest bomber and the heaviest combat aircraft ever built, being some 20 per cent larger than the American B-1B. Evolved through the Samolet 70 programme under the leadership of Valentin Bliznyuk and flown by Boris Veremey, the prototype (70-01) made its maiden flight on 18 December 1981 at Zhukovsky. Unlike the cancelled American B-1 that was subsequently resurrected in October 1981 as a low-level subsonic penetration bomber flying at transonic speeds and relying on its low observability (reduced radar cross-section) to evade detection, the Tu-160 was designed for low-level penetration at transonic speeds and high-level penetration at supersonic speeds, above Mach 1.9.

Variable geometry and full-span leading-edge and trailing-edge double-slotted flaps gave the aircraft good low-speed handling as well as high supersonic speed. Wing sweep was manually selected with three settings: 20 degrees for take-off and landing, 35 degrees for cruise, and 65 degrees for high-speed flight. A unique feature of the design was that the trailing edge of the inboard section of the flaps (immobilised with the wings swept) had no fuselage slot to retract into when the wing was swept, instead folding upwards to be aligned with the aircraft's centreline and thereby acting as a fence. Some aircraft had a 'double-jointed' folding section that could fold up to be a fence at either 35 or 65 degrees.

Powered by four SSPE Trud (Kuznetsov) NK-321 turbofans each rated at 137.2 kN (30,843 lbf) dry and 245.16 kN (55,115 lbf) with afterburner, the Tu-160 had a crew of four sitting side by side on pairs of Zvezda K-36D ejection seats, entry to the cockpit being via a ladder in the rear part of the nose-gear bay. The pilot and co-pilot were provided with fighter-type control columns, but although the aircraft had an FBW control system, all cockpit displays were conventional, with analogue instruments and no MFDs, CRTs, HDDs or HUDs. The Tu-160 had a long pointed radome housing the terrain-following radar, with a fairing below it for the forward-looking TV camera used for weapon aiming. A retractable in-flight refuelling probe was also fitted. The offensive war load was carried in two tandem fuselage weapons bays, each normally fitted with rotary carousels that could carry either six RK-55 (AS-15 Kent) cruise missiles with 200-kT nuclear warheads at a range in excess of 3,000 km (1,865 miles) or twelve AS-16 (BL-10) Kickback supersonic short-range attack missiles or 'SRAMskis'.

The Blackjack suffered considerable development and operational problems and was often grounded whilst numerous changes were made to the systems and airframe, due mainly to lack of funding. The aircraft generally had a good safety record (principally because of the low hours flown), although at least one prototype (70-01) was lost. Fortunately the crew survived. Prolonged development meant that the second prototype (70-03) did not fly until 6 October 1984. In fact, just a few days later, on 10 October, the first series production aircraft took off from Kazan, but it would be another two and a half years before the Tu-160 entered service with the Soviet Air Force. Series production had started in 1984 and continued until July 1992, by which time thirty to forty aircraft (including prototype and PP aircraft) had been built.

On 20 August 1989, the Tu-160 made its public debut over Tushino, the second prototype making two record-breaking flights on 31 October and 3 November 1989, gaining speed-with-load and altitude-with-load records respectively. The aircraft was shown at the Paris Air Show at Le Bourget in June 1991, but the following January, Russian President Boris Yeltsin stated that no further strategic bombers would be produced. However, it was announced in 1995 that limited production of the bomber would resume at the Kazan plant, but it is unlikely that the initial requirement for 100 Blackjacks will ever be fulfilled.

On the orders of the Politburo, two Blackjacks were deployed to Ukraine on 25 April 1987, entering service with the VVS 186th Guards Heavy Bomber Regiment at Pryluky Air Base in May 1987, a third aircraft being delivered by the end of the year. Deliveries continued at a very slow rate, each separate series aircraft being literally 'hand made' and production suffering from the multitude of design and development problems that existed. Even after delivery there were a number of ongoing problems with the aircraft, many of which severely restricted operations and at times had to be supported by teams of engineers from the Kazan production plant and the Tupolev OKB. The aircrew lacked basic flying equipment, and ground crews working in close proximity to the aircraft suffered from a lack of anti-vibration boots and ear-defenders. Problems with the K-36D ejection seats meant that they could not be adjusted to suit individual crew members, and general reliability of the engines and systems bordered on the unacceptable despite the 'systems' utilising around 100 computers and processors.

In spite of all these outstanding problems, the type continued to be delivered to the 121st Guards Heavy Bomber Regiment at Engels Air Base, even though a common standard and configuration had not been agreed. Thus wingspans, equipment fits and intake configurations differed from aircraft to aircraft. It should also be mentioned that the Tu-160 incorporated a unique pivoting upper tail fin (as on the Lockheed SR-71 Blackbird) in place of the more standard fixed vertical tail surface and rudder. It had an unrefuelled range of 7,300 km (4,536 miles) and a maximum speed of over 2,000 kph (1,243 mph).

Temporarily, in the early 1990s, due to airfield construction work at Engels, additional aircraft were deployed to the 184th Guards Heavy Bomber Regiment at Pryluky. However, on 24 August 1991, the aircraft were grounded and became stranded there as a result of the collapse of the Soviet Union and a lack of funds and technical expertise to support them. Subsequently several rounds of talks were held between the CIS and Ukraine with regard to the return of the aircraft to Russia, but, as might be expected, no agreement could be reached, due mainly to money. A number of Russian experts inspected the aircraft at Pryluky and Uzyn airfields in 1993 and 1996, reporting that although most were unserviceable they were in good condition technically. Even so, the price of $3 billion demanded by the Ukrainians for returning the aircraft and ground support equipment was considered unreasonable by the Russians. Still unable to reach an agreement, and with most of the aircraft unairworthy due to lack of maintenance, in 1995 the Ukraine Council of National Security and Defence decided that a number of aircraft would be scrapped. Raytheon Technical Services were awarded the contract on 15 June 1998 by the US Department of Defense, but it was agreed that eight would be returned to Russia in lieu of unpaid bills for natural gas supplies to Ukraine. The first flew back to Engels on 5 November 1999, the remainder arriving by 21 February 2000.

With the twelve that remained in Russia (five at Engels Air Base with the 121st Guards Heavy Bomber Regiment, one almost complete at Kazan, and the other six at the Zhukovsky test centre) the CIS inventory totalled twenty aircraft, and an order was placed for an additional unfinished aircraft at Kazan to be completed and delivered to allow the CIS to match the Boeing B-2 Spirit long-range bomber inventory on a one-for-one basis. Although earlier pressure had been made by the Soviet Defence Ministry to withdraw the Tu-160 totally from service use, after the Kosovo rebuff in 1999, it was decided to keep at least fifteen aircraft operational with Russian Long Range Aviation under the command of Lieutenant-General Mikhail Oparin.

Yakovlev (Yak-)

Alexander Sergeyevich Yakovlev, the youngest of the principal wartime Soviet aircraft designers, was born in Moscow on 1 April 1906. Whilst his patrons were the victims of numerous purges and other forms of disgrace, Yakovlev managed to retain his premier position in Soviet aviation for some fifty years. After spending time as a mechanic at Moscow Central Aerodrome, he entered the Zhukovsky Aviation Academy after winning a light plane design competition in 1927, Yakovlev redesignating the aircraft AIR-1 to please Commissar A. I. Rykov, who was head of the TsS Osoaviakhim where he worked. Graduating in 1931, Yakovlev joined the TsKB at Menzhinsky Factory No. 39, but his preoccupation with light sports planes led to his expulsion in 1933. Following a successful appeal to leading government and party officials he was given the use of an old bed factory and this became his base for light aircraft production, the factory being rebuilt in 1935. His first design to enter series production was the AIR-6, 400 of which were built at Leningrad, and he soon established himself as a successful designer of training and sports aircraft.

Yakovlev had travelled abroad on at least two occasions before the Second World War to study developments outside of the Soviet Union and now turned his attention to military aircraft, consolidating his position as an aircraft designer and receiving a Stalin Prize for his BB-22 high-speed bomber in 1939. The Yakovlev series of single-seat fighters remained in production throughout the war, more being built (37,000) than any other type of Soviet wartime fighter. In addition, large numbers of UT-2 trainers were produced, together with a much smaller number of light twin-engine liaison aircraft such as the Yak-6. His fighters were distinguished by their clean lines, and after the war the basic design was successfully adapted to take the new turbojets in place of piston engines.

In total, Yakovlev designed more than 100 aircraft. His success was no doubt helped by the fact that from 1940 until 1948 he was Deputy Minister of Aviation Industry, and it has been said that his designs almost monopolised TsAGI's T-101 full-scale wind tunnel during that period. After the war Yakovlev trainers such as the UT-2, Yak-11 and Yak-18 were the universal types used throughout the communist world until eventually Czechoslovakian, Polish and Yugoslavian turbine-engined primary trainers were adopted. Despite an initial lead in pod-and-boom jet fighter design, Yakovlev's straight-through jet fighters were not adopted; neither was his first post-war transport design. He was equally unsuccessful in the helicopter field, despite the fact that a special design bureau of rotary wing experts was set up and produced three widely differing designs. In 1952, the Yak-25 series was launched, and his twin-engined, all-weather reconnaissance fighter was in service in one form or another throughout the early years of the Cold War.

Yakovlev's designs included a Douglas DC-3 transport replacement with bypass engines, which flew for the first time towards the end of 1966. Widely used by Aeroflot, it was also exported. The Yak-36 Freehand, a VTO aircraft, was demonstrated for the first time at the 1967 Soviet Aviation Day and entered Soviet Navy service as the Yak-38 Forger VTOL ship-borne fighter. The Yakovlev OKB also produced the Yak-40/42 jet transport and a series of light planes such as the Yak-50, Yak-52, Yak-53 and Yak-55.

Yakovlev was also known as the writer of several excellent aviation books. He died on 22 August 1989, aged 83, and was succeeded by Alexander Nikolayevich Dondukov. In 1992, the OKB was reorganised as the Yakovlev Aircraft Corporation, with its main production plant at Smolensk embracing the airframe plants and the ZMDB Progress and Zaporozhye engine plants.

Yakovlev UT-2 Mink

By the mid-1930s, aircraft designers were already beginning to opt for monoplane configuration rather than the then well-established biplane. In many ways Soviet designers actually led the way: Polikarpov with his I-16 fighter; Tupolev with his giant bombers and civil types; and of course Yakovlev with his newly established OKB.

Amongst the types produced by his design bureau was the AIR-10, a two-seater that first flew on 11 July 1935 and went on to win that year's 'All-Union' contest for trainer and sports aircraft, although the Soviet Air Force demanded a series of changes and improvements before it would accept the aircraft as a service machine. By 1937, the revised design had been completed, the original steel tubular fuselage having been replaced by pine and, for ease of production, the 'Gottingen 387' wing profile had been modified to have a flat underside, the whole aircraft having been significantly strengthened. Two versions were built under the designation Ya-20. One had a 112 kW (150 hp) M-11E 5-cylinder radial engine, whilst the other was fitted with an imported Renault air-cooled inline engine. Although somewhat heavier than the AIR-10, the Ya-20 proved successful. The M-11-powered floatplane variant won several international records, and a second Renault-engined version won the 1937 Moscow–Sevastopol–Moscow air race.

The M-11-powered Ya-20 was the variant accepted by the Soviet Air Force as its primary trainer aircraft, under service designation UT-2. It was a single-engined, twin-seat monoplane with a low-mounted cantilevered wing, open cockpits for the instructor and pupil, and a fixed undercarriage. Production machines, initially built in five factories, were fitted with 82 kW (110 hp) M-11M or M-11G engines, which actually reduced performance significantly. However, these powerplants were readily available and familiar to maintenance personnel. The aircraft was simple and easy to maintain and, above all, cheap to produce, and in the hands of experienced instructor pilots the UT-2 initially appeared to have excellent flying characteristics. However, when subsequently flown by novice pilots some worrying defects came to light. The worst was a tendency to enter a flat spin, caused by the centre of gravity being too far towards the rear of the aircraft. An attempt was made to correct this by fitting an anti-spin parachute—the first time this idea had been used in the Soviet Union.

Extensive research into the aircraft's problems by engineers and test pilots at TsAGI resulted in a number of solutions, and these were incorporated into an improved production-standard model designated '1940 standard' in order to distinguish it from the earlier '1938 standard'. The improved UT-2 incorporated some fifty changes, including a nose lengthened by 150 mm (6 inches), which moved the centre of gravity forward by 3 per cent, and the fitting of an uprated 93 kW (125 hp) M-11D engine. Along with the new engine, two sets of removable cylinder head fairings were introduced—a high winter one and a low summer one—but the fairings were removed completely from aircraft operated in hot regions. A new design of air intake pre-heater was also used. In addition, several changes to the airframe were made to counter a number of weaknesses, although fortunately these did not lead to any great increase in weight. To bring the main wheels forward, the rear undercarriage strut was lengthened by 38 mm (1½ inches) and the cockpit seats were made height-adjustable and could be removed completely to facilitate maintenance. Instrument panels were changed and fitted with anti-vibration dampening, whilst the main-wheel undercarriage shock absorbers were improved and a tail wheel was fitted in place of the skid, which had tended to act as a plough on the grass airfields used. At the request of the VVS, a blind flying hood was fitted.

The improved UT-2 served as the principal basic trainer for the VVS for many years, and post-war also served with the air forces of Poland, Bulgaria, Romania and Hungary, but a number of captured aircraft were already in use in the Second World War with Finland, Germany, Hungary and Romania. The UT-2 Mink took over from the Polikarpov Po-2 (U-2) biplane as the Soviets' primary trainer, although the latter did remain in service and production as a night bomber and trainer.

The Yakovlev UT-2 was one of the few Soviet aircraft to carry a three-colour upper fuselage camouflage paint scheme, first introduced in 1943 and believed to be similar in tone to earlier colours introduced on Luftwaffe aircraft (RLM 70 black-green and RLM 71 dark green). A total of 7,243 UT-2s were built in the period from 1935 to 1945, before the aircraft was eventually superseded in Soviet use by another Yakovlev trainer design, the Yak-18.

Yakovlev-1 (I-26) and Yak-7

The high-altitude Ya-26 (I-26) was first flown on 1 January 1940, two years after design work had begun, securing Yakovlev the Order of Lenin and a number of other more material honours. The aircraft was fitted with a Klimov 820 kW (1,100 hp) M-105P 12-cylinder V-type liquid-cooled engine in place of the intended 1,007 kW (1,350 hp) M-106. Entering production in the late spring of 1941, the Yak-1 was in service by early 1942, successive versions incorporating progressive improvements in armaments. Initial planned armament was one engine-mounted ShVAK 20 mm cannon and two synchronised ShKAS 7.62 mm machine guns.

The I-26 was of mixed construction, with a plywood covering, a wooden wing and a steel tube fuselage, with duralumin panelling forward and fabric-covered plywood skinning aft. Later modifications included cutting down the rear fuselage as well as the installation of a new cockpit enclosure with all-round visibility. The initial designation was Yak-1M, but this model was later re-engined with the 940 kW (1,260 hp) M-105PF engine and became the Yak-7B. A total of 8,721 Yak-1s were built from 1940 to 1944.

The Soviet Air Force required the Yak OKB to develop a two-seat trainer from the Yak-1 fighter, as there was already sufficient room behind the pilot to facilitate a pupil and also because Yakovlev specialised in trainer aircraft. Development of the UTI-26 started in January 1940, and the prototype made its first flight in July 1940, the second 'improved' prototype being built in September. The first Yak-7UTI was built in May 1941 at Khimki (GAZ-301), but the plant was evacuated later that year and production transferred to GAZ-153 at Novosibirsk. The aircraft was used for training, reconnaissance and artillery observation.

Early in 1942, a new version was built, the Yak-7V, which featured a fixed undercarriage and was without armament. This variant entered series production in May 1942, with a total of 783 aircraft built between May 1941 and December 1943. Of these, only 186 were UTI variants, the remainder being Yak-7Vs. After the German attack in June 1941, GAZ-301 transformed a Yak-7UTI trainer into a single-seat fighter with the same armament as that of the Yak-1, and two months later Stalin ordered the construction of the 'new' fighter at GAZ-301 and GAZ-153. As a result, production started in September 1941, and by the end of the year sixty-two Yak-7s had been built. Later, from January to May 1942, GAZ-153 built 277 Yak-7As, fitted with radio and other improvements, which were used by 434ºIAP and 519ºIAP of the VVS.

Production of the Yak-7B had started In April 1942 at both GAZ-153 and GAZ-261, the latter building the type until July. Fitted with an M-105PA engine and heavier machine guns (twelve 12.7 mm ShKAS), this aircraft was at the time the best fighter available to the VVS, and it was for this reason that GAZ-82 at Moscow also started production. In reality, however, the Yak-7 was underpowered in Soviet Air Force operation and was no match for the Messerschmitt Bf 109F and 109G. Consequently a Yak-7 was tested with the more powerful M-82 radial engine, but without success, before finally the new M-105PF engine was selected. From the summer of 1942, both GAZ-82 and GAZ-153 produced Yak-7 aircraft fitted with this powerplant. The weight of this variant was also reduced by 30 kg (66 lb) as the provision to carry rockets was removed.

The first re-engined Yak-7B was delivered in August 1942, and the aircraft was used in the Battle of Stalingrad. Earlier, in May 1942, the revised Yak-7V had replaced the Yak-7UTI on the production lines. During the summer of 1942, due to the poor performance of the Lavochkin LaGG-3, GAZ-21 at Gorky was ordered to build the Yak-7B, but only five were constructed there as Lavochkin had developed the very capable radial engine La-5 and GAZ-21 turned to production of this aircraft instead. In December 1942, a new version of the Yak-7B was introduced with a better all-round vision canopy, and three months later an improved aerodynamic fuselage variant was on the production lines. Finally, in December 1943, production of the Yak-7V trainer ceased. The success of the Yak-7B can be judged by the fact that on 1 October 1944, there were still 764 in service with the Soviet Air Force on the German Front.

Yakovlev Yak-3

A late-1941 VVS requirement for a low-level close support fighter for the battlefront led to possibly the most agile monoplane of the Second World War, the Yak-3 short-range dogfighter. The object was to produce a small low-drag, all-metal, lightweight fighter using the M-107 engine and carrying armament of one ShVAK gun and one UBS. The programme was managed by Konstantin V. Sinelshchikov, who was also responsible for the Yak-1M. Owing to the need to concentrate on Yak-1M production, work on the Yak-3 (as the new aircraft had been designated) was suspended for one year. This was unfortunate, as development of the M-107A engine suffered an even longer delay, leading to adoption of the 970 kW (1,300 hp) M-105PF-2 instead.

The Yak-3 project was restarted under Oleg Antonov in August 1943. At the outset of work in October 1941, a decision had been taken to use the small wing of 9.2 m (30 feet) span and 14.85 m2 (160 square feet) area. A wing of this design was completed in early 194,2 although it is believed that it was not flown until later that year on a modified Yak-1M. This aircraft had the cut-down rear fuselage and rear-view canopy of the Yak-18, a fully retractable tail wheel and a new streamlined radiator installation with a long duct aft of the wing, a more streamlined air-cooler installation under the engine, and a low-drag frameless windscreen. The designation of this aircraft is unknown. Further refinements actually increased the weight slightly but continued to reduce drag, which was achieved mainly by replacing the oil cooler by twin parallel oil radiators inside the wing spars inboard of the wing roots served by symmetric enlarged wing-root inlets and discharging via ejectors under the centre-section lower skin.

Soviet records on the development of the Yak-3 are sketchy, but the first prototype with that designation flew in 1943 and suffered a structural failure, delaying the development programme. Consequently the aircraft was not submitted for NII VVS testing until 3 March 1944, and not officially cleared for series production until three months later. However, despite the delay, by this time a small number of pre-series aircraft were under construction at GAZ-286 at Kamensk-Uralsky. On completion, the aircraft were immediately assigned to an operational regiment for service trials and in the event saw combat during the Soviet counter-offensive to Operation Zitadelle, acquitting themselves well. After official NII clearance the Yak-3 entered Red Air Force service with 91 IAP in June 1944, and the regiment was able to claim the destruction of twenty-four Bf 109Gs and Fw 190s on 16 July 1944 in a single low-altitude attack involving eighteen of 91 IAP's Yak-3s.

Having been cleared for production two years later than it should have been, the Yak-3 was built with remarkable speed. Twenty-one aircraft were delivered in July 1944, and by the end of the following month over 100 had been produced. When production ceased in May 1945, a total of 4,111 had been built. This brought the final total of wartime Yak single-engined fighters, excluding experimental models, to 36,737 aircraft.

The Yak-3 was an outstandingly easy aircraft to fly, with precision control of rate of roll, turning circle, and manoeuvres in the vertical plane. A vital fact heavily stressed by Soviet historians is that the aircraft could outmanoeuvre the Bf 109 and Fw 190 A, especially at altitudes below 6,096 m (20,000 feet). The French Normandie-Niemen squadron unanimously selected the Yak-3 in preference to any other Allied aircraft available in the late summer of 1944, using the excellent little fighter to shoot down 119 German aircraft over a ten-day period in the October of that year. Extensive history of the Yak-3's brief operational life is full of its remarkable ascendancy over the depleted Luftwaffe. For example, when eighteen Yak-3s engaged twenty-four Messerschmitts and Focke-Wulfs in a dogfight, the Luftwaffe lost fifteen of its fighters whilst the Soviets lost only one Yak-3, with one damaged.

By 1944, GAZ-31 at Tbilisi had already built 498 Yak-3s and GAZ-292 at Saratov another 1,682, making a total of 2,180 aircraft. This was a rapid increase in production, as on 1 October only 265 Yak-3s had served on the German Front. GAZ-31 built 436 aircraft in the first five months of 1945, by 10 May in fact, GAZ-292 producing another 1,495—a total of 1,931 aircraft produced in about five months, or an average of 386 per month. Production of the Yak-3 did continue after May 1945, but at a reduced rate in both factories. GAZ-31 built only another twenty-six aircraft in the remaining months of the year, and only a further forty-eight in 1946. GAZ-292 built a further 423 aircraft after 10 May 1945, and 240 aircraft in 1946, bringing the total production of the Yak-3 to 4,848, of which 4,111 were produced during the Second World War.

In May 1945, large numbers of Yak-3s could be found on the German Front with the VVS. The Normandie-Niemen squadron had forty, although only thirty-seven arrived in Paris on 20 June 1945. The Polish Air Force also had a small number of the type, and these were retired from service in September 1946. Early in 1947, the last of the Soviet Yak-3 fighters were scrapped, but the Yugoslav Air Force had a larger number which continued in use until 1949. However, this was not the end of the Yak-3 story. In the mid-1990s, a number of Yak-3M flying copies were ordered by the US Gunnell Company due to the demand for historical aircraft. Fitted with American Allison engines, the aircraft were built at Orenburg and the first 'new/old' Yak-3M was flight tested almost fifty years after the type's creation.

Yakovlev Yak-2/Yak-4

In May 1938, Yakovlev was invited to build a high-speed reconnaissance plane to replace the obsolete R-10. This resulted in the AIR-22, Yakovlev's first warplane. The first prototype had a bright red fuselage and silver wings and made its first flight on 22 February 1939 at Tushino, piloted by J. I. Piontkovsky. The two 716 kW (960 hp) M-103 engines gave the aircraft a maximum speed of 567 kph (352 mph) which at this time was an excellent performance.

The Soviet Air Force accepted the aircraft as the R-12 reconnaissance plane, but unfortunately Stalin noticed the aircraft was 150 kph (93 mph) faster than the SB-2 bomber and ordered it to be produced as a short-range bomber. The order was issued on 15 March 1939. Getting the B-22 (as the aircraft was then designated) into production was a major task, complicated by the need for over 100 engineering changes. Yakovlev organised a special group, KB-70, to speed up production by copying over 3,300 drawings. As a reward, he was called to the Kremlin on 27 April 1939, where Stalin bestowed on him the Order of Lenin and gave him a ZIS car and 100,000 roubles. The first aircraft was completed on 31 December 1939, its maiden flight taking place on 20 February 1940.

In 1940, GAZ-1 at Moscow and GAZ-81 at Tushino started production of the B-22 fitted with two M-103 engines. Later these were replaced by the uprated

783 kW (1,050 hp) M-105, the additional power being needed to offset the curtailed performance of the aircraft due to the fitting of guns and armour and to facilitate the carriage of bombs. The Soviet Air Force proposed to replace the SB-2 bombers in the mixed divisions with the B-22. The requirement was for sixty bombers for each of the thirty-four divisions, amounting to 2,040 aircraft. A fighter version, designated BB-22IS or I-29, was also built and tested. GAZ-1 produced eighty-one B-22s and GAZ-81 built fifty-seven. The first Soviet unit to receive the bomber was 18°BAP in the Moscow MD.

Early in 1941, the M-103 version was designated the Yak-2, the 820 kW (1,100 hp) M-105 version being given the designation Yak-4. Unfortunately the performance with maximum bomb load, guns and armour fitted was very poor. Maximum low-level speed was only 290 kph (180 mph). As the much superior Pe-2 bomber was now available, the Soviet Air Force opted for mass-production of this aircraft instead, so series production of the Yak bombers was later terminated. GAZ-1 concentrated on MiG-3 fighter production, although GAZ-81 did continue with production of a further sixty-three Yak-4 bombers in 1941, bringing total production of the type to just 201 aircraft. On 22 June 1941, only a few Soviet units had a small number of Yak bombers. For example, 1 BAP in the 11th Composite Aviation Division at Lida had twenty-four. Most had been destroyed on the ground during the first day of the war, and due to the aircraft's poor performance, those that were not were soon shot down by the superior German fighters. The 118°BAP in the Moscow area was the only unit left with the type still in use in 1945. Such was the story of how a small reconnaissance aircraft with excellent performance was transformed into a 'bad' bomber due to Stalin's obsession with high performance.

Yakovlev Yak-9

Although short on firepower by most standards, the Yak-9 soon became by far the most important fighter on all Soviet fronts by 1944, even remaining in production after the war until 1946. The aircraft entered production in late 1942 as a refined derivative of the long-range Yak-7D1 fighter. The Yak-7D1 was notable for its mixed wood and metal primary structure, especially the wing, permitting an increase of 147 kg (324 lb) in payload. External changes included a slightly larger rudder with a more vertical hinged axis, improved oil and coolant radiator duct profiles and standardisation of the trim tabs on the ailerons, plus a 360-degree vision three-piece canopy.

The Yak-9 was a pilot's aircraft. It was light and easy on the controls, with excellent manoeuvrability and performance at altitudes up to about 4,875 m (16,000 feet). The first series aircraft came off the production line at GAZ-153 in October 1942, and the type was soon in action—at Stalingrad in November 1942, and on all fronts by February 1943. Production continued until 1948, totalling 16,769 aircraft in several main variants and some lesser ones. These included the original Yak-9 with the 969 kW (1,300 hp) Klimov VK-105PF-1 engine or the 1,015 kW (1,360 hp) VK-105PF-3 inline engine, armed with one 20 mm cannon and one or two 12.7 mm machine guns.

The Yak-9M that followed had revised armament.

The first major production variant, the Yak-9D long-range escort fighter requested by Stalin in March 1943, was fitted with the VK-105PF-3 engine and had greater fuel capacity. It was followed by an anti-tank variant, designated Yak-9T, with greater armour penetration power in the form of a 37 mm cannon or a 45 mm cannon and provision for anti-tank bomblets under the wings. The Yak-9K heavy anti-tank variant came next, with a 45 mm cannon fitted in the nose. Despite proving highly successful in attacks against PZKW VI tanks and bomber attacks with HE rounds, the 'T' and 'K' variants were produced only in small numbers. The Yak-9B variant was a high-speed light bomber with provision for four 100 kg (220 lb) bombs internally as part of a total 600 kg (1,320 lb) internal and external payload. It had first been tested in March 1943, and although successful, Yakovlev was against the fitting of external bomb loads or drop tanks.

The Yak-9P was a night interceptor fitted with an FS-55 searchlight for illumination of its quarry. It had a landing light in the port wing leading edge and was also fitted with a RPK-10 radio compass in the rear fuselage, often under a transparent dorsal hatch. The Yak-9DD very long-range fighter was based on the Yak-9D and fitted with nine fuel tanks that gave it a range of up to 2,285 km (1,420 miles) at cruising speed or 1,325 km (825 miles) at maximum speed. The aircraft could remain airborne for up to 6½ hours, making it ideal for escort missions and deep penetration work. It was used to escort American B-17 and B-24 bombers in 1944, and also in support of Josip Tito's partisans in Yugoslavia, escorting C-47 Dakota transports on resupply missions. In 1944/45, 399 Yak-9DDs were built. The second-generation Yak-9 was developed in mid-1943 as the Yak-9U and replaced the original variant in production in the autumn of 1944. The first Yak-9U was flown in December 1943 with the original powerplant, differing mainly in a thorough revision of the airframe to reduce drag. Even with the original engine a substantial gain in all-round performance was achieved.

On 1 October 1944, the Red Air Force had 2,692 Yak-9s on the German Front in 100 regiments. The Yak-9P post-war interceptor used the 1,230 kW (1,650 hp) Klimov VK-107A inline engine, which had been cleared for production in late August 1944. Some 800 Yak-9Ps were built, the type also being used by the air forces of Yugoslavia, Hungary, China, Poland and Albania. A third series variant of the Yak-9U was a reconnaissance version equipped with cameras and designated Yak-9R. Final wartime production introduced a modified airframe with D1 flush-riveted stressed skin throughout. This was the result of prolonged structural research and could have led to further major improvement in fuel capacity, but Yakovlev had lost interest in piston-engined aircraft by 1945. A metal-skinned two-seat trainer, the Yak-9UT, went into production in early 1945, but only a few were built. The final variant, the Yak-9UV, was a tandem-seat trainer with the original VK-105PF-2 engine and fabric and wood fuselage. Of the 16,769 aircraft built, 3,900 were of the 'U' variant and its derived versions. Post-war, many local and national (exported variant) modified versions were built. A common modification was the fitting of the RPK-10 radio compass as in the wartime Yak-9P interceptor.

Yakovlev Yak-12

Early in 1947, Yakovlev decided to build a replacement for the Yak-10. The Yak-12S ambulance version appeared in 1948. It was fitted with a 120 kW (160 hp) M-11FR engine and could carry one stretcher. This was followed by the Yak-12SKh, a version for agricultural use. The aircraft entered civil use and military service in 1949. This was followed by the Yak-12GR hydroplane fitted with twin wooden floats. However, these variants were produced only in small numbers, the first mass-produced variant being the Yak-12R fitted with the AI-14R engine. This version had been ordered by Stalin on 6 April 1950, ten aircraft appearing at the Tushino Aviation Day parade in 1951. The AI-14R engine was rated at 194 kW (260 hp) and was fitted to the 'R', 'M' and 'A' models. The aircraft was produced initially for the VVS as a two-seat liaison aircraft, with an occasional third seat. There were also some small civil transports.

In 1955, the OKB produced the Yak-12M with better overall distribution of mass and areas, balancing the heavier engine by a longer rear fuselage and enlarged tail. The vertical tail area was increased by 41 per cent and the horizontal tailplane by 36 per cent with two bracing struts added. This aircraft had a duralumin wing and was a true four-seater, with a substantial increase in allowable weights, and was produced for use in the agricultural and ambulance roles. In December 1955, a model for sport parachuting was produced, with a door on the starboard side equipped with a running board.

The final production variant was the Yak-12A in 1957. It was a greatly improved aircraft, fitted with a wing of Cessna trapezoidal plan profile. The vertical tail was that of the Yak-12R but with a new horizontal tail with wire bracing above and below. Larger fuel tanks were fitted in the tapered space between wing and spars, and a landing light was fitted for the first time. The aircraft had a completely revised cabin interior including a US-style control panel with a control 'wheel' instead of a stick, and more comfortable seats. The pilot was seated in the front left seat beside one passenger, the rear passengers being accommodated on a two-seat divan. Despite its considerably increased weight, the aircraft was significantly faster and had a longer range. An experimental model Yak-12B using a 224 kW (300 hp) AI-14RF engine was produced, designed with STOL capability particularly in mind.

Yakovlev Yak-25/27/28

Around 2,000 Yaks of over twenty different versions were built and delivered to the Soviet forces for a variety of duties, ranging from all-weather interception to reconnaissance and electronic warfare. Most were produced at the Irkutsk factory (GAZ-90) between 1953 and 1970. The all-weather, twin-engined Yak-25 (II) was the second Yakovlev design to use this designation. The Yak-25 was the military designation of the Yak-120 two-seat interceptor that had made its first flight on 16 June 1952, having been designed and built in a very short time to a VVS requirement issued in November 1951. It should be said that the aircraft bore an uncanny resemblance to the French Sud Aviation Vautour N, also developed in the early 1950s.

Yakovlev Yak-38

Specifications for a VTOL aircraft were issued in 1962, but it was not until five years later that two Yak-36 VTOL prototypes were demonstrated in Moscow. From these aircraft the Yak-38 was derived, making its first flight in 1971. Series production started in 1975 and the type entered Soviet Naval Aviation service the following year.

The single-seat Yak-38 represented the Soviets' first V/STOL combat aircraft. Unlike the British FRS.1 Sea Harrier, the aircraft used two lift jet engines in addition to the vectored thrust main engine, which initially was thought to be an 80 kN (17,989 lbf) Lyulka AL-21F but is now known to have been a 66.7 kN (14,991 lbf) Tumansky R-27V-300 unit. The aircraft was capable of short take-off using an automatic control system that managed the operation of the lift jets and vectoring nozzles. In flight, the lift jet doors above and below the fuselage were activated automatically. The lift jets were also used to correct pitch and trim. For carrier operation the aircraft had folding outer wing panels. Avionics included a small ranging radar and IFF.

Although the Yak-38 was designed principally to provide Soviet naval forces with experience in the operation of such aircraft, the type was lacking in performance, warload capability and avionics. However, it provided Soviet aircraft carriers and helicopter carriers with a useful interception and attack capability and was a much better aircraft than was generally acknowledged by the West. All Yak-38s were withdrawn from operational use in 1994, although some are still used in the land-based training role for Naval Aviation. The Yak-38U was the unarmed two-seat training version with a fuselage lengthened to 17.7 m (58 feet) and the radar removed in order to accommodate the pupil's cockpit ahead of the tutor pilot. A number of these aircraft also remain in use for land-based training.

Yakovlev Yak-140

The Yak-140 was the little-known losing contender for the Soviet Air Force's lightweight jet fighter requirement of the 1950s. In the late 1940s, the Yakovlev OKB designed and tested a number of lightweight fighters such as the Yak-17, Yak-23, Yak-30 and Yak-52. Of these aircraft only the first two types entered production, for limited home and foreign use, until ousted by the superior Mikoyan MiG-15. Another significant factor was the fact that Artem Mikoyan's brother Anastas held high position in the Soviet hierarchy and that since Stalin's death Yakovlev had lost much of the credibility he had built up in the Second World War. However, as result of the VVS requirement, a new project was started in 1953 on a lightweight single-seat fighter to be powered by the yet to be built 50 kN (11,240 lbf) Mikulin AM-11 engine.

The aircraft was a mid-wing monoplane with wings swept at 55 degrees at 25 per cent of mean chord. It was to have a central intake housing a small radar antenna, and a typical Yak undercarriage with two main legs in the fuselage and two supporting outriggers at the wing tips. Armament was to comprise two 30 mm NR-30 cannon and two under-wing pylons for ten ARS-70 or sixteen ARS-57 unguided rocket launchers. The aircraft was to be capable of a top speed of at least 1,700 kph (1,056 mph) at

15,000 m (49,212 feet), attainable within 3 minutes of take-off. Production of the first prototype was started in 1954, but it was soon realised that the new engine would not be available, so it was decided to fit the older and less powerful AM-9. As this power unit offered only 31.87 kN (7,165 lbf) of thrust, the Yakovlev OKB was forced to make modifications to reduce the weight by reducing its armament and fuel capacity.

However, this was to have a serious effect on the aircraft's firepower and range, and of course on its maximum speed, which was reduced to Mach 1.3. The MiG OKB had built two prototypes, the Ye-2 and Ye-4, both designed to meet the same specification as the Yak-140 but with different wing shapes. The Ye-2 had a conventional swept-wing and the Ye-4 a delta. It was intended that both would use the AM-11 engine, but again lack of availability forced Mikoyan to revert to the AM-9W. Competitive lightweight fighter trials began with the Ye-2 reaching a speed of 1,920 kph (1,193 mph) and a height of 19,000 m (62,336 feet). However, by the end of 1955, the more powerful Tumansky R-11 engine (the new designation for the dissolved Mikulin OKB's AM-11) was ready and was fitted to the new Mikoyan delta prototype, the Ye-5, giving a considerable improvement in performance and speed over a Ye-2A fitted with the same engine. Consequently it was decided not to continue work on the Yak-140 and the programme was cancelled, the Mikoyan E-5 delta eventually leading to the famous MiG-21 aircraft.

Yermolayev

Vladimir Grigoryevich Yermolayev was born in 1909 and graduated from Moscow State University in 1931. He made a major contribution to the development of Bartini's Stal-7 aircraft and became head of GAZ-240 in 1939 after Bartini's arrest and exile to Siberia. Yermolayev died of typhoid on 31 December 1944.

Yermolayev Yer-2/Yer-4

In January 1939, Stalin invited Yermolayev to develop a new long-range bomber from the Stal-7 transport aircraft. A large OKB was immediately established and the design of the DB-240 (as the bomber was designated) was started at GAZ-240, followed by construction of the prototype, which was flown in June 1940 with excellent results. The aircraft was fitted with two M-105 engines. OKB testing was concluded by September 1940, NII state testing being completed the following month. Production of the aircraft, designated Yer-2, started at GAZ-64 at Voronezh and the second prototype was completed in September 1940. Series production gained momentum and aircraft became available from the spring of 1941, with around twenty being delivered by 22 June.

Early in 1941, Stalin ordered that the aircraft be modified to carry ACh-30 diesel engines in order to increase its operational range, but unfortunately there was not enough time to complete this task before Germany attacked the Soviet Union in the

June of that year. Operational service of the Yer-2 began immediately, with virtually no training of the two new regiments that were hastily formed with the aircraft in early July at Voronezh. These initial crews were mainly test pilots selected from local Aeroflot line crews, forming the 420 DBAP and 421 DBAP (long-range bomber) units. Long-range missions to Konigsberg and Berlin commenced almost immediately and Berlin was attacked for the first time by a Yer-2 on the night of 7/8 August 1941. The factory at Voronezh was evacuated in October, but in the event the evacuation came earlier than was necessary. Voronezh was not attacked until July 1942, by which time GAZ-64 had produced a total of seventy-one Yer-2s.

It was not until 1942 that Yermolayev was able to equip the Yer-2 with the new ACh-30 diesel engines that had been requested by Stalin. The aircraft retained the twin fins and rudders of the earlier versions but differed in having wing and tail surfaces of increased area and a new cockpit layout. Initial service models had the cockpit offset to port, with the pilot and co-pilot seated in tandem. Both versions of the Yer-2 served with Long Range Bomber squadrons engaged in attacking the German hinterland. In 1943, Yermolayev built the slightly enlarged Yer-4 with the improved ACh-30B 1,119 kW (1,500 hp) diesel engines. The aircraft passed its NII certification tests in December 1943, winning major competitive evaluation over the Ilyushin Il-6, and for this reason the Yer-4 was ordered into series production.

In January 1944, Stalin requested a fast transport plane capable of carrying ten or twelve passengers a distance of 4,000-5,000 km (2,485-3,100 miles). The proposal was to transform a Yer-4 bomber into a transport—effectively a complete reversal of an upgraded Stal-7 transport from which the original bomber was derived. However, this proved difficult and the Ilyushin Il-12 was finally selected for series production. Between 1941 and 1945 a total of 462 Yer-2/4s were built, the aircraft being used against Germany in 1944/45. Post-war, 310 Yer-4s were built at GAZ-39 at Irkutsk in 1946/47, and prior to the Tupolev OKB's reverse-engineered Tu-4 development, the Yer-4 was the Soviet Union's main long-range bomber, continuing in VVS service until 1951.

Experimental, Prototype and Demonstrator Designations

Until the 1950s, the only Soviet protocol for prototype designations that existed was for fighters. Until that time most prototypes were prefixed 'I'. For example, the prototype MiG-1/3 was designated I-200, the Sukhoi Su-1 was I-330, and the LaGG-3 prototype, I-301. Other types of aircraft, such as bombers and attack types, did not have special designations. Therefore under normal circumstances the particular aircraft would initially be presented for NII VVS tests under its OKB designation. Then, if accepted for series production, the State Commission would redesignate the aircraft. As an example it is of interest to note that the Su-27 Flanker prototypes were all designated T-10.

As the Sukhoi OKB appeared to utilise 'S' and 'T' symbols to annotate its prototypes, for a while Sukhoi prototype designs with swept wings (*Strelovidnoye*) were designated 'S' and those with delta wings (*Treugolnoye*) were designated 'T'. However, in the 1960s this protocol was ignored when the delta-wing Su-24 was designated T-6-1, and later, for example, the Su-25 Frogfoot sturmovik was designated S-8.

From 1954 the Mikoyan OKB designated all prototypes 'E' for Experimental, but it should be noted, as seen on Soviet photographs, that the westernised designation 'Ye' is incorrect and in Soviet terminology all 'Ye' prefixes are in fact 'E'. For example, Ye-2 = E-2, Ye-4 = E-4 and Ye-166 = E-166. However, the MiG OKB did not keep to the 'E' designation in more recent years. For example, the MiG-23 prototype received the designation 23-11, and the MiG-27 and MiG-29 prototypes did not carry the 'E' prefix.

Another Soviet OKB anomaly was with aircraft concerned in record attempts, where the specific aircraft involved in the test was often denoted by only part of its original designation. This was sometimes presented differently to the West. For example, the record-breaking MiG-27 was presented to the West as the E-66, but in the Soviet Union was designated simply E-6, and the E-166 MiG-25 engine test bed was flown as the E-66. Such were the vagaries of Soviet experimental and prototype aircraft designations.

Mikoyan MiG-21-based technology demonstrators

The Mikoyan OKB used the basic aerodynamic shape of the MiG-21 to develop several larger designs in order to meet other Soviet Air Force requirements. Some that flew are listed below:

I-320: A Mikoyan jet prototype fitted with RD-45F engines. Its first flight took place in April 1949.

I-350M: The first Mikoyan supersonic jet fighter designed to accept TR-3A engine (later AL-5). It was derived from the earlier MiG-17, but had 60-degree wing sweeps with four prominent wing fences to prevent stall. The aircraft engine failed on its first flight in July 1951 at 1,000 m (3,281 feet), although it was skilfully recovered by test pilot Colonel Grigory Sedov.

I-360: A parallel prototype to the I-350M with a similar wing design to the MiG-19 prototype.

I-370: A large swept-wing fighter-bomber based on the Ye-2's shape and aerodynamics.

I-380: The I-380 was built as the I-3U fighter-bomber and the I-3P interceptor. Both variants were overtaken by successful evaluation and selection for series production of the Sukhoi Su-7 and Su-9 aircraft.

I-75F: A relative of I-370/380 aircraft and fitted with a Lyulka engine, Uragan-5B radar and AA-3 Anab K-8 missiles, the I-75F interceptor was capable of Mach 2.25 or 2,756 kph (1,713 mph).

Ye-150: Dating from *circa* 1958, the Ye-150 was basically a scaled-up Ye-6 fitted with a 93 kN (20,935 lbf) Tumansky R-15M-300 engine and K-8 and K-9 missiles. It did not fly until July 1960.

Ye-152: An improved Ye-150 developed in 1959 and powered by a 100 kN (22,478 lbf) R-15A engine, with minor airframe modifications, a new integrated navigation and intercept system and clipped wings for the fitting of wing-tip-mounted AAMs. It did not fly until April 1961.

Ye-152A Flipper: It featured a redesigned fuselage to accommodate two Tumansky R-11F-300 engines mounted side by side and was capable of Mach 2.35 or 2,879 kph (1,789 mph). Only one was built, but the Chinese Shenyang Company built a copy, designated J-8 Finback I, less than 200 of which were built, production ceasing in favour of the upgraded Finback II.

Ye-166 (E-166): A development aircraft test bed for MiG-25 Foxbat engines, it featured a new tail and a streamlined fuselage and canopy. It set the world speed record in 1961 at 2,681 kph (1,666 mph) and achieved a sustained altitude record of 22,670 m (74,376 feet) in 1962, designated E-66.

Glossary of Abbreviation

AP	Aviation Regiment
ASW	Anti-submarine Warfare
AV-MF	Soviet Naval Aviation
BAP	Bomber Aviation Regiment
CRT	Cathode Ray Tube Display
DA	Soviet Long Range Aviation
ECCM	Electronic Counter-countermeasures
ECM	Electronic Countermeasures
ELINT	Electronic Signals Intelligence
EW	Electronic Warfare
FA	Soviet Frontal Aviation
FAI	Fédération Aéronautique Internationale
GLIT	State Flight Test Centre
HDD	Head-Down Display
HUD	Head-Up Display
IA-PVO	Fighter Aviation/Air Defence Force
IAP	Fighter Aviation Regiment
LII	Flight Research Institute
MAD	Magnetic Anomaly Detector
MAP	Ministry of Aircraft Production
MAPO	Moscow Aircraft Production Organisation
MFD	Multi-Function Display
NII	Scientific Research Institute
PVO	Soviet Air Defence Force
RFAF	Russian Federation Air Force
SAR	Search and Rescue
SIGINT	Signals Intelligence
TsAGI	Central Aerohydrodynamic Institute
TsIAM	Central Institute of Aviation Motors

TsKB	Central Design Bureau
VTA	Soviet Transport Aviation
VVF	Soviet Military Air Fleet
VVS	Soviet Air Force